Communications in Computer and Information Science 2128

Rationale
The CCIS series is devoted to the publication of proceedings of computer science conferences. Its aim is to efficiently disseminate original research results in informatics in printed and electronic form. While the focus is on publication of peer-reviewed full papers presenting mature work, inclusion of reviewed short papers reporting on work in progress is welcome, too. Besides globally relevant meetings with internationally representative program committees guaranteeing a strict peer-reviewing and paper selection process, conferences run by societies or of high regional or national relevance are also considered for publication.

Topics
The topical scope of CCIS spans the entire spectrum of informatics ranging from foundational topics in the theory of computing to information and communications science and technology and a broad variety of interdisciplinary application fields.

Information for Volume Editors and Authors
Publication in CCIS is free of charge. No royalties are paid, however, we offer registered conference participants temporary free access to the online version of the conference proceedings on SpringerLink (http://link.springer.com) by means of an http referrer from the conference website and/or a number of complimentary printed copies, as specified in the official acceptance email of the event.

CCIS proceedings can be published in time for distribution at conferences or as post-proceedings, and delivered in the form of printed books and/or electronically as USBs and/or e-content licenses for accessing proceedings at SpringerLink. Furthermore, CCIS proceedings are included in the CCIS electronic book series hosted in the SpringerLink digital library at http://link.springer.com/bookseries/7899. Conferences publishing in CCIS are allowed to use Online Conference Service (OCS) for managing the whole proceedings lifecycle (from submission and reviewing to preparing for publication) free of charge.

Publication process
The language of publication is exclusively English. Authors publishing in CCIS have to sign the Springer CCIS copyright transfer form, however, they are free to use their material published in CCIS for substantially changed, more elaborate subsequent publications elsewhere. For the preparation of the camera-ready papers/files, authors have to strictly adhere to the Springer CCIS Authors' Instructions and are strongly encouraged to use the CCIS LaTeX style files or templates.

Abstracting/Indexing
CCIS is abstracted/indexed in DBLP, Google Scholar, EI-Compendex, Mathematical Reviews, SCImago, Scopus. CCIS volumes are also submitted for the inclusion in ISI Proceedings.

How to start
To start the evaluation of your proposal for inclusion in the CCIS series, please send an e-mail to ccis@springer.com.

Naveen Chauhan · Divakar Yadav ·
Gyanendra K. Verma · Badal Soni ·
Jorge Morato Lara
Editors

Machine Learning, Image Processing, Network Security and Data Sciences

5th International Conference, MIND 2023
Hamirpur, India, December 21–22, 2023
Revised Selected Papers

Springer

Editors
Naveen Chauhan
National Institute of Technology Hamirpur
Hamirpur, Himachal Pradesh, India

Divakar Yadav
Indira Gandhi National Open University
New Delhi, Delhi, India

Gyanendra K. Verma
National Institute of Technology Raipur
Raipur, Chhattisgarh, India

Badal Soni
Computer Science and Engineering
National Institute of Technology Silchar
Silchar, Assam, India

Jorge Morato Lara
Carlos III University
Madrid, Spain

ISSN 1865-0929 ISSN 1865-0937 (electronic)
Communications in Computer and Information Science
ISBN 978-3-031-62216-8 ISBN 978-3-031-62217-5 (eBook)
https://doi.org/10.1007/978-3-031-62217-5

This Springer imprint is published by the registered company Springer Nature Switzerland AG
The registered company address is: Gewerbestrasse 11, 6330 Cham, Switzerland

Preface

The Department of Computer Science and Engineering at the National Institute of Technology, Hamirpur, was immensely pleased to extend a warm invitation to researchers, experts, and practitioners worldwide for the 5th International Conference on Machine Learning, Image Processing, Network Security, and Data Sciences (MIND 2023). The conference took place on the 21st and 22nd of December 2023 at the picturesque premises of the National Institute of Technology, Hamirpur, India, and it was indeed an enriching and intellectually stimulating event.

Over the years, MIND conferences have served as crucial platforms for the convergence of leading minds in academia, industry, and government, fostering collaborative endeavors and facilitating the exchange of cutting-edge research and insights in the domains of machine learning, image processing, network security, and data sciences. Building upon the successes of its predecessors hosted by NIT Kurukshetra, NIT Silchar, NIT Raipur, and MANIT Bhopal in 2019, 2020, 2021, and 2022 respectively, MIND 2023 successfully upheld and further enhanced the spirit of interdisciplinary collaboration and knowledge dissemination.

This year's conference featured distinguished keynote speakers, comprehensive technical sessions, and engaging panel discussions covering a diverse array of topics pertinent to the aforementioned domains. Participants were invited to contribute their research findings, innovative methodologies, and practical experiences, thereby enriching the discourse and collectively advancing the frontiers of knowledge in these rapidly evolving fields.

MIND 2023 provided an exceptional opportunity for participants to forge new connections, deepen existing collaborations, and explore avenues for interdisciplinary research and development. Researchers, academicians, professionals, and policymakers actively engaged in this dynamic forum, leveraging the invaluable networking opportunities and intellectual exchange it afforded.

We are delighted to share insights into the rigorous peer review process undertaken for MIND 2023. The peer review process was single-blind, ensuring impartial evaluation of submissions. Each manuscript submitted underwent scrutiny by a minimum of three reviewers, ensuring thorough assessment and maintaining the highest standards of quality. A total of 173 submissions were received, reflecting the robust interest and engagement of the research community. Out of these, 29 full-length papers were accepted for presentation at the conference, following a meticulous selection process.

On behalf of the organizing committee, we extend our heartfelt gratitude to all participants, sponsors, and supporters for their invaluable contributions towards making MIND 2023 a resounding success. We are confident that their participation greatly enriched the conference proceedings, and we eagerly anticipate their presence at future events.

We are grateful for everyone's participation in MIND 2023 and trust that their experience was both enlightening and inspiring.

December 2023

Naveen Chauhan
Divakar Yadav
Gyanendra K. Verma
Badal Soni
Jorge Morato Lara
Organizing Team

Organization

Chief Patron

H. M. Suryawanshi	National Institute of Technology Hamirpur, India

Patron

Anoop Kumar	National Institute of Technology Hamirpur, India

Honorary Chairs

Lalit Awasthi	National Institute of Technology Uttarakhand, India
Jorge Morato	Universidad Carlos III de Madrid, Spain

General Chairs

Bharat K. Bhargava	Purdue University, USA
Pradip K. Das	Indian Institute of Technology Guwahati, India

General Co-chairs

Siddharth Chauhan	National Institute of Technology Hamirpur, India
Kamlesh Dutta	National Institute of Technology Hamirpur, India
T. P. Sharma	National Institute of Technology Hamirpur, India
Gyanendra K. Verma	National Institute of Technology Raipur, India

Organizing Chair

Naveen Chauhan	National Institute of Technology Hamirpur, India

Organizing Secretaries

Arun Kumar Yadav	National Institute of Technology Hamirpur, India
Mohit Kumar	National Institute of Technology Hamirpur, India
Rajeev Kumar	National Institute of Technology Hamirpur, India
Badal Soni	National Institute of Technology Silchar, India

Publication Chairs

Rajesh Doriya	National Institute of Technology Raipur, India
Nitin Gupta	National Institute of Technology Hamirpur, India
Divakar Yadav	IGNOU, India

Publicity Chairs

Jerry Chun-Wei Lin	Western Norway University of Applied Sciences, Norway
Prashant Kumar	National Institute of Technology Jalandhar India
Dharmendra P. Mahato	National Institute of Technology Hamirpur, India
Sangeeta Sharma	National Institute of Technology Hamirpur, India
John Wang	Montclair State University, USA

Technical Chairs

Pardeep Singh	National Institute of Technology Hamirpur, India
Jyoti Srivastava	National Institute of Technology Hamirpur, India
Priyanka	National Institute of Technology Hamirpur, India

Advisory Committee

Mansaf Alam	Jamia Millia Islamia, India
Ashish Anand	Indian Institute of Technology Guwahati, India
Mahesh Chandra Govil	National Institute of Technology Sikkim, India
Asif Iqbal	Management & Science University, Malaysia
Z. A. Jaffery	Jamia Millia Islamia, India
Sangeeta K.	Keele University, UK
Dinesh K. Vishwakarma	DTU, India
Binod Kumar Kanaujia	National Institute of Technology Jalandhar, India

Vivek Kumar Singh	BHU, India
Sandeep Kumar Sengar	Cardiff Metropolitan University, UK
Brijesh Kumar	IGDTUW, India
Manoj Kumar	University of Wollongong in Dubai, UAE
Pinaki Mitra	IIT Guwahati, India
Poornima Mittal	DTU, India
Balakrishna Pailla	Reliance Jio AICoE, India
Danila Parygin	Volgograd State Technical University, Russia
Ramana Reddy	NIT Kurukshetra, India
Raghuraj Singh	HBTU Kanpur, India
Bhuvan Unhelkar	University of South Florida, USA
Suresh Vishwakarma	BC Hydro, Canada

Technical Program Committee

Rashi Agarwal	HBTU Kanpur, India
Mayank Agarwal	IIT Patna, India
Utkarsh Agrawa	University of Oxford, UK
Mohammad Ahsan	UPES Dehradun, India
Zahid Akhtar	SUNY Polytechnic Institute, USA
Madhulika	Amity University, India
Akash Anil	Cardiff University, UK
Sangeeta Babu	King Khalid University, Saudi Arabia
Gaurav Baranwal	BHU, India
Mahip Bartere	P. R. Pote Patil College of Engg. and Management, India
Sathisha Basavaraju	Beltech, India
Jatin Bedi	Thapar Institute of Engineering and Technology, India
Swarup Behera	Reliance Jio AICoE, India
P. Bhagath	LBRCE, India
Megha Bhusan	DIT Dehradun, India
Shilpa Budhkar	Ericsson, India
Jatoth Chandrasekhar	NIT Raipur, India
Prasenjit Chatterjee	MCKV Institute of Engineering, India
Sadu Chiranjeevi	RGUKT, India
Deepti Chopra	Jagan Institute of Management Studies, India
Rajendra Choudhary	PDEU, India
Subrata Chowdhury	Sreenivasa Institute of Technology, India
Shirshendu Das	IIT Hyderabad, India
Rajesh Devaraj	Nvidia, India

Sukanta Dey	Intel, USA
Anshuman Dhuliya	Intel, India
Neelam Duhan	J. C. Bose University of Science and Technology, India
Sibaji Gaj	Qualcomm, USA
Mirza Ghalib Baig	IIIT Kottayam, India
Sonam Gupta	AKGEC, India
Deepak Gupta	Maharaja Agrasen Institute of Technology, India
Rajeev Gupta	Microsoft IDC, India
Swati Gupta	Jain University, India
Sailesh Iyer	Rai University, India
Arti Jain	JIIT, India
Amita Jain	Dr. B. R. Ambedkar University Delhi, India
Pooja Jain	IIIT Nagpur, India
Sudhansu Josh	Doon University, India
Piyush Joshi	IIIT Sri City, India
Subhadeep Karan	Meta, USA
Ashish Khanna	Maharaja Agrasen Institute of Technology, India
P. Kiran Sree	SVECW, India
Sangram Kishor Jena	West Virginia University, USA
Lella Kranthi Kumar	VIT AP, India
Divya Kulkarni	Eli Lilly, India
Pramod Kumar Yadav	NIT Srinagar, India
Naveen Kumar Gupta	Dr. B. R. Ambedkar NIT Jalandhar, India
Rajeev Kumar Gupta	PDEU, India
Santosh Kumar Bharti	PDEU, India
Deepak Kumar Sharma	IGDTUW, New Delhi
Abhay Kumar Agarwal	KNIT Sultanpur, India
Sunil Kumar Sahu	IIAI Abu Dhabi, UAE
Rohit Kumar Tiwari	MMMUT, India
Soumava Kumar Roy	EPFL, Switzerland
Sanjay Kumar	NIT Raipur, India
Mohit Kumar	Dr. B. R. Ambedkar NIT Jalandhar, India
Ankit Kumar	UPES Dehradun, India
Sanjay Kumar	REC Azamgarh, India
Rahul Kumar	RGIPT, India
Dinesh Kumar	NIT Jamshedpur, India
Satish Kumar	Airspan Networks, UK
Hima M. Bindu	North Orissa University, India
Shrikant Malviya	Durham University, UK
Monika Mehta	NIFT Patna, India
Anasua Mitra	Eli Lilly, India

Deepankar Nankani	Eli Lilly, India
Aditya Nigam	IIT Mandi, India
Piyoosh P.	College of Engineering Trivandrum, India
Rakesh Pandey	Synopsis, India
Karthik Pandia	Uniphore, India
Akshay Parekh	Eli Lilly, India
Yamuna Prasad Shukla	IIT Jammu, India
Mahendra Pratap Yadav	IIIT Pune, India
Saptarshi Pyne	University of Wisconsin-Madison, USA
Deepak Rai	Bennett University, India
U. S. N. Raju	NIT Warangal, India
Balaprakasa Rao Killi	NIT Warangal, India
Sudheer Reddy K.	Anurag University, India
Pallabi Saikia	RGIPT, India
Parikshit Saikia	NIT Silchar, India
Sonia Sanchez	University Carlos III of Madrid, Spain
Tushar Semwal	Microsoft IDC, India
Sonia Semwal	Eli Lilly, India
Diganta Sen Gupta	Meghnad Saha Institute of Technology, India
Santoshi Sengupta	Graphic Era Hill University, India
Sayantan Sengupta	TU Denmark, Denmark
Shivi Sharma	Jain University, India
Priyanka Sharma	SKIT Jaipur, India
Shashi Shekhar Jha	IIT Ropar, India
Vivek Singh Verma	HBTU Kanpur, India
Amrendra Singh Yadav	ABV-IIITM Gwalior, India
Pawan Singh Mehra	DTU, India
Shyam Singh Rajput	National Institute of Technology Patna, India
Karan Singh	JNU, India
Simranjit Singh	Bennett University, India
Meenakshi Sood	NITTTR Chandigarh, India
Ganji Sreeram	Reliance Jio AICOE, India
Basant Subba	IIT Ropar, India
Mayank Swarnkar	IIT BHU, India
Bhanu Teja Nellore	Reliance Jio AICoE, India
Prabhat Verma	HBTU Kanpur, India
Akhilesh Verma	AKGEC, India
Anshul Verma	BHU, India
Sandeep Vidyapu	CS Group, Germany
Vibhas Yadav	REC Banda, India
Ashima Yadav	Bennett University, India

Contents

Machine Learning

Network Security

Data Science

Machine Learning

SynText - Data Augmentation Algorithm in NLP to Improve Performance of Emotion Classifiers

Sahil Chawla(✉), Deepanshu Yadav, Santosh, Ashish Kumar, Divya Gupta, and Shampa Chakraverty

Netaji Subhas University of Technology, New Delhi, India
schawla516@gmail.com, shampa@nsut.ac.in

Abstract. Emotion classification is a common task in natural language processing (NLP) where the goal is to classify the emotion expressed in a given text, such as joy, sadness, anger, or fear. Emotion Classification in natural language is an integral task in application domains like marketing, data analysis, and pattern recognition. However, building accurate emotion classifier models can be challenging due to several factors, such as the subjective nature of emotions, the complexity of language, and the scarcity of labeled data. To tackle these problems, research related to different methods of data augmentation has been performed, to increase both, the quantity, and the quality of labeled data. The major challenge faced with labeled data is that the preservation of the label and meaning of the sentence is of top priority while performing augmentation, which is what this research aims to tackle. This research aims to improve existing methods of data augmentation in the field of NLP with the aim of enhancing emotion classifier models. Previous methods focus on augmentation but don't keep the increase of diversity as the main aim of augmentation. We propose a novel data augmentation technique "SynText" which performs augmentation by using contextually meaningful synonyms, with a focus on increasing the diversity of emotion-related words, while also preserving the label of the given data point. The technique is applied on some benchmark datasets mentioned in literature, like the GoEmotions Dataset and the SST5 dataset, and it is found that emotion classification models trained on datasets augmented using "SynText" tend to give better results for metrics like F1 Score and Accuracy.

Keywords: Emotion Classification · Natural Language Processing · Data Augmentation · Synonym Replacement

1 Introduction

Emotion detection, classification, and analysis, being at the intersection of many application domains, like psychology or marketing, has gained special importance and hence is a widely researched topic. With the boom of online services, especially social media, the digital footprint of a user has increased exponentially, and has resulted in great potential for analysis. For example, marketing companies are continually using emotion analysis to identify the type of products suiting certain type of people. Similarly, social media

N. Chauhan et al. (Eds.): MIND 2023, CCIS 2128, pp. 3–14, 2024.
https://doi.org/10.1007/978-3-031-62217-5_1

services like Twitter, Instagram, are also regularly mining emotional information, to give better recommendations which results in higher screen time for users. Apart from the business aspects, emotion classification is also actively used in areas like calculation of a country's Happiness Index, or identifying trends of how people are reacting to new laws etc. Hence, improving the methods of emotion classification has numerous use cases and is a core research area.

There are various datasets which are available in literature, which are specially curated for the task of emotion classification. But, even after much research, the datasets are majorly still small-sized, and the ones having large amounts of data, suffer from issues like class-imbalance. For resolving these problems, solutions like Data Augmentation techniques have also been researched, and is still an active area of research.

Data augmentation (DA) encompasses methods of increasing training data diversity without directly collecting more data (Feng et al., 2021) [1]. It plays a major role in Computer Vision tasks and is now also seeing increasing application and use in NLP tasks. Research related to Data Augmentation has been taken up in the Machine Learning (ML) field, ranging from basic techniques like EDA (Wei et al., 2019) [2], which introduced methods like Synonym Replacement, Random Insertion, Random Swap and Random Deletion, to advanced techniques including the use of Language Models. For example, Kobayashi et al. (2018) [3] introduced contextual synonym replacement using a bi-directional LSTM language model, yet there is still a scope of improvement in the field to improve the quality of emotion classification datasets.

BERT (Bidirectional Encoder Representations from Transformers), a newer language model, has exactly the needed power to understand the context provided and convert given textual data to mathematical embeddings. These embeddings can be different for same words, appearing in different sentences, encompassing the context of the entire sentence.

By this research, we aim to improve the synonym replacement data augmentation technique, by including contextual similarity criterion on every stage of the algorithm. We aim to use BERT for capturing the context of sentences and generating synonyms based on that. We also aim to introduce a novel Word Choosing mechanism, wherein the algorithm will initially find certain words in the sentence which provide emotional context to the sentence related to the emotion label given to that sentence. By only choosing such words, we ensure that the emotional diversity of the dataset is increased, and also the label of the sentence has higher chances to be preserved and not changed due to augmentation. Further, once synonyms are generated, we also plan to create a Scoring mechanism, which will discard results that are not contextually similar to the original sentence, and hence will further strengthen the final results.

The structure of the report is organized as follows: Sect. 2 describes the related work done in the field of emotion classification, with a focus on synonym-based data augmentation methods and presents a brief literature survey, including various Emotion Taxonomies proposed previously. Section 3 describes the methodology we propose, with flowcharts and examples. Section 4 provides observations and results in the experiments we devised. Section 5 concludes the discussion and gives an insight into the possible future work. Thereafter follow the references in Sect. 6.

2 Literature Review

2.1 Emotion Taxonomy

Emotion taxonomy builds on the basic emotions and dimensional models by providing a more detailed and comprehensive framework for understanding emotional experiences.

The basic emotions model, as proposed by Ekman et al. (1972) [4], identifies six basic emotions that are universally recognizable across cultures: anger, disgust, fear, joy, sadness, and surprise. This model has been criticized for its simplicity and lack of granularity, as it overlooks the complex and nuanced nature of emotional experiences.

To address some of the limitations of the basic emotions model, Shaver et al. (1987) [5] proposed a more complex categorization system. This system consisted of six basic emotion classes: fear, love, joy, surprise, sadness, and anger. Each of these classes was further divided into subclasses of more fine-grained emotions, resulting in a hierarchical tree-like structure of emotions. This categorization system attempted to capture the complexity and diversity of emotional experiences, accounting for both universal and culturally specific emotional expressions.

Most recently, Demsky et al. (2020) [6] introduced the fine-grained emotion taxonomy. The GoEmotions dataset consists of comments from a wide range of topics, such as news, politics, sports, entertainment, and technology, and in different styles, such as formal and informal language, sarcasm, and irony. The emotion categories are based on Plutchik's wheel of emotions, which is a widely used and influential model of basic emotions. The 27 categories are divided into seven groups: joy, sadness, anger, fear, surprise, disgust, and neutral. Each comment is annotated with one or more emotion labels, indicating the emotions expressed in the text. One of the strengths of the GoEmotions dataset is its size and diversity. The large number of comments and emotion categories make it suitable for training and evaluating deep learning models, which require large amounts of data to achieve high performance.

2.2 Benchmark Datasets

During the literature survey, we observed several datasets being used in related research. Some of these were specifically curated by the authors to solve a problem pertaining to a specific domain, while other datasets used included social media data (like Twitter) for sentiment and further emotion classification.

One such example is the JIRA dataset annotated by Ortu et al. (2016) [7] in which the dataset is divided into three groups: The first group has 392 data points, classified into Anger, Love, Fear, Joy, Surprise, and Sadness; The second group having 1600 data points, has categorization into 3 emotions: Joy, Love, and Sadness; The third group has 4000 data points, categorized into 4 emotions: Sadness, Joy, Love, and Anger. Another benchmark dataset is the International Survey on Emotion Antecedents and Reaction (ISEAR) given by Wallbott et al. (1994) [8].

The SST2 (Stanford Sentiment Treebank 2) dataset was given by Socher et al. (2013) [9]. In this dataset, there are only 2 sentiments which are positive and negative. The dataset consists of 11855 movie review data points which are labeled by humans. Similarly, the SST5 dataset contains the same 11855 data points which are classified into 5

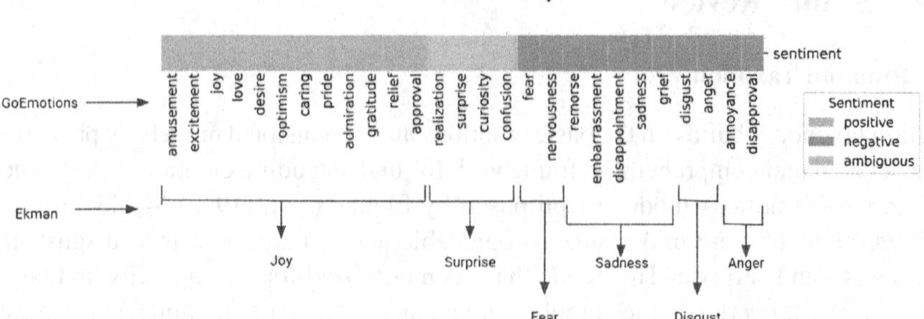

Fig. 1. GoEmotions and Ekman Taxonomy Explained

sentiment labels such as negative, somewhat negative, positive, somewhat positive, and neutral. Labels in this dataset are fine-grained versions of the SST2 dataset.

The GoEmotions dataset [6] has 58000 data points which were carefully selected from the Reddit comments, and they were labeled into 27 fine-grained emotions or Neutral. This dataset is in the English language and the main objective to create this dataset was to increase the capability of chat bots to understand the customer, by having a better understanding of the emotions portrayed in customer feedback.

The limitation with most of the datasets is that they are manually annotated and the size of data available in them is small. The GoEmotions dataset has a huge data size, and it is annotated into 28 fine-grained emotions including Neutral, as shown in Fig. 1, in which we can see the GoEmotions emotion taxonomy [6], along with its representation in Ekman terminology.

2.3 Data Augmentation

Data augmentation techniques are used to artificially create data to increase the diversity in the existing data so that algorithms could perform better on the test data or in a real-world task that they are designed to work on. A few of the already existing popular data augmentation techniques are presented by Wei et al. (2019) [2] in which there are examples of techniques like Synonym replacement, Random Insertion into the data, Random swap of words in the data, and Random deletion of words in the data. These prove to be one of the simplest, yet most effective techniques.

Data Augmentation methods have also been explored previously using Language Models. As mentioned by Fadaee et al. (2017) [10], the main focus was on the machine translation task, where they were replacing the words in the input sentence with rare words only, in which the top k rare words were predicted by leftwards and rightwards LSTM language models independently.

The synonym work which is most similar to our synonym augmentation technique was proposed by Kobayashi et al. [3] where the author introduced a technique of replacing words in the sentence using a language model. To prevent the newly generated words from changing the label of the sentence, the author had used a conditional constraint in order to preserve the label of the sentence. They used a bi-directional LSTM language model to gather the context of variable length from both directions together. Their method didn't need knowledge from any task and could be used for any task of classification in various domains.

In the paper by Imran et al. (2022) [11], the author first applied the basic techniques of word insertion, word substitution, word deletion, and random shuffling and on observing that the emotion of text was not always preserved, the author took some steps to ensure it. For example, he created a lexicon dictionary for the augmentation of data in the text to make the text suitable for that emotion.

These data augmentation techniques have significantly helped to improve the quality of the dataset, in order to improve the performance of the classifier on datasets, but still, with the advancement of technology in terms of Language Models, and introduction of new datasets, scope for improvement remains.

3 Methodology

Before understanding the algorithm, let's have a look at the core requirements of the algorithm:

- Given a sentence, the algorithm must find words which are suitable for replacement and generate synonyms for those words.
- Here, "Synonyms" don't just refer to dictionary-based synonyms of a word, but words which are possible replacements, while considering the context of the word in the sentence it is being used in.
- The words added must preserve the semantic meaning of the sentence and must conform with the label which was assigned to that sentence.

Hence, the algorithm is divided into 3 modules:

- Choosing words with high semantic similarity with the label
- Generation of synonyms of all candidate words
- Ranking and scoring of generated synonyms depending on contextual similarity with the original sentence.

A Module-wise flowchart is shown in Fig. 2.

Given below is the process of the algorithm in each module:

1. Choosing Words in a sentence:

   We choose words depending on the amount of effect the word has on determining the emotion (label) of the sentence. We do this so that we can increase the diversity of words related to that specific emotion. For this, we consider the words and find their contextual similarity with the label of that sentence.

   For each data point:

   a. We first obtain the embeddings of the entire sentence (token wise embeddings) using BERT.

   a. Next, we consider each word one by one, and replace the word with the emotion label. Again, we find the token wise embeddings of this new sentence (with the emotion label replaced).

b. Now, we have embeddings of both the word and the emotion label which are inclusive of the context of the entire sentence. We use these to find the cosine similarity of the embeddings of the word and the emotion label.
c. The words are then sorted according to highest similarity and are chosen by setting a threshold (0.6).

A flowchart representing this word choosing process is shown in Fig. 3.
Once the words are selected, we move on to the second step.

2. Generating Synonyms of the chosen words:
For generation of synonyms, we consider the words chosen one by one. In this part, we use BERT which encodes the embeddings of a word, uses softmax activation and finally uses multinomial classification on the vocabulary of BERT, and gives us possible synonyms (we retrieve max(5, 2 * numberOfAugmentationsRequired synonyms)).

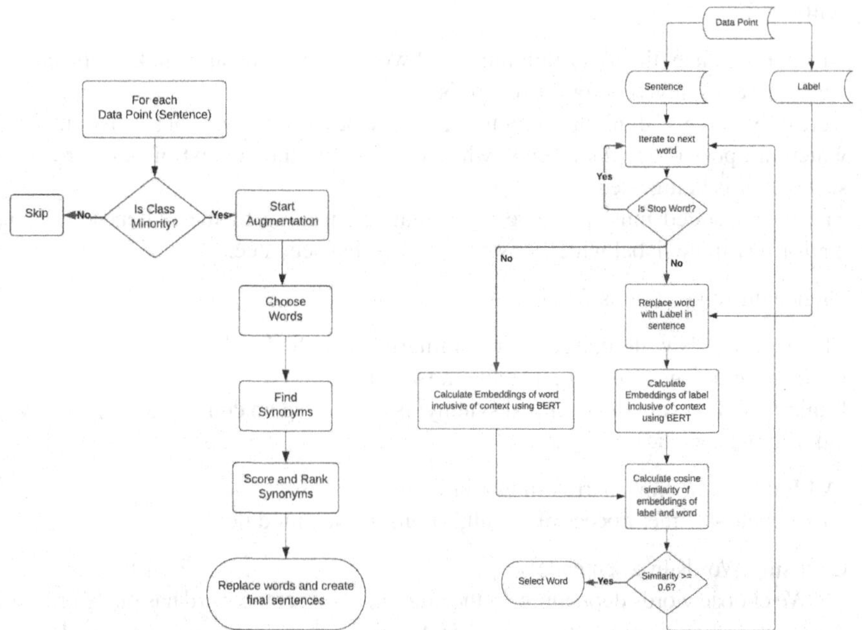

Fig. 2. Modules of algorithm

Fig. 3. Word Choosing Module

3. Ranking the synonyms based on a scoring system:
As stated before, a synonym is considered a good replacement if it fits the context of the sentence, and if it is similar to the original word (so that the emotion is portrayed as it is supposed to be)
Hence, we propose a scoring system consisting of the following scores:
a. Contextual Similarity of the original word and the synonym proposed: This process is like that portrayed in the word choosing module. We calculate embeddings of both the original word and the synonym with the context of the entire sentence.

Cosine similarity is then applied, and a threshold is set (0.6) to consider the worth of the synonym.

b. Non-Contextual similarity of the word and the synonym: For this, we calculate the similarity of the original word and the synonym using BERT itself. In this part, BERT gives us embeddings of the word itself but doesn't use the context of the sentence. This gives us a dictionary-based similarity of both the words. After observation, we set the dictionary-based similarity threshold to be 0.6.

Both the scores are averaged and again a joint threshold of 0.6 has been taken by observation. A flowchart of the scoring system is also given in Fig. 4.

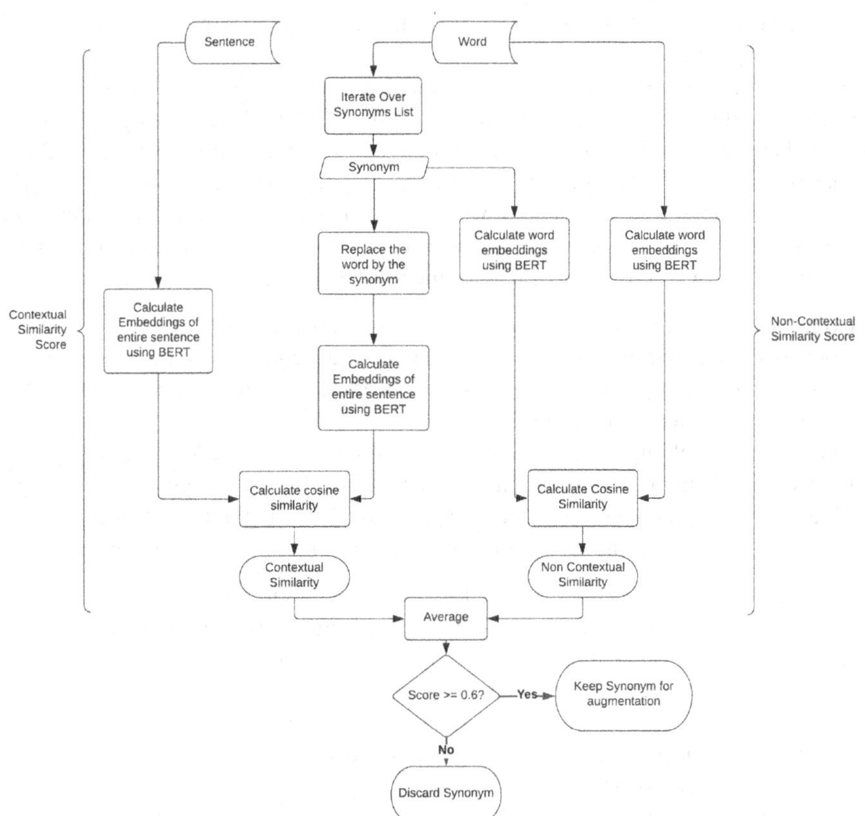

Fig. 4. Synonym Scoring Module

4 Experimentation

Which sentences were to be augmented, how much augmentation was required, these questions were answered using the analysis we performed on the data, which showed us the label-wise count in the dataset. The main purpose of augmentation was to increase the quantity of sentences of the label which had less data. Also, in this case, we considered only those sentences which had a single label, to make augmentation focused on the label itself. For this, we considered the class with the most data as the majority class (Admiration – around 4000). In this, we didn't consider the neutral class as the majority, as the amount of neutral data points was exceedingly high compared to other classes, while the rest classes had a relatively comparable number of data points. Next, whichever classes had data less than 20% (80:20 ratio) of the majority class, were augmented until they had enough data.

For Testing our methodology, the methodology was to choose a dataset and run a baseline model on the dataset. Then, we augmented the dataset using the process explained above and ran the same model on the new dataset. Finally, we compared the metrics of both the runs, to check for any improvement by augmentation.

Before any operation on a dataset, we apply some basic preprocessing which helps the model understand the text better, and also which boosts the performance of our augmentation. The preprocessing includes the following steps:

- Conversion of all text into lower case (as we use bert-base-uncased)
- Conversion of all emojis and emoticons into their text equivalents. For example, 😊 is converted to "smiling face" and:) is also converted to "smiling face". This is done using emot and demoji libraries in python
- Contraction unfolding has been done. An example of this includes changing "we'll" to "we will". This is done using the "contractions" library in python. Further, this library also helps in conversion and fixing of text containing Internet Slang. This was done as it is better for the algorithm if there is a minimum of unknown vocabulary.

The first benchmark dataset we used was the GoEmotions dataset which contains about 57,000 sentences classified into 28 fine grained emotions. The count of data points with single labels before and after augmentation are shown in Table 1.

The classes in bold are those which were under the 80:20 ratio specified above and were considered for augmentation. The classification task was done using a BERT model as specified by J. Devlin et al. (2019) [12] and the results of the model before and after augmentation are as shown in Table 2.

It was observed that amongst the 14 classes that were augmented, 11 classes showed improvement in the F1 Score, with the most significant improvements in classes like Grief (0.36 from 0.00) and Relief (0.69 from 0.15). This is an important improvement as this shows that as the model was previously not even able to identify a single sentence as grief, it now has drastically improved performance over it. This is an indicator that the algorithm is generating synonyms which are portraying the meaning of the label correctly and hence the diversity of the emotion is increased. Similar drastic increase can be seen in the Relief class. Apart from this, there were some classes like Embarrassment or Pride, which showed reduced performance, but not by a large factor. Overall, the augmentation technique proved to be useful for the model, increasing the macro-average F1 score from 0.46 to 0.52.

Table 1. Before and After Augmentation label-wise count (only single-label sentences)

S. No	Label	Before	After
1	Admiration	2710	2710
2	Amusement	1652	1652
3	Anger	1025	1025
4	*Annoyance*	1451	1451
5	*Approval*	1873	1873
6	*Caring*	649	78
7	*Confusion*	858	858
8	*Curiosity*	1389	1389
9	*Desire*	389	773
10	*Disappointment*	709	846
11	*Disapproval*	1402	1402
12	*Disgust*	498	781
13	*Embarrassment*	203	699
14	*Excitement*	510	753
15	*Fear*	430	757
16	*Gratitude*	1857	1857
17	*Grief*	39	546
18	*Joy*	853	853
19	*Love*	1427	1427
20	*Nervousness*	85	510
21	*Neutral*	12823	12823
22	*Optimism*	861	861
23	*Pride*	51	553
24	*Realization*	586	803
25	*Relief*	88	622
26	*Remorse*	353	608
27	*Sadness*	817	817
28	*Surprise*	720	850

In the SST2 and SST5 datasets, accuracy is a reasonable metric as there is less class imbalance, and the classification is a multi-class classification and not a multi-label

Table 2. Class-wise F1 score of the GoEmotions Dataset

S. No	Label	F1 Score	
		Before *	After
1	Admiration	0.65	0.66
2	Amusement	0.80	0.83
3	Anger	0.47	0.51
4	*Annoyance*	0.34	0.35
5	*Approval*	0.36	0.41
6	*Caring*	0.39	0.47
7	*Confusion*	0.37	0.42
8	*Curiosity*	0.54	0.57
9	*Desire*	0.49	0.50
10	*Disappointment*	0.28	0.29
11	*Disapproval*	0.39	0.40
12	*Disgust*	0.45	0.46
13	*Embarrassment*	0.43	0.39
14	*Excitement*	0.34	0.44
15	*Fear*	0.60	0.68
16	*Gratitude*	0.86	0.92
17	*Grief*	0.00	0.36
18	*Joy*	0.51	0.62
19	*Love*	0.78	0.80
20	*Nervousness*	0.35	0.4
21	*Neutral*	0.68	0.60
22	*Optimism*	0.51	0.5
23	*Pride*	0.36	0.26
24	*Realization*	0.21	0.36
25	*Relief*	0.15	0.69
26	*Remorse*	0.66	0.53
27	*Sadness*	0.49	0.54
28	*Surprise*	0.50	0.69

* Before Results were taken from the GoEmotions paper [6]

classification (i.e., exactly one classification for each data point). The accuracy of the GoEmotions model is also given for sake of completeness (Table 3).

Table 3. Comparison of BERT on datasets before and after augmentation

Dataset	Accuracy	
	Without Augmentation	With Augmentation
GoEmotions	42.19	44.59
SST2	91.10	91.76
SST5	48.82	50.31

5 Conclusion

Data Augmentation in NLP proves to be a challenging, yet effective task to improve the quality and quantity of existing textual datasets. Our proposed algorithm aims at improving the synonym replacement data augmentation technique for emotion classification datasets. We employ BERT for this task and devise a novel word choosing and scoring system to increase diversity of data points in a dataset. After performing augmentation using our algorithm, we evaluate the performance of an emotion classifier model which was first trained on the original dataset, and then compare its performance when it is trained on the augmented dataset, keeping all the characteristics and hyperparameters of the model the same. We iteratively developed our algorithm while working on the GoEmotions dataset, which is one of the largest manually annotated datasets for emotion classification. For this dataset, we observed an improvement in the model's performance when trained after augmentation. After augmentation, the model was able to even identify classes for which it didn't classify a single correct data point earlier. We also ran our algorithm on two other benchmark datasets, the SST2 and SST5 datasets, and saw improved performance after augmentation on those datasets too. Hence, according to our results, we conclude that the proposed algorithm helps in increasing the quality and diversity of the datasets, which further improves the emotion classification task.

6 Future Scope

In this project, we have proposed an algorithm that is able to generate contextually similar synonyms in a sentence. It can choose the most emotion portraying words and is able to score and rank final replacements according to their similarity with the original sentence. As a result, the diversity of emotion labeling datasets can be increased, and the scarcity of some emotion classes can be removed. As technology progresses, and new research occurs, there are some aspects of the algorithm which may be improved. It is possible that the algorithm flow be further extended to datasets other than emotion classification tasks. For this, the word choosing and scoring part may have to be altered slightly according to the types of labels being processed. Apart from this, another improvement can be related to the thresholds that are assigned. Currently, the thresholds are assigned solely by observation. A possible improvement can be to develop a fixed standard for setting the thresholds used in calculating similarities, which would be dependent upon the amount of diversity and quantity increase required in the dataset. This would make the algorithm more easily accessible and usable.

References

1. Feng, S.Y., et al.: A survey of data augmentation approaches for NLP. arXiv preprint arXiv: 2105.03075 (2021)
2. Wei, J., Zou, K.: Eda: easy data augmentation techniques for boosting performance on text classification tasks. arXiv preprint arXiv:1901.11196 (2019)
3. Kobayashi, S.: Contextual augmentation: data augmentation by words with paradigmatic relations. arXiv preprint arXiv:1805.06201 (2018)
4. Ekman, P.: Facial expressions of emotion: new findings, new questions. Psychol. Sci. **3**(1), 34–38 (1992). https://doi.org/10.1111/j.1467-9280.1992.tb00253.x.S2CID9274447
5. Shaver, P., Schwartz, J., Kirson, D., O'connor, C.: Emotion knowledge: further exploration of a prototype approach. J. Pers. Soc. Psychol. **52**(6), 1061–1086 (1987). https://doi.org/10.1037/0022-3514.52.6.1061.PMID3598857
6. Demszky, D., Movshovitz-Attias, D., Ko, J., Cowen, A., Nemade, G., Ravi, S.: GoEmotions: a dataset of fine-grained emotions. arXiv preprint arXiv:2005.00547 (2020)
7. Ortu, M., et al.: The emotional side of software developers in JIRA. In: Proceedings of the 13th International Conference on Mining Software Repositories, MSR 2016, Austin, Texas, pp. 480–483. Association for Computing Machinery, New York (2016)
8. Scherer, K.R., Wallbott, H.G.: Evidence for universality and cultural variation of differential emotion response patterning. J. Pers. Soc. Psychol. **66**(2), 310 (1994)
9. Socher, R., et al.: Recursive deep models for semantic compositionality over a sentiment treebank. In: Proceedings of the 2013 Conference on Empirical Methods in Natural Language Processing, pp. 1631–16422013
10. Fadaee, M., Bisazza, A., Monz, C.: Data augmentation for low-resource neural machine translation. In: ACL, pp. 567–573 (2017)
11. Imran, M.M., Jain, Y., Chatterjee, P., Damevski, K.: Data augmentation for improving emotion recognition in software engineering communication. arXiv (2022)
12. Devlin, J., Chang, M.-W., Lee, K., Toutanova, K.: BERT: pre-training of deep bidirectional transformers for language understanding. arXiv [cs.CL] (2019)

Internet of Medical Things: Empowering Mobility and Health Monitoring with a Smart Walking Stick

Tushar Bhatia, Madhulika Bhaduria(✉), and Subash Chand Gupta(✉)

Department of Computer Science and Engineering, Amity University, Noida, Uttar Pradesh, India
{mbhaduria,scgupta}@s.amity.edu

Abstract. This paper presents the design of low-cost Smart Walking Sticks that aims to provide a comprehensive set of features to enhance user experience and functionality. The device provides various features including Step Count, Heart Rate and SpO2 measurement, Stress Measurement, Smart Home Control, Stopwatch, and Weather Information. These features enable users to monitor their physical activity, vital signs, and stress levels and promote overall well-being. The Smart Walking Stick is designed with modularity in mind, ensuring easy installation and replacement of components. The Raspberry Pi Pico W microcontroller serves as the main board for device operations, providing a powerful and flexible platform. The MAX30102 sensor is utilized for Heart Rate Measurement, while the MPU6500 sensor enables Fall Detection and Step Count functionalities. To offer a user-friendly interface, an SSD1306 0.96-in. OLED display is incorporated. Furthermore, the device incorporates a critical safety feature by integrating Amazon Web Services (AWS) to enable Help Request. In the event of Fall Detection, an SMS is sent to predefined contacts for prompt assistance. The device also contains a 5-W Speaker to emit a loud noise to request assistance from anyone nearby. The device also provides the ability to request Help if required, using the same SMS service. The device can also be used to control Smart Home devices such as Lights, Fans, Switches, and other Smart Devices using Amazon Alexa and AWS. The device achieves fall detection accuracy of 98%, heart rate accuracy of 96% and SpO2 accuracy of 98%.

Keywords: IoMT · AWS · Smart Walking Stick · Assistive aids · Fall Detection · Smart Home Control · Heart Rate · SpO2 · Stress detection · Step Count · Weather · MQTT

1 Introduction

The rapid evolution of IoMT (Internet of Medical Things) has revolutionized healthcare systems by introducing advanced devices and technologies. Common IoMT devices include Fitness Wearables, Smart Pills, Smart Pacemakers, and other Point Care devices that are generally seen in a Healthcare Environment. These devices allow us to generate real-time data and have streamlined clinical processes. Additionally, assistive aids

N. Chauhan et al. (Eds.): MIND 2023, CCIS 2128, pp. 15–27, 2024.
https://doi.org/10.1007/978-3-031-62217-5_2

such as Walking sticks, Crutches, and Walkers have significantly benefited the elderly and differently-abled individuals. Assistive Technology enables people to live healthy, productive, and independent lives and to participate in their daily lives, without these technologies, people are often excluded, and isolated thereby depriving themselves of their mental and physical health.

It is estimated by the WHO (World Health Organization) that by the year 2050, more than 3.5 billion people will need at least one assistive product, with many older people needing two or more [1]. These technologies are designed to have a positive impact on the health and well-being of an individual and their families. It may also provide socioeconomic benefits to such individuals. With the use of IoMT devices, individuals can live independent and dignified lives. To empower elderly and differently-abled individuals, a Smart Walking Stick is designed which includes various sensors and connectivity features.

2 Related Works

There have been significant advances in the field of Smart Assistive Aids. Da-Ming Ding et al. [2], have designed a Fall detection method based on the SPRT method. Their method uses an STM32 with multiple sensors to achieve a Fall detection rate of about 160 ms. They have been able to achieve accuracy higher than 94.6% than traditional algorithms.

Yusheng Wang et al. [3] have designed an adaptive threshold for the ZUPT algorithm. Their work uses a modified ZUPT algorithm to provide a Pedestrian Navigation System. The inertial system is mounted on the shoe of the pedestrian and uses a VN-200 IMU.

Wan-Jung Chang et al. [4] designed an assistive system for Visually Impaired People by designing a Smart Stick for Aerial Obstacle Avoidance and Fall Detection.

Sathya Narayanan E et al. [5] have designed an IoT-based smart walking cane for typhlotic with voice assistance. They have designed a Smart Walking Stick that uses an Ultrasonic Sensor, Global Positioning System (GPS), and other sensors to help navigate the elderly.

M. Alwan et al. [6] Designed an IoT-based passive Floor-Vibration detector for the Elderly. They have designed a vibration-based fall detector, for differently-abled individuals.

Adnan Dabir [7] developed a GPS and IoT-equipped Smart Walking stick. They used a GSM-GPRS module, Raspberry Pi Zero W and used a 3-axis accelerometer, and a PPG sensor with a module to avoid any false alarms.

Pedro Batoca et al. [8] have designed a physical rehabilitation center with walking aids. The developed system is based on an ESP32 with an IMU (Inertial Measuring Unit) mounted in a crutch. They have used Cloud data storage and MQTT protocol and has designed a server application for physiotherapist and patients to view and analyze data from each session.

Carlos Nave et al. [9] have designed an IoT-based Physical Rehabilitation solution based on Smart Walkers, a Multimodal sensing solution including IMU, Load Cells, and Ultrasound sensor was designed and implemented. Their approach uses Arduino Mega to calculate Walking Metrics and store them in the cloud, where the data can be analyzed using a web app.

Maria Martins et al. [10] developed a smart walker to detect the user's movement and guide the walker. The designed device uses a fuzzy logic algorithm to control the walker's movement and permits the user to manipulate the smart walker at their own pace. Various advancements have been made to target different audiences, however the cost of manufacturing such devices on a large scale is expensive such as walking device designed by [6] costs INR 9000, whereas the proposed device costs INR 2000. This proposed device offers a low-cost alternative to other proposed devices.

3 Material and Design

The device is designed to offer a low-cost and lightweight approach while offering a comprehensive suite of features. To ensure interoperability a modular approach was used, this allows the module to be mounted on any assistive aid such as a Walking Stick or a Walker. To support this idea a general-purpose Walking Stick is used, this allowed us to prioritize user comfort and reduce fatigue. The incorporation of these features allows us to provide a user-friendly grip while ensuring optimal usability for the user. As the module is mounted on an off-shelf stick, it can be adjusted easily to any custom-made stick for the user. This ensures that the user is provided with optimum comfort.

The Walking Stick supports a maximum weight of 80 to 100 kg. The total weight of the module is 300 g. It is equipped with a power bank of 4400 mah. The Raspberry Pi Pico W [11] offers sleep and dormant mode. If the device is used continuously, it can be powered for 2 days and consumes 150 mA as peak consumption. If the device is in dormant mode, it consumes 0.8 mA which can last the device around 6 months. Along with the module, as shown in Fig. 1, an SSD1306 [12] Display module is mounted at the handle of the walking stick. The Module uses a White OLED display, providing great viewing angles, even in an outside environment. A MAX30102 [13] Sensor is also mounted just below the display along the handle to measure Heart Rate and SpO2.

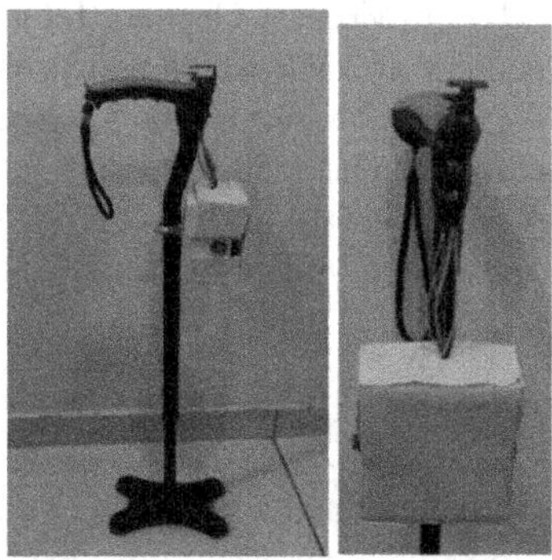

Fig. 1. Module mounted on a walking stick. (Side view/Front view)

The device as shown in Fig. 2 shows a Raspberry Pi Pico W, mounted on top of a breadboard along with an MPU6500 [14] which acts as a Gyroscope and Accelerometer

Sensor, providing 6 DOF (Degrees of Freedom). The module also shows us a speaker along with an LM386 [15] module to provide PWM signals to the speaker. The device is powered at 5 V through the VSYS Pin of the Pico W. An Interactive User Interface is designed for the Walking Stick, which can be controlled using 2 buttons as shown in Fig. 1. The modules are designed to offer a set of I2C addresses that can be used to communicate with the device.

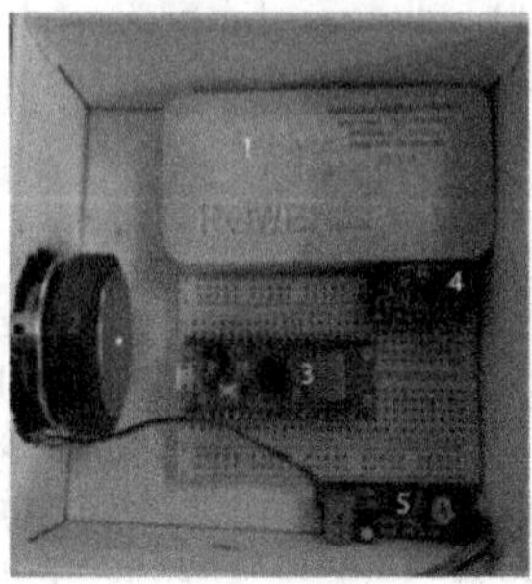

Fig. 2. Inside the module (without connecting wires)

The main board offers 2 I2C (Inter-Integrated Circuit) buses along with other protocols such as SPI, and UART, however, to ensure the timing signals are synchronized, I2C is used. The device first detects if the required sensors are present on the I2C bus before performing other operations. This allows the device to perform a hardware check before executing any other operation. The main board powers the modules using the VSYS (System input voltage (1.8 V to 5.5 V)) pin of the device as it uses the onboard SMPS supply to generate 3.3 V which allows us to power all the sensors using the 3v3(OUT) pin and it also protects against any hikes that may occur during the usage of the device. The main board also supports an onboard Wi-Fi module which allows us to directly use Wi-Fi and Bluetooth without requiring any additional configuration. It allows us to connect to Amazon Web Services using MQTT (Message Queuing Telemetry Transport). The main board has an onboard flash memory of 2 MB which allows us to store the configuration files required to connect to AWS IoT Core service, thus providing the power to leverage Cloud Services. The flash memory can be configured during the operations, it allows us to perform CRUD operations on the device itself using AWS services. Multithreading was also implemented to ensure smooth functioning.

4 Material and Methods

This section presents the various features and functionalities that have been implemented. These features are designed to provide an easy-to-use experience along with critical safety features such as Helpline requests and Fall detection. The following subsections detail each implemented feature.

4.1 Fall Detection and Step Count

To facilitate continuous fall detection and step count, a custom trigger-based algorithm was designed to calculate fall detection and step counts. Initially, a custom offset is applied to convert the raw values into meaningful readings. A low pass filter is applied with subsequent calibration to initialize the sensor. The sensor provides readings as a tuple of ax,ay,az each being raw accelerometer values and gx,gy,gz as raw gyroscope values along each axis. The Euclidean Norm [16] of the Acceleration vector is calculated by using the formulae:

$$Rawamplitude = \sqrt{ax^2 + ay^2 + az^2}$$

The formulae square the acceleration values along each axis, sum them, and then take the square root to obtain the magnitude of the acceleration vector. The raw amplitude is multiplied by 10 for final conversion. The same formulae are used to calculate gyroscope values. The Fall Detection algorithm uses these values as a basis to detect falls using custom Triggers.

The fall detection algorithm is divided into several stages:

- Trigger 1: This stage detects an initial acceleration that exceeds a threshold value. When this threshold is crossed, a trigger flag is activated. The threshold is 39 units for this stage as amplitude value.
- Trigger 2: Once Trigger 1 is activated, the algorithm checks if the acceleration remains above a certain level for a specified duration and if there is a significant change in the gyroscope readings. If these conditions are met, Trigger 2 is activated, indicating a potentially dangerous situation. The amplitude value is greater than 12.
- Trigger 3: When Trigger 2 is activated, the code checks if the gyroscope readings remain within a specific range for a certain duration. If these conditions are satisfied, Trigger 3 is activated, indicating a possible fall. The threshold angle change for this step is between 700 and 800.

Fall detection: When Trigger 3 is activated, the code performs a final check to confirm if the gyroscope readings indicate a fall. If the readings fall within a specified range, a fall is detected. When a fall is detected, a PWM (Pulse Width Modulation) signal is sent to the speaker to alert anyone in the presence of the stick. As well as the display also shows a Fall Icon and Text as shown in Fig. 3. The next step is to send a Help Request to all the family contacts stored on the Mainboard. The Device uses MQTT with AWS IoT Core to facilitate and call a custom AWS Lambda Function which then processes the message and uses AWS SNS (Simple Notification Service) to send a custom SMS message to all the family members. The Recorded Latency was 200 ms for the complete execution.

The flowchart in Fig. 4 shows the order of execution and the message that is published on the edge device indicating successful execution of the algorithm.

For the Step Counter Application, the device maintains a step counter and uses the calculated acceleration and gyroscope values to calculate each step. A custom message is also played when the user reaches a certain target. Figure 5 shows the step counter interface.

Fig. 3. Fall Detection icon with Fall Detected text.

Fig. 4. Flow chart indicating AWS architecture used for Help Request and Help Message

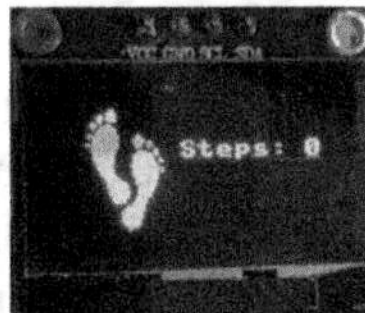

Fig. 5. Step Counter User Interface

4.2 Heart Rate and SpO2 Measurement

The sensor is mounted in a favorable position for the user. The sensor provides the raw readings of Red and IR(Infrared) LED. The data collected by the sensor represents the intensity of red light detected by the sensor after passing through blood vessels in the fingertip. As the heart pumps blood through the vessels, the amount of absorbed and reflected changes, resulting in a pulsatile signal. The collected data is then converted into meaningful values by applying a Low-pass Filter to remove any noise and high-frequency components from the signal. The low-pass filter smooths the data and makes it easier to identify any peak. The Filtered data is then added to the FIFO Buffer which maintains a window of the most recent data points. The algorithm then finds peaks by comparing each data point in the buffer with its adjacent points. If the data point is higher than both its previous and next points, it is considered a peak.

The algorithm dynamically adjusts the peak detection thresholds based on the previous peak intervals and keeps track of the time intervals between two consecutive peaks and the first peak of the previous and current cycle. A peak threshold is also defined to identify any valid peaks and reduce the likelihood of false positives due to any noise in the signal. Using the onboard IR Led, the sensor detects if a finger is placed on the sensor or not. If the sensor detects a finger, it calculates the BPM using the following formulae [17]:

$$BPM = 60 * \frac{SamplingRate}{AveragePeakInterval}$$

Here the sampling rate is the rate at which data is collected by the sensor. The sensor is also used to calculate SpO2(Peripheral Capillary Oxygen Saturation). The algorithm estimates the oxygen saturation level in the blood, specifically the percentage of hemoglobin saturated with oxygen, using data from the Red and IR signals. This is done specifically by using IR signals as it is observed that Infrared light is absorbed more by oxygenated blood than deoxygenated blood.

The red and IR signals consist of both AC and DC components. The AC component represents the pulsatile changes in the signal due to the heartbeat, while the DC component represents the baseline intensity of the signal. To calculate the AC component the algorithm uses the previous buffer and peak lists used in the heartbeat algorithm and subtracts the mean value of the signal from the current signal. To calculate the DC component of the signals the algorithm is equal to the fractional value of the sum of the values in the buffer and peak, divided by the number of peaks.

The algorithm then uses the AC and DC components of the individual signals to calculate absorbance, by using the following formulae:

$$Absorbance = \log_{10} \frac{DC}{AC}$$

The SpO2 value is calculated based on the ratio of the absorbance of Red and IR light. The following formulae is based on the Beer-Lambert Law which allows us to calculate the light absorbance to the concentration of the absorbing material.

$$SpO2 = a + b * \left(\frac{red_{absorbance}}{ir_{absorbance}} \right) + c$$

Here the values of a, b, and c are empirically derived, where a = 110, b = -25, and c = -36.5. A constant c was also added in addition to the previous work by Pattana Kainan et al. [17] to reach the required accuracy when compared to a general-purpose Pulse Oximeter. The values are calculated and displayed on the display as shown in Fig. 6.

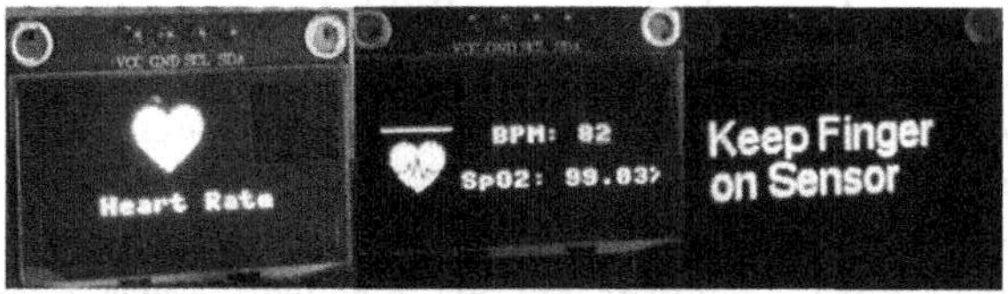

Fig. 6. Heart Rate and SpO2 measurement user interface

4.3 Smart Home Control

To promote independent lifestyle, the device is designed to control Smart Home devices such as Switches, Lights, Fans, Doors, and other smart home devices. To facilitate such a service, Amazon Web Services (AWS) is used. AWS is a very popular cloud platform, and its integration with Amazon Alexa, which is a very popular voice assistant, allows the device to be integrated with existing smart home environments. Amazon allows developers to create custom smart home skills which act as an API for Alexa to be used in conjecture with cloud services, a Custom Home Skill is designed to allow the user to configure a Virtual Button with Alexa Smart Routines to control their Smart Home Devices. The Virtual Button is made using API gateway, another popular service that allows us to design REST and HTTP API and provides us with endpoints that can be used to call the Alexa Skill to control the Smart Home devices. The Button information is stored in DynamoDB, a NoSQL service, with their subsequent requests. Figure 7 shows the flow chart for a successful request sent using AWS. The main board connects to AWS using MQTT protocol.

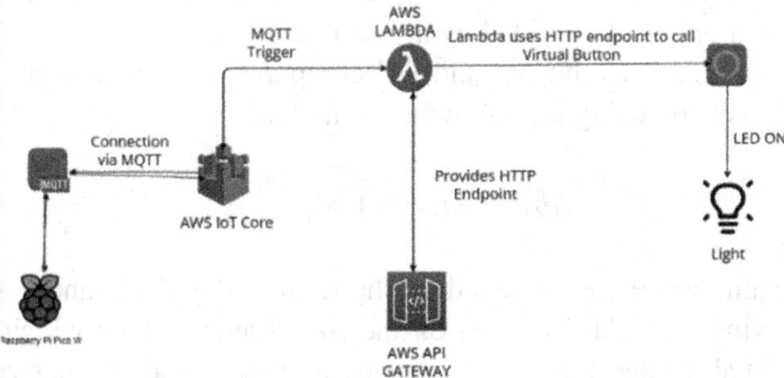

Fig. 7. Flow Chart of AWS services used for Smart Home Control

MQTT is a very popular communication protocol for IoT devices. It is an event-driven protocol and uses a Pub/Sub architecture. AWS offers the capability to connect IoT devices using AWS IoT core service, which allows us to leverage the power of AWS Services. It can be configured to subscribe to a particular Topic where messages can be published. AWS allows us to use their MQTT broker to connect to AWS IoT Core. Once such a connection is established, the device is ready to send messages to a specific topic. Lambda functions were designed to connect AWS IoT Core with our HTTP endpoints to allow the device to send a message which can act as a trigger to the function to turn on the device. To indicate a successful execution, the boto3 library is used in the lambda function which publishes a success message back to the Topic, which is received by the device. A success message as shown in Fig. 8 is shown on the display. If the device is not available or the routine is not triggered due to network issues, a failed message is displayed. The average latency recorded for a successful operation is about 2 s.

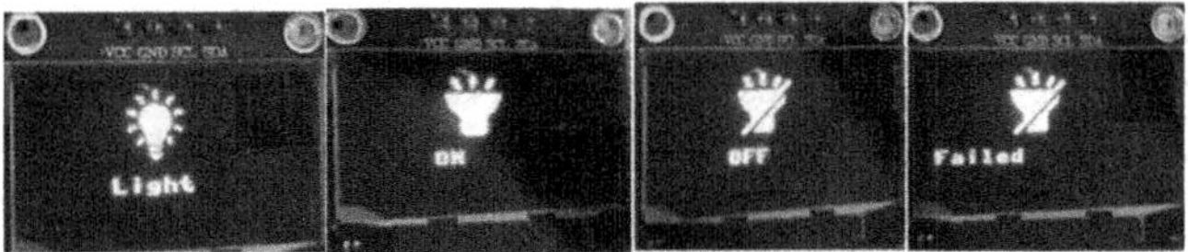

Fig. 8. Message Received after successful execution.

4.4 Stopwatch

A Stopwatch functionality is offered by the device, for the user. The user can take advantage of such functionality for Exercise and Physiotherapy. The device uses the NTP (Network Time Protocol) to reset the clock to the current time. The user can use the navigation buttons to Start, Stop or Reset the clock. The Elapsed time is performed by subtracting the start time and the end time. The device uses the display to show the Elapsed time as shown in Fig. 9.

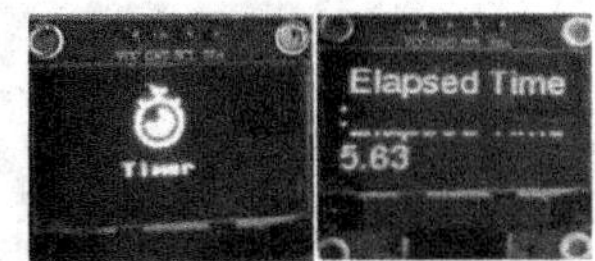

Fig. 9. Stopwatch user interface

4.5 Weather and Helpline

The device can also show weather reports using freeweatherAPI which is an API service designed by weather API. The response generated is then forwarded to a Lambda function using REST API made by using API Gateway of a Lambda Function. The lambda function is designed to receive the input and publish the required response to the MQTT broker of the AWS IoT core. Figure 10 shows the flow of subsequent request from device to AWS services. The device uses Wi-Fi to connect to the available Wi-Fi networks and uses a database of City names stored on Flash Memory to load up city names.

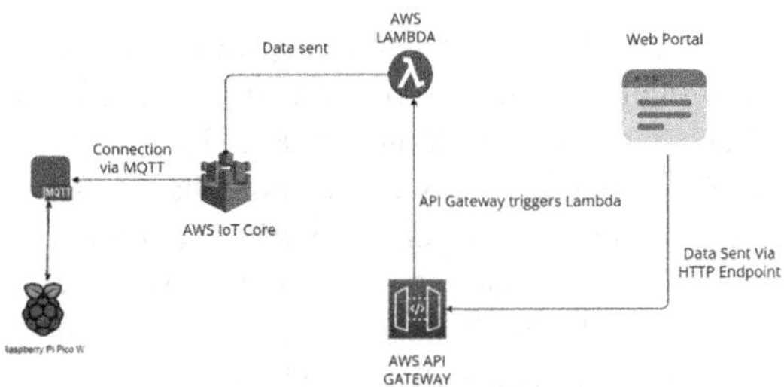

Fig. 10. Flow chart of AWS services used for CRUD operations by Web Portal

The device makes an HTTP request to the freeweatherAPI to receive the required JSON response. The device processes the JSON response and displays the current Temperature, Weather conditions, and Location as shown in Fig. 11.

A user can request help by using the Helpline function of the device. The device publishes the phone number and name of the Contacts in the Contact database present in the Flash memory to the MQTT broker, to send the required Helpline information to AWS IoT Core which is forwarded to a Lambda function. The lambda function uses Amazon SNS (Simple Notification Service) to send a custom Help Message to all the individuals present in the Contact List. The Contact List can be edited using a website portal. The portal allows the user to perform CRUD (Create, Read, Update, Delete) operations on the database stored on the flash memory. If the User sends a response. The response is forwarded to a Lambda function which receives the JSON response and publishes a message to the MQTT broker to perform the required operation on the device. The device displays the Name and the phone number received, indicating a successful operation as shown in Fig. 11.

Fig. 11. Weather user interface and Helpline interface

4.6 Stress Monitoring and Wi-Fi Reset

The devices use the same algorithm stated in the previous section to calculate Heart Rate. A custom algorithm based upon the peak detection method is used to calculate HRV (Heart Rate Variability) to calculate the HRV index to measure Stress. The algorithm calculates the RR intervals using the peak detection method, the algorithm then uses the RR interval to calculate the Mean RR and the standard deviation of the RR interval. It uses the following formulae [18] to calculate the HRV index.

$$HRV\ Index = \frac{RR\ Mean}{RR\ Standard\ Deviation}$$

The algorithm then uses the BPM calculated using earlier methods and the calculated HRV index and BPM to monitor stress based on a custom threshold. The Stress index is thereby calculated and displayed as shown in Fig. 13. The device also offers the capability to reset the Wi-Fi details if any connection change is required. The device achieves this by using a website portal to perform CRUD operations on a Wi-Fi database stored on the flash memory of the device. A user can thereby register themselves on the Portal which is used to change the Wi-Fi details of the device. If any request is received by the device. It displays the Name and SSID of the Wi-Fi indicating a successful change in the database. The user can use the Wi-Fi reset function to reset the Wi-Fi as shown in Fig. 12.

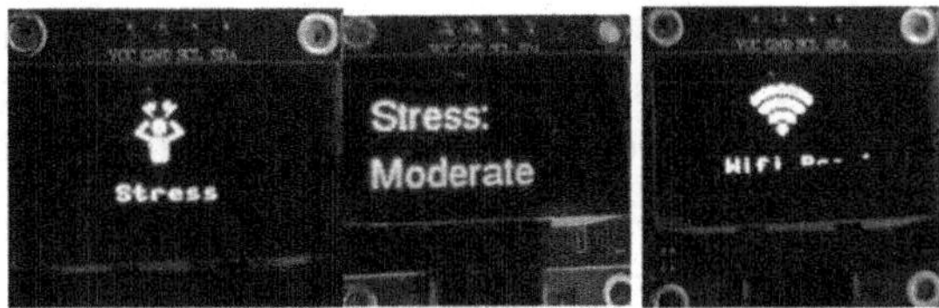

Fig. 12. Stress interface and Wi-Fi Reset

5 Results and Discussion

This section provides an opportunity to delve deeper into the findings and implications of the study.

- Evaluation of Design Features:
  A simple modular approach is adopted to ensure interoperability. The module can be easily installed on any system such as a walker. The module weighs about 300 g, allowing it to be lightweight, and providing optimum comfort to the individual.
- Impact on User Mobility and Health Monitoring:
  The Fall Detection algorithm was tested in a controlled environment and detected fall with a success rate of 98% and was calculated by using a similar method to [19]. To avoid any false alarms a similar approach as in [6, 11] can be followed to filter out any false readings. The Heart Rate and SpO2 algorithm was tested in accordance with a general-purpose Pulse Oximeter. The accuracy for Heart Rate was found to be 96% whereas the accuracy for SpO2 was found to be 98%. To allow the Fall detection and other operations to be performed simultaneously, multi-threading was used. This allowed us to use Fall Detection feature along with other functions of the device.
- Security Considerations
  To ensure security is maintained at each step, various measures were taken. As the device is turned on, a sensor check is performed to ensure all sensors are working correctly. To ensure that the keys are safe. They are encrypted in cryptographic formats by the AWS and stored as environment variables in the device. The device with the correct client key and secret key is allowed to access AWS services. For the web portals, AWS API gateway has been used. The APIs are protected against any DDOS and DOS attacks to ensure security [20].

6 Conclusion

This research paper acts as a foundation for the design of new assistive aids, by leveraging the power of embedded systems and cloud to provide a comprehensive suite of features. Development in other fields such as Artificial intelligence offers exciting opportunities to address specific challenges and reach a wider audience. Additionally, with the development of newer sensors and modules alternatives to the current design can be produced at a cheaper cost, along with device certifications for protection against physical phenomena such as rain, humidity, etc. This device is designed for closed environments such as homes, offices, and hospitals. The future work will include the addition of a SIM module to provide seamless connectivity and the ability to receive phone calls directly from the walking stick, it will also include integration with popular fitness APIs such as Google Fit, which can be used as a cloud-native hub to review the performance of an individual. A Body Area Network can also be designed to offer seamless integrations with other environments.

References

1. Lindström, A.: Assistive technology. Assistive technology (who.int) (2023)
2. Ding, D.-M., et al.: Fall detection system on smart walker based on multisensor data fusion and SPRT method. IEEE Access **10**, 80932–80948 (2022)
3. Wang, Y., Shkel, A.M.: Adaptive threshold for zero-velocity detector in ZUPT-aided pedestrian inertial navigation. IEEE Sens. Lett. **3**(11), 1–4 (2019)
4. Chang, W.-J., et al.: Design and implementation of an intelligent assistive system for visually impaired people for aerial obstacle avoidance and fall detection. IEEE Sens. J. **20**(17), 10199–10210 (2020)
5. SathyaNarayanan, E., Nithin, B.P., Vidhyasagar, P.: IoT based smart walking cane for typhlotic with voice assistance. In: 2016 Online International Conference on Green Engineering and Technologies (IC-GET). IEEE (2016)
6. Alwan, M., et al.: A smart and passive floor-vibration based fall detector for elderly. In: 2006 2nd International Conference on Information & Communication Technologies, vol. 1. IEEE (2006)
7. Dabir, A., et al.: GPS and IOT equipped smart walking stick. In: 2018 International Conference on Communication and Signal Processing (ICCSP). IEEE (2018)
8. Batoca, P., Postolache, O., Correia, A.: Physical therapy gait assessment based on smart sensing and cloud services. In: 2022 International Symposium on Sensing and Instrumentation in 5G and IoT Era (ISSI). IEEE (2022)
9. Nave, Carlos, and Octavian Postolache. "Smart walker based IoT physical rehabilitation system." 2018 International Symposium in Sensing and Instrumentation in IoT Era (ISSI). IEEE, 2018
10. Martins, M.M., et al.: Assistive mobility devices focusing on smart walkers: classification and review. Rob. Auton. Syst. **60**(4), 548–562 (2012)
11. Raspberry Pi. Raspberry Pi Pico W Datasheet (2023). https://datasheets.raspberrypi.com/picow/pico-w-datasheet.pdf datasheets.raspberrypi.com/picow/pico-w-datasheet.pdf
12. Solomon Tech, 2008, SSD1306, SSD1306 (adafruit.com)
13. Maxim Integrated. Max30102 High-Sensitivity Pulse Oximeter and Heart-Rate Sensor for Wearable Health, MAX30102--High-Sensitivity Pulse Oximeter and Heart-Rate Sensor for Wearable Health (analog.com) (2018)
14. TDK InvenSense. MPU-6500, PS-MPU-6500A-01-v1.3.pdf (2020). https://www.tdk.com/en/index.html
15. Texas Instruments. LM386 Low Voltage audio amplifier (2023). https://ti.com/lit/ds/symlink/lm386.pdf
16. Lindfield, G., Penny, J.: Chapter 2-linear equations and eigensystems. Numer. Methods 73–156 (2019)
17. Kainan, P., et al.: New pulse oximetry detection based on the light absorbance ratio as determined from amplitude modulation indexes in the time and frequency domains. Biomed. Signal Process. Control **75**, 13627 (2022)
18. Stein, P.K.: Assessing heart rate variability from real-world Holter reports. Cardiac Electrophysiol. Rev. **6**, 239–244 (2002)

19. Wang, J., et al.: An enhanced fall detection system for elderly person monitoring using consumer home networks. IEEE Trans. Consum. Electron. **60**(1), 23–29 (2014)
20. Corbett, N.: Understanding the AWS IoT Security Model. Understanding the AWS IoT Security Model | The Internet of Things on AWS – Official Blog (2017). https://www.amazon.com/

MRI Based Spatio-Temporal Model for Alzheimer's Disease Prediction

S. Harshanandhini and J. Aravinth(✉)

Department of Electronics and Communication Engineering, Amrita School of Engineering, Amrita Vishwa Vidyapeetham, Coimbatore, India
j_aravinth@cb.amrita.edu

Abstract. Alzheimer's disease (AD) is a leading cause of memory loss and eventually leads to the mortality of affected individuals. It is characterized by structural changes in the brain, including the shrinkage of specific regions and the development of abnormalities. AD is a progressive neurodegenerative disease that worsens over time. Spatial analysis helps identify the affected brain regions, while temporal analysis provides insights into the disease progression and temporal patterns of change. Integrating both spatial and temporal information allows for a more accurate and detailed characterization of AD. Consequently, the development of a spatio-temporal model holds promise for early diagnosis of AD. This work proposes a spatio-temporal analysis using deep neural networks this utilizes Magnetic Resonance Imaging (MRI) data obtained from two sources: the Alzheimer's Disease Neuroimaging Initiative (ADNI) database and the Open Access Series of Imaging Scans (OASIS). Demographic information such as Mini-Mental State Examination (MMSE), Clinical Dementia Rating (CDR), Global Clinical Dementia Rating (GCDR), and whole brain volume are important in Alzheimer's prediction, as they provide valuable insights into cognitive function, disease progression, and brain health, aiding in the identification and assessment of individuals at risk or in the early stages of Alzheimer's disease. A spatio-temporal model called Convolutional Long Short-Term Memory (ConvLSTM) was developed for the analysis of spatio-temporal features using deep neural networks. The proposed ConvLSTM-based spatio-temporal model achieves an accuracy of 98% for all types of datasets, both with and without demographic information, enabling early prediction of AD.

Keywords: Alzheimer's disease · mild cognitive impairment · Alzheimer's Disease Neuroimaging Initiative · convolution neural network · Long Short-Term Memory · Convolutional Long Short-Term Memory · Open Access Series of Imaging Scans

1 Introduction

Alzheimer's disease (AD) is a neurological brain disorder that causes dementia, characterized by the loss of cells and shrinkage of the brain. It primarily affects

N. Chauhan et al. (Eds.): MIND 2023, CCIS 2128, pp. 28–44, 2024.
https://doi.org/10.1007/978-3-031-62217-5_3

the temporal lobe and hippocampus of the brain. Dementia has both physical and psychological effects, leading to impaired communication, behavioral changes, and difficulties in handling day-to-day activities [1]. A recent survey predicts that the prevalence of Alzheimer's disease is influenced by various factors, such as aging populations, advancements in healthcare, and changes in lifestyle, resulting in projections that may vary over time. Mild cognitive impairment (MCI) is an early stage of AD. Identifying AD at the MCI stage is crucial for detection and management. However, if MCI is detected in later stages, it becomes irreversible [2] and ultimately leads patients to death.

To predict and diagnose Alzheimer's disease, several demographic factors play a crucial role. These include the Mini-Mental State Examination (MMSE), Clinical Dementia Rating (CDR), Global Clinical Dementia Rating (GCDR), and whole brain volume. The MMSE assesses cognitive decline, while the CDR and GCDR scales evaluate the severity of dementia and functional impairment, aiding in understanding disease progression [1]. Additionally, measuring whole brain volume through imaging techniques like magnetic resonance imaging (MRI) reflects the loss of brain tissue associated with AD, thus enhancing accuracy in diagnosis and early detection [2].

Initially, traditional diagnosis methods for AD involved physical and neurological examinations, such as assessing coordination, reflexes, balance, and sense of sight, but these methods have their own limitations. Subsequently, lab tests and neuropsychological testing were introduced. To overcome these limitations, imaging modalities like computed tomography (CT), Positron emission tomography (PET), and MRI are now used [3]. MRI images are obtained from databases like Open Access Series of Imaging Scans (OASIS) and the Alzheimer's Disease Neuroimaging Initiative (ADNI), along with demographic information [4]. Due to overlapping symptoms in various stages of AD, detecting the disease requires specialized knowledge and can be time-consuming.

To address the different stages of AD, features were extracted from imaging modalities and initially classified using Machine Learning (ML) [5]. Subsequently, convolutional neural networks (CNNs) have been introduced for spatial analysis [6]. To enhance the accuracy of the diagnosis, temporal variations need to be examined for the progression of AD [3].

This study proposes a novel solution that involves analyzing spatio-temporal features using deep neural networks, particularly the Convolutional long short-term memory (ConvLSTM) model, to detect Alzheimer's disease in its stages [7]. These models were trained and evaluated with various datasets, both with and without demographic information, to improve the understanding and early detection of Alzheimer's disease.

The contribution of the paper is summarized as follows.

1. A new spatio-temporal model was developed for the timely prediction of AD.
2. ConvLSTM was introduced for analysis of spatio-temporal features using deep neural network.

The paper is structured as follows: Sect. 2 provides an overview of related works, which establishes the foundation for the proposed research. In Sect. 3, the proposed methodology is presented, outlining the workflow of the study. Section 4 is dedicated to presenting the experimental results and its analysis. Finally, Sect. 5 offers the conclusion, summarizing the key findings and contributions of the proposed work.

2 Related Work

This section focuses on a literature survey, which elucidates the relevant existing works related to the proposed study.

Imaging Modalities like MRI and FMRI were used for better prediction of AD from the ADNI and OASIS datasets by researchers [8,9]. However, OASIS has limited usage for AD detection research [10,11]. AD has five stages, and researchers have considered either two [1,2], three, or four [12,13] classes in their studies, with a focus on binary classification. OASIS contains two stages: Demented and non-Demented.

Initially, features like ROI, slice, and subject-based CNN were presented by [14,15] for the detection of AD. Subsequently, multiple feature fusion techniques like CCA [16] and multi-modality feature fusion [17] were adopted in most research [18,19] for better classification. Moreover, in the present state of the art, textural and correlation features were incorporated into the artificial intelligence system to classify AD into three different stages [20].

Spatial and temporal dimensions were addressed individually. [2,3] devised various CNN models and an Improved CNN+LSTM. These methods combine neural networks to process large datasets. While these models may have a lower computation speed in comparison to other models, they demonstrate higher computation complexity. In this study, a single neural network was devised to perform parallel analysis of spatio-temporal features.

3 Proposed Methodology

This section focuses on the development of the spatio-temporal model to improve the prediction of AD. Initially, three different datasets, namely OASIS, ADNI, and ADNI with temporal variation and demographic information, are used. Secondly, spatio-temporal models like CNN+LSTM, (2+1) D CNN, and ConvLSTM are evaluated using these datasets. Finally, classification is performed for both binary and multiple classes, further enhancing the accuracy of AD prediction. Figure 1 shows the proposed model.

3.1 Dataset

ADNI: 90 subjects were selected from the ADNI database which includes 30 AD, 30 MCI, and 30 CN to avoid imbalance. It incorporates 5066 2D T1 weighted images of baseline scans with demographic information [21] shown in Table 1. For classification data has been spilt into 60 subjects for training, 15 subjects for testing and 15 subjects for validation.

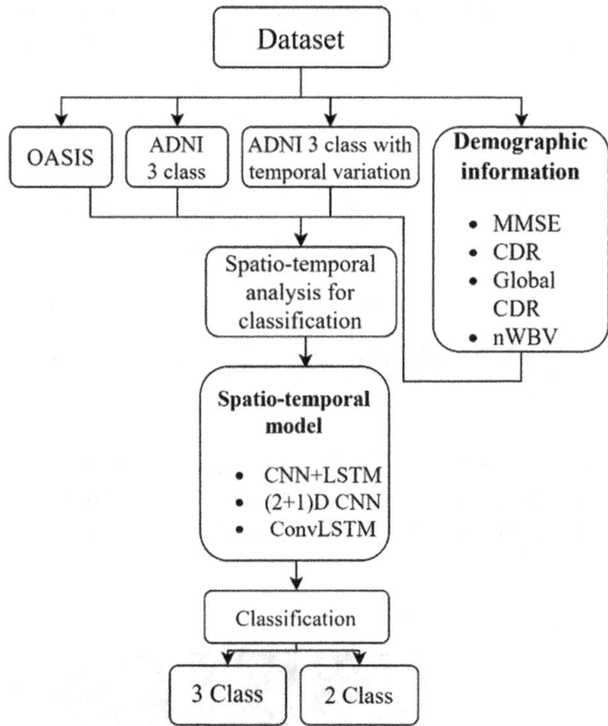

Fig. 1. Proposed Methodology.

ADNI Dataset with Temporal Variation: 10302 2D T1 weighted MRI images were collected at baseline,6 months, 12 months, and 24 months with demographic information [3] shown in TABLE I. 90 subjects including 30 subjects for each CN, MCI, and AD taken from the ADNI database and spilt into multiple class and binary classes such as CN vs MCI, MCI vs AD and AD vs CN. Spatial and temporal variations of the taken images are shown in Fig. 2. For classification data has been spilt into 60 subjects for training, 15 subjects for testing and 15 subjects for validation.

OASIS: OASIS-2 is a longitudinal collection of subjects with annotations as demented and non-demented [22]. T1-weighted MRI scans for 60 subjects were taken with calculations of the whole-brain volume and other demographic information shown in Table 1. For classification data has been spilt into 40 subjects for training, 10 subjects for testing and 10 subjects for validation.

Table 1 presents the dataset information along with its corresponding demographic information. The OASIS dataset consists of binary classes, namely demented and non-demented. The ADNI dataset and ADNI dataset with temporal variation contain three classes: CN, MCI, and AD, with 30 subjects per class. The MMSE score is measured on a 30-point scale, the CDR value is assessed on

Table 1. Dataset usage with number of subjects and classes with demographic information

Dataset	Class	Subjects	Demographic information				
			Sex M/F	MMSE	CDR	Global CDR	nWBV
ADNI (temporal variation)	CN	30	16/14	30	0	0	0.89
	MCI	30	19/11	26.9	0.5	1	0.73
	AD	30	17/13	17	1	1	0.66
ADNI	CN	30	16/14	29.8	0	0	0.89
	MCI	30	19/11	23.98	0.5	1	0.73
	AD	30	17/13	16.5	1	1	0.66
OASIS	Demented	30	18/12	24.96	0.5–1	1	0.722
	Non demented	30	22/8	29.29	0	0	0.74

a five-point scale, and the Global CDR is a two-point scale with values of 0 and 1. Additionally, whole brain volume was extracted using a toolkit. The inclusion of demographic information enhances the prediction of AD.

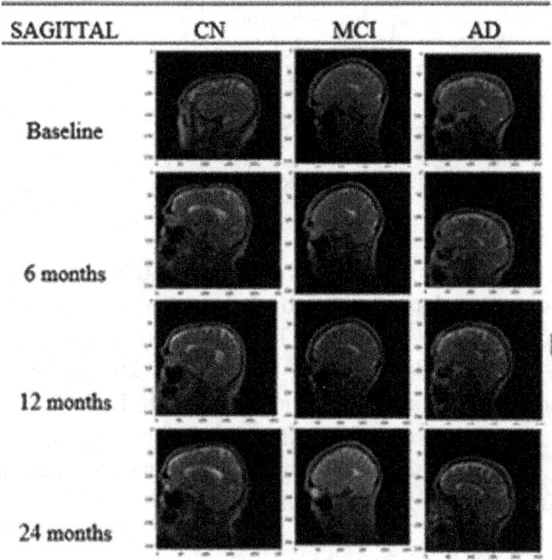

Fig. 2. Visualization of Dataset.

3.2 Spatio-Temporal Model

A spatiotemporal model is computational framework used to analyze and predict relationships in images that vary both in spatial and temporal. It combines spatial and temporal dimensions to capture the dynamics and interactions between different variables over time and across different locations or regions. Initially various datasets like OASIS ADNI and ADNI with temporal variation have been taken for analysis of spatial and temporal features. Later, it performs binary and multiple class classification for better prediction of AD with metrics like Accuracy, precision, recall, F1-Score [23,24].

CNN+LSTM. The combination of CNN and LSTM networks forms a deep learning architecture known as CNN+LSTM. It is commonly used for analyzing sequential data with spatial variations [3]. CNNs are effective at capturing spatial features in images and it consist of convolutional and pooling layer that automatically analysis the spatial and local features from input data. Later features have been extracted from flatten layer and given as input for LSTM. LSTMs captures long-term information and it is a recurrent neural network (RNN) that stores and update information over time [3]. LSTMs can effectively handle temporal variations and remember important information from previous time steps for prediction of AD shown in Fig. 3.

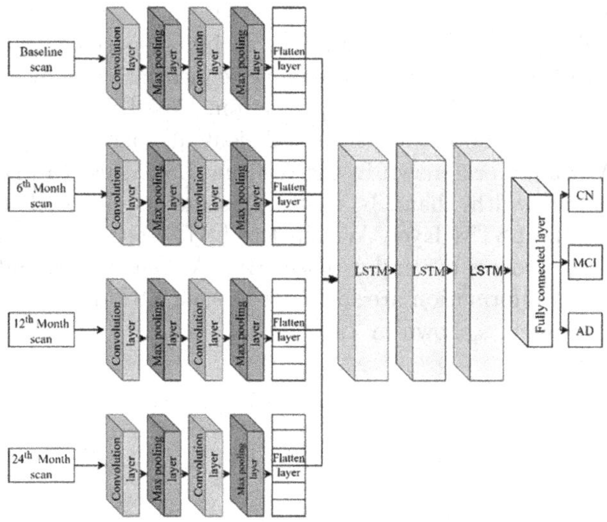

Fig. 3. CNN+LSTM Model

(2+1) D CNN. A convolutional neural network called a (2+1) D CNN uses both 1D and 2D convolutions [2]. Analysis of spatiotemporal characteristics, which have both a spatial and a temporal component, is frequently done using this technique. In a (2+1) D CNN, the temporal component reflects the temporal dimension, and the spatial component refers to the two-dimensional spatial information. Overall, a (2+1) D CNN has proved effective in the prediction of

AD and offers an efficient method for spatiotemporal data, exploiting both the spatial and temporal features of the input shown in Fig. 4.

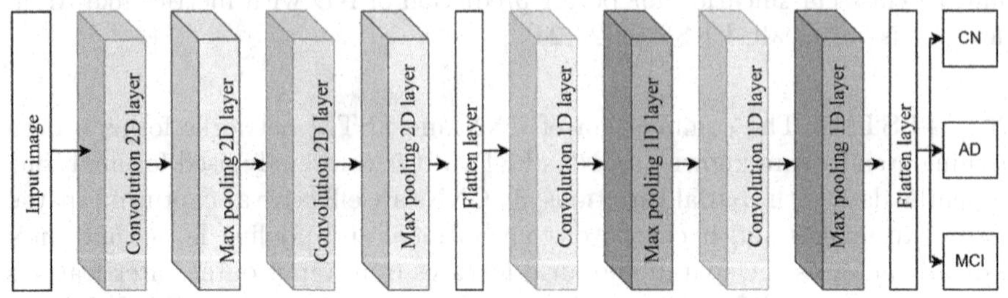

Fig. 4. (2+1) D CNN Model.

ConvLSTM. A convolutional LSTM network called ConvLSTM integrates convolutional operations into the LSTM architecture [7]. It has been created primarily to handle spatiotemporal data that includes spatial information. This particular kind of RNN excels in modelling sequential data by accumulating long-term knowledge. For better AD prediction, ConvLSTM aims to incorporate convolutional operations which are efficient at collecting spatial features into the LSTM framework shown in Fig. 5. Conv_LSTM uses a 2D tensor with dimensions (height, width, channels) that represents a series of 2D feature maps as the input to the LSTM layer. Within the LSTM cells, convolutional techniques are used to process this input tensor [10]. A memory cell and three gates control the flow of information are included in each LSTM cell shown in Fig. 6 and its Hyperparameters shown in Table 2.

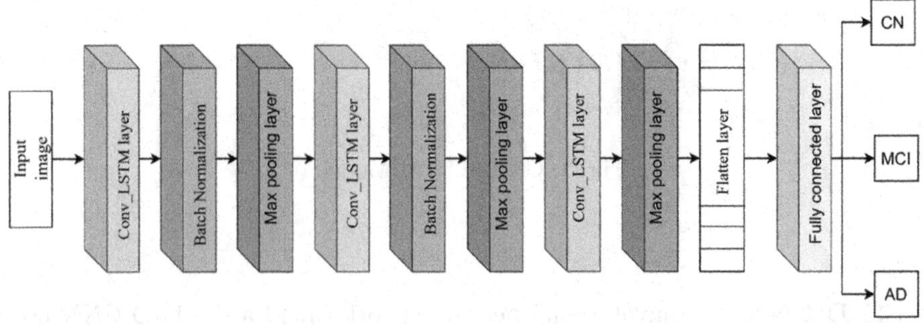

Fig. 5. ConvLSTM Model.

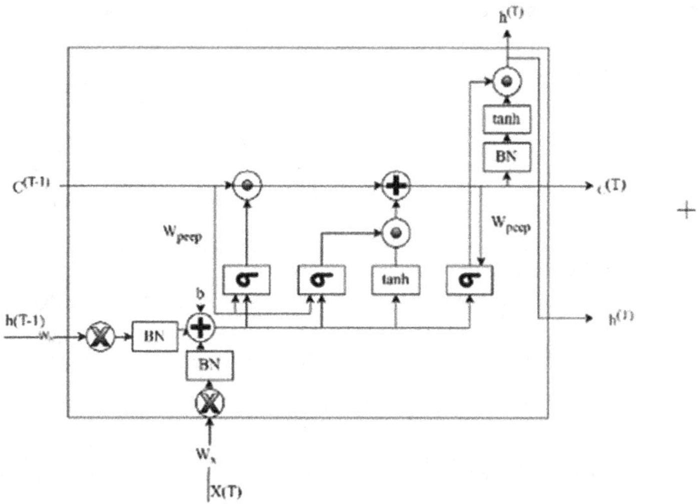

Fig. 6. Conv_LSTM layer.

Table 2. Hyperparameter for the proposed model

Hyperparameter	Name/value
Activation function	ReLu, Softmax
Epochs	20
Batch size	8
Loss function	Sparse_categorical_cross entropy
Optimizer	adam
Recurrent activation	sigmoid

4 Results and Discussion

In this chapter, the findings and discussions of the proposed work are presented.

4.1 ConvLSTM

ConvLSTM model have been developed for analyzing both spatial and temporal features in single layer to avoid computation complexity for better prediction of AD. The developed model has been examined by 3 different datasets with and without demographic information and the result have been shown in Tables and Training and validation accuracy and loss for ConvLSTM model is plotted in Fig. 7 and 8.

Table 3 shows the performance analysis of developed ConLSTM with various datasets like ADNI, ADNI with temporal variation, and OASI. The developed model performs better for ADNI dataset with temporal variation and OASIS dataset with accuracy of 98% respectively.

Table 3. Performance analysis of ConvLSTM for different dataset.

Spatio-temporal model Dataset	Class	ConvLSTM			
		Accuracy %	Precision	Recall	F1-score
ADNI	CN	97	0.99	0.99	0.99
	AD		0.98	1.00	0.99
	MCI		1.00	0.93	0.93
ADNI (with temporal variation)	CN	98	1.00	0.98	0.99
	AD		0.99	1.00	0.99
	MCI		0.99	0.99	0.99
OASIS	Demented	98	0.98	0.99	0.99
	Non-Demented		0.99	0.98	0.99

Table 4. Performance analysis of ConvLSTM for different dataset with demographic information.

Spatio-temporal model	Class	ConvLSTM with demographic information			
Dataset		Accuracy %	Precision	Recall	F1-score
ADNI	CN	98	1.00	0.99	0.99
	AD		0.98	1.00	0.99
	MCI		1.00	0.98	0.99
ADNI (with temporal variation)	CN	98	1.00	0.98	1.00
	AD		1.00	0.98	0.99
	MCI		0.98	1.00	1.00
OASIS	Demented	98	0.99	0.99	0.99
	Non-Demented		0.99	0.99	0.99

Table 4 displays the performance analysis of the developed ConvLSTM model using various datasets, including ADNI, ADNI with temporal variation, and OASIS with demographic information. The results indicate that the developed model exhibits superior performance, achieving an accuracy of 98% across all datasets that include demographic information.

Table 5 shows binary class classifications of datasets such as ADNI and ADNI with a temporal variation using ConvLSTM. ADNI with temporal variation dataset performs better than the ADNI dataset with accuracy of 98% respectively.

Table 6 shows binary class classification for datasets such as ADNI and ADNI with a temporal variation using ConvLSTM. The features were extracted from ConvLSTM and combine with demographic information and classified using Random Forest, dataset with demographic information archives 99% accuracy than datasets without demographic information.

Figure 7 displays the training and validation accuracy plot, revealing a minimal gap between the accuracy values in both training and validation phases. On

Table 5. Performance analysis of ConvLSTM for binary classes.

Spatio-temporal model	Class	ConvLSTM			
Dataset		Accuracy %	Precision	Recall	F1-score
ADNI	CN	97	0.98	0.98	0.98
	AD		0.98	0.97	0.98
	MCI	98	0.98	0.99	0.99
	AD		0.98	0.97	0.98
	CN	97	0.99	0.97	0.98
	MCI		0.97	0.98	0.98
ADNI (with temporal variation)	CN	98	1.00	0.98	0.99
	AD		0.98	1.00	0.99
	MCI	98	0.99	1.00	1.00
	AD		0.98	1.00	0.99
	CN	98	1.00	0.99	1.00
	MCI		0.99	1.00	1.00

Table 6. Performance analysis of ConvLSTM for binary classes with demographic information

Spatio-temporal model	Class	ConvLSTM with demographic information			
Dataset		Accuracy %	Precision	Recall	F1-score
ADNI	CN	99	0.99	0.99	0.99
	AD		0.99	0.98	0.99
	MCI	99	0.99	0.98	0.99
	AD		1.00	0.99	0.98
	CN	99	0.99	0.98	0.98
	MCI		0.99	0.99	1.00
ADNI (with temporal variation)	CN	99	0.99	0.97	0.98
	AD		0.99	1.00	0.98
	MCI	99	0.98	0.99	0.99
	AD		0.99	1.00	1.00
	CN	99	0.99	0.98	0.97
	MCI		0.98	0.97	0.98

the other hand, Fig. 8 shows the training and validation loss plot, demonstrating a consistent difference between the training and validation loss, which indicates a well-fitted model. This observation confirms that ConvLSTM performs effectively for all datasets, both with and without demographic information, resulting in improved classification of AD.

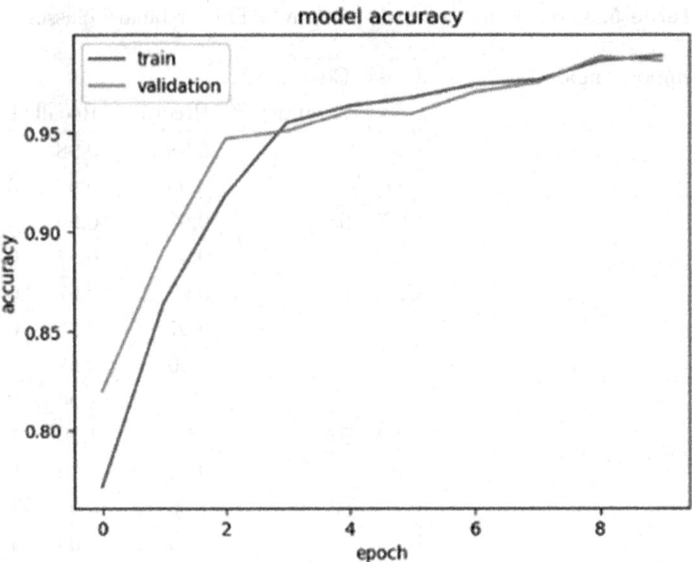

Fig. 7. Training and validation accuracy plot of ConvLSTM model.

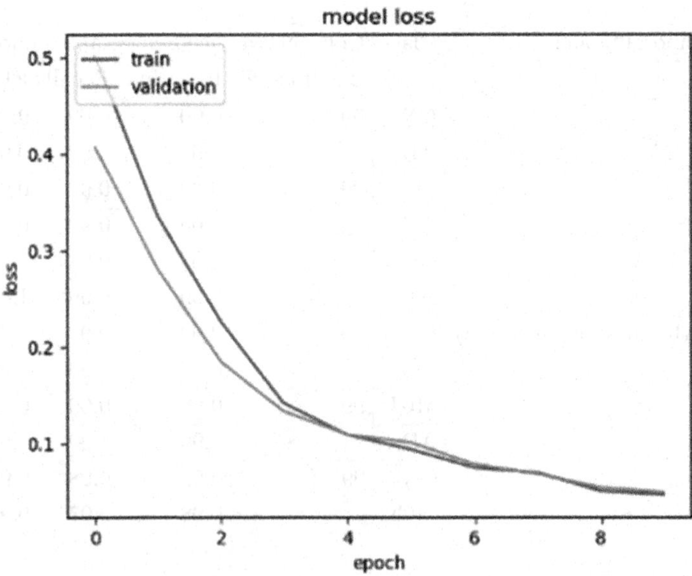

Fig. 8. Training and validation loss plot of ConvLSTM Model.

4.2 ConvLSTM with Other Spatio-Temporal Model

Spatial and temporal features have been extracted and trained automatically via developed Spatio-temporal models. The proposed ConvLSTM was campared with CNN+LSTM and (2+1) D CNN models for better prediction of AD.

Table 7. A Comparison of different approaches employed in the study.

Model	Accuracy	Precision	Recall	F1-Score	Parameters
CNN+LSTM	96	0.95	0.95	0.96	932,182
(2+1) D CNN	94	0.93	0.92	0.94	822,090
ConvLSTM	98	0.98	0.98	0.98	100,688

Table 7, the accuracy, precision, recall, and F1 score values for the different spatio-temporal models utilized in this study are presented. Among these models, CNN+LSTM and (2+1) D CNN are combinations of deep neural networks, resulting in higher training parameters compared to ConvLSTM. However, despite the higher complexity, ConvLSTM outperforms the other models in spatio-temporal analysis, achieving an impressive accuracy of 98%.

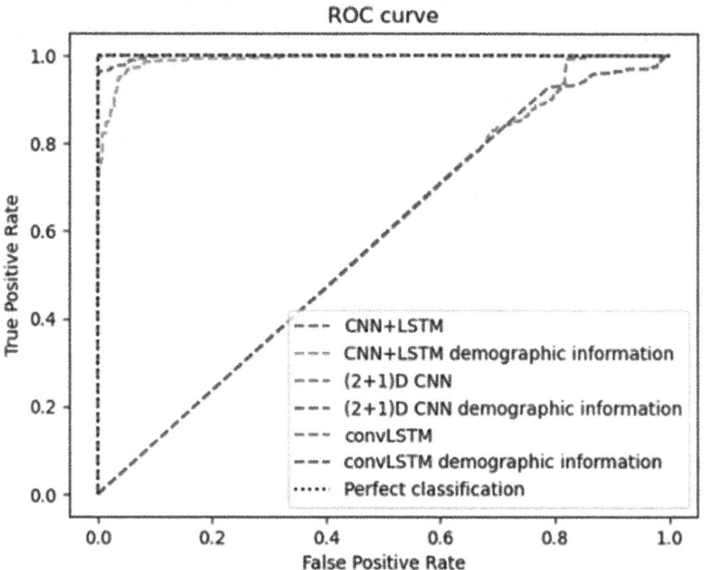

Fig. 9. ROC plot for spatio-temporal models.

Figure 9 the ROC curve of ConvLSTM model would reach the top left corner of the plot compared with other models, representing perfect classification. The ROC plot of (2+1) D CNN diagonal line from the bottom left to the top right represents decisions are no better than random chance.

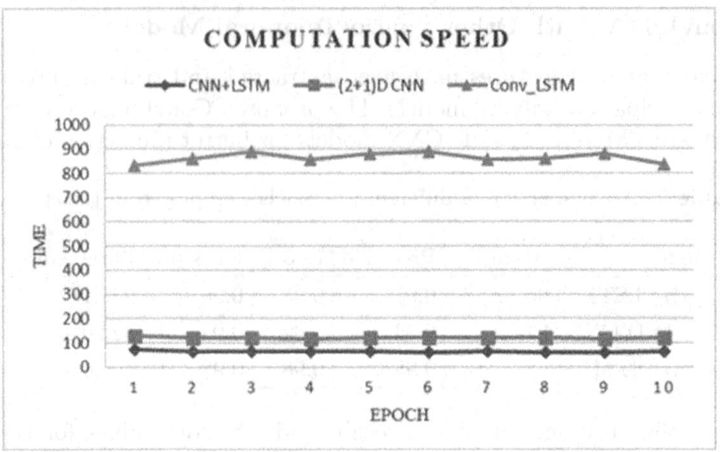

Fig. 10. Computation Speed of spatio-temporal models.

Figure 10 showcases the computation speed of the developed spatio-temporal models across different datasets. The ConvLSTM model exhibits a higher computation speed due to its ability to perform parallel analysis of the spatio-temporal model using a single deep neural network. In contrast, other spatio-temporal models perform series analysis using a combination of neural networks. It is important to note that the computation speed is dependent on the size of the dataset.

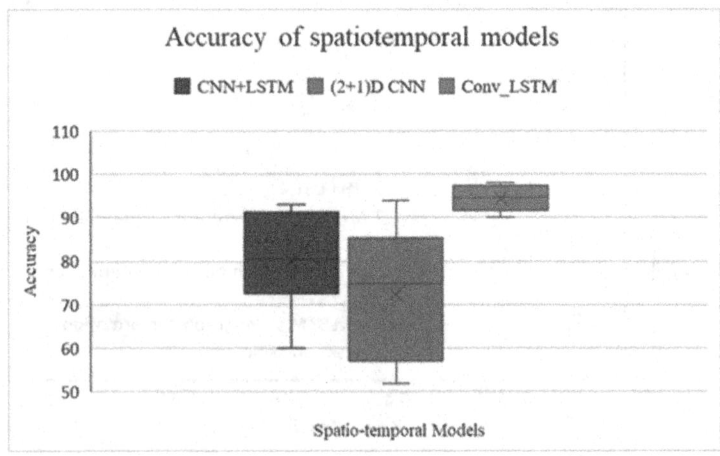

Fig. 11. Box plot for accuracy of spatiotemporal models.

Figure 11 presents a comparison of training accuracies among different spatio-temporal models using a box plot. The ConvLSTM model consistently exhibits higher accuracy across all datasets in comparison to other spatio-temporal models.

4.3 ConvLSTM with State of the Art

Considered preprocessing and convolutional incorporated LSTM network, the proposed ConvLSTM model achieved a high accuracy rate compared with other state of the art shown in Table 8 and Table 9.

Table 8. Performance comparision on the ADNI dataset.

Method	Description	Classes	Accuracy (%)
(2+1) D CNN [2]	Sequence based (2+1) D CNN with spatial and temporal analysis	AD vs MCI	78
CNN+LSTM [3]	Improved Convolutional Neural Network with temporal and spatial analysis	NC vs AD (12 months)	93.3
SSBIN [1]	shearlet Subbabd energy feature -Based individual network with features like NV and LV	MCI vs HC	89.71
		AD vs MCI	90
		AD vs HC	94.78
Hybrid (CNN+LSTM) [25]	Hybrid (CNN+LSTM) with multimodality feature fusion	AD, NC, MCI,EMCI, LMCI	98.5
ConvLSTM	Convolutional Long Short-Term Memory with spatio-temporal analysis	AD, CN vs MCI	97
		CN vs AD	97
		MCI vs AD	98
		CN vs MCI	97
		AD, CN vs MCI	98
		CN vs AD	99
		MCI vs AD	99
		CN vs MCI	99

Table 8 compares proposed ConvLSTM model with state-of- the art models for datasets like ADNI and ADNI with temporal variation different combination of classes. The developed ConvLSTM is better for automatic analyzation of spatio-tempormal features using deep neural network compared with other models and it also archives 99% accuracy for all kind of datasets and its combination of classes.

Table 9 presents a comparison of the proposed ConvLSTM model with state-of-the-art models using the OASIS dataset. The developed ConvLSTM model outperforms other models in automatically analyzing spatio-temporal features through deep neural networks, achieving an impressive accuracy of 98% for the OASIS dataset.

Table 9. Performance comparison on the OASIS dataset

Method	Description	Classes	Accuracy (%)
Random forest	ML classifiers	CN, MCI vs AD	88.99
Logistic Regression [1]			88.46
Gradient Boost	ML classifiers	Demented vs non-Demented	97.58
SVM			96.77
Logistic Regression			96.77
Randomforest			96.77
Naive Bayes [22]			95.96
Brain Net 2D	Brain Net and Residual Network with deep feature extraction	CN vs AD	79
Brain Net 3D			80
Brain Net 2D		CN vs AD	82
		AD vs MCI	88
Brain Net 3D		CN vs AD	84
		AD vs MCI	77
Res Net 18 [10]		CN vs AD	93
		AD vs MCI	89
Conv_LSTM	Convolutional Long Short-Term Memory with spatio-temporal analysis	Demented vs non-Demented	98

5 Conclusion

Alzheimer's disease, a leading cause of brain cell loss, brain shrinking, and progressive memory decline, poses a significant threat worldwide. Spatial analysis identifies affected brain regions, while temporal analysis reveals disease progression and temporal patterns of change. Integrating spatial and temporal information enables more accurate prediction. The proposed work focuses on developing spatio-temporal models for early AD prediction. To overcome computational complexity and sample limitations, the ConvLSTM model is introduced, utilizing various datasets with demographic information. Compared to other spatio-temporal models, ConvLSTM excels in analyzing spatio-temporal features, exhibiting extraordinary accuracy of 98% across different datasets, using demographic information, for early AD prediction. In future, the spatio-temporal model for classifying Alzheimer's disease can be expanded to five classes, incorporating temporal variation and demographic information. This advancement allows for better tracking of disease progression and enables yearly predictions, particularly in the early mild cognitive impairment (EMCI) stage. By considering temporal changes and demographic factors, the model provides valuable insights for personalized interventions and improved disease management.

References

1. Feng, J., Zhang, S.-W., Chen, L., Zuo, C., Initiative, A.D.N., et al.: Detection of alzheimer's disease using features of brain region-of-interest-based individual network constructed with the smri image. Comput. Med. Imaging Graph. **98**, 102057 (2022)
2. Turhan, G., Küçük, H., Isik, E.O.: Spatio-temporal convolution for classification of alzheimer disease and mild cognitive impairment. Comput. Methods Prog. Biomed. **221**, 106825 (2022)
3. Sun, H., Wang, A., He, S.: Temporal and spatial analysis of alzheimer's disease based on an improved convolutional neural network and a resting-state fmri brain functional network. Int. J. Environ. Res. Public Health **19**(8), 4508 (2022)
4. Attur, S.S., Harikumar, M.E.: Detection of alzheimer's disease using fuzzy inference system. In: 2022 4th International Conference on Smart Systems and Inventive Technology (ICSSIT), pp. 1235–1241. IEEE (2022)
5. Wen, J., et al.: Convolutional neural networks for classification of alzheimer's disease: overview and reproducible evaluation. Med. Image Anal. **63**, 101694 (2020)
6. Kishore, P., Kumari, C.U., Kumar, M.N.V.S.S., Pavani, T.: Detection and analysis of Alzheimer's disease using various machine learning algorithms. Mater. Today Proc. **45**, 1502–1508 (2021)
7. Zheng, H., Lin, F., Feng, X., Chen, Y.: A hybrid deep learning model with attention-based CONV-LSTM networks for short-term traffic flow prediction. IEEE Trans. Intell. Transp. Syst. **22**(11), 6910–6920 (2020)
8. Houria, L., Belkhamsa, N., Cherfa, A., Cherfa, Y.: Multi-modality MRI for Alzheimer's disease detection using deep learning. Phys. Eng. Sci. Med. **45**(4), 1043–1053 (2022)
9. Li, J., Zhang, X., Zhou, Q., Chan, F.T., Hu, Z.: A feature-level multi-sensor fusion approach for in-situ quality monitoring of selective laser melting. J. Manuf. Processes **84**, 913–926 (2022)
10. Saratxaga, C.L., Moya, I., Picón, A., Acosta, M., Moreno-Fernandez-de Leceta, A., Garrote, E., Bereciartua-Perez, A.: MRI deep learning-based solution for Alzheimer's disease prediction. J. Pers. Med. **11**(9), 902 (2021)
11. Alroobaea, R., et al.: Alzheimer's disease early detection using machine learning techniques (2021)
12. Zhou, T., Thung, K.-H., Zhu, X., Shen, D.: Effective feature learning and fusion of multimodality data using stage-wise deep neural network for dementia diagnosis. Hum. Brain Mapp. **40**(3), 1001–1016 (2019)
13. Arco, J.E., et al.: Data fusion based on searchlight analysis for the prediction of Alzheimer's disease. Expert Syst. Appl. **185**, 115549 (2021)
14. Khan, R., Qaisar, Z.H., Mehmood, A., Ali, G., Alkhalifah, T., Alturise, F., Wang, L.: A practical multiclass classification network for the diagnosis of Alzheimer's disease. Appl. Sci. **12**(13), 6507 (2022)
15. Sudharsan, D., et al.: Analysis of machine learning and deep learning algorithms for detection of brain disorders using MRI data. In: Gupta, M., Ghatak, S., Gupta, A., Mukherjee, A.L. (eds.) ISCMM 2021. LNCS, vol. 37, pp. 39–46. Springer, Heidelberg (2022). https://doi.org/10.1007/978-981-19-0151-5_4
16. Zhao, F., Qiao, L., Shi, F., Yap, P.-T., Shen, D.: Feature fusion via hierarchical supervised local CCA for diagnosis of autism spectrum disorder. Brain Imaging Behav. **11**, 1050–1060 (2017)

17. Afzal, S., et al.: Alzheimer disease detection techniques and methods: a review (2021)
18. Jia, H., Lao, H.: Deep learning and multimodal feature fusion for the aided diagnosis of Alzheimer's disease. Neural Comput. Appl. **34**(22), 19585–19598 (2022)
19. Jiang, M., Yan, B., Li, Y., Zhang, J., Li, T., Ke, W.: Image classification of Alzheimer's disease based on external-attention mechanism and fully convolutional network. Brain Sci. **12**(3), 319 (2022)
20. Silva, J., Bispo, B.C., Rodrigues, P.M., Alzheimer's Disease Neuroimaging Initiative.: Structural MRI texture analysis for detecting Alzheimer's disease. J. Med. Biol. Eng. **43**(3), 227–238 (2023)
21. Lau, A., Beheshti, I., Modirrousta, M., Kolesar, T.A., Goertzen, A.L., Ko, J.H.: Alzheimer's disease-related metabolic pattern in diverse forms of neurodegenerative diseases. Diagnostics **11**(11), 2023 (2021)
22. Battineni, G., et al.: Improved Alzheimer's disease detection by MRI using multimodal machine learning algorithms. Diagnostics **11**(11), 2103 (2021)
23. Aravinth, J., et al.: Alzheimer's disease prediction by spatio-temporal feature fusion for MRI data. In: 2023 Third International Conference on Secure Cyber Computing and Communication (ICSCCC), pp. 580–585. IEEE (2023)
24. Shrinithi, S., Aravinth, J.: Detection of melanoma skin cancer using dermoscopic skin lesion images. In: 2021 International Conference on Recent Trends on Electronics, Information, Communication & Technology (RTEICT), pp. 240–245. IEEE (2021)
25. Balaji, P., Chaurasia, M.A., Bilfaqih, S.M., Muniasamy, A., Alsid, L.E.G.: Hybridized deep learning approach for detecting Alzheimer's disease. Biomedicines **11**(1), 149 (2023)

Comparative Analysis of Economy-Based Multivariate Oil Price Prediction Using LSTM

Babita Pathik[1], Rajeev Kumar Gupta[2](✉), and Nikhlesh Pathik[3]

[1] Department of CSE, Technocrats Institute of Technology, Bhopal, India
[2] Department of CSE, Pandit Deendayal Energy University, Gandhinagar, Gujarat, India
rajeevmanit12276@gmail.com
[3] Department of CSE, Bansal Institute of Science and Technology, Bhopal, India

Abstract. Predicting unrefined petroleum prices is crucial for decision-makers, financiers, and academics in the energy industry. This paper presents an economic system-based multivariate oil price forecasting model that utilizes LSTM, a sophisticated deep learning algorithm that could capture tricky and nonlinear interactions in data with temporal order. Our model takes WTI crude price and numerous economic variables, containing US Dollar Index Futures, Gold Futures, Ten-year US Bond Yield, and S&P 500, as input characteristics. Before model training, we executed data pre-processing to eliminate outliers and enhance model accuracy. Via exploratory file study, we diagnosed and identified 482 outliers between 2007 and 2009, which were influenced by the financial crisis. We also expelled data from 2020 and after, as the hurricane of COVID-19 should distort our judgments. To choose our model's efficiency, we used metrics such as square (R2), Mean Square Error (MSE), and Mean Absolute Error (MAE). Our findings display that the LSTM version has powerful predicting talents and can correctly forecast oil price bases on economic indicators. This review paper also stresses the significance of macroeconomic indicators in oil price forecasting.

Keywords: LSTM · Crude Oil · West Texas Intermediate (WTI) · Mean Square Error (MSE) · Pre-processing · R2 Score

1 Introduction

Petrol, diesel fuel, and polymers are just a few of the items made from crude oil, a valuable commodity. A multitude of variables, such as supply and demand, prevailing economic circumstances, and geopolitical developments, affect the price of crude oil. Crude oil price forecasting is a difficult task [1] that calls for comprehensive models that can capture the intricate and nonlinear interactions between these variables. Using a machine learning model is one way to forecast the price of crude oil [6, 9, 10]. In order to discover the links between the numerous elements that affect the price of crude oil, machine learning models are trained using historical data. Once trained, a model may be used to forecast crude oil prices in the future [11, 12].

Variables, such as supply and demand, prevailing economic circumstances, and geopolitical developments, affect the price of crude oil. Crude oil price forecasting

N. Chauhan et al. (Eds.): MIND 2023, CCIS 2128, pp. 45–54, 2024.
https://doi.org/10.1007/978-3-031-62217-5_4

is a difficult task [1] that calls for comprehensive models that can capture the intricate and nonlinear interactions between these variables. Using a machine learning model is one way to forecast the price of crude oil. Machine learning models are trained using historical data to discover the links between the numerous elements that affect the price of crude oil. Once trained, a model may be used to forecast crude oil prices in the future.

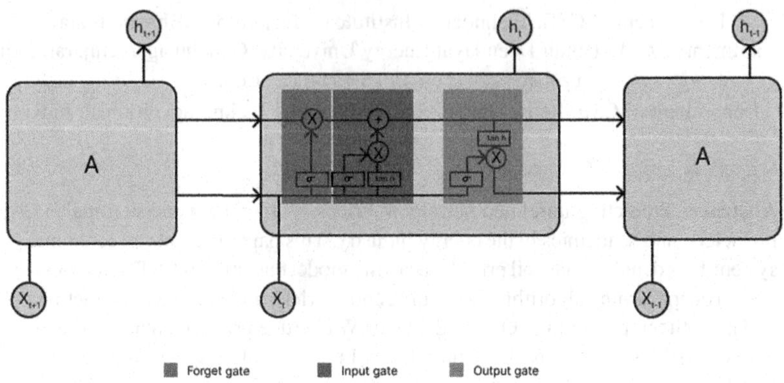

Fig. 1. LSTM structure [3].

The LSTM is a promising [2] model for time series data in finance. It differs from a typical recurrent neural network in that it has a unique topology where memory cells in lieu of regular nodes in the buried layers. Because of its distinctive structure, LSTM has stronger fitting capabilities. Each of the cells that make up an LSTM has an intricate internal structure. Three different types of gates, an internal state, and a number of inputs make up a cell's internal structure, as seen in Fig. 1. The connections between the gates and nodes represent weighted values for the connection signals. These weighted values are crucial for artificial neural networks since choosing weights is the most crucial factor in LSTM. For predicting oil prices using a multivariate time series analysis, LSTM is employed here because it has a significant processing capability for data with temporal order.

2 Literature Survey

A new method for forecasting crude oil prices using artificial neural networks is presented in the paper by Nalini Gupta and Shobhit Nigam [1]. By determining the ideal lag and quantity of delay effects that regulate crude oil prices, the authors emphasise the key benefit of their strategy, which is the capacity of the ANN to capture the unstable pattern of crude oil prices continually.

To get the most precise and close findings, the authors also touch on the significance of adjusting the latency over a period of time. The findings obtained using the suggested model greatly exceed those obtained using other approaches, with a best Root Mean Squared Error (RMSE) of 7.68.

In order to forecast the price of West Texas Intermediate (WTI) crude oil, the study "Evolutionary Neural Network model for West Texas Intermediate crude oil price prediction" suggests an alternate strategy based on a genetic algorithm and neural network (GA-NN) [5]. The authors show that their GA-NN technique surpasses baseline approaches in terms of prediction accuracy and computing efficiency by comparing it to them. The WTI crude oil price predicted by the suggested GA-NN model and the observed price are both statistically equivalent, according to the authors' Mann-Whitney test, which they also used to compare. Potential uses for the suggested model include the creation of worldwide crude oil price estimation, development strategies, and industrial production policies. The study of a cutting-edge method that combines a genetic algorithm with a neural network makes a significant addition to the field of crude oil price prediction. The benefit of this method is that it uses genetic information to adjust the neural network parameters, increasing prediction accuracy. The R2 score of 0.91722, a strong measure of the model's capacity to capture the variance in crude oil prices, is another way in which the authors illustrate the viability of their strategy.

The performance of the Multi-recurrent Network (MRN) in predicting crude oil prices over a range of prediction horizons is assessed in the study by O. Orojo, et al. [7]. The MRN is a recurrent neural network model that demonstrates intricate, flexible, and rigid state-based memory. In order to explicitly represent the shocks in oil prices brought on by the financial crisis, the authors compare the MRN with various models, including Feedforward Multi-layered Perceptron (FFMLP), Simple Recurrent Network (SRN), and Long Short-Term Memory (LSTM).

To assess the models, the authors combine out-sample data from October 2003 to March 2015 with in-sample data made up of important indicator variables collected across the pre-financial crisis era (July 1969 to September 2003). They discover that the MRN performs better than the FFMLP, SRN, and LSTM models in predicting crude oil prices, especially when it comes to simulating shocks brought on by the financial crisis. Five years before the 2008 financial crisis, the MRN was able to identify significant latent characteristics buried in the input signal. This implies that the indicator variables may be used as early warning signs of future financial disturbances.

The research makes a significant addition to the field of crude oil price forecasting by proving the efficacy of the MRN, a very straightforward yet potent recurrent neural network model. Policymakers and market participants who want to comprehend the factors influencing crude oil prices and make wise decisions based on their estimates should consider the authors' conclusions.

In order to increase the accuracy of crude oil price predictions, further research has expanded on the work described in this study by looking at additional MRN method adjustments or switching to completely other machine learning approaches. Using the MRN methodology suggested by the authors of this research as an example, a recent study titled "Deep learning for crude oil price forecasting: A complete evaluation" explores several deep learning approaches for crude oil price forecasting.

3 Proposed Method

After conducting a thorough investigation of various models to forecast daily oil prices based on historical daily oil price data, Multivariate LSTM has emerged as a promising approach. A diagram outlining the methodology used is provided in Fig. 2.

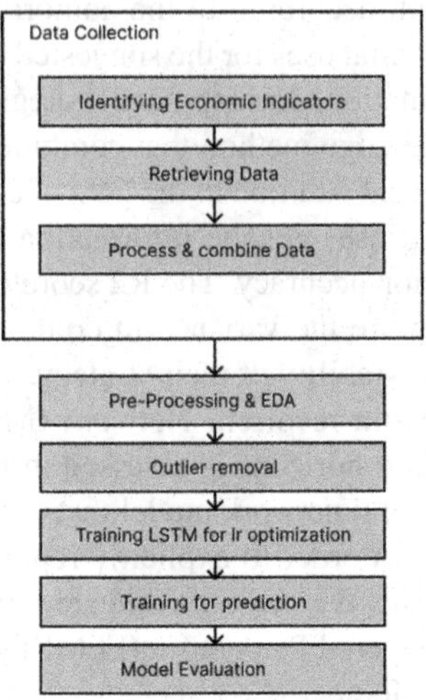

Fig. 2. Method Architecture diagram

3.1 Data Collection

Oil prices are affected by a variety of factors, including economic indicators such as gold, stocks, and the US dollar index [4]. To represent the economy and crude oil price, we have taken the historical data of the following indicators to create the dataset used for this work:

- West Texas Intermediate, or WTI [5], is a blend of crude oil traded on the NYMEX that includes spot prices. Together with Brent and Dubai Crude, (WTI) crude oil is a particular grade of crude oil and one of the three primary benchmarks for oil price.
- Gold Futures: When inflation rises in response to rising oil prices, so do GOLD futures. A reliable indication of economic conditions is gold futures [4].
- US Dollar Index Futures
- Ten-Year US Bond Yield represents the yield on US 10-Year Bonds is a certificate for the 10-year-old loan with the federal government, a good reflection of how investors feel about the economy [4].
- The S&P 500 and Dow Jones Utility Average, which measure the performance of 15 utility stocks and 500 major publicly traded corporations in the United States, respectively, using market capitalization weighting [5].

The target variable is the West Texas Intermediate (WTI) crude oil price. It is used for training because future prices are dependent on previous trends. Historical data of the target variable and other features, such as gold prices, US dollar index, and stock indicators, is collected from openly available sources for the period 2000 to 2019. The data is then combined for coinciding dates.

3.2 Data Pre-processing and Exploratory Data Analysis (EDA)

The first stage of pre-processing entails the construction of a date index. Imputations from the day before are then used to replace any null values in the dataset. This is as a result of the finding that short-term changes in oil prices are often comparable. After processing, the data is next exposed to exploratory data analysis (EDA), which looks for trends, patterns, and connections between the target variable and other variables. To find outliers for each year, a box and whisker plot is used specifically, making it possible to spot data points that need to be removed. Oil prices can vary dramatically during financial crises and other big events, thus it is crucial to spot and eliminate outliers. These data points can be eliminated to improve model training.

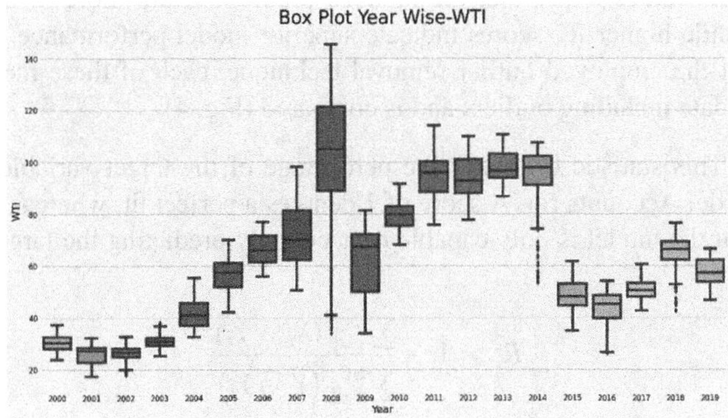

Fig. 3. Box plot for year wise WTI prices

In the years 2007, 2008, and 2009, there were notable shifts in the prices of West Texas Intermediate (WTI) which can be seen in the box plot shown in Fig. 3. In instance, WTI oil prices ranged between $30 and $140 in 2008, a year marked by the financial crisis and high volatility. The financial crisis that lasted from 2007 to 2009 was notable for causing significant changes in oil prices. We eliminated data points between 2007 and 2009 to lessen the influence of this crisis on our findings. This elimination procedure resulted in the removal of 482 outliers. We have also purposely left out data from 2020 and after, as that would also say a similar story due to the outbreak of COVID-19.

3.3 Model Training

To avoid overfitting, we first do a train-test split before standardization. We store data using the Long Short-Term Memory (LSTM) model, which accepts a predetermined amount of time steps for each output. For instance, if we provide 60 time steps, the model will use days 1 through 60 as a sequence to forecast the results for days 61 and beyond.

We enlarge the learning rate vs. epoch graph in order to establish the ideal learning rate for our model. We choose the learning rate that results in the smallest loss, which in this instance seems to be somewhere around 3e−5. One of the most important factors in the model training process is fine-tuning the learning rate. We see that the training and validation loss curves are close to each other, demonstrating the absence of overfitting. Also, the flat loss curves are a good thing. We would have concluded that overfitting was taking place if we had seen a sizable degree of validation loss reducing with an increase in the number of epochs. Yet given that this doesn't seem to be the case, we can say that overfitting is not an issue.

3.4 Model Training

(LSTM) model, which makes use of the financial outlier elimination method, performed. The following metrics [8] were used to evaluate the model:

As the main indicators of the effectiveness of our model, we report these data. Lower MSE and MAE values imply that the model's predictions are more in line with the actual data, while higher R2 scores indicate superior model performance. To evaluate the efficacy of the employed outlier removal technique, each of these metrics is also generated for data including outliers and is compared (Fig. 4).

- R2 Score: This statistic estimates the percentage of the target variable's variation that the model Accounts for. A score of 1 denotes a perfect fit, whereas a score of 0 denotes that the model is only capable of accurately predicting the target variable's mean.

$$R^2 = 1 - \frac{\sum_{i=1}^{m} (X_i - Y_i)^2}{\sum_{i=1}^{m} \left(\overline{Y} - Y_i\right)^2} \tag{1}$$

- Mean Squared Error (MSE): This measure shows the average of the squared variations between the target variable's expected and actual values. It is a statistic that is frequently utilised in regression issues.

$$MSE = \frac{1}{n} \sum_{i=1}^{n} \left(Y_i - \widehat{Y}_i\right)^2 \tag{2}$$

MSE = Mean Squared Error
n = number of data points
Yi = Observed Values
$\widehat{Y}_i$ = Predicted Values

- Mean Absolute Error (MAE): This statistic shows the average of the absolute discrepancies between the target variable's expected and actual values. It is a frequently employed statistic in regression issues, similar to MSE.

$$MAE = \frac{1}{m} \sum_{i=1}^{m} |X_i - Y_i| \tag{3}$$

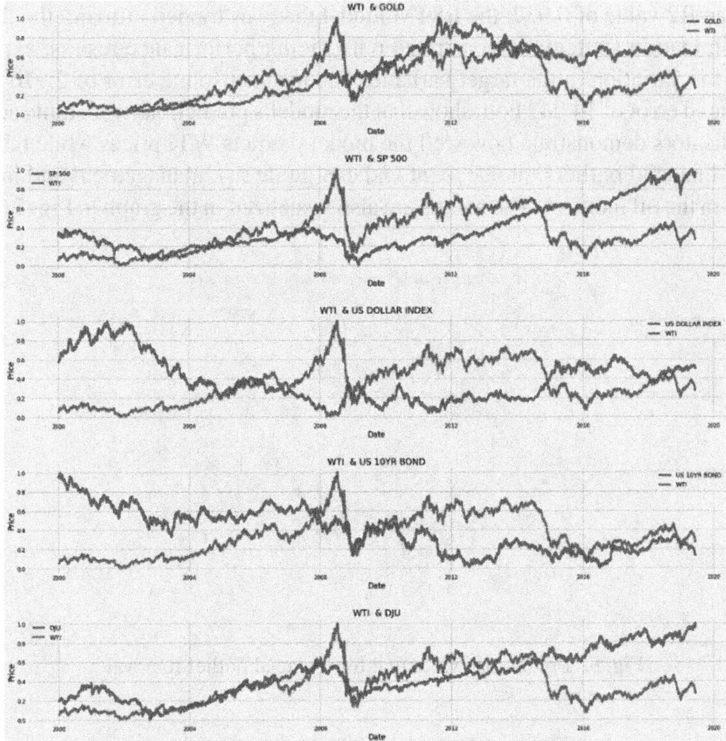

Fig. 4. Bivariate Analysis of Every Economic Indicator V/S WTI Price

4 Results and Discussion

Bivariate feature analysis was used in this study to better understand the connections between various factors and how they affect WTI pricing. The findings reveal that both WTI and SP 500 saw significant declines in 2009, proving that both series were influenced by the same outside forces and moved in tandem. With the exception of rare time periods, such as 2000, 2007–09, and 2010–16, when their connection seems to be inverse, the US Dollar index and WTI have a high correlation. This implies that there may be other variables at play in addition to the US Dollar's movement having a substantial influence on the price of WTI.

Prices for WTI and gold have been seen to fluctuate in tandem, with gold occasionally appearing to lag behind WTI, especially in 2007, when there was little difference between the two values. Because that changes in US 10-year Bond interest rates can predict impending financial crises, they appear to be a leading indication of WTI price volatility. Lastly, there is a strong link between 2003 and 2009 between the movements of the DJU and WTI. Overall, these findings offer insightful information on the connections between various factors and how they affect WTI prices, which may be utilized to guide risk management and trading tactics in the oil industry.

With an R2 value of 0.937, the LSTM model that was trained utilizing the financial outlier elimination strategy demonstrated outstanding performance results, explaining 93.7% of the variation in the target variable. The mean absolute error of 2.976 and the mean squared error of 14.242 both show that the model's predictions were quite accurate. These indicators demonstrate how well the model predicts WTI prices while taking the effects of financial outliers into account and can guide risk management and investing strategies in the oil industry. The results are also visualized in the graph in Fig. 5 (Fig. 6).

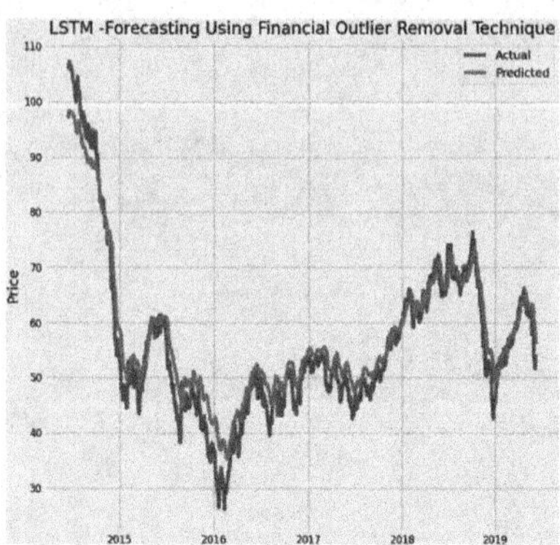

Fig. 5. Predictions v/s actual for financial outlier removal

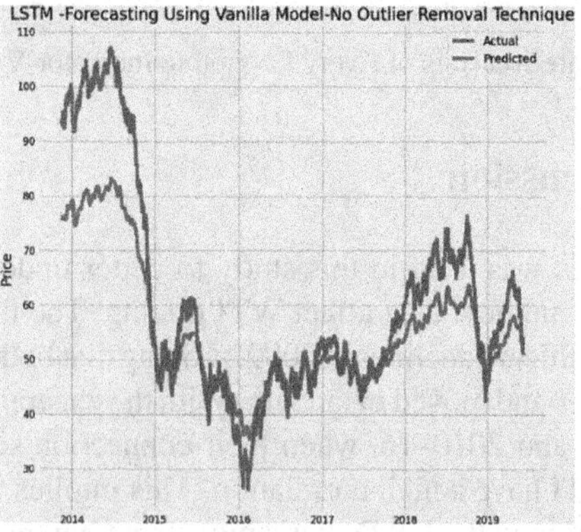

Fig. 6. Predictions v/s actual for no outlier removal technique

The LSTM model trained using the financial outlier reduction method performed noticeably better than the base model without outlier removal. The outlier removal enhanced the model's capacity to explain the variance in the target variable, as seen by the R2 score of 0.937 for the outlier-removed model, which was greater than the R2 score of 0.767 for the vanilla model. Furthermore, the outlier removal enhanced the model's predictive accuracy as evidenced by the fact that the mean squared error for the outlier-removed model was 14.242 while the mean squared error for the vanilla model was 87.915. Last but not least, the outlier-removed model performed better than the vanilla model, as evidenced by the fact that its mean absolute error, which was 2.976 instead of 6.583, was lower.

Overall, the LSTM model's performance in forecasting WTI prices was greatly enhanced by the outlier removal approach, demonstrating the significance of taking financial outliers into account in financial modelling and analysis (Table 1).

Table 1. Comparing financial outlier removal technique v/s vanilla model

	Financial outlier	Vanilla
R2 Score	0.937	0.767
MSE	14.242	87.915
MAE	2.976	6.583

5 Conclusion

We used a new method to predict WTI crude oil prices using a type of artificial intelligence called a long short-term memory (LSTM) model. We also removed any unusual data points (outliers) from our data set, which improved the accuracy of our predictions. Our model with outlier removal had an R2 score of 0.937, Mean Squared Error of 14.242, and Mean Absolute Error of 2.976. This was better than the model without outlier removal, which had an R2 score of 0.767, Mean Squared Error of 87.915, and Mean Absolute Error of 6.583.

We used a multivariate approach by including various economic indicators as inputs to our model. This allowed us to capture complex relationships and dependencies between different factors, which improved the accuracy and robustness of our predictions.

Our study highlights the importance of considering multiple factors when predicting financial outcomes. It also demonstrates the effectiveness of LSTM models in such scenarios. Overall, our research provides valuable insights into the predictive modeling of WTI crude oil prices and could potentially be used to improve financial decision-making.

References

1. Gupta, N., Nigam, S.: Crude oil price prediction using artificial neural network. Procedia Comput. Sci. **170**, 642–647 (2020)
2. Cen, Z., Wang, J.: Crude oil price prediction model with long short-term memory deep learning based on prior knowledge data transfer. Energy **169**, 160–171 (2019)
3. Kanani, S., et al.: An AI-enabled ensemble method for rainfall forecasting using long-short term memory. Math. Biosci. Eng. **20**(5), 8975–9002 (2023)
4. Sharma, A., Tselykh, A.: Machine learning-enabled estimation system using fuzzy cognitive mapping: a review. In: 3rd International Conference on Computing, Communications, and Cyber-Security, IC4S 2021, pp. 487–500 (2021)

5. Zhang, K.: Hong M, Forecasting crude oil price using LSTM neural networks. Data Sci. Financ. Econ. **2**(3), 163–180 (2022)
6. Aziz, N., Abdullah, M.H.A., Zaidi, A.N.: Predictive analytics for crude oil price using RNN-LSTM neural network. In: IEEE International Proceedings on Computational Intelligence (ICCI), pp. 173–178 (2020)
7. Jovanovic, L., et al.: Multi-step crude oil price prediction based on LSTM approach tuned by Salp Swarm algorithm with disputation operator. Sustainability **14**(21), 14616 (2022)
8. Chiroma, H., Abdulkareem, S., Herawan, T.: Evolutionary neural network model for West Texas intermediate crude oil price prediction. Appl. Energy **142**, 266–273 (2015)
9. Orojo, O., Tepper, J., McGinnity, T.M., Mahmud, M.: A multi-recurrent network for crude oil price prediction. In: IEEE Symposium Series on Computational Intelligence (SSCI), Xiamen, China, pp. 2940–2945 (2019)
10. Arfaoui, M., Rejeb, A.B.: Oil, gold, US dollar and stock market interdependencies: a global analytical insight. Eur. J. Manag. Bus. Econ. **26**(3), 278–293 (2017)
11. Geman, H., Kharoubi, C.: WTI crude oil futures in portfolio diversification: the time-to-maturity effect. J. Bank. Finan. **32**(12), 2553–2559 (2008)
12. Prabowo, H., Hidayat, A.A., Cenggoro, T.W., Rahutomo, R., Purwandari, K., Pardamean, B.: Aggregating time series and tabular data in deep learning model for university students GPA prediction. IEEE Access **9**, 87370–87377 (2021)

Deep Learning Based EV's Charging Network Management

Ishaan Mehta, Santosh Bharti(✉), and Rajeev Gupta

Pandit Deendayal Energy University, Gandhinagar, India
{ishaan.mmtds22,Santosh.Bharti}@sot.pdpu.ac.in

Abstract. Efficient management of charging networks is crucial as EVs become more popular in transportation systems. This study focuses on two main aspects: deploying EV charging stations using a binary Quadratic model and using reinforcement learning for optimal path selection. Additionally, the paper explores the accurate estimation of SoC in EVs using deep neural networks. The binary Quadratic model considers factors like location, population density, transportation patterns, and infrastructure availability to strategically place charging stations. Reinforcement learning helps EV users find the best path to charging stations based on traffic, station availability, and preferences. Deep neural networks use historical data and real-time factors to estimate SoC precisely, optimizing charging strategies and improving EV performance and reliability. The findings contribute to the advancement of charging network management, promoting accessibility, cost-effectiveness, user experience, and sustainable transportation.

Keywords: EV-Electric Vehicle · Charging station · DNN · SoC

1 Introduction

Nowadays, electric vehicles (EVs) are gaining significant attention and are considered an important aspect of our modern world. One of the limitations of EVs is their limited cruising range, necessitating frequent recharging. As the population continues to grow exponentially, there is a corresponding increase in business volume. Given the finite stock of energy on Earth, it is essential to transition to alternative energy sources, with electricity being a stylish option. EVs serve as an illustration of this transition.

Currently, plug-in charging systems are widely used for charging EVs. This system requires connecting a plug to the vehicle for charging. However, wireless charging eliminates the need for plugging and unplugging, reducing physical effort and the risk of electric shock. Wireless charging technology offers advantages such as increasing the traveling range, reducing battery size, and alleviating charging time. These benefits contribute to the profitability and environmental advantages of EVs.

Similar to conventional vehicles that require petrol pumps, EVs require charging stations. Integrating charging and parking systems based on IoT technology

N. Chauhan et al. (Eds.): MIND 2023, CCIS 2128, pp. 55–62, 2024.
https://doi.org/10.1007/978-3-031-62217-5_5

makes the process more efficient and user-friendly. Information can be uploaded simultaneously on panels and smartphones, providing convenience and real-time updates. IoT also facilitates vehicle parking monitoring and charging. Additionally, IoT enables data storage on panels, allowing access from anywhere, simplifying life. Combining parking areas with EV charging stations provides numerous advantages. However, the current transportation and parking infrastructure struggles to accommodate the growing number of vehicles, resulting in environmental and economic damage due to time spent searching for parking spots. Therefore, there is a need for efficient approaches to support EVs and their charging requirements by utilizing parking and charging architectures effectively. Overall, the integration of EV charging and parking systems through IoT technology offers convenience, efficiency, and sustainability in the transportation sector.

2 Literature Review

2.1 EV Charging Stations

Electric vehicles (EVs) have been gaining popularity in recent years as a sustainable and environmentally friendly mode of transportation. However, one of the main challenges associated with the adoption of EVs is the availability of charging infrastructure. The management of EV charging networks is a crucial aspect in ensuring that there is enough charging infrastructure to support the growing number of EVs on the road [1].

Conducted a study focusing on the optimization of EV charging station placement and sizing. Their research introduced a mathematical model that takes into account EV users' travel patterns and charging station characteristics to determine the optimal placement and sizing of charging stations. By considering these factors, the study aimed to improve the utilization of charging infrastructure, resulting in more efficient charging network management [9].

Proposed a charging coordination strategy specifically designed for scenarios where multiple EVs are charging at the same station. Their strategy aimed to reduce peak loads on charging stations and ensure timely and efficient completion of the charging process. By employing a simulation approach, the study demonstrated the effectiveness of their proposed strategy, which can contribute to more balanced charging loads and improved overall charging network performance [10].

Presented a smart charging management system that integrates renewable energy sources and energy storage systems. The study focused on optimizing the charging process to reduce energy consumption and enhance the utilization of renewable energy sources. By effectively managing the charging process and leveraging renewable energy, the proposed system has the potential to contribute to more sustainable and environmentally friendly charging network operations [11].

Conducted a comprehensive review of the challenges and opportunities associated with the management of EV charging networks. The review emphasized the need for advanced charging technologies to meet the increasing demands of EVs and highlighted the importance of collaboration between stakeholders in the EV charging industry. By addressing these challenges and fostering cooperation, the review suggests that effective management of EV charging networks can be achieved, promoting the widespread adoption of EVs and sustainable transportation.

2.2 State of Charge (SoC)

State of Charge (SOC) estimation is a critical component in the development of battery management systems (BMS) for electric vehicles (EVs) and other energy storage systems. Accurate SOC estimation is necessary to ensure the safe and efficient operation of the battery system. A literature review of recent research on SOC estimation reveals several key approaches and techniques.

A comprehensive review emphasizing the significance of model-based approaches in state of charge (SOC) estimation [12]. The review highlighted various types of models employed in SOC estimation, including equivalent circuit models, electrochemical models, and machine learning models. The study concluded that model-based approaches offer the highest level of accuracy and reliability in SOC estimation.

A proposed approach of hybrid SOC estimation approach that combines a dynamic system model with the unscented Kalman filter (UKF) algorithm. This approach demonstrated improved accuracy in SOC estimation across diverse operating conditions [13].

A deep neural network (DNN) model for SOC estimation, incorporating temperature and current information [14]. Training the DNN model using a large dataset of battery performance data resulted in superior performance compared to other machine learning models.

A review that shed light on the challenges associated with SOC estimation in lithium-ion batteries, such as temperature effects, aging effects, and dynamic operating conditions. The review discussed potential approaches to address these challenges, including the utilization of advanced sensor technologies and machine learning algorithms [15].

3 Methodology

3.1 Deploy EV Charging Station

The Binary Quadratic Model (BQM) is a mathematical optimization technique used in many applications, including the deployment of electric vehicle (EV) charging stations.

The methodology for using BQM for deploying EV charging stations typically involves the following steps:

- Defining the optimization objective: The first step is to define the objective of the optimization, such as maximizing the utilization of the charging stations or minimizing the cost of the deployment.

- Formulating the problem as a BQM: The optimization problem is then formulated as a BQM, which is a mathematical expression of the objective function and the constraints on the variables. The BQM is typically expressed as a quadratic equation with binary variables.
- Solving the BQM: The BQM is then solved using a suitable optimization solver that can find the optimal values of the binary variables that satisfy the objective function and constraints.
- Interpreting the results: The optimal solution of the BQM provides a set of values for the binary variables that determine the deployment of the charging stations. These results are then interpreted and used to guide the deployment strategy.

The methodology for using BQM for deploying EV charging stations involves defining the optimization objective, formulating the problem as a BQM, solving the BQM, and interpreting the results. BQM is a powerful optimization technique that can be used to optimize the deployment of charging stations while considering various constraints and objectives.

3.2 Optimal Path to the EV Charging Station

The methodology for using reinforcement learning (RL) for finding the optimal path to an EV charging station typically involves the following steps:

- Problem formulation: The first step is to define the problem of finding the optimal path to an EV charging station as a Markov Decision Process (MDP). In an MDP, the problem is modeled as a set of states, actions, and rewards.
- State representation: The next step is to define the state representation, which captures the relevant information about the environment that affects the decision-making process. In the context of finding the optimal path to an EV charging station, the state representation could include the location of the EV, the distance to the charging station, the traffic conditions, and the availability of charging stations.
- Action selection: The RL agent then selects an action based on the current state. In the context of finding the optimal path to an EV charging station, the actions could include turning left or right at an intersection, choosing a particular lane, or taking a certain route.
- Reward function: After taking an action, the RL agent receives a reward based on the new state. The reward function incentivizes the agent to take actions that bring it closer to the charging station. In the context of finding the optimal path to an EV charging station, the reward function could assign a positive reward for reaching the charging station and a negative reward for running out of battery.
- Learning: The RL agent then uses the experiences gained from interacting with the environment to update its policy for selecting actions. This learning process involves updating the values of the state-action pairs based on the received rewards and selecting actions that maximize the expected future rewards.

- Evaluation: The RL agent's policy is evaluated by testing it on a set of test scenarios to ensure that it performs well under different conditions.

The methodology for using RL for finding the optimal path to an EV charging station involves defining the problem as an MDP, selecting a state representation, defining an action selection policy, defining a reward function, learning the optimal policy, and evaluating the performance of the policy. RL is a powerful technique that can optimize the path to the charging station while considering various factors, such as traffic conditions, charging station availability, and battery level of the EV.

3.3 SoC Estimation

The methodology for estimating State of Charge (SoC) using Deep Neural Networks (DNNs), Convolutional Neural Networks (CNNs), and Long Short-Term Memory (LSTM) typically involves the following steps:

- Dataset collection: The first step is to collect a dataset of battery voltage and current measurements and their corresponding SoC values. This dataset should include a diverse range of operating conditions, such as different temperatures, discharge rates, and charging rates.
- Data preprocessing: The raw dataset is then preprocessed to remove any noise or outliers and normalize the data. The voltage and current measurements are also converted to time-series data (Table 1).

Table 1. SoC estimation using different models

Sr. No.	Model	Dataset	Loss		MSE	
			Train	Validation	Train	Validation
1	CNN	COMB	0.068	0.241		
2	DNN	COMB	0.066	0.0351	0.066	0.0351
3	LSTM	COMB	0.00723	0.0012	0.014	0.0025
4	CNN	LG	0.0071	0.019		
5	DNN	LG	0.07	0.019	0.00926	0.0067
6	LSTM	LG	0.0016	0.0028	0.031	0.0057
7	CNN	PANASONIC	0.0037	0.0359		
8	DNN	PANASONIC	0.038	0.0199	0.027	0.0068
9	LSTM	PANASONIC	0.001	0.0085	0.002	0.0967

- Model selection: The next step is to select a suitable DNN, CNN, or LSTM model architecture for SoC estimation. DNNs are a basic type of neural network that consists of an input layer, one or more hidden layers, and an output layer. CNNs are a type of neural network that is well-suited for image processing tasks and can extract features fromthe data. LSTM is a type of neural network that is well-suited for time-series data and can model temporal dependencies.

- Training and validation: The selected model is then trained and validated on the preprocessed dataset. The dataset is typically divided into training and validation sets, and the model is trained on the training set and validated on the validation set to ensure that it generalizes well to unseen data.
- Hyperparameter tuning: The hyperparameters of the selected model are then tuned to optimize its performance on the validation set. These hyperparameters include the learning rate, number of hidden layers, number of neurons per layer, and activation functions.
- Testing: The final step is to test the performance of the trained model on a separate test dataset. The test dataset is used to evaluate the model's ability to accurately estimate the SoC under different operating conditions (Table 2).

Table 2. SoC estimation using different models

Sr. No.	Model	Dataset	MAE		RMSE		Time
			Train	Validation	Train	Validation	Mins
1	DNN	COMB	0.0066	0.0351	0.087	0.0485	14
2	LSTM	COMB	0.0186	0.0319	0.038	0.0499	450
3	DNN	LG	0.007	0.0199	0.0096	0.026	11
4	LSTM	LG	0.0016	0.0028	0.0557	0.0754	328
5	DNN	PANASONIC	0.038	0.0199	0.0049	0.0247	8
6	LSTM	PANASONIC	0.0159	0.0967	0.0451	0.1305	188

4 Result

The table provided represents the results of different models in the task of state of charge (SoC) estimation. SoC estimation is a crucial aspect of battery management systems, as it determines the remaining capacity of a battery, enabling efficient utilization and accurate monitoring. The models evaluated in this study include CNN, DNN, and LSTM, which are commonly used deep learning architectures. These models were trained and validated on three different datasets: COMB (a combination of multiple datasets), LG (a specific dataset named LG), and PANASONIC (a specific dataset named Panasonic).

COMB Dataset: For the COMB dataset, the DNN model emerged as the top performer in SoC estimation. It achieved an MSE of 7.64E–05 for the training set and an MSE of 0.0351 for the validation set. The DNN model also demonstrated a low MAE of 0.0066 and an RMSE of 0.0351. However, it should be noted that the DNN model required a longer execution time of 1160637.125 min, indicating more computational resources.

LG Dataset: On the LG dataset, the LSTM model showcased the best performance among the evaluated models. It achieved an MSE of 0.0031 for the training set and an MSE of 0.0057 for the validation set. The LSTM model exhibited an MAE of 0.023 and an RMSE of 0.031. With an execution time of 328 min, the LSTM model demonstrated its effectiveness in accurately estimating the state of charge on the LG dataset.

PANASONIC Dataset: The DNN model outperformed other models on the PANASONIC dataset for state of charge estimation. It achieved an MSE of 2.37E–05 for the training set and an MSE of 0.0038 for the validation set. The DNN model showed an MAE of 6.08E-04 and an RMSE of 0.0199. With a relatively shorter execution time of 8 min, the DNN model proved to be efficient in estimating the state of charge on the PANASONIC dataset.

These results highlight the effectiveness of deep learning models, specifically the DNN and LSTM architectures, in accurately estimating the state of charge for batteries. The choice of model may vary depending on the specific dataset and computational requirements. The provided results can serve as a reference for selecting an appropriate model for state of charge estimation in battery management systems (Fig. 1).

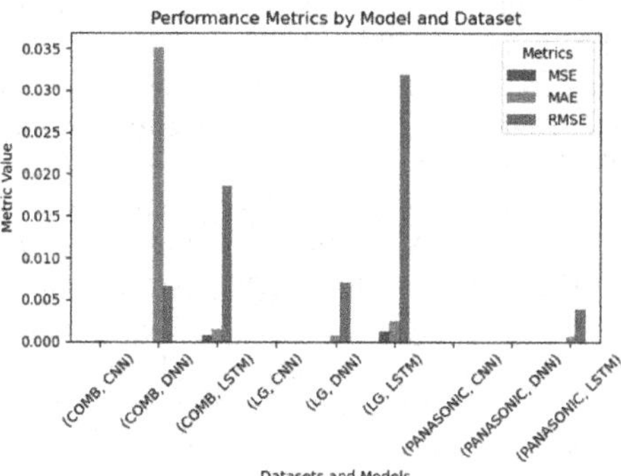

Fig. 1. Comparison of Models with different datasets

5 Conclusions

In conclusion, the development of EV's charging network management and SoC estimation technologies is crucial for the widespread adoption of electric vehicles (EVs) and the transition to sustainable mobility. The charging network management system should be designed to ensure that EV users have access to a reliable and convenient charging infrastructure. This can be achieved through the deployment of intelligent charging stations, integration with renewable energy sources, and the implementation of V2G technology. Moreover, accurate and reliable SoC estimation is crucial for the safe and efficient operation of EVs. The development of advanced SoC estimation techniques, such as DNNs, CNNs, and LSTMs, can help to improve the accuracy of SoC estimation and ensure that EVs are charged to the appropriate level. This, in turn, can help to improve the performance and lifespan of EV batteries.

Future developments in charging network management and SoC estimation should focus on the integration of these technologies to create a comprehensive and efficient charging infrastructure for EVs. Additionally, the standardization of charging protocols is important to ensure that EV users have a seamless charging experience regardless of their location or the type of EV they own.

Overall, the development of EV's charging network management and SoC estimation technologies is critical for the widespread adoption of EVs, the reduction of greenhouse gas emissions, and the promotion of sustainable mobility.

References

1. Liu, J., Zhang, L., Wang, Y.: Review of electric vehicle charging infrastructure planning research. J. Clean. Prod. **210**, 1484–1494 (2019)
2. Li, Y., Wu, X., Li, M., Wang, X., Lin, X.: A review of electric vehicle charging station planning models and methods. Energy **194**, 116875 (2020)
3. Wang, Z., Wen, F.: A comprehensive survey of EV charging station management systems. J. Clean. Prod. **289**, 125306 (2021)
4. Liu, H., Cui, S., Zhang, L.: Battery state of charge estimation for electric vehicles using deep learning: a review. J. Power Sources **469**, 228372 (2020)
5. Yan, W., Zhang, X., Zhang, J.: A review on battery state of charge estimation methods for electric vehicles. Renew. Sustain. Energy Rev. **102**, 259–278 (2019)
6. Tao, W., Chen, Y., Zhang, Y.: A review on battery state of charge estimation for electric vehicles. IEEE Access **8**, 34706–34722 (2020)
7. Zhao, J.H., Dong, Z.Y., Li, X., Wong, K.P.: A framework for electricity price spike analysis with advanced data mining methods. IEEE Trans. Power Syst. **22**(1), 376–385 (2007)
8. Ayob, A., et al.: Review on electric vehicle, battery charger, charging station and standards. Res. J. Appl. Sci. Eng. Technol. **7**(2), 364–373 (2014). https://doi.org/10.19026/rjaset.7.263. ISSN: 2040- 7459. eISSN: 2040-7467
9. Tang, Y., Sun, K., Zhang, L., Li, K.: Charging coordination strategy for multiple electric vehicles at the same station. IEEE Trans. Power Syst. **36**(2), 977–987 (2021)
10. Li, X., Zhao, J., Zhang, Y., Zhang, X., Wang, Y., Li, Y.: Smart charging management system for electric vehicles with renewable energy integration. IEEE Trans. Ind. Inf. **16**(6), 3707–3717 (2020)
11. Peng, L., Zhang, X., Fang, X., Zhang, T., Wu, J.: Challenges and opportunities in the management of electric vehicle charging networks: a review. IEEE Trans. Intell. Transp. Syst. **22**(5), 2874–2885 (2021)

Crop Yield Prediction Using Machine Learning Approaches

Dhvanil Bhagat, Shrey Shah, and Rajeev Kumar Gupta(✉)

Pandit Deendayal Energy University, Gandhinagar, Gujarat, India
rajeev.gupta@sot.pdpu.ac.in

Abstract. Crop yield prediction plays an essential role in agricultural planning and decision-making. The present research offers a comprehensive study into the use of machine learning algorithms for agricultural production prediction based on a variety of fertilizers consumption and area production of various crops. The study's essential process includes data gathering which is gathered in two parts and then combined into one, preprocessing, and model selection. Random Forest Regressor, Decision Tree Regressor, Linear Regression, LSTM, and more such regression models were among the algorithms tested and compared. According to the data, Random Forest Regressor and linear Regression had the greatest accuracy in crop yield prediction. By utilizing machine learning methods and bridging the gap between technology and the agriculture sector, this study contributes to the progress of agricultural practices. The results may help farmers choose the best crops for future years, therefore optimizing agricultural operations and increasing production and yield.

Keywords: Crop Yield · Fertilizers · LSTM · Random Forest

1 Introduction

Agriculture is one of the highly employed sectors of the nation. The agriculture sector, performing various agro-related activities, contributes enormously to India's finances. Thus, this sector is regarded as the most diverse way of earning money. Consequently, it serves the needs of around 1.4 billion people in India. [1] The sudden rise in demand for processed foods can be attributed to several factors, including increasing urbanization, rising population, natural weather variability, soil loss, increasing funds to spend, changing spending habits, the creation of split families, and the growing need for food in two-earner nuclear families. The need for agricultural products will increase as the world's population grows, necessitating effective farmland development and an increase in crop output. [2] The demand for organic products in the Indian market is growing and is anticipated to rise with a CAGR of 25.25% between 2022–27. So, there is greater room for the development of an accurate prediction system for crop production which is acutely required.

The present crop yield forecasting method mainly relies on field reports, crop development models, satellite imagery, statistical models, and multiple combinations of them.

N. Chauhan et al. (Eds.): MIND 2023, CCIS 2128, pp. 63–74, 2024.
https://doi.org/10.1007/978-3-031-62217-5_6

These methods concentrate on slightly different elements of projecting agricultural yield.[3] Ground research is to document the reality of the field. Based on interactions between the plant, the environment, and the management, crop growth models duplicate crop growth and development. In remote sensing methods, satellite imaging is utilized to record the current crop condition and subsequently calculate the eventual yield. The results from the three preceding procedures as well as weather data are employed as predictors in statistical models to create non-varying relationships between various parameters and crop yield. Most of the time, the farmers use his/her experience to predict the crop yield and accordingly allocate required resources and execute appropriate financial planning. But this process has a major flaw that can negatively impact the crop yield which can substantially affect the resources of the farmer and can hamper financially. Due to a variety of circumstances, such as soil fertility, climatic disparities, floods, shortage of groundwater, and other similar issues, a farmer cannot predict crop production with a higher level of accuracy.[4] Because many factors contribute to predicting crop yields, it is important to take these factors into account while choosing crops concerning the changing seasons.

Machine learning uses an empirical methodology to identify significant connections and patterns in input data. This strategy has a lot of potential for improving crop yield projections. Approximations of functions that link predictors, such as features, to labels, like agricultural yield, are produced by various machine learning algorithms. These algorithms can incorporate results from different approaches as features, much like statistical models. Notably, machine learning algorithms have several benefits: they are great at capturing complex non-linear relationships between different data sources; their performance tends to improve with larger training datasets; and they can effectively handle noisy data through regularization techniques that lower variance and generalization errors.[2] ML is used widely due to its usefulness in a range of domains such as forecasting, identifying faults, recognition of patterns, and so on. When there is a loss due to bad weather conditions, the ML algorithms also help to increase the crop yield production rate. Regardless of the distracting environment, machine learning algorithms are utilized in crop selection to reduce yield output losses. As a result, machine learning can augment the benefits of complementary techniques such as crop growth models and remote sensing by combining data-centric modeling to give reliable agricultural production projections.

This research article is organized as follows: a step-by-step explanation of crop yield analysis. The evaluation of different ML techniques used to assess crop yield prediction is provided, and the most accurate technique is recommended. The goals and problem statements for agricultural yield prediction are then displayed, followed by a comparison of several study types. Finally, future work and conclusion are discussed.

2 Related Works

Aruvansh et al. [1] carried out tests using data from the Indian government, and it was found that among the models used, including Random Forest, K Nearest Neighbors, Artificial Neural Network, XGBoost, and Logistic Regression, the Random Forest algorithm provides the best yield prediction accuracy with a score of 67.80%. A simple

Recurrent Neural Network is a sequential model that predicts rainfall better than the LSTM does temperature. For yield prediction, the article takes into account a variety of variables, including temperature, precipitation, season, and area. When all factors are taken into consideration, the findings show that Random Forest is the best classifier.

Sonal et al. [2], implemented the hybrid approach by collecting a crop dataset from Kaggle.com and used it to train and test their model. They found that their hybrid approach was able to achieve an accuracy of 97% by applying Long Short-Term Memory, Recurrent Neural Networks, and Support Vector Machine algorithms together, which was higher than the accuracy achieved when using Artificial Neural Networks and Random Forest algorithms. The authors concluded that their approach could aid farmers who experience losses on their farms because they lack understanding of how to cultivate in various soil and climatic conditions.

Balamurugan et al. [3], described the data used in the research, which includes a large dataset of experimental maize hybrids planted in different locations across the United States and Canada between 2008 and 2016. The authors propose a deep neural network model for yield prediction and present the results of their model. The model's performance was discovered to be extremely susceptible to the accuracy of the weather forecast, demonstrating the importance of climate forecasting systems. The article also discusses the feature selection method used in the research and the potential applications of deep neural networks in agriculture and crop management.

Dilli et al. [4], discuss several past research that demonstrated the potential of machine learning to forecast crop yields and suggest that future applications may consider the advantages of combining machine learning with other methodologies like crop development models and satellite imaging. The essay also emphasizes the significance of creating a general machine-learning methodology that can be used across many crops and regions and underscores the design concepts of accuracy, modularity, and reusability. Information on the data sources and indicators used in feature design is provided in the article.

Mosleh et al. [5], proposed a system for modeling and forecasting crop yield in Saudi Arabia using artificial intelligence. The approach considers numerous environmental conditions, like temperature, precipitation, and insecticide use, that affect crop yields of different crops, including potatoes, rice, sorghum, and wheat. To estimate and anticipate Saudi Arabia's agricultural yields, the study built a prediction model using a Multi-Layer Perceptron (MLP) model which had an RMSE value of 0.04493. This study's main goal is to forecast future values for significant crop yields in Saudi Arabia to assist farmers and the government in improving local, regional, and national post-harvest management practices for transportation, storage, and distribution.

Saeed et al. [6] describe the data used in the research i.e. the deep neural networks used for yield prediction and explain the results of the model. The research used a comprehensive dataset of corn hybrids and yield performances to predict the performance of maize hybrids in different regions. The research found that deep neural networks can accurately predict crop yield with validation RMSE of 23.14, and that weather prediction has a significant impact on the performance of the model.

WASI et al. [7] propose a novel hybrid approach combining ARIMA and ANN for long-term crop yield forecasting. It corrects short-term ARIMA predictions using ANN-modeled residuals. Applied to rice yield data in Uttar Pradesh, the hybrid approach significantly improves accuracy, reducing MAPE from 17.677% (ARIMA) to 4.65%. Using hybrid-predicted yield for 2020 as a baseline, the method extends forecasts to 2025 to meet future population demands.

Mayank et al. [8] explain how crop production can be predicted using machine learning algorithms, which can assist farmers in making informed choices and policymakers in taking the proper actions for marketing and storage. The paper offers information about the project's particular algorithm, the data collection procedure, and the effects of climate change on agricultural products in India. The created website is user-friendly, and the study's districts and crops all had forecast accuracy levels above 75%, indicating higher prediction accuracy.

Priyanga et al. [9] thoroughly analyzed how deep learning algorithms are used to estimate crop production using data from remote sensing. The most well-known deep learning algorithms, including Long Short-Term Memory (LSTM) and Convolutional Neural Networks (CNN), are described in the paper, which also underlines the significance of vegetation indicators and environmental characteristics in predicting agricultural production. Deep learning approaches outperform classic machine learning methods, with CNN and LSTM being particularly effective, according to the research. The most influential features in crop yield forecasts are vegetation indices and weather data. The study provides valuable insights into the current state and future directions of deep learning-based crop yield prediction.

P.S. Maya et al. [10] presented an MLR-ANN hybrid model for precise crop yield prediction. The study investigates the interaction between Artificial Neural Network (ANN) and Multiple Linear Regression (MLR) models and analyses performance indicators to assess the efficacy of the suggested hybrid model. According to the study, the ANN model's prediction accuracy is increased by utilizing MLR coefficients to initialize the input layer weights and bias. For MLR and ANN, the root-mean-square error (RMSE) was found to be 9.8% and 5.1%, respectively. The proposed hybrid model, specifically for paddy in Tamil Nadu State, has overall positive results for predicting crop production. The Table 1 below shows a comparison of different research papers.

Table 1. Comparison of various research studies

S. No	Authors	Methodology	Features used	Performance matrix
1	Aruvansh Nigam et al. [1]	Random Forest, KNN, ANN, XGBoost, Logistic Regression	temperature, rainfall, area, and season	Random Forest = 67.80
				XGBoost = 63.63
				KNN = 43.25
				Logistic Regression 25.81
2	Sonal Agarwal et al. [2]	LSTM, RNN, SVM	Temperature, Rainfall,	Accuracy = 97%
			pH value, relative	
			humidity, area	
3	Priya P et al. [3]	Developed a deep neural network (DNN) approach, Lasso, Shallow neural networks (SNN), Regression Tree(RT)	crop type, yield performance, Nitrogen value	NA
4	Mosleh Hmoud et al. [4]	Multi-layered Perceptron (MLP)	crop yield, temperature, rainfall, and insecticides	RMSE = 0.04493, R = 96.02
5	Saeed Khaki et al. [5]	Deep Neural Network (DNN)	crop genotype, yield performance, and environment (weather and soil)	Validation RMSE = 23.14
6	Wasi Alam et al. [6]	ARIMA and ANN	genetic markers, soil conditions, and weather components	MAPE for ARIMA (2,1,0) = 17.677% and MAPE for hybrid approach = 4.65%
7	Mayank Champaneri1 et al. [7]	KNN and Support Vector Regressor	weather, temperature, humidity, rainfall, moisture	Accuracy > 75%
8	P.S. Maya Gopal et al. [8]	Artifical Neural Network(ANN) and Multiple Linear Regression (MLR)	rainfall, maximum and minimum temperatures and solar radiation	MLR: RMSE = 9.8%, MAE = 6.9%, R = 89%; ANN: RMSE = 5.1%, MAE = 6.4%, R = 99%

3 Proposed Work

The figure (Fig. 1) below is a flowchart of our proposed work on crop yield prediction.

3.1 Data Collection

For crop yield prediction, we prepared a dataset comprising various features. We have gathered the data from the ICRISAT government website. Under the crops section, we obtained individual crop Areas and production values of the state we wanted, and then

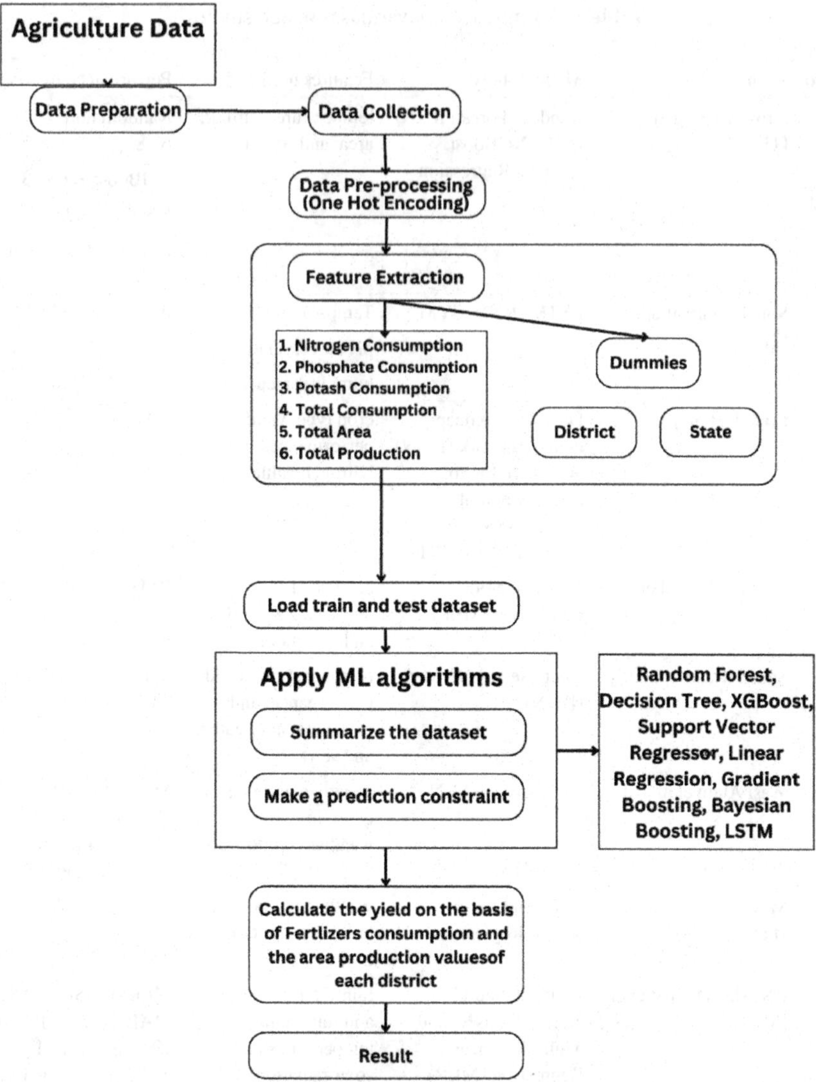

Fig. 1. Workflow diagram of crop yield prediction

under the inputs section; we obtained fertilizer consumption values. We gathered two types of data: the first is one consisted of the area and production values of various types of crops which we used to calculate yield; and the other fertilizers consumption consisted of nitrogen, phosphate, and potash consumption. We have gathered these two data from 18 districts of Gujarat and the yearly consumption of fertilizers is given over the years 2000–2017, so we have 324 observations in total. [16].

3.2 Data Preprocessing

In data preprocessing for the crop yield prediction dataset, several steps were taken to ensure the quality and suitability of the dataset. As discussed in dataset preparation, we gathered two datasets; so, our task was to combine those two datasets in the correct order in over to prevent any errors which could affect our results. If we had any field missing in any of one data, we removed those rows as using a mean or median value in those data would be of no use as every district had different values and in such a small dataset, variation of even a small observation can create a big effect in our results. We simply added the area & and production values of every crop into 2 different columns which we used to calculate yield using the below-mentioned formula. Columns like state code and district code were removed as they served no purpose to the dataset. After calculating yield, we applied the min max scaler to the area column and removed the production column as the features and the area column were only necessary for the independent variables, and the yield column was used as the dependent variable. The equation given below is what we used for calculating Yield.

$$\text{Yield} = \frac{\text{P(1)} + \text{P(2)} + \ldots + \text{P(n)}}{A(1) + A(2) + \ldots + A(n)} \tag{1}$$

where P1, P2,P3…Pn are the production values of the various crops in 1000 hectares & A1, A2, A3… An are the areas of that crop irrigated in 1000 tons.

We have considered the data from the dataset after 2000, as the data before it had many outliers and did not give good accuracy, so we selected the data after 2000 and it gave the best results. The dataset is shown below (Fig. 2).

	Dist Code	Year	State Code	State Name	Dist Name	RICE AREA (1000 ha)	RICE PRODUCTION (1000 tons)	WHEAT AREA (1000 ha)	WHEAT PRODUCTION (1000 tons)	KHARIF SORGHUM AREA (1000 ha)	...	FRUITS AND VEGETABLES AREA (1000 ha)	POTATOES AREA (1000 ha)	ONION AREA (1000 ha)	FODDER AREA (1000 ha)
0	121	2000	3	Gujarat	Ahmedabad	92.17	60.60	58.18	98.60	0.00	...	17.74	1.62	0.16	131.25
1	122	2000	3	Gujarat	Amreli	0.00	0.00	3.90	8.70	14.70	...	2.80	0.00	0.20	33.30
2	123	2000	3	Gujarat	Banaskantha	0.00	0.00	46.70	118.30	12.40	...	18.80	14.30	0.90	212.70
3	124	2000	3	Gujarat	Bharuch	21.70	11.80	8.10	13.40	20.10	...	13.30	0.00	0.30	30.70
4	125	2000	3	Gujarat	Vadodara / Baroda	54.40	10.80	13.90	30.50	13.50	...	21.80	1.30	0.50	38.40
...	...	...	...	...	...	...	...	...	...	...	...	...	...	...	...
319	134	2017	3	Gujarat	Panchmahal	127.96	144.13	72.68	168.60	0.06	...	0.00	0.06	1.09	0.00
320	135	2017	3	Gujarat	Rajkot	0.00	0.00	71.17	255.44	0.00	...	0.00	0.00	5.10	0.00
321	136	2017	3	Gujarat	Sabarkantha	8.66	29.87	154.25	447.87	0.00	...	0.00	28.47	0.62	0.00
322	137	2017	3	Gujarat	Surat	105.79	273.93	8.10	20.80	20.25	...	0.00	0.00	0.27	0.00
323	138	2017	3	Gujarat	Surendranagar	0.85	1.57	41.71	128.75	0.04	...	0.00	0.01	1.24	0.00

324 rows × 63 columns

Fig. 2. Dataset

After we added values in the respective Area & Production columns, we only took those two columns in our dataset instead of every crop. There were many columns with the categorical data like District Name; so we used one-hot encoding on those specific columns which creates binary vectors for each unique value in the columns, effectively converting them into multiple binary indicator columns and converting them into float. Because of one-hot encoding, we got many features in our model, but that didn't affect us in any way. The final dataset after pre-processing used for training is shown below (Fig. 3).

	Year	NITROGEN CONSUMPTION (tons)	PHOSPHATE CONSUMPTION (tons)	POTASH CONSUMPTION (tons)	T. Area	Ahmedabad	Amreli	Banaskantha	Bharuch	Bhavnagar	...	Kutch	Mehsana	Panchmahal
0	2000	32660	9873	5329	553.37	1	0	0	0	0	...	0	0	0
1	2000	12010	9722	386	868.90	0	1	0	0	0	...	0	0	0
2	2000	42866	16320	2781	957.80	0	0	1	0	0	...	0	0	0
3	2000	21069	6385	4835	458.30	0	0	0	1	0	...	0	0	0
4	2000	35249	7814	2435	540.60	0	0	0	0	0	...	0	0	0
...	...	...	...	...	...	...	...	...	...	...	...	...	...	...
319	2017	70498	9727	1359	647.18	0	0	0	0	0	...	0	0	1
320	2017	108519	54681	12824	825.11	0	0	0	0	0	...	0	0	0
321	2017	81747	23767	14109	549.26	0	0	0	0	0	...	0	0	0
322	2017	80074	30311	27213	368.32	0	0	0	0	0	...	0	0	0
323	2017	83525	31749	2648	600.02	0	0	0	0	0	...	0	0	0

324 rows × 24 columns

Fig. 3. Dataset after one-hot encoding

3.3 Model Selection

The selection of an appropriate model is crucial. Factors such as prediction accuracy, computational efficiency, and interpretability should be considered to identify the most suitable model for the task. We have taken 70% of data as training data and 30% as testing data as our dataset is small. The algorithms applied are given below:

Random Forest Regressor: Random Forest which is a popular machine learning algorithm, is an effective supervised learning method. It is often used to solve ML classification and regression problems. It uses the basic concept of ensemble learning, which is the act of combining several classifiers to solve a difficult problem and improve the model's performance.

Decision Tree Regressor: The decision tree is one of the most commonly used practical methods for supervised learning. It can be used to complete classification and regression tasks, with the latter being more commonly used in real-world scenarios. Its tree-structured classifier is made up of three main node kinds. The root node, which can be further subdivided, is the first node that represents the entire sample.

XGBoost: The XGBoost algorithm has emerged as a popular and powerful machine learning technique for a wide range of predictive tasks, including crop yield prediction. XGBoost stands for Extreme Gradient Boosting and is known for its ability to handle complex, non-linear relationships in data. By iteratively building an ensemble of weak prediction models, XGBoost optimizes the model's performance and provides robust predictions. Its efficiency, scalability, and feature importance analysis make XGBoost a valuable tool for accurate prediction and decision-making in the agricultural domain.

Support Vector Regression (SVR): Support Vector Regression is a regression-specific variation of the recognized Support Vector Machine (SVM) method. It seeks a hyperplane that best matches the data points while keeping a given margin around the anticipated values. [21] SVR tries to minimize the discrepancy between expected and actual values while regularizing the model's complexity. It uses a kernel function to transfer the data into a higher-dimensional space, allowing the technique to capture non-linear relationships. SVR is adaptable when dealing with complicated data patterns and may be fine-tuned.

Linear Regression: Linear regression is a basic and extensively used machine learning algorithm for predicting numerical outcomes. The primary goal is to fit a linear equation to the data and illustrate the relationship between one or more independent variables. By estimating the coefficients of the equation, linear regression enables the prediction of new outcomes based on the input variables. Its simplicity, interpretability, and effectiveness make linear regression a valuable tool for various applications.

Gradient Boosting: Gradient Boosting Regression is a sophisticated ensemble learning approach that combines numerous weak learners (usually decision trees) to produce a robust prediction model. It works by fitting new models to the residual errors of prior models repeatedly. Each new model focuses on decreasing the ensemble's previous mistakes. Gradient Boosting Regression is distinguished by its ability to efficiently handle non-linearity and feature interactions. It uses gradient descent to optimize a loss function and changes the model parameters to minimize the loss. Gradient Boosting Regression has a high prediction accuracy and can handle complicated data interactions.

Bayesian Boosting Regression: Another ensemble approach that uses the Bayesian framework to generate a strong prediction model is Bayesian Boosting Regression. It combines the benefits of both boosting and Bayesian modeling approaches. Bayesian approaches offer a sound foundation for incorporating previous information and uncertainty into the modeling process. Multiple weak learners are trained sequentially in Bayesian Boosting, and Bayesian updating is used to improve the model's predictions. This method quantifies uncertainty and provides plausible ranges for predictions. Bayesian Boosting Regression is very beneficial when dealing with limited data and estimating interpretability and uncertainty.

Long Short-Term Memory (LSTM): The Long Short-Term Memory (LSTM) algorithm is a specialized form of recurrent neural network (RNN) that excels at capturing long-term dependencies in sequential data. [22] With its unique architecture, including memory cells and gating mechanisms, LSTM can effectively process and retain information over extended sequences. This makes it particularly well-suited for time series analysis and prediction tasks. LSTM's ability to model temporal relationships and handle sequential data has proven valuable in capturing patterns and making accurate predictions in diverse fields. The data is divided into 70% for training data and 30% for test data. Our model runs on 50 epochs, with batch size 32, this is tuned after trying various combinations. We've selected the parameters that gives the best outcomes.

3.4 Evaluation

Model evaluation is crucial for determining the efficiency of the trained model. We have used Mean-Squared Error (MSE), Mean Absolute Error (MAE), and R2-score as the evaluation metrics. The less the MSE & MAE, and more the R2 Score, the better the model will be in predicting the yield of the unknown data (Table 2).

Table 2. Evaluation of different models

Algorithm	Mean Squared Error (MSE)	Mean Absolute Error (MAE)	R2 score
Random Forest Regressor	0.1026	0.2267	0.8070
Support Vector Regression	0.1261	0.2417	0.7626
Decision Tree	0.2708	0.3433	0.4906
XGBoost	0.1383	0.257	0.7397
Gradient Boosting Regression	0.1178	0.246	0.7782
Bayesian Regression	0.1173	0.2295	0.7791
Linear Regression	0.1122	0.2304	0.7889
Long Short Term Memory	0.1595	0.3	0.654

4 Results

The machine learning models used in these papers are focused on identifying the trend or pattern in the target variable 'yield' and improving it as its main purpose. The dataset is a combination of two data; one is the yearly fertilizer's consumption, and the other one consisted of area, and production values of each crop which after adding, we found the yield of all crops per year. After merging the datasets, we plotted a heatmap to see the correlation between different features and we found that they're very correlated. We applied 8 different ML models to see which one gives the best r2 score. From the above given table, we can infer that the best R2 Score for crop yield prediction is provided by Random Forest Regressor and linear Regression which gave r2 scores of 0.80 & 0.79 respectively. Similarly, a nearer R2- score is obtained from Bayesian Regression, Gradient Boosting, and Support Vector Regression. The models with greater r2 scores represent how good they are fit for predicting data. Decision Trees didn't provide a good outcome which means they're not fit to predict values on the current data. We can use these models to predict the yield and production of crops by entering the area value and the other features and get good predictions using the model with the highest r2-score.

5 Conclusion

This research presented the various machine learning algorithms for predicting the yield of the crop based on fertilizer consumption, area & and yield of certain crops. Our Dataset had very less observations as the fertilizer consumption was counted yearly, if we had monthly data, the model could have worked even better. We tried on fewer districts too, and the accuracy we were getting was not so good. So, we can conclude that more data can produce better predictions in yield. It has been established that Random Forest gives the highest yield prediction accuracy of all. Overall, this research contributes to the advancement of crop yield prediction by evaluating and comparing different machine-learning algorithms.

6 Future Work

This research work can help develop a crop recommendation system that can be helpful for farmers in the production and distribution of various crops which will enhance the decision-making of the farmers and guide them to the best crop for their field. Right now, we have only used Gujarat's dataset; we can use a dataset containing every district in India, then this model can be useful nationwide. We don't have fertilizers data for each crop, but if we can get that then we can find yield for every crop. We can also include weather data to see if there are any correlations to it. Also, ML algorithms can be applied to time-series data such as ARIMA & SARIMA for better accuracy in crop yield prediction. The final results that have been displayed currently can be transformed into a web application and our future work would be developing an application where the farmers can use it as an app and also enabling the whole system in the regional language of farmers.

References

1. Nigam, A., Garg, S., Agrawal, A., Agrawal, P.: Crop yield prediction using machine learning algorithms. In: 2019 Fifth International Conference on Image Information Processing (ICIIP), Shimla, India, pp. 125–130 (2019)
2. Breiman, L.: Random forests. Mach. Learn. **45**, 5–32 (2001)
3. Priya, P., Muthaiah, U., Balamurugan, M.: Predicting yield of the crop using machine learning algorithm. Int. J. Eng. Sci. Res. Technol. **7**(1), 1–7 (2018)
4. Mishra, S., Mishra, D., Santra, G.H.: Applications of machine learning techniques in agricultural crop production: a review paper. Indian J. Sci. Technol. **9**(38), 1–14 (2016)
5. Van Klompenburg, T., Kassahun, A., Catal, C.: Crop yield prediction using machine learning: a systematic literature review. Comput. Electron. Agric. **177**, 105709 (2020)
6. Rashid, M., Bari, B.S., Yusup, Y., Kamaruddin, M.A., Khan, N.: A comprehensive review of crop yield prediction using machine learning approaches with special emphasis on palm oil yield prediction. IEEE Access **9**, 63406–63439 (2021)
7. Khaki, S., Wang, L.: Crop yield prediction using deep neural networks. Front. Plant Sci. **10**, 621 (2019)
8. Muruganantham, P., Wibowo, S., Grandhi, S., Samrat, N.H., Islam, N.: A systematic literature review on crop yield prediction with deep learning and remote sensing. Remote Sens. **14**(9), 1990 (2022)
9. Gopal, P.S.M., Bhargavi, R.: A novel approach for efficient crop yield prediction. Comput. Electron. Agric. **165**, 104968 (2019)
10. Alpaydin, E.: Introduction to Machine Learning. MIT press, Cambridge 2020
11. Venugopal, A., Aparna, S., Mani, J., Mathew, R., Williams, V.: Crop yield prediction using machine learning algorithms. Int. J. Eng. Res. Technol. (IJERT) NCREIS **09**(13) (2021)
12. https://www.ibef.org/industry/agriculture-india
13. Reddy, D.J., Kumar, M.R.: Crop yield prediction using machine learning algorithm. In: 2021 5th International Conference on Intelligent Computing and Control Systems (ICICCS), Madurai, India, pp. 1466–1470 (2021)

14. Paudel, D., et al.: Machine learning for large-scale crop yield forecasting. Agric. Syst. **187**, 103016 (2021)
15. Kumari, P., Rathore, S., Kalamkar, A., Kambale, T.: Predicition of crop yield using SVM approch with the facility of E-MART system. Easychair (2020)
16. http://data.icrisat.org/
17. Gupta, M., et al.: Crop yield prediction techniques using machine learning algorithms. In: 2022 8th International Conference on Smart Structures and Systems (ICSSS). IEEE (2022)
18. Sri, B. Swathi, et al. "An Improved Machine Learning based Crop Recommendation System." *2023 International Conference on Sustainable Computing and Data Communication Systems (ICSCDS).* IEEE, 2023
19. Gupta, S., Jasrasaria, R., Kalonia, S., Khurana, A.: Farmer's guide: crop prediction using random forest regression. IRE J. **6**(12), 591 (2023). ISSN: 2456–8880
20. Patel, J., et al.: A machine learning-based water potability prediction model by using synthetic minority oversampling technique and explainable AI. In: Computational Intelligence and Neuroscience: CIN 2022 (2022)
21. Gupta, R.K., Sahu, Y., Kunhare, N., Gupta, A., Prakash, D.: Deep learning based mathematical model for feature extraction to detect corona virus disease using chest X-ray images. Int. J. Uncertain. Fuzz. Knowl.-Based Syst. **29**(06), 921–947 (2021)
22. Kanani, S., Patel, S., Gupta, R.K., Jain, A., Lin, J.C.W.: An AI-Enabled ensemble method for rainfall forecasting using Long-Short term memory. Math. Biosci. Eng. **20**(5), 8975–9002 (2023). https://doi.org/10.3934/mbe.2023394

Detection and Classification of Waste Materials Using Deep Learning Techniques

Abisek Dahal[1(✉)], Oyshi Pronomy Sarker[1], Jahnavi Kashyap[1], Rakesh Kumar Gupta[1], Sheli Sinha Chaudhuri[2], and Soumen Moulik[1]

[1] Deptartment of CSE, National Institute of Technology, Meghalaya Shillong, India
{abiseknitskm,01oyshipronomy,kashyapjahnavi2018,rakeshgupta1004, mouliksoumen}@gmail.com

[2] Department of Electronic and Telecommunication, Jadavpur University, Jadavpur, West Bengal, India
shelism@rediffmail.com

Abstract. This paper deals with the detection and classification of waste materials by performing an analysis of the deep learning-based computer vision techniques. Object detection and classification algorithms use machine learning to produce meaningful results. Thus, in real-life following this approach we can get benefits of enhanced performance in waste identification and increase in recycled materials. We review existing research and solutions for waste object detection,focusing on deep-learning models and frameworks employed in similar object detection problems. Subsequently,we describe the creation and composition of our data sets,which include fourteen waste categories encompassing various items commonly found in waste streams such as glass waste,chip packets and plastic bags. We then discuss the object detection models that were utilized to classify and detect waste materials within our data sets. Specifically,we employ SSD MobileNet V2 FPN Lite, EfficientDet-D0, YOLOv7,and YOLOv8 models to achieve accurate waste identification and classification. Finally, we present and analyze the results obtained by these models. Our evaluation indicates that YOLO v8 achieves the highest accuracy,with a confidence level of 0.5 and a Mean Average Precision (mAP) of 76.6%.

Keywords: Waste Object Detection · Efficient Recycling · Deep learning · SSD MobileNet V2 FPN Lite · EfficientDet-D0 · YOLOv7 · YOLOv8

1 Introduction

As a result of growing environmental concerns and the demand for sustainable practices, waste management has turned into a substantial problem in recent years. Waste management plays a pivotal role in pollution management and reducing negative impact of waste on our planet. The effectiveness of recycling procedures depends on the precise identification and categorization of waste

N. Chauhan et al. (Eds.): MIND 2023, CCIS 2128, pp. 75–85, 2024.
https://doi.org/10.1007/978-3-031-62217-5_7

items. Deep learning techniques have emerged as a promising solution to address this challenge. The classification of waste is necessary to increase the recycling efficiency. Traditional waste sorting and recycling techniques demand lot of time, money, and resources, which limit its efficiency. To address this issue, deep learning algorithms must be integrated into garbage and waste recognition systems for effective waste classification,recycling and disposal [1]. Deep learning is a branch of machine learning that employs artificial neural networks to simulate model and solve complex problems. It has been widely applied in waste detection and classification, achieving high accuracy rates and improving the efficiency of waste management systems. Moreover, researchers have developed deep learning-based intelligent garbage detection systems that employ Convolutional Neural Networks (CNNs) to automate the entire process by decreasing the time spent in sorting the garbage and increasing profitability [2]. WasteNet [3] a waste classification system at the leading edge for Smart bins – proposed a waste sorting system that uses a CNN to sort and classify waste at edge layer, reducing the need for cloud computing and improving response times. Various studies have been conducted on trash detection and classification by using machine learning and deep learning. For instance, a waste and trash recognition and classification system based on CNN VGG-16 classifies domestic garbage into the hazardous, bio-waste, recyclable, non-recyclable, and other garbage [4]. Another study suggests the smart fusion of deep learning features for improved trash and waste classification optimally combines multiple deep learning features to achieve reliable waste classification capabilities [5]. By employing Artificial Intelligence (AI) powered systems, we can significantly improve the accuracy, speed, and cost-effectiveness of waste sorting processes. This, in turn, will contribute to optimizing recycling facilities, reducing landfill waste, and overall environmental sustainability. We enable these models to precisely distinguish between various types of waste by training them on large dataset containing labeled waste samples. We enable these models to precisely differentiate distinct forms of waste by training deep learning models on massive dataset. This strategy makes waste classification more effective and advances waste management procedures as a whole.

2 Related Works

Waste management is a critical issue for pollution management and garbage classification determines recycling efficiency. The objective of this literature review is to present a comprehensive summary of an existing research on deep learning-based trash and waste items detection and classification for efficient recycling. The author in [4] proposed guidelines for training CNN to classify various objects as recyclable, non recyclable or others. They also suggested a CNN-based system for distinguishing between trash and other items. They leverage Alexanet CNN-based architecture to propose two CNN,to find waste materials in an image and separate them as materials that can be recycled from sanitary landfill waste to train the model. The benchmark TrashNet indoor picture dataset serves as the initial training and testing ground for the proposed model. Then the model is trained and tested using outdoor images for which it was meant to be used. They were able to attain a commendable level of accuracy by leveraging the CNN model. They also suggest to integrate this technique to replicate existing manual cleaning and garbage collection in smart cities. The authors in [6] introduced an algorithm for real-time detection of domestic garbage in rural areas. This algorithm utilizes an enhanced YOLOv5s network model,aiming to achieve accurate and efficient garbage detection in real-world scenarios. Their research aimed to improve garbage detection algorithms with limited dataset in 13 categories. They suggested further improvements in small and multiple target detection,optimization of real-time performance by reducing network complexity and enhancing bounding box prediction detection. The author in [7] highlights the lack of global benchmarks and standards for automatic waste detection metrics and tries to address those issues using ten existing open-source waste dataset. They replicate the existing model to create a base for waste detection. They further create a new benchmark dataset i.e. *Identify waste and categorize waste.* to categories waste into different categories like bio waste, glass waste, metal waste,etc. They presented, EfficientDet-D2 for localization and EfficientNet-B2 for classification of trash and waste materials into 7 categories and trained their model in a semisupervised way by making use of unlabeled images. The authors in [8] proposed a state of art AquaTrash dataset and AquaVision model that offer a potential solution to address the growing concern of water pollution. Their model has an ability to identify and categorize pollutants and hazardous waste materials,aiding in restoration and maintenance of clean water bodies. Deep learning-based waste detectors typically require extensive annotated samples for training,which can be time-consuming and labor-intensive.

To address this challenges authors in [9] proposed versatile detection system capable of flexibly detecting various waste categories with limited labeled samples. Experimental results showcase that framework attains a mean average precision of 31.16% across 12 waste categories when trained with only a few samples (30 instances per category).

3 Proposed Model

In our experimental study,we utilized,we used our custom dataset as the baseline. The dataset comprises a total of 212 images,encompassing 20,297 annotations in total. Each image on average contains 97.5 annotations representing 14 distinct classes. These classes include board boxes,burnt paper,glass waste,plastic bottles, packets, plastic bags,non-plastic bottles,paper cups,paper waste, plastic spoons,plastic bowls, plastic plates and plastic cups. The class balance representation of dataset is shown in Fig. 1. To ensure proper evaluation,we divide the dataset into three distinct sets: training,validation and test sets of 93%, 5%, and 2%, respectively. Additionally, the input data maintains a consistent resolution of 416×416 pixels.

3.1 Data Collection

The data collection process for model involved collaborating with waste management facilities,capturing high-resolution images of diverse waste materials and ensuring accurate labeling through expert annotation. Environmental factors like lighting conditions and backgrounds were carefully consider capturing waste items under different setups to enhance model robustness. The dataset underwent rigorous review ensuring precise labeling with bounding boxes or segmentation masks.

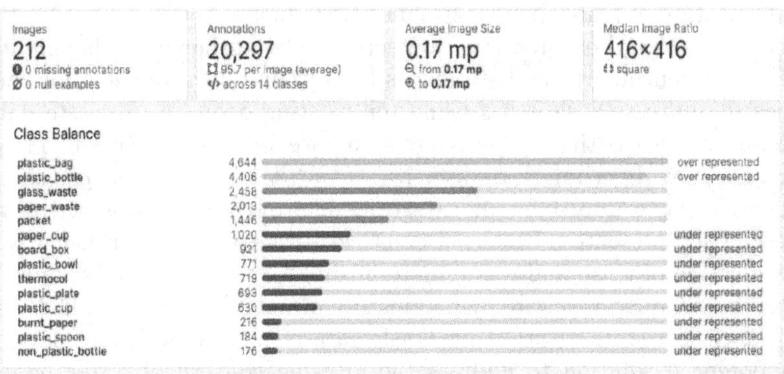

Fig. 1. Class Balance Representation of the Datasets.

3.2 Pre Processing and Augmentation

For data pre-processing and augmentation,we leveraged the capabilities of Roboflow, a robust platform that facilitates the use of custom data for object detection tasks. Roboflow offers a streamlined workflow, allowing for seamless image upload, annotation as shown in Fig. 3,using its built-in tools,model training using its training engine,and deployment of the trained model for production use.

The dataset annotations were performed using the LabelMe tool, an open-source Python-based annotation tool that supports manual polygonal annotation for object detection,classification and segmentation tasks. LabelMe offers various shape options such as polygons,circles,rectangles,lines, line strips and points allowing for flexible and precise labeling as shown in Fig. 2. The resulting labels were saved as JSON files directly from the application. To align the dataset with the desired format,a Python script provided by the LabelMe repository was utilized to convert the annotations to PASCAL VOC format.

In order to optimize the dataset, several pre-processing steps were applied. These steps included automatic orientation adjustment,resizing and remapping redundant classes. The original dataset contained 20 classes, of which four were

Fig. 2. Annotated images.

Fig. 3. Proposed architecture.

deemed redundant and subsequently remapped,resulting in a final set of 14 distinct waste material classes. We have consider these class for consideration as board boxes,burnt paper,glass waste, plastic bottles,packets,plastic bags,plastic bottles,paper cups, paper waste,plastic spoons, plastic bowls,plastic plates, plastic cups,plastic straws and non-plastic bottles.

To augment the dataset's variety and enhance the performance of the mode l performance,various augmentations were applied using Roboflow. These augmentations included horizontal and vertical flips 90° clockwise and counterclockwise rotations,upside-down flips,saturation adjustments ranging from -32% to +32%, brightness adjustments between -14% and +14%, and exposure adjustments ranging from -13% to +13%.

3.3 Evaluation Metrics

We evaluate the effectiveness and performance of our model using the mAP metric, which is calculated as the average precision across all classes at a specific Intersection over Union (IoU) threshold. The precision is calculated by dividing the number of true positives (TP) by the sum of true positives (TP) and false positives (FP). Mathematically, *Precision (P)* may be defined as follows:

$$P = \frac{TP}{TP + FP} \tag{1}$$

Recall (R) is calculated as ratio of true positives to the sum of true positives and false negatives, quantifying the ability of a model to correctly identify positive instances. Mathematically,

$$R = \frac{TP}{TP + FN} \tag{2}$$

Furthermore, mAP is a performance metric employed to assess the effectiveness of object detection and recognition systems. It is calculated as the average precision for each class then takes the mean across all the classes, providing a comprehensive measure of the model's precision in identifying and localizing objects in various categories.

$$mAP = \frac{1}{n}\sum_{i=1}^{n} AP_i \tag{3}$$

where n is the total number of classes and AP_i is average Precision for class i. Average Precision (AP) is a performance metric used in object detection and information retrieval tasks to measure the quality of ranked predictions. Mathematically,

$$AP = \frac{1}{TP}\sum_{TP} IR \tag{4}$$

where TP represents true positives at each interpolated recall (IR) level.

The *F1-score (F1)* is a metric which combines precision as well as recall which is calculated as the harmonic mean of the two, providing a balanced measure of a model's accuracy. Mathematically,

$$F1 = \frac{2 * PR}{P + R} \tag{5}$$

Accuracy (A) is the ratio of correctly classified class to the total number of class,reflecting the overall correctness of a model's predictions.Mathematically,

$$A = \frac{TP + TN}{TP + TN + FP + FN} \tag{6}$$

The Intersection over Union (IoU) metric holds significant importance in object detection and segmentation tasks. It quantifies the level of overlap between the predicted and true regions by calculating the ratio of their intersection to their union. IoU provides a valuable measure to assess the accuracy and precision of the model's predictions in relation to the ground truth regions. Mathematically,

$$IoU = \frac{\text{Area of Intersection}}{\text{Area of Union}} \tag{7}$$

3.4 Waste Garbage Detection Algorithms

To conduct our experiment, we applied four supervised machine learning algorithms on original and feature selection dataset. Our objective is to determine the algorithm that achieves the highest accuracy in detecting waste garbage. The algorithms used in our experiment are as follows:

1. SSD MobileNet v1 FPN Lite
2. EfficientDet-D0
3. YOLOv7
4. YOLOv8

We compare the performance of these algorithms based on their accuracy in garbage detection.

4 Result and Simulation

The experiment was conducted using Keras, a popular Python framework for deep learning model development. Additional libraries employed included Scikit-learn, pandas, roboflow and NumPy, enhancing the experimentation process. The experiment necessitated a dedicated Graphical Processing Unit (GPU) on a computer server in google colab with the GPU with 15GB GDDR5 VRAM for computational capabilities to facilitate efficient computations.

4.1 SSD MobileNet

SSD MobileNet V2 is an object detection model that combines feature pyramid network (FPN) with a lightweight MobileNet V2 backbone. It utilizes a single-shot multibox detector (SSD) framework for efficient and accurate object detection tasks. We trained the model for 40,000 steps, with batch size 16 (with our waste dataset-198 train images). The evaluation metrics at 40,000 steps are calculated. The threshold for the model accuracy is determined using the mAP of the model, which was created by evaluating test images and test results obtained during real-time waste detection. The mAP is obtained at 0.50 IoU is 0.235. To improve the accuracy of the model batch size cab be increase and the number of steps as well. An additional metric employed for evaluation is the loss function the presence of a low loss function indicates reduced confidence and localization loss, indicating accurate predictions as demonstrated in the graph above, showcasing a classification loss of around 0.08 and localization loss of 0.10 at 40k steps.

4.2 EfficientDet-D0

EfficientDet-D0 is an efficient object detection model that balances accuracy and computational efficiency for various computer vision tasks. We conducted training for our model over 28,000 steps, utilizing a batch size of 8 and a dataset consisting of 198 train images. The evaluation metrics were calculated at the 28k step, resulting in a mAP score of 0.266403 for an IoU of 0.50. In an attempt to enhance accuracy,we explored increasing the batch size,but due to limitations on training duration (Collab GPU ran out of limit),We settled for 16,000 steps with a total loss of 0.33. Our objective was to achieve a total loss below 0.24, as attained by the SSD MobileNet Model. Consequently, we reduced the number of epochs to 8 and conducted training up to the 28k step,achieving a loss of 0.23. Since there were no significant increases in loss over the preceding 10k steps,we concluded training at the 28k step. Total loss obtained at 28k is 0.2237 which is not so good but less than the SSD MobileNetv2 which was 0.2489.We can increase the Performance could have been increased with better infrastructure i.e. more GPUs Fig. 3 (Fig. 4).

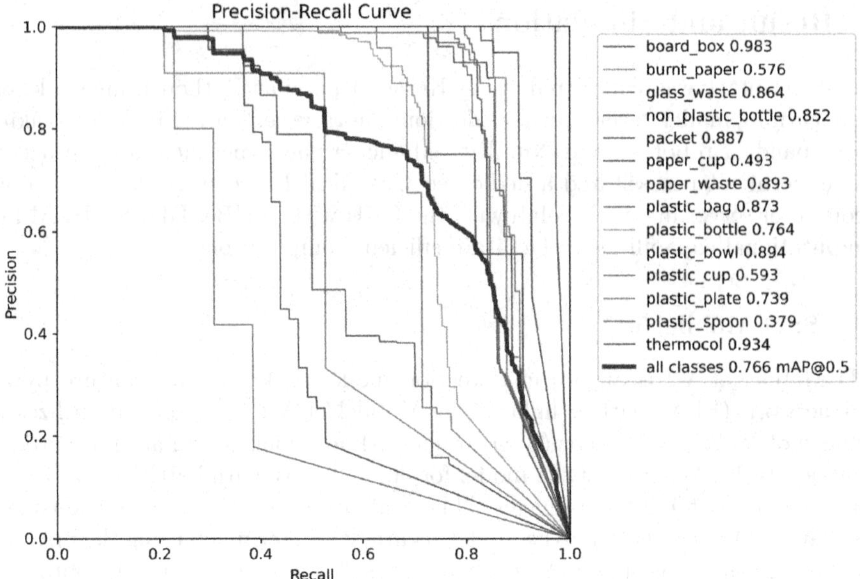

Fig. 4. PR Curve YOLOv8.

4.3 YOLOv7 and YOLOv8

YOLOv7 and YOLOv8 are object detection model and YOLOv8 has some improvement with a number of new features.We utilized the YOLOv7 tiny variant with a batch size of 8, training it for 300 epochs. The YOLOv7 tiny is a scaled-down version of the YOLOv7 object detection model,optimized for speed and efficiency at the expense of accuracy. The batch size refers to the number of images processed simultaneously during training, impacting training speed and memory requirements. The number of epochs indicates how many times the model was trained using the complete dataset,influencing accuracy,but prolonging training time. With an IoU of 0.5,the YOLOv7 achieved an average precision of 41.3%,indicating a reasonable level of accuracy that could be enhanced through additional epoch training. Evaluating object detection performance,mAP@0.5 considers precision and recall,offering insights into both accuracy and completeness of the model. Higher mAP@0.5 values signify improved accuracy and completeness. On the other hand YOLOv8 uses a new backbone network that is even more efficient and accurate. It also uses a new head network that is better at predicting object,considering PR curve as shown in Fig. 4 we can conclude that model is performing well. In our case YOLOv8 gave an mAP@0.5 value of 76.6% for 200 epochs which is the highest accuracy of all the models as shown in Fig. 5.

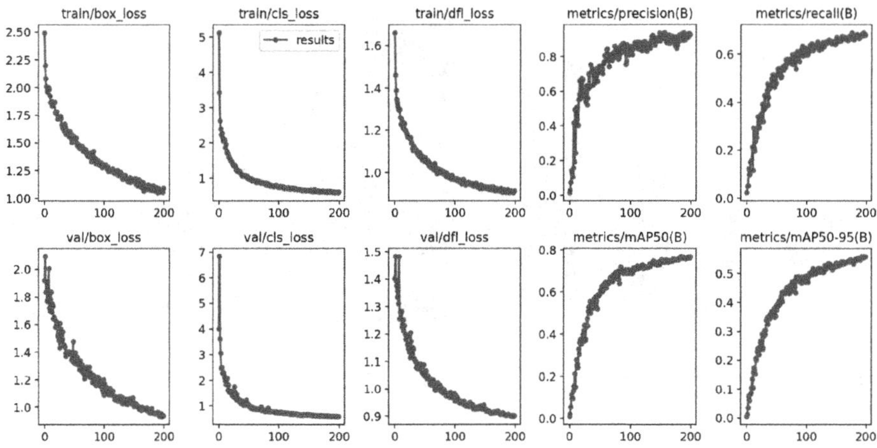

Fig. 5. Performance Analysis of Model.

4.4 Comparison of Model

After completion of training the various models, the accuracy results were obtained as shown in Table 1. The graph in Fig. 6 depicts a comparison of mAP values across various models as it measures the accuracy and quality of detected objects by comparing the predicted bounded boxes to the ground truth bounding box. Here, mAP@0.5 specifically refers to the mean Average Precision is calculated at an IoU threshold of 0.5 which establishes the minimal overlap needed between a prediction's and the ground truth's bounding boxes for a detection to be declared accurate. While mAP@0.5:0.95 calculates the mAP across multiple IoU thresholds,ranges from 0.5 to 0.95 with increments of 0.05.It helps in assessment of the model's detection performance by considering a range of IoU thresholds,reflecting both stringent and lenient matching criteria for object localization.

Table 1. Accuracy Table

Sl. No.	Model	Accuracy
1	MobileNet V2 FPN Lite	23.5%
2	EfficientDet-d0	26.6%
3	Yolo v7	41.3%
4	Yolo v8	76.6%

From Table 1,it is quite evident that our YOLOv8 has recorded best performance matrices as compared to the other standard algorithms Fig. 7 represents the model's understanding and interpretation by processing an input image. It

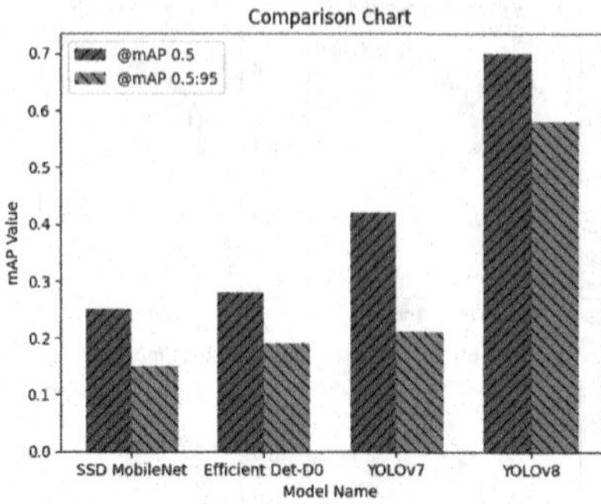

Fig. 6. Comparison of mean average precision.

Fig. 7. Predicted Image.

also also depicts the detection of objects, such as plastic, bottles, etc., from the input images.

5 Conclusion

Deep learning algorithms have shown remarkable promise in the detection and classification of waste products and they have the potential to significantly alter waste management processes. We can precisely identify and categorise waste materials using computer vision algorithms and neural networks, resulting in more effective sorting and recycling procedures. Deep learning models beat conventional methods in terms of accuracy and speed.After training for 200 epochs, Yolo v8 exhibited the highest mAP of 76.6% at an IoU threshold of an 0.5.Our aim is to enhance models results by expanding the sample size of the dataset.Additionally,we plan to refine the existing algorithm by fine-tuning the model and its associated constraints. To facilitate waste collection, detection, and classification in real-time scenarios, we intend to develop an application. This app will contribute from waste material detection and classification to recycling efforts, which will help us reduce carbon footprints. In the future, we can design waste management systems that are more efficient, long-lasting, and economically viable by using techniques like expanding the dataset, real-time implementation, multimodal fusion, transfer learning, deployment in developing countries and robots integration. A mobile app will be developed to detect and help segregate garbage and waste items at a lower level. Adopting these advances will contribute to a cleaner, greener future for our planet. This efficient solution will contribute towards achieving the UN sustainability goals.

References

1. Chen, Y., et al.: Classification and recycling of recyclable garbage based on deep learning, J. Cleaner Prod. Vol 414, 2023, 137558, ISSN 0959-6526
2. Chauhan, R., Shighra, S., Madkhali, H., Nguyen, L., Prasad, M.,: Efficient future waste management: a learning-based approach with deep neural networks for smart system (LADS). Appl. Sci. 2023; 13(7):4140. https://doi.org/10.3390/app13074140
3. White, G., Cabrera, C., Palade, A., Li, F., Clarke, S.: Waste classification at the edge for smart bins. arXiv:2006.05873. https://doi.org/10.48550/arXiv.2006.05873
4. Wang, H.:"Garbage recognition and classification system based on convolutional neural network VGG16," 2020 3rd International Conference on Advanced Electronic Materials, Computers and Software Engineering (AEMCSE), Shenzhen, China, 2020, pp. 252-255. https://doi.org/10.1109/AEMCSE50948.2020.00061
5. Ahmad, K., Khan, K., Al-Fuqaha, A.: Intelligent fusion of deep features for improved waste classification. IEEE Access **8**, 96495–96504 (2020)
6. Jiang, X., Hu, H., Qin, Y., Hu, Y., Ding, R.: A real-time rural domestic garbage detection algorithm with an improved YOLOv5s network model. Sci. Rep. **12**(1), 16802 (2022)
7. Majchrowska, S., Mikołajczyk, A., Ferlin, M., Klawikowska, Z., Plantykow, M.A., Kwasigroch, A., Majek, K.: Deep learning-based waste detection in natural and urban environments. Waste Manage. **138**, 274–284 (2022)
8. Panwar, H., et al.: Automating the detection of waste in water bodies using deep transfer learning, Case Studies in Chemical and Environmental Engineering, Vol 2, 2020, 100026, ISSN 2666-0164, https://doi.org/10.1016/j.cscee.2020.100026
9. Zhou, W., Zhao, L., Huang, H., Chen, Y., Xu, S., Wang, C.: Automatic waste detection with few annotated samples: Improving waste management efficiency, Eng. Appl. Artif. Intell. Vol 120, 2023, 105865, ISSN 0952-1976, https://doi.org/10.1016/j.engappai.2023.105865
10. Abuga, D., Raghava, NS.:Real-time smart garbage bin mechanism for solid waste management in smart cities, Sustain. Cities Soc. Vol 75, 2021, 103347, ISSN 2210-6707, https://doi.org/10.1016/j.scs.2021.103347
11. Aral, R. A., et al.: Classification of TrashNet Dataset Based on Deep Learning Models.In :2018 IEEE International Conference on Big Data (Big Data), Seattle, WA, USA, 2018, pp. 2058-2062, https://doi.org/10.1109/BigData.2018.8622212.

A Comparative Analysis of ML Based Approaches for Identifying AQI Level

Nairita Sarkar, Pankaj Kumar Keserwani[(✉)], and Mahesh Chandra Govil

Computer Science and Engineering, National Institute of Technology Sikkim, Ravangla, India

pankaj.keserwani@gmail.com

Abstract. Monitoring Air Quality Index (AQI) is a significant research concern within the realm of intelligent urban planning and the sustainable development of cities, with a particular focus on enhancing air quality in Asian nations such as India. Over the recent years, the utilization of machine learning (ML) techniques has experienced a substantial surge in popularity for predicting the AQI. The primary goal of this work is to assess the air quality levels of four metropolitan cities: Ahmedabad, Bengaluru, Chennai, and Delhi, using various ML models and a comparative analysis of the models' performance is also done. The AQI data for the four metropolitan cities mentioned are collected from CPCB website. Several preprocessing strategies are employed to control the data before it is fed into the classification models. The outcomes of the utilized models are represented in respect of F1-score, recall, precision and accuracy.

Keywords: Air Quality Index · Logistic Regression · Support Vector Machine · K-Nearest Neighbor · Random Forest · Decision Tree

1 Introduction

Clean air is an essential element for sustaining life on Earth, and its importance cannot be overstated. It has a crucial significance in numerous physiological processes within human bodies, ensuring accurate functioning of the respiratory system. Fresh air supports the growth of plants and maintains the ecosystems of countless animal species. Now a days, with the continuous increase in industrialization, urbanization, and vehicular emissions, the quality of air is getting worse [15]. Breathing in polluted air can have detrimental effects on our respiratory health, cardiovascular system, and immune system. Inhalation of contaminants like Particulate Matter (PM), Nitrogen Oxides (NO_x), Sulphur Dioxide (SO_2), and Volatile Organic Compounds (VOCs) can irritate respiratory system, leading to coughing, wheezing, asthma, bronchitis etc. These factors also contribute to the development and progression of cardiovascular diseases. So, improving the air quality is a significant matter today. Many initiatives, such as awareness campaigns, increasing tree plantation, sustainable transportation, clean energy

N. Chauhan et al. (Eds.): MIND 2023, CCIS 2128, pp. 86–97, 2024.
https://doi.org/10.1007/978-3-031-62217-5_8

promotion, etc. have been taken to improve air quality and solve the health issues caused by air pollution. Air quality monitoring and prediction are one of the most effective solutions to maintain well-being of human. AQI is a standardized metric helps to assess level of air pollution in a specific area. People may avoid visiting any place with a higher AQI value to prevent health issues. Built upon the AQI values, air pollution levels are categorized into six classes: Fair (0–50), Satisfactory (51–100), Medium (101–200), Unfair (201–300), Very Unfair (301–400), Severe (401–500).

The development of ML approaches has significantly impacted air quality prediction by revolutionizing the accuracy [1]. ML models can learn from historical air quality data and meteorological parameters to establish complex relationships and generate predictive models. This research work aims to make a comparative analysis framework on some ML approaches and analyse the performance efficiency of the models. By leveraging historical data of air quality from four cities in India (Ahmedabad, Bengaluru, Chennai, Delhi) various ML models namely Logistic Regression (LR), Support Vector Machine (SVM), K-Nearest Neighbor (KNN), Random Forest (RF), Decision Tree (DT) have been analysed and evaluated. The motivation behind this research work stems from the pressing need to address the adverse consequences of polluted air on human body and environment. The claimed contributions of this work are summarized below:

1. The AQI data for four metropolitan cities of India are accumulated from official website of Central Pollution Control Board (CPCB) of India.
2. The gathered data are preprocessed using a variety of approaches namely handling of missing values, normalising the data, and elimination of outliers.
3. Various ML models: LR, SVM, KNN, RF, DT are explored and evaluated on the preprocessed data and DT provides the superior outcome.

1.1 Arrangement of the Paper

The remaining sections are organized in the following manner: Sect. 2 illustrates a concise survey, specificity of the ML models is presented in Sect. 3 whereas the exploratory outcomes are explained in Sect. 4 and Sect. 5 briefs conclusion of this work along with future scope.

2 Related Work

Now-a-days AQI analysis is required to assess the quality of ambient air and its influence on health of human being and environment. Current research trends indicates that various ML approaches are used by various researchers for prediction of AQI. Zhu et al. [26] formulated a multi task learning based network with reduced complexity to forecast air contaminants. Liu et al. [15] utilized RFR (RF Regressor), SVR (Support Vector Regressor) to estimate Beijing's AQI and NO_2 concentration. The SVR model forecasts better AQI, with Root

Mean Square Error= 7.666, R^2 = 0.9766. In the same year, Lendrum et al. [5] demonstrated the application of DT and SVM algorithms to forecast $PM_{2.5}$ level from meteorological data of Quito, Ecuador with 89% of accuracy. Again in 2020, Castelli et al. [6] used RBF (Radial-basis-function) and SVR to estimate the score of AQI, and showed that SVR provided best result with accuracy of 94.1%. Later, Pant et al. [17] used DT approach to accurately estimate air quality in Dehradun, Uttarakhand with an accuracy of 98.63%. Very recently, Van et al. [22] established a technique to deal with air pollutants and in this work XGBoost outperformed with an RMSE of 0.03684. S.Abu et al. [1] employed RF to assess the time series pattern of particulate matter of Ras Garib city, Egypt. Ketu [11] invented a recursive feature exclusion strategy dependent on linear regression and RF to anticipate the AQI value along with density of contaminants. The authors assessed the efficacy of the model using metrics such as the Mean Squared Error (MSE), Root Mean Squared Error (RMSE), Mean Absolute Percentage Error (MAPE), Mean Absolute Error (MAE) and R^2 score. In addition to this, the author also addressed the consequence of air pollution on people's health. Kishor et al. [12] emphasized ML and IoT based advanced technologies for analysis and purification of quality of air. Again, Shrivastava et al. [20] crafted a device which is capable of capturing the poisonous gases. To accumulate the data authors employed Arduino-based sensors and by leveraging historical data on toxic gases, they used machine learning methods to identify air pollution. Islam et al. [10] employed machine learning models for forecasting PM2.5 levels and air quality within the larger Dhaka region in Bangladesh. To achieve this objective, four models namely random tree, additive regression, reduced error pruning tree and random sub-space were employed. Out of all the monitoring stations in Darus Salam and Gazipur, random sub-space yielded the most favorable outcomes when considering evaluation metrics like R^2, MSE, and RMSE. Rahi et al. [18] conducted a thorough examination of existing systems to suggest a smart air pollution tracking system that leverages two a meta-heuristic approaches to proficiently enhance chosen attributes. Furthermore, these features undergo classification using a SVM, which forecasts the air quality index with false positive rates of 99% and recall rate of 89.6%. Lei et al. [14] made an analysis of ML approaches to predict the volume of $PM_{2.5}$ and PM_{10} in the air and the RF model performed best.

The review of existing literature indicates that previous scholars have utilized various ML methods for forecasting AQI. However, they have faced difficulties in attaining a high level of prediction accuracy. To address these challenges, this study has conducted a comprehensive investigation to categorize the levels of AQI for four metropolitan cities in India.

3 Materials and Methods

This section outlines the data sources and methodologies utilized in this study for classifying AQI categories. Figure 1 depicts the workflow diagram for this work.

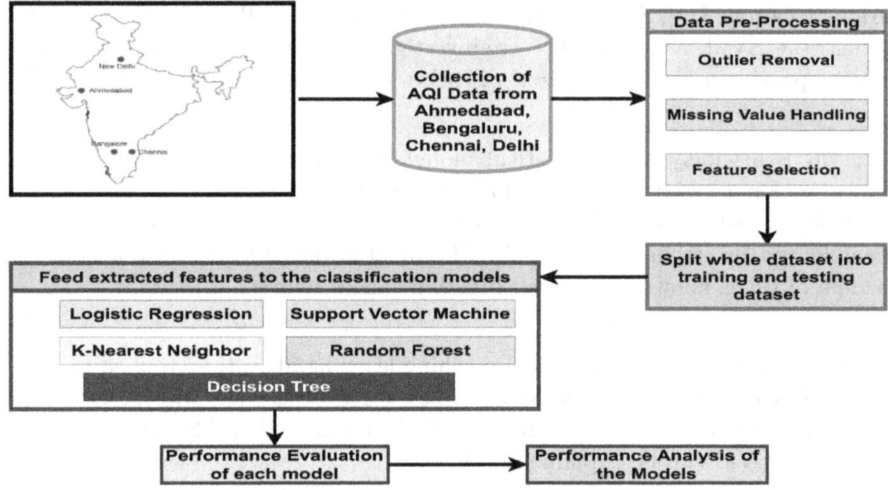

Fig. 1. Flow diagram of the work

3.1 Accumulation of Data and Dataset Description

Data were retrieved from the official website of CPCB, covering the period from 1st January, 2015 to 3rd July, 2021, and were sourced from various air quality monitoring stations located in four major metropolitan areas: Ahmedabad, Bengaluru, Chennai, and Delhi. In India, AQI is determined by considering ten pollutant indices in accordance with the prevailing air quality guidelines established by CPCB. The collected dataset is containing the detail of concentration of PM_{10}, $PM_{2.5}$, NO, NO_2, CO, SO_2, O_3, NO_x, NH_3, Benzene, Toluene, Xylene along with a target column which is containing various AQI classes.

3.2 Pre-processing of Data

Preprocessing of data is an influential phase that involves preparing and cleaning raw data to improve its quality and usability [13]. It enhances the accuracy and reliability of the results obtained from various models. In this study, the applied data preprocessing methods encompass handling missing values, eliminating outliers, and selecting relevant features. To replace missing values mean imputation method is used whereas outliers are removed using z-score approach [8]. To pick out the most informative and discriminative features correlation based feature selection strategy is used and finally the columns for Benzene, Toluene, Xylene and NH_3 are removed due to low correlation value.

3.3 Different ML Models

Predicting AQI accurately using an environmental quality model can be a challenging task because of the constantly changing nature of environmental data in various locations [16]. So, to accurately determine the AQI levels, separate ML models: LR, SVM, KNN, RF, DT are investigated in this study. The subsequent sections provide a concise overview of each model utilized in this study.

LR: LR is a widely used statistical model that predicts the probability of a binary outcome based on one or more independent variables. It is particularly useful for classification tasks, where the dependent variable is categorical for example: yes/no, true/false etc. [24]. The function helps to derive the numeric formula of LR is known as sigmoid function ranges between 0 to 1.

SVM: SVM is a robust supervised machine learning algorithm applied in classification task. The aim is to construct an effective hyperplane which maximizes separation of data points belonging to distinct classes [7]. The mathematical formula for SVM can be explained by Eq. 1.

$$wt^T * x + bi = 0 \tag{1}$$

where, x represents the input feature vector, wt and bi are the weight and bias respectively. The objective is to find the optimal values of wt and bi that maximize the margin.

KNN: KNN is a simple effective ML algorithm applied for classification purposes. KNN is non-parametric approach that makes predictions based on the similarities between data points [4]. For a classification problem the class label is determined by majority voting among the K neighbors [23].

DT: DT is a predictive modeling tool which utilizes a tree-type structure to make decisions or predictions based on input data. It's commonly used in machine learning for classification tasks, where it recursively splits the data into subsets to reach final decisions or outcomes [21].

RF: RF integrates more than one number of decision trees for prediction and follow the ensemble learning concept. For a given dataset, RF constructs an ensemble of decision trees [3]. When making predictions, new data is passed through each tree, and the ultimate result is acquired by assembling distinct prediction of each tree.

4 Results and Discussion

In this section, we present the key findings of our study, providing a comprehensive overview of the ML models and their performance analysis. Below are the performance evaluation metrics utilised in this study:

1. **Confusion Matrix:** To assess how well a classification model performs a table is used which is known as confusion matrix [9]. This matrix is typically a square matrix with rows and columns representing the predicted and actual classes, respectively. Model correctly predicts the positive class is called True Positive (TP), incorrectly predicted positive class is known as False Negative (FN), incorrectly predicted negative class is called False Positive (FP) and correctly predicted negative class is called True Negative (TN). This matrix helps to evaluate various evaluation metrics (accuracy, precision, recall, and F1-score) to check out the efficacy of model.
2. **Accuracy:** It calculates the percentage of accurately categorized instances among all instances in the dataset [19]. Mathematically, accuracy is expressed by Eq. 2.
$$Accuracy = \frac{TN + TP}{FN + FP + TN + TP} \tag{2}$$
3. **Precision:** It computes measurement of true positive analysis for all the occurrences that the model predicted as positive [19]. Mathematically, precision is formulated as:
$$Precision = \frac{TP}{TP + FP} \tag{3}$$
4. **Recall:** It quantifies the proportion of correct positive predictions among all the authentic positive instances [25]. Mathematically, recall is denoted as:
$$Recall = \frac{TP}{FN + TP} \tag{4}$$
5. **F1-score:** A balanced measure of recall and precision is provided by F1-score [2] and mathematically represented by Eq. 5.
$$F1 - score = \frac{2 * (Precision * Recall)}{(Precision + Recall)} \tag{5}$$

4.1 Experimental Result Analysis and Discussion

The experimental setup for this study involves simulations and modeling conducted within a Python programming environment. These operations were carried out on a system equipped with an Intel Core i7 CPU running at 2.40 GHz and boasting 16 GB of RAM. This system operated on Microsoft Windows 10 Professional. In this section, we investigate the exploration and evaluation of various ML approaches performed on the dataset accumulated from CPCB website. After applying several pre-processing techniques on the raw dataset, the pre-processed dataset is partitioned into 80% and 20% of training and testing samples respectively. After that training data are fed into the classifier models. First the confusion matrix is obtained for each of the city. Determining the confusion matrix is the utmost importance when implementing a classification problem because it provides a comprehensive and detailed evaluation of the models' performance. In this work a multi class classification of AQI data has been done using LR, SVM, KNN, RF, DT models. From the confusion matrix generated from each of the model the number of correct prediction and false prediction are evaluated. From the values of true and false prediction the corresponding evaluation parameters: accuracy, precision, recall and F1-score values are calculated on the basis of which effectiveness of the classification models are analysed. The graphical representation of the confusion matrix for LR, SVM, KNN, DT, RF are shown in Figs. 2, 3, 4, 5, 6 respectively.

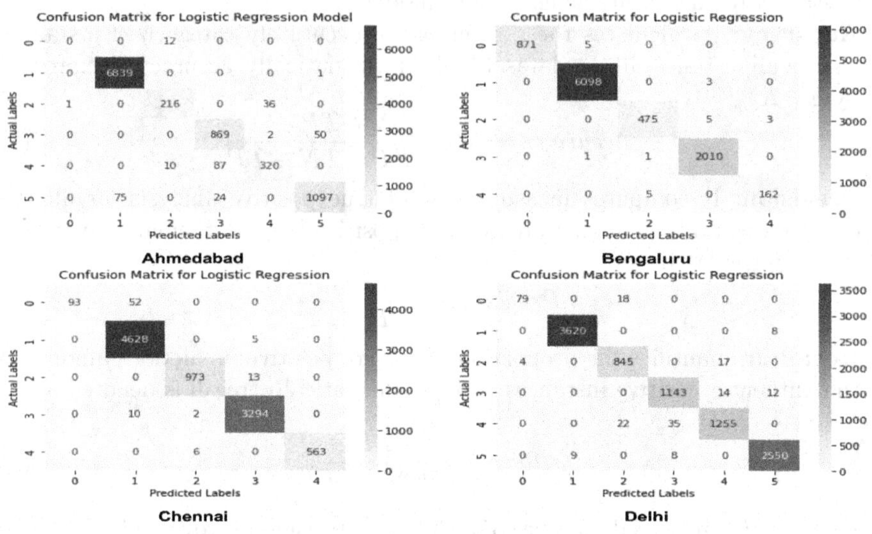

Fig. 2. Confusion matrix for four cities using LR

City-wise performance comparison of the explored models are presented in Table 1.

It is depicted from Table 1 that the LR model achieved an accuracy of 96.90%, 99.76%, 99.08% and 98.47% for Ahmedabad, Bengaluru, Chennai and Delhi respectively which indicates a relatively high level of overall correctness in its true predictions. The efficacy of SVM model is almost nearer to the LR model which shows accuracy of 96.46%, 98.34%, 97.61% and 97.33% for Ahmedabad, Bengaluru, Chennai and Delhi respectively. In the implementation the SVM model RBF kernel is used. RF and DT models shows comparatively better performance than LR and SVM models in regard to all the four evaluation metrics. But the performance of KNN has been declined for the dataset of all the four cities with respect to all metrics. The KNN model exhibits slightly improved values for all four evaluation metrics when applied to the cities of Bengaluru and Chennai. Table 1 shows that DT performs best for all the datasets and it also shows the superior result in terms of all the evaluation metrics. DT model provides best performance by achieving an accuracy of 99.99%, 99.97%, 99.98% and 99.98% for Ahmedabad, Bengaluru, Chennai and Delhi respectively. This

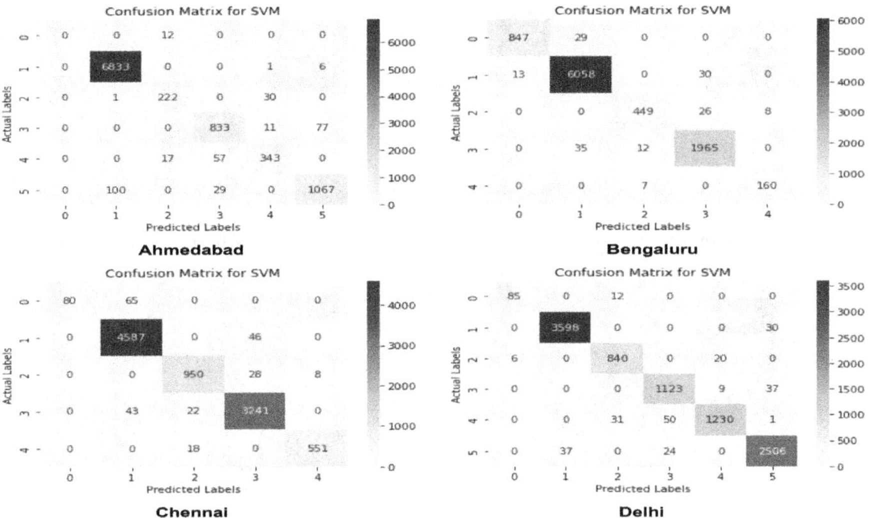

Fig. 3. Confusion matrix for four cities using SVM

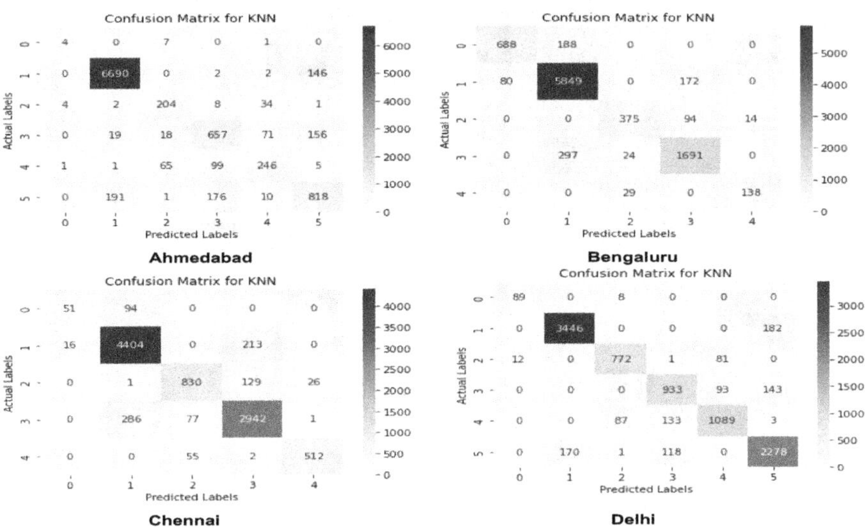

Fig. 4. Confusion matrix for four cities using KNN

indicates a relatively high level of overall correctness in its predictions. The precision of DT model is 99.98%, 99.97%, 99.99% and 99.99% for Ahmedabad, Bengaluru, Chennai and Delhi respectively which indicates a high level of accuracy in identifying true positive cases. The obtained recall values are 99.97%, 99.96%, 99.96% and 99.99% for Ahmedabad, Bengaluru, Chennai and Delhi respectively. The F1-score is found to be 99.98%, 99.97%, 99.95% and 99.98%

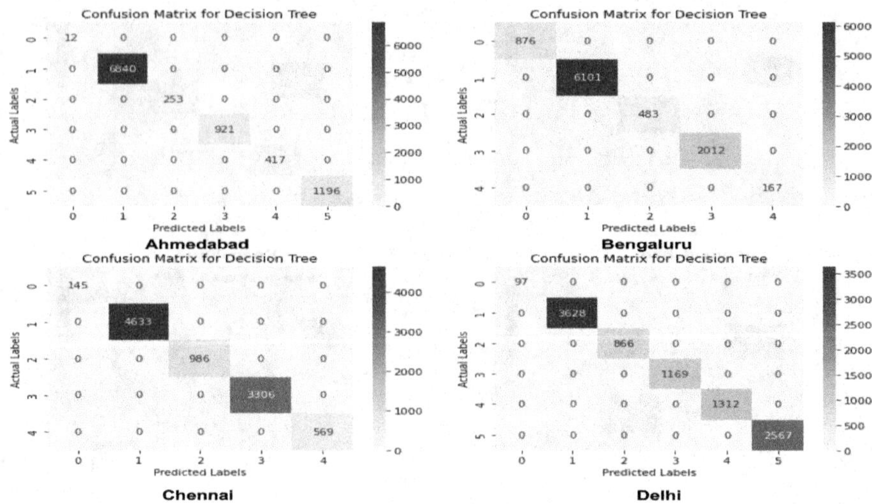

Fig. 5. Confusion matrix for four cities using DT

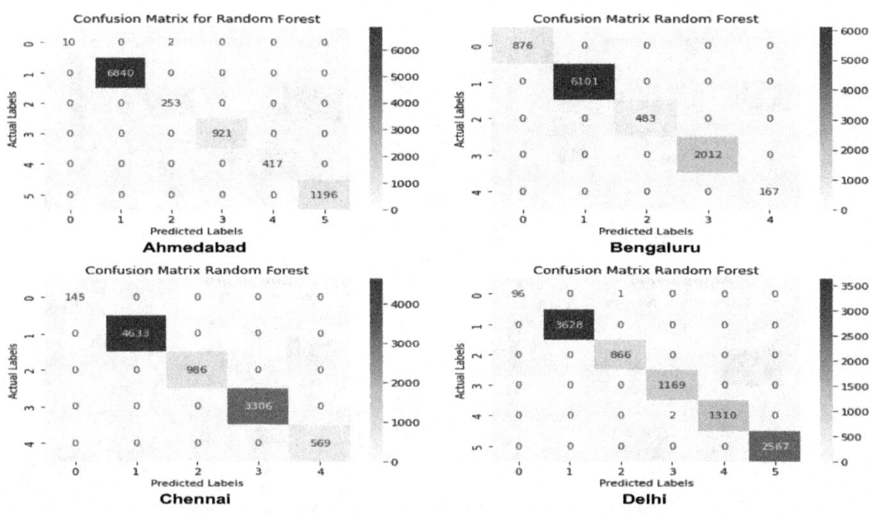

Fig. 6. Confusion matrix for four cities using RF

for Ahmedabad, Bengaluru, Chennai and Delhi respectively which suggests a good balance between the accuracy of positive predictions and the ability to capture actual positive instances. The model-wise comparative analysis based on accuracy, precision, recall and F1-score are presented in Fig. 7.

Table 1. City-wise performance comparison based on different models

Model	City	Accuracy(%)	Precision(%)	Recall(%)	F1-score(%)
LR	Ahmedabad	96.90	96.77	96.90	96.80
	Bengaluru	99.76	99.76	99.76	99.76
	Chennai	99.08	99.09	99.08	99.02
	Delhi	98.47	98.47	98.47	98.47
SVM	Ahmedabad	96.46	96.28	96.46	96.35
	Bengaluru	98.34	98.33	98.34	98.33
	Chennai	97.61	97.63	97.61	97.52
	Delhi	97.33	97.34	97.33	97.33
KNN	Ahmedabad	89.41	89.24	89.41	89.29
	Bengaluru	90.68	90.58	90.68	90.56
	Chennai	90.66	90.52	90.66	90.46
	Delhi	89.29	89.31	89.29	89.29
DT	Ahmedabad	99.99	99.98	99.97	99.98
	Bengaluru	99.97	99.97	99.96	99.97
	Chennai	99.98	99.99	99.96	99.95
	Delhi	99.98	99.99	99.99	99.98
RF	Ahmedabad	99.00	99.00	99.00	99.00
	Bengaluru	99.97	99.98	99.96	99.97
	Chennai	99.00	99.00	99.00	99.00
	Delhi	99.99	99.99	99.98	99.98

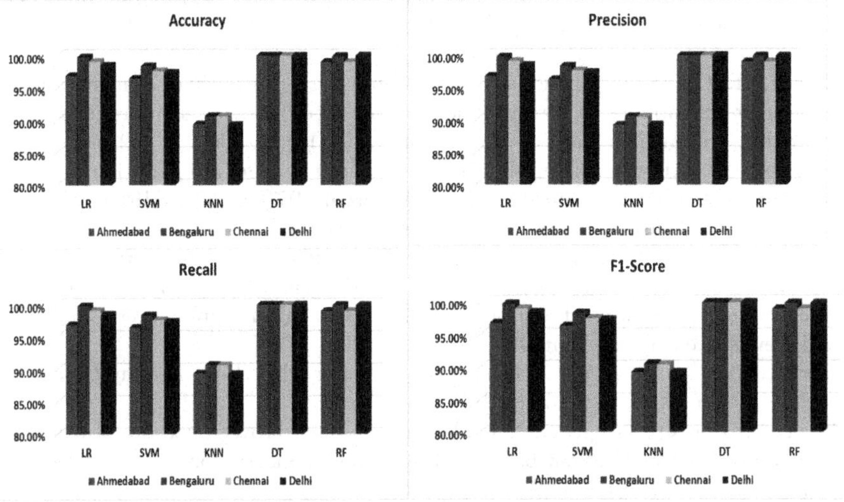

Fig. 7. Model-wise comparative analysis of evaluation metrics

5 Conclusion and Future Scope

This task focused on comparative inspection of machine learning framework for categorizing the AQI classes based on AQI values. In this work AQI prediction is accomplished on four Indian metropolitan cities. Different data pre-processing techniques: missing value handling, outlier removal, feature selection are used to enhance the data representation for further processing. The comparative analysis of different modeling techniques revealed that DT model exhibited better performance for predicting air quality for all the four metropolitan cities. In future, this work can be enhanced to predict the AQI of other geographic locations with various features by combining additional pollution indices at various levels and the work can be expanded to predict all those indices. Again, future research could look into integrating time series models like LSTM or RNN to capture the seasonal trends and fluctuations related to events like festivals in order to improve the accuracy of AQI predictions.

References

1. Abu El-Magd, S., Soliman, G., Morsy, M., Kharbish, S.: Environmental hazard assessment and monitoring for air pollution using machine learning and remote sensing. Int. J. Environ. Sci. Technol. **20**(6), 6103–6116 (2023)
2. Asri, H., Mousannif, H., Al Moatassime, H., Noel, T.: Using machine learning algorithms for breast cancer risk prediction and diagnosis. Procedia Comput. Sci. **83**, 1064–1069 (2016)
3. Azar, A.T., Elshazly, H.I., Hassanien, A.E., Elkorany, A.M.: A random forest classifier for lymph diseases. Comput. Methods Programs Biomed. **113**(2), 465–473 (2014)
4. Bansal, M., Goyal, A., Choudhary, A.: A comparative analysis of k-nearest neighbour, genetic, support vector machine, decision tree, and long short term memory algorithms in machine learning. Decis. Anal. J. **3**(11), p. 100071 (2022)
5. Campbell-Lendrum, D., Prüss-Ustün, A.: Climate change, air pollution and noncommunicable diseases. Bull. World Health Organ. **97**(2), 160 (2019)
6. Castelli, M., Clemente, F.M., Popovič, A., Silva, S., Vanneschi, L.: A machine learning approach to predict air quality in California. Complexity **2020** (2020)
7. Cervantes, J., Garcia-Lamont, F., Rodríguez-Mazahua, L., Lopez, A.: A comprehensive survey on support vector machine classification: applications, challenges and trends. Neurocomputing **408**, 189–215 (2020)
8. Curtis, A.E., Smith, T.A., Ziganshin, B.A., Elefteriades, J.A.: The mystery of the z-score. Aorta **4**(04), 124–130 (2016)
9. Deng, X., Liu, Q., Deng, Y., Mahadevan, S.: An improved method to construct basic probability assignment based on the confusion matrix for classification problem. Inf. Sci. **340**, 250–261 (2016)
10. Islam, A.R.M.T., et al.: Estimating ground-level PM2. 5 using subset regression model and machine learning algorithms in asian megacity, dhaka, bangladesh. Air Quality, Atmosphere and Health, pp. 1–23 (2023)
11. Ketu, S.: Spatial air quality index and air pollutant concentration prediction using linear regression based recursive feature elimination with random forest regression (rferf): a case study in India. Nat. Hazards **114**(2), 2109–2138 (2022)

12. Kishor, K., Pandey, D.: Study and development of efficient air quality prediction system embedded with machine learning and IoT. In: International Conference on Innovative Computing and Communications: Proceedings of ICICC 2022, Vol 2, pp. 313–326. Springer (2022)
13. Krouska, A., Troussas, C., Virvou, M.: The effect of preprocessing techniques on twitter sentiment analysis. In: 2016 7th International Conference on Information Intelligence Systems and Applications (IISA), pp. 1–5. IEEE (2016)
14. Lei, T.M., Siu, S.W., Monjardino, J., Mendes, L., Ferreira, F.: Using machine learning methods to forecast air quality: a case study in macao. Atmosphere **13**(9), 1412 (2022)
15. Liu, H., Li, Q., Yu, D., Gu, Y.: Air quality index and air pollutant concentration prediction based on machine learning algorithms. Appl. Sci. **9**(19), 4069 (2019)
16. Maltare, N.N., Vahora, S.: Air quality index prediction using machine learning for Ahmedabad city. Digital Chem. Eng. **7**(1), p. 100093 (2023)
17. Pant, A., Sharma, S., Bansal, M., Narang, M.: Comparative analysis of supervised machine learning techniques for AQI prediction. In: 2022 International Conference on Advanced Computing Technologies and Applications (ICACTA), pp. 1–4. IEEE (2022)
18. Rahi, P., Sood, S.P., Bajaj, R.: Meta-heuristic with machine learning-based smart e-health system for ambient air quality monitoring. In: Recent Innovations in Computing: Proceedings of ICRIC 2021, Vol 2, pp. 501–519. Springer (2022). https://doi.org/10.1007/978-981-16-8892-8_38
19. Saito, T., Rehmsmeier, M.: The precision-recall plot is more informative than the roc plot when evaluating binary classifiers on imbalanced datasets. PLoS ONE **10**(3), e0118432 (2015)
20. Shrivastava, A.L., Dwivedi, R.K.: Air quality prediction using supervised machine learning techniques. In: ICT with Intelligent Applications: Proceedings of ICTIS 2022, Vol 1, pp. 305–312. Springer (2022). https://doi.org/10.32628/CSEIT206435
21. Suthaharan, S., Suthaharan, S.: Decision tree learning. Machine Learning Models and Algorithms for Big Data Classification: Thinking with Examples for Effective Learning, pp. 237–269 (2016)
22. Van, N., Van Thanh, P., Tran, D., Tran, D.T.: A new model of air quality prediction using lightweight machine learning. Int. J. Environ. Sci. Technol. **20**(3), 2983–2994 (2023)
23. Vijila Rani, K., Joseph Jawhar, S.: Lung lesion classification scheme using optimization techniques and hybrid (KNN-SVM) classifier. IETE J. Res. **68**(2), 1485–1499 (2022)
24. Wang, P., Zheng, X., Li, J., Zhu, B.: Prediction of epidemic trends in COVID-19 with logistic model and machine learning technics. Chaos, Solitons Fractals **139**, 110058 (2020)
25. Zhang, X., Feng, X., Xiao, P., He, G., Zhu, L.: Segmentation quality evaluation using region-based precision and recall measures for remote sensing images. ISPRS J. Photogramm. Remote. Sens. **102**, 73–84 (2015)
26. Zhu, D., Cai, C., Yang, T., Zhou, X.: A machine learning approach for air quality prediction: model regularization and optimization. Big data Cognitive Comput. **2**(1), 5 (2018)

Marker-Based Augmented Reality Application in Education Domain

Sudesh Rani[1(✉)], Saptarshi Mazumdar[2], and Mayank Gupta[1]

[1] Punjab Engineering College (Deemed to be university), Chandigarh, India
{sudeshrani,mayankgupta}@pec.edu.in
[2] Nokia Solutions and Networks, Noida, India

Abstract. Augmented Reality (AR) technology has the potential to revolutionize the way education is delivered, by enhancing the learning experience and making it more interactive and engaging. One way that augmented reality can be used in education is through the use of AR-based applications and educational games that allow students to interact with virtual objects and environments in the real world. These applications can be used to teach subjects such as science, math, and history in a more interactive and engaging way. This paper demonstrates the development process of building a marker-based AR application for the education domain. The application uses a laptop screen as a marker and computer hardware 3D models as augmented objects. The app developed displays some components of a laptop such as the motherboard which can be extended to include many more components.

Keywords: Augmented reality · Marker-based technique · 3D model

1 Introduction

Augmented Reality (AR) is a technology that blends virtual elements with the real world, enhancing user's perception and interaction with the environment. It overlays computer-generated objects such as images, videos or 3D models, onto the physical world in real-time, creating an immersive and interactive experience [6]. AR has gained significant popularity in various fields, including gaming, marketing, healthcare and entertainment. In recent years, educators and researchers have recognized the potential of AR to transform the education domain, providing new opportunities for enhanced learning experiences.

Traditional educational approaches often rely on static textbooks, lectures, and two-dimensional visual aids. While these methods have been effective to some extent, they fail to fully engage students and cater to different learning styles. This has led to a growing demand for innovative teaching methodologies that can bridge the gap between theoretical concepts and practical understanding. AR applications in education have the ability to address these challenges by creating dynamic and interactive learning environments. AR integrates digital

N. Chauhan et al. (Eds.): MIND 2023, CCIS 2128, pp. 98–109, 2024.
https://doi.org/10.1007/978-3-031-62217-5_9

content into the physical world, enabling students to visualize complex concepts, manipulate objects, and engage in hands-on experiences, fostering enhanced understanding, critical thinking, problem-solving skills, and creativity.

AR technology in education enhances learning through interactive experiences that engage students in virtual experiments and collaborative activities, catering to diverse learning styles. AR can be utilized for various fields in classroom setting. Few potential examples from history and geography domain are: interactive historical tours, geographical exploration, 3D models of historical artifacts [8], real-time translation of geographical key-terms, customized applications for various users etc. Studies confirm AR's positive impact on student engagement, motivation, and knowledge retention across various educational disciplines. Platforms like Unity 3D simplify AR application development for educators and developers, potentially transforming traditional education methods [2].

After highlighting AR's significance in diverse applications, the paper is structured as follows: Sect. 2 offers an overview of augmented reality approaches. Section 3 analyzes prior research. Section 4 details the developed solution and its theoretical basis. Section 5 covers practical development and methodologies. Section 6 showcases implementation outcomes. Finally, Sect. 7 concludes the findings, discusses implications, and suggests future research directions.

2 AR Approaches

There are various AR approaches [26] used in different applications to make improvements in the education domain. Some of the approaches are listed below.

- **Marker-based AR:** Utilizes specific markers or images for precise tracking, commonly used in educational applications to provide interactive learning experiences.
- **Marker-less AR:** Makes use of device sensors such as GPS, accelerometer, and compass to overlay virtual content without the need for physical markers. This approach is suitable for outdoor and location-based learning.
- **Projection-based AR:** Projects virtual content onto physical surfaces, enhancing classroom engagement through interactive whiteboards, tables, and walls.
- **Superimposition-based AR:** Overlays virtual content onto real-world materials without markers, enriching printed materials like textbooks and posters with multimedia elements.
- **Recognition-based AR:** Combines aspects of marker-based and marker-less approaches by recognizing and tracking real-world objects, enabling interactive learning experiences based on real-world objects.

The integration of AR technology in the education domain holds tremendous potential to revolutionize traditional teaching methodologies [4]. As educators and researchers continue to explore and harness the power of AR, we can expect to see transformative changes in the way we teach and learn. Objectives of the research presented in this paper are as follows:

- To develop a marker-based AR application to address the need for innovative and interactive teaching methodology.
- To provide thorough insights into the potential of marker-based AR applications as a tool for educational enhancement by in-depth analysis of the development process, challenges, and outcomes.
- To explore the potential of Unity 3D as a development platform for creating AR applications and to highlight its potential for future educational endeavors.

3 Related Work

AR and VR technologies, fueled by platforms such as Microsoft HoloLens, Oculus Rift, and Oculus Quest [19], have gained substantial attention, including applications in education. Recent years have seen growing enthusiasm for these technologies in education, with numerous studies showing positive impacts on learning outcomes. For example, VR-based instruction enhances learning effectively, although the challenge is to move beyond traditional classroom replication [23].

AR and VR have expanded into various domains. In construction management, AR is effectively used for scheduling, worker training, safety management, cost and time control, and quality assurance [1]. These technologies are pivotal in managing automobile construction projects [16]. In cultural tourism, AR and VR enhance visitor experiences, but factors influencing engagement remain under-explored. Museums benefit from AR and VR, enhancing visitor engagement [18]. These technologies, if used effectively, can boost tourist engagement, despite appearing as substitutes for physical tourism experiences [10].

Vuforia, a marker-based tracking system, excels in target detection, particularly in applied scenarios [24]. It shows potential in maintaining AR-based facilities, despite factors like distance, position, and ambient light. In education, AR projects in universities and schools foster e-learning ecosystems and allow project monitoring [14]. In healthcare, AR aids healthcare professionals by providing seamless access to critical patient information without diverting their focus [12]. Another study presents an AR software suite for assisting human operators in assembly tasks within a Human-Robot Collaboration (HRC) environment [9].

AR enhances interactive learning experiences and revolutionizes healthcare [11]. It empowers students to engage with virtual objects in real time, improving education. In healthcare, AR provides real-time patient data, enhancing surgical precision and medical education. By integrating digital content into practitioners' field of view, it streamlines decision-making during medical procedures. AR supports interactive virtual object manipulation and telemedicine, expanding healthcare accessibility. AR technology offers precise visualization of virtual models from MRI images, particularly in cardiac scar tissue, with implications for research and education [5].

In [13], authors used System Usability Scale (SUS) and Human AR User Study (HARUS) models to assess two mobile AR apps: one with multiple markers

(MAR) and another with a keypad (MAR with keypad). The keypad-based AR (MAR with keypad) outperformed, excelling in usability, interaction quality, and learning, especially for complex subjects like Karnaugh Map (K-map). This suggests its potential for teaching engineering concepts related to K-Map. In [27], authors discuss integrating augmented reality educational games to enhance teaching and learning. Using a case study, they emphasize game rating, ease of use, usefulness, motivation, and attitudes in creating effective educational games.

In science education, AR enhances learning with immersive elements, improving outcomes. The diverse applications of AR span education [21], construction, manufacturing [17], healthcare, entertainment & gaming [22], tourism, retail & e-commerce [7], market research, and science. Ongoing research solidifies AR's potential as an emerging, broadly beneficial technology. However, recent publications do not emphasize on the development process of an AR-based mobile application specifically for education domain. This paper provides a step-by-step procedure for developing the mobile application and also showcases the same through an example.

4 Proposed Solution

The proposed solution entails the development of a marker-based AR application tailored for the educational domain. The application development process is structured around four distinct phases to ensure a systematic and efficient approach for the development and deployment of this AR application. These four phases are outlined as follows:

- **Research and Planning:** This initial phase involves collecting key information, setting objectives, and the creating a comprehensive project road-map. It includes an extensive literature review, research studies, and relevant case studies on AR technology in education. The analysis of existing AR applications identifies advantages, challenges, and the best practices for the usage of AR in education.
- **Requirement Analysis:** In this phase, the specific needs, preferences, and challenges of the intended user group, namely high school students seeking a practical learning experience in computer hardware, are thoroughly assessed. The choice of the laptop screen as the marker allows students to employ their own laptops to use the developed application.
- **Development and Implementation:** The development and implementation phase revolves around the creation of application components, such as 3D models, Unity 3D assets, and C# scripts for the implementation of animations and interactive elements. The Unity 3D game engine serves as the development platform for assembling the application and integrating all its components. Marker detection and tracking are facilitated through the use of the Vuforia engine.
- **Evaluation and Testing:** The final phase focuses on evaluating the performance and effectiveness of the developed marker-based AR application. User

testing is conducted to gather feedback from high school students who engage with the application. Evaluation metrics include usability, educational effectiveness, and user satisfaction, all of which are assessed based on the feedback received.

The above-mentioned phases collectively facilitate the systematic development and deployment of a marker-based AR educational application, ensuring comprehensive research, user-centered design, robust implementation, and rigorous evaluation to create an effective and engaging learning tool for high school students.

4.1 Development Architecture

The general architectural framework of the proposed AR-based mobile application follows the design presented in [21] and is composed of four key components, as represented in Fig. 1. The specific attributes of each element are described as follows:

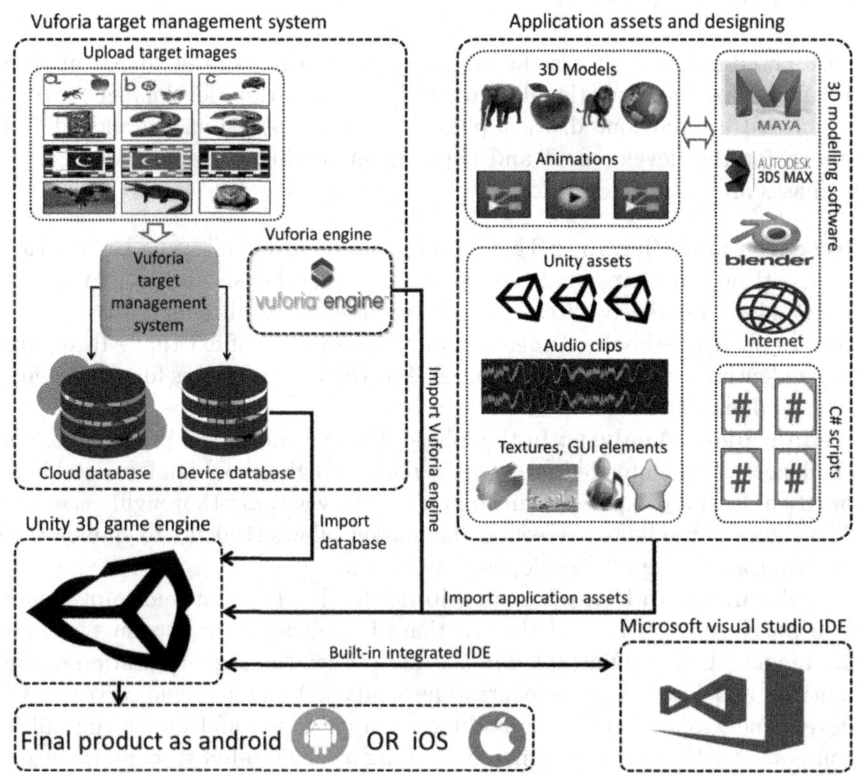

Fig. 1. AR-based mobile application development architecture [21]

Component 1 - Vuforia Target Management System
Description: This component focuses on the management of target images crucial for the AR application's marker detection functionality.
Key Features:

- **Target Image Database:** Utilizes a cloud storage and database system for the storage and management of target images.
- **Vuforia Engine Integration:** Seamlessly integrates the Vuforia engine to enable marker-based AR functionalities.

Component 2 - Application Assets and Designing
Description: This component is responsible for the assets and design elements essential for the AR application.
Key Features:

- **3D Models:** Creation and seamless integration of 3D models representing augmented objects that will overlay the marker.
- **Unity Assets:** Utilizes pre-existing assets from the Unity Asset Store to enhance the application's visual aesthetics.
- **3D Modeling Software:** Employs software tools such as Blender or Autodesk Maya for the creation and modification of 3D models.
- **C# Scripts:** Development of C# scripts to enable animations and interactive behaviors for augmented objects.

Component 3 - Unity 3D Game Engine
Description: This component serves as the core engine for the AR application.
Key Features:

- **Scene Creation:** Establishes scenes within the Unity 3D engine where augmented objects and interactions are staged.
- **Integration with Components 1 and 2:** Seamlessly integrates with the Vuforia Target Management System and the Application Assets and Designing component to enable marker detection and the overlay of augmented objects.
- **Logic Implementation:** Encompasses the coding of logic within Unity 3D to manage user interactions, animations, and other functionalities.

Component 4 - Android-based Application
Description: This component represents the final application intended for deployment on Android devices.
Key Features:

- **Integration with Component 3:** Integrates the Unity 3D game engine into an Android application for a complete AR experience.
- **User Interface:** Designs an intuitive user interface to facilitate seamless interaction with the AR content.
- **Testing and Deployment:** Rigorously tests the application on Android devices to ensure optimal performance and then deploys it on the target platform.

Further, the mobile application development and deployment process comprises several steps, as outlined below, to ensure efficient execution.

1. Install Unity 3D and the Vuforia engine.
2. Set up a new Unity project, selecting a 3D template as the starting point.
3. Import and configure the Vuforia package by providing a valid license key.
4. Create an Image Target to display the AR content by uploading a suitable image as a marker and setting its size.
5. Integrate an AR Camera into the scene to display the AR content.
6. Develop 3D models and animations within the Unity project, adjusting their position, rotation, and scale in accordance with the marker's dimensions and position.
7. Thoroughly test the application by building and running it on an Android device.

5 Implementation

The steps involved in the implementation and development of the AR-based mobile application are outlined below.

5.1 Building a Raw Mesh on the Marker Image and Marker Detection

AR transforms user interactions by overlaying digital content on the real world. Marker-based tracking, a common technique, uses identifiable markers like images to align virtual content with the environment. This alignment requires precise calculation of the camera's position and orientation, which can be complex and time-consuming in unfamiliar settings. Yet, using easily recognizable markers simplifies this estimation process.

An AR system utilizes image processing techniques to identify markers, such as QR codes, as reference points as shown in Fig. 2 - examples from ARToolkit [20] and ARTag [15] tools. Effectively recognized markers are essential for providing accurate location and orientation information to the camera, enabling the seamless integration of digital visuals into the physical world. Square markers, in particular, are favored for their simplicity and ability to offer a minimum of four identifiable points for precise camera pose calculation. These markers are typically designed with high visibility, prioritizing variations in brightness over color differences.

While marker-based tracking offers advantages like simple setup and fast detection, it's not universally applicable. Challenges arise when the environment lacks preset markers, making tracking complex. In such scenarios, developers can leverage content creation tools like Unity 3D to interact with AR frameworks like Vuforia. Unity 3D acts as a platform for building 3D environments and embedding models into them. It enables real-time interaction by instantly reflecting model changes on the screen. Furthermore, Unity 3D eases the creation of static

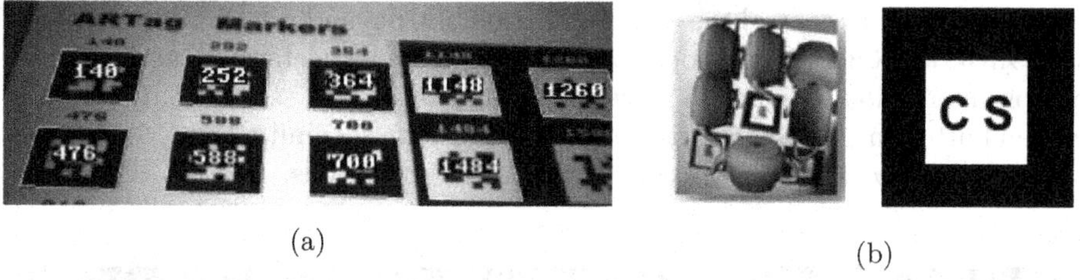

Fig. 2. Examples of marker detection (a) ARTag Markers (b) ARToolkit Markers

AR markers for seamless integration into AR applications [28]. While marker-based tracking offers numerous advantages, its suitability may vary depending on the specific AR scenario.

5.2 Feature Extraction Using Vuforia Image Scanner

Vuforia Engine, a computer vision platform for AR applications, relies on Image Targets for real-time recognition. These Image Targets are recognized by comparing camera images to a known target resource database [24].

The process starts with uploading target images to the Vuforia Target Manager for assessment. These Image Targets can be downloaded for Unity or native app integration, streamlining development and testing. Alternatively, Image Targets can be dynamically generated at runtime. During the image capture phase, users capture marker patterns-typically simple black squares on a white background. These patterns are saved with a .patt extension. In the marker tracking phase, the tracking module locates the 3D model in relation to the physical marker. In the rendering phase, the original marker picture blends with the 3D model, creating a seamless augmented environment [25].

The Vuforia Target Manager plays a pivotal role in Image Target feature extraction. It processes uploaded images, assesses their detection and tracking capabilities, and provides data and visual representations of the target's properties. Once downloaded, Unity Editor or native apps can utilize these Image Targets, eliminating the need for repeated photo uploads. Figure 3a shows the significance of Image Targets in the Vuforia Engine, enabling real-time image detection and tracking. This approach ensures the precise identification and tracking of target properties within AR applications [29].

5.3 Implementing Virtual Buttons with C# Scripting

Virtual buttons are integral components of AR experiences created using Unity 3D, serving as user interface elements that trigger specific actions when users tap on them. Developed using the Vuforia AR platform within Unity 3D, virtual buttons are often placed on Image Targets, which are markers recognized by the Vuforia engine in the real environment. Users interact with these virtual buttons through their device's camera. A C# script includes a public variable named "virtualButton" to control the assigned virtual button, and the OnButtonPressed and OnButtonReleased methods can be implemented to determine actions upon button interactions. Figure 3b shows some part of the c# script created for the virtual button in Unity 3D. This combination of Vuforia, Unity, and C# scripting empowers developers to create interactive AR applications.

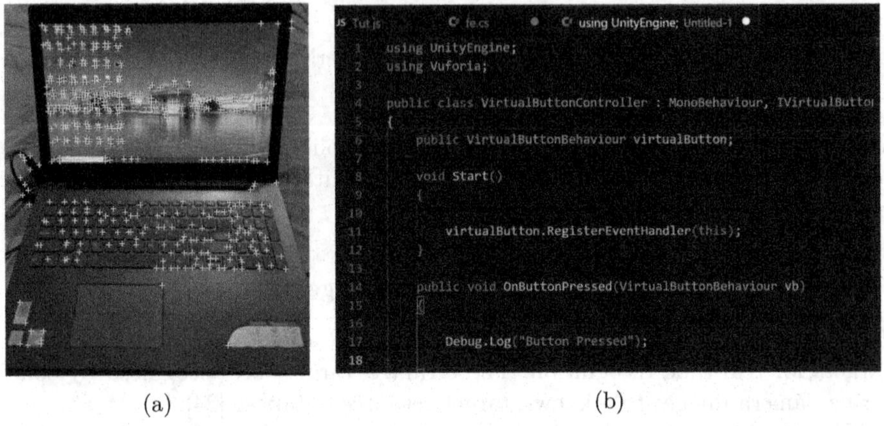

Fig. 3. (a) Feature Extraction (b) C# script for Virtual Button Implementation

5.4 Creating 3D Models with Blender

The process of 3D modeling using Blender involves several steps for building, refining, and finalizing digital creations. These steps include object creation, mesh editing, sculpting, UV unwrapping, texture painting, material and shader assignment, lighting and rendering setup, animation using keyframes, and exporting in various file formats such as such as .obj, .fbx, or .stl etc. These steps enable the creation of detailed 3D models for diverse applications [3]. The major challenge in this application development process was to create a good quality 3D model of the hardware components. Although, Blender has been used in the proposed approach for 3D model creation, however, it resulted in a very basic 3D model. To create more visually appealing models, it is suggested to explore other 3D model creation tools available in the research community.

6 Results

Running the marker-based AR application on an Android device displays a laptop as the target image, serving as an anchor for augmented objects, including a motherboard and a graphics cooling system, seamlessly integrated with the laptop. An accompanying audio narration introduces users to object details and

Fig. 4. AR application output screen

functionalities, enhancing their understanding and engagement. Additionally, a floating 3D text element provides supplementary information.

Figure 4 shows the overlaid augmented objects on the laptop screen as marker image in Unity 3D framework. It also shows a green plane, functioning as a virtual button through C# script. When users interact with the plane, associated augmented objects perform predefined actions, allowing for engaging gestures or touch interactions. This combination of marker detection, augmented content, audio narration, and interactive buttons creates an interactive AR experience, seamlessly integrating virtual elements into the real world.

7 Conclusion

The potential of AR extends across various domains, from smartphones to car windshields, offering opportunities for enhanced productivity, safety, and accessible information. However, one of the most significant impacts lies in education. In the education domain, AR has proven an efficient technology to enhance learning and understanding of users in visual and interactive way. This paper has detailed the development process of a marker-based augmented reality application tailored for educational purposes. The application leverages a laptop screen as the marker, with augmented computer hardware 3D models enhancing the educational experience. With this AR application, students can immerse themselves in complex subjects, such as computer hardware, gaining a profound understanding. This hands-on approach fosters not only engagement but also knowledge retention.

Furthermore, the developed application is not limited to computer science or any specific field of study. AR has the potential to revolutionize various disciplines, including history and geography. By overlaying 3D models onto images or books, AR transforms traditional classroom settings into captivating and interactive learning environments. Students are provided with the means to explore historical landmarks and geographical features in a tangible, hands-on manner. This kindles curiosity, deepens appreciation, and sparks enthusiasm for learning. As we delve deeper into exploring the vast potential of AR, its capacity to redefine our perceptions and interactions with the world becomes increasingly evident.

References

1. Ahmed, S.: A review on using opportunities of augmented reality and virtual reality in construction project management. Organ. Technol. Manage. Constr. Int. J. **10**(1), 1839–1852 (2018)
2. Ali, A.M., Radwan, A.E., Abd El-Gawad, E.A., Abdel-Latief, A.S.A.: 3D integrated structural, facies and petrophysical static modeling approach for complex sandstone reservoirs: A case study from the coniacian–santonian matulla formation, july oilfield, gulf of suez, egypt. Natural Resources Research **31**(1), 385–413 (2022)
3. Aristov, M.M., Geng, H., Pavelic, A., Berry, J.F.: A new library of 3D models and problems for teaching crystallographic symmetry generated through blender for use with 3D printers or sketchfab. J. Appl. Crystallogr. **55**(1), 172–179 (2022)
4. Avila-Garzon, C., et al.: Augmented reality in education: an overview of twenty-five years of research. Contemp. Educ. Technol. **13**(3) (2021)
5. Barcali, E., Iadanza, E., Manetti, L., Francia, P., Nardi, C., Bocchi, L.: Augmented reality in surgery: a scoping review. Appl. Sci. **12**(14), 6890 (2022)
6. Barhorst, J.B., McLean, G., Shah, E., Mack, R.: Blending the real world and the virtual world: exploring the role of flow in augmented reality experiences. J. Bus. Res. **122**, 423–436 (2021)
7. Billewar, S.R., et al.: The rise of 3D e-commerce: the online shopping gets real with virtual reality and augmented reality during Covid-19. W. J. Eng. **19**(2), 244–253 (2022)
8. Challenor, J., Ma, M.: A review of augmented reality applications for history education and heritage visualisation. Multimodal Technol. Interact. **3**(2), 39 (2019)
9. Chouchene, A., Ventura Carvalho, A., Charrua-Santos, F., Barhoumi, W.: Augmented reality-based framework supporting visual inspection for automotive industry. Appl. Syst. Innovation **5**(3), 48 (2022)
10. Cranmer, E.E., tom Dieck, M.C., Fountoulaki, P.: Exploring the value of augmented reality for tourism. Tourism Manag. Perspect. **35**, 100672 (2020)
11. Dolega-Dolegowski, D., et al.: Application of holography and augmented reality based technology to visualize the internal structure of the dental root-a proof of concept. Head face Med. **18**(1), 1–6 (2022)
12. Doughty, M., Ghugre, N.R.: Head-mounted display-based augmented reality for image-guided media delivery to the heart: a preliminary investigation of perceptual accuracy. J. Imaging **8**(2), 33 (2022)
13. Dutta, R., Mantri, A., Singh, G.: Evaluating system usability of mobile augmented reality application for teaching karnaugh-maps. Smart Learn. Environ. **9**(1), 6 (2022)
14. Farshid, M., Paschen, J., Eriksson, T., Kietzmann, J.: Go boldly!: explore augmented reality (AR), virtual reality (VR), and mixed reality (MR) for business. Bus. Horiz. **61**(5), 657–663 (2018)

15. Fiala, M.: Comparing ARTag and Artoolkit plus fiducial marker systems. In: IEEE Int. Workshop Haptic Audio Vis. Environ. Appl, p. 6. IEEE (2005)
16. Hajirasouli, A., Banihashemi, S.: Augmented reality in architecture and construction education: state of the field and opportunities. Int. J. Educ. Technol. High. Educ. **19**(1), 39 (2022)
17. Ho, P.T., Albajez, J.A., Santolaria, J., Yagüe-Fabra, J.A.: Study of augmented reality based manufacturing for further integration of quality control 4.0: A systematic literature review. Appl. Sci. **12**(4), 1961 (2022)
18. Jung, T., tom Dieck, M..C., Lee, H., Chung, N.: Effects of Virtual Reality and Augmented Reality on Visitor Experiences in Museum. In: Inversini, A., Schegg, R. (eds.) Information and Communication Technologies in Tourism 2016, pp. 621–635. Springer, Cham (2016). https://doi.org/10.1007/978-3-319-28231-2_45
19. Kelly, J.W., Doty, T.A., Ambourn, M., Cherep, L.A.: Distance perception in the oculus quest and oculus quest 2. Frontiers Virtual Reality **3**, 850471 (2022)
20. Khan, D.: Robust tracking through the design of high quality fiducial markers: an optimization tool for artoolkit. IEEE access **6**, 22421–22433 (2018)
21. Muhammad, K., Khan, N., Lee, M.Y., Imran, A.S., Sajjad, M.: School of the future: a comprehensive study on the effectiveness of augmented reality as a tool for primary school children's education. Appl. Sci. **11**(11), 5277 (2021)
22. Muñoz, E.G., Fabregat, R., Bacca-Acosta, J., Duque-Méndez, N., Avila-Garzon, C.: Augmented reality, virtual reality, and game technologies in ophthalmology training. Information **13**(5), 222 (2022)
23. Scavarelli, A., Arya, A., Teather, R.J.: Virtual reality and augmented reality in social learning spaces: a literature review. Virtual Reality **25**, 257–277 (2021)
24. Sendari, S., Firmansah, A., et al.: Performance analysis of augmented reality based on vuforia using 3D marker detection. In: 2020 4th International Conference on Vocational Education and Training (ICOVET), pp. 294–298. IEEE (2020)
25. Simon, J.: Augmented reality application development using unity and Vuforia. Interdisc. Description Complex Syst.: INDECS **21**(1), 69–77 (2023)
26. Theodoropoulos, A., Lepouras, G.: Augmented reality and programming education: a systematic review. Int. J. Child-Comput. Interact. **30**, 100335 (2021)
27. Videnovik, M., Trajkovik, V., Kiønig, L.V., Vold, T.: Increasing quality of learning experience using augmented reality educational games. Multimedia tools Appl. **79**(33–34), 23861–23885 (2020)
28. Westfahl, S., Meyer-Renner, D., Bagula, A.: A framework for the design, implementation and evaluation of a multi-variant augmented reality application. In: 2022 ITU Kaleidoscope-Extended reality how to boost quality of experience and interoperability, pp. 1–9. IEEE (2022)
29. Zaina, L.A., Fortes, R.P., Casadei, V., Nozaki, L.S., Paiva, D.M.B.: Preventing accessibility barriers: guidelines for using user interface design patterns in mobile applications. J. Syst. Softw. **186**, 111213 (2022)

Hate Speech Detection Using Machine Learning and Deep Learning Techniques

Divya Singh, Sonam Gupta(✉), and Rekha Baghel

Ajay Kumar Garg Engineering College, Ghaziabad, India
Guptasonam6@gmail.com

Abstract. This paper delves into the pressing issue of hate speech in the digital era, which undermines inclusive online conversations. It investigates various methods for detecting hate speech, utilizing both conventional machine learning techniques and state-of-the-art deep learning architectures. The study focuses on deep learning models such as Convolutional Neural Networks, Recurrent Neural Networks, and Transformers, assessing their effectiveness in identifying textual patterns. Additionally, the practicality of machine learning algorithms, including ensemble methods, is examined. To ensure fairness, class inequality and ethical considerations are thoroughly taken into account when evaluating the efficiency of hate speech detection systems. Furthermore, the report addresses emerging challenges like context-dependent hate speech and evolving linguistic patterns. It places great importance on the ongoing necessity for research efforts and moral obligations to combat hate speech on online platforms.

Keywords: machine learning · deep learning · hate speech · convolutional neural network · recurrent neural network · transformers

1 Introduction

The rise of social media and the internet has transformed global communication, but it has also unfortunately given rise to an increase in instances of racism. Hate speech, in particular, involves targeting individuals or groups based on factors such as their race, ethnicity, gender, religion, or national origin, and it can have the potential to incite or promote violence. In response to these challenges, scientists and engineers have developed electronic systems that harness the power of machine learning and artificial intelligence to identify and combat hate speech. These technological solutions analyze vast amounts of data generated on social media platforms and online forums, with the goal of recognizing and preventing hate speech from spreading.

This study takes a deep dive into a comprehensive exploration of hate speech detection systems. It specifically focuses on the evolution from traditional rule-based methods to cutting-edge machine learning and deep learning techniques, highlighting the advancements in technology that aim to address this critical issue. It also explores the challenges involved, such as prejudice, ethical issues

N. Chauhan et al. (Eds.): MIND 2023, CCIS 2128, pp. 110–124, 2024.
https://doi.org/10.1007/978-3-031-62217-5_10

and the rapid pace of hate speech. In the present era, the prevalence of hate speech has become a concerning issue with significant consequences. The extensive utilization of social networks and online platforms has contributed to a surge in hate speech, resulting in substantial harm to individuals, groups, and entire communities.

This paper is about hate speech, a difficult topic that can be destructive, cause hatred, and incite hatred and fear. Deep learning and machine learning algorithms have the potential to expand hate speech analysis, allowing platforms and organizations to quickly respond to negative information. While hate speech vocabulary and context-sensitive phrases are continuously changing, standard rule-based techniques find it difficult to keep up. In order to detect hate speech using machine learning and deep learning methods, this paper provides a thorough description of methodology, datasets, models, assessment metrics, and ethical issues.

The structure of this paper is as follows: The taxonomy for classifying the realm of hate speech is found in Sect. 2, which comes after the introduction. The literature review and associated activities are covered in Sect. 3, which provides details on how the survey's paper was gathered. Section 4 discusses the difficulties in recognizing hate speech. The datasets used in various research investigations are covered in Sect. 5 along with their sources. The algorithms that were used by researchers in their investigations are described in Sects. 6 and 7. The measures used to assess the datasets are given in Sect. 8. Finally, Sect. 9 shows comparisons based on the selected metrics and summarizes the researchers' conclusions in their individual investigations. At the end of this study, we have highlighted future research areas with conclusion.

2 Definitions and Taxonomy

Hate speech may take many different forms and occur in a variety of settings. To comprehend its principles and offer clarity for our study, taxonomy is constructed.

Definition of Hate Speech Definition of Hate Speech Offensive Language: An offensive or disturbing statement is called a swear word. This may include swearing, profanity, blasphemy, and sentiments that violate morality or morality, but these must not be motivated by hatred or Violent violence.

Taxonomy of Hate Speech. We provide a taxonomy that divides hate speech into many aspects in order to better comprehend the variety of hate speech expressions: **Explicit vs. Implicit Hate Speech:** Hate speech can be explicit, with overt expressions of hatred and discrimination, or implicit, with subtle or coded language that conveys similar sentiments. **Individual vs. Group Targeting:** Hate speech can target specific individuals or groups. Group targeting may involve broad generalizations or stereotypes about a particular category of people. **Contextual Variations:** Hate speech can vary significantly based on the context in which it occurs. This includes social networking website, chat room, news articles, and confidential discussion. **Severity and Intensity:** Hate speech can range from mild forms of derogatory language to extreme calls for violence or harm. **Intersectionality:** Hate speech often involves intersecting categories of discrimination, where individuals may be targeted for multiple attributes simultaneously (e.g., race and gender). **Motivations:** Hate speech can be motivated by various factors, including prejudice, ideology, political beliefs, or cultural biases. **Medium:** Hate speech can appear in different media, such as text, images, videos, or symbols.

3 Comprehensive Review of the Literature

The author identified the following research questions (RQ) based on the gaps identified in previous studies conducted prior to the literature survey on hate speech detection: **RQ1.** What machine learning algorithm exhibited superior precision?
RQ2. Which methodology is best deep learning or machine learning?

3.1 Fact-Finding Process

The author conducted a survey for this paper by searching for hate speech detection on the Google Scholar search engine.

3.2 Sources

The study utilized resources from IEEE, Springer, Google Scholar, and Science Direct for paper collection.

3.3 Study Method Criteria

For this research paper, data collection spanned from 2019 to 2023, encompassing the latest developments in this field to gain insights into the ongoing research in this area.

3.4 Research Focus

The study focuses on analyzing the most widely used deep learning and machine learning methods for detecting hate speech. This study intends to investigate several methods to improve the comprehension of recognizing hate speech on social media sites. Table 1 below presents the compilation of relevant research papers.

Table 1. Overview of survey articles on automated hate speech detection (2019–2023)

Cite	Abstract	Publications
[1]	With a focus on datasets, features, and machine learning models and an emphasis on inconsistent results, small datasets, and inadequate reliability for diverse applications, this paper examines textual hate speech detection systems	MDPI Journal Information
[2]	A particular emphasis on NLP and DL technologies is placed on the topic of hate speech recognition and monitoring inside social networking sites in this research review. Additionally, it clarifies current restrictions and identifies promising areas for further study	Published by Elsevier B.V
[3]	The SNO Against Hate Crimes uses HaterNet, an artificial technology, to observe and visualize hate speech on Twitter. With an AUC of 0.828, it performs better than earlier techniques by introducing a new public dataset, contrasting classification strategies, and comparing methodologies	MDPI Journal Information
[4]	This paper examines machine learning methods for detecting hate speech in Twitter data streams with a particular emphasis on fragmentation difficulties, general metadata design, and threshold settings.	Elsevier Inc
[5]	Social friction and cyber conflict can result from hate speech on social media. Due to its complexity and resource shortage, automatic detection of hate speech is essential, especially in difficult to learn languages like Arabic.	CS & IT
[6]	Annotated corpora and Lexica have become more important in the field of NLP for the identification of hate speech on social media.	Springer
[7]	It looks at recent advances in the study of racism and hate speech on social media, stressing a lack of platform and geographical diversity, a lack of reflective conversation, and little interaction with critical racial viewpoints.	Television and new media
[8]	With an emphasis on English and Spanish output, this study analyses works on hate speech in legal and communication studies. It tackles multidisciplinary and transversality issues and suggests mapping hate speech for cross-national comparisons	Sage Open
[9]	The study collects 197,566 comments from four platforms, 80% non-hateful, and 20% hateful, using various algorithms and feature representations. Results show XGBoost performs best, with BERT features being most impactful. The code is publicly available for further development	Springer
[10]	To detect hate speech across online platforms, DeepHate is a cutting-edge deep learning model that combines numerous textual properties including word embedding, feelings, and topical information. It outperforms existing state-of-the-art methods and provides helpful insights on key aspects	ACM Conference
[11]	A deep NLP model for the automatic recognition of hate speech in social media data is presented in the study. When tested on the HASOC2019 dataset, this model, which combines convolutional and recurrent layers, had a macro F1 score of 0.63	Springer

4 Challenges in Defining and Categorizing Hate Speech and Detection with ML/DL

Due to its subjectivity, contextual unpredictability, and ever-evolving modalities of expression, categorising hate speech is a difficult task. Intelligent, context-aware strategies, automatic detection technologies, human judgement, and the always changing nature of online communication are required to counteract it. Effective prevention systems depend on collaboration between researchers, platform providers, and policymakers, as well as on ML and DL approaches. Here are some key challenges:

4.1 Personalization and Explanation

Racism is context-dependent and can vary across culture, region, and time. Understanding context and intent for ML/DL models is difficult.

Contextual Sensitivity: Hate speech interpretation is influenced by context, intent, and tone, as what is considered offensive or hateful in one circumstance may not be in another.

Subjective Perception: Hate speech can be interpreted differently by different individuals, with some viewing it as legitimate criticism or free expression, highlighting the varying perceptions of such expressions.

4.2 Evolving Language

Hate speech often involves subtle linguistic nuances, sarcasm, and irony that can be difficult to detect, especially for rule-based models.

Rapid Linguistic Evolution: Hate speech language evolves quickly to adapt to changing social norms, online communities, and communication platforms. New terms, phrases, or symbols emerge, making it challenging to keep definitions up to date.

Coded Language: Hate speech can be expressed through coded or veiled language, making it difficult to detect using traditional linguistic analysis. Such expressions may require contextual understanding to identify.

4.3 Legal and Cultural Variations

Legal Differences: Definitions of hate speech and its legal implications vary significantly across countries and regions. What is considered hate speech in one jurisdiction may not be in another.

Cultural Differences: Cultural norms and values influence the perception of hate speech. What is acceptable or offensive can differ widely among cultures and communities.

4.4 Subtlety and Micro-aggression

Hate speech is not always overt; it can manifest subtly through micro-aggression or coded language. Recognizing these subtle expressions can be challenging.

4.5 Data Quality and Labeling

High-quality labeled datasets for training models are essential. However, labeling hate speech is subjective, and datasets can contain biases based on annotators' perspectives.

4.6 Data Imbalance

Hate speech is typically a minority class, leading to imbalanced datasets. This can result in models that perform well on non-hate speech but poorly on incitement of hatred.

4.7 Multilingual and Multi Modal Content

Hate speech exists in multiple languages and across various media types, including text, images, audio, and video. Developing models that can handle this diversity is challenging.

4.8 Evolution of Hate Speech

Online hate speech evolves rapidly as new terms, phrases, and tactics emerge. Models may become outdated quickly, necessitating continuous model updates.

4.9 Adversarial Attacks

Adversaries can craft content specifically to evade detection systems. Models need to be robust against adversarial inputs.

4.10 Privacy Concerns

Hate speech detection often involves analyzing sensitive and potentially personally identifiable information. Safeguarding privacy is crucial.

4.11 Bias and Fairness

ML/DL models can inherit biases from training data, leading to unfair outcomes, especially concerning minority groups. Ensuring fairness is a significant challenge.

4.12 Real-Time Detection

Hate speech often requires real-time detection to mitigate its immediate impact. Achieving low-latency detection while maintaining accuracy is challenging.

4.13 Scalability

Social media platforms process vast amounts of data daily. Hate speech detection models need to scale efficiently to handle this volume.

4.14 User Behavior

Detecting hate speech is not only about identifying content but also understanding its impact on user behavior, including engagement, influence, and response.

4.15 Legal and Ethical Considerations

Determining appropriate responses to hate speech; involves ethical considerations, including privacy, oversight, and user consent. Different laws have different definitions of hate speech, and some terms may be protected under freedom of expression. Being legal and ethical is difficult.

4.16 Intersectionality

Complex Identities: Hate speech can single out individuals based on a multitude of intersecting attributes, such as ethnic inclusiveness, demographic features and sexual preference. This complexity makes categorization challenging.

4.17 Ambiguity

Some cases may fall in a gray area where it is unclear whether the expression qualifies as hate speech or not. These ambiguous cases require careful analysis and contextual understanding.

4.18 Freedom of Speech

Finding equilibrium between curbing hate speech and upholding the tenets of free expression remains an ongoing challenge. Overzealous censorship may stifle legitimate discourse.

4.19 Digital Evolution

Digital Evolution: The digital environment introduces unique challenges. Hate speech can spread rapidly on social media, and platforms must develop automated detection systems to keep up.

4.20 Diverse Expressions

Diverse Expressions: Hate speech can encompass a wide range of expressions, from racial slurs to religious discrimination, making it challenging to create a comprehensive categorization.

5 Hate Speech Detection Datasets

This section examines the process of choosing and evaluating noteworthy hate speech datasets, describing their characteristics and addressing the inherent difficulties involved in their development and assessment. These datasets, which include posts, comments, and forum debates, are crucial tools for developing machine learning and deep learning models as well as for testing them. They cover a wide spectrum of target groups delineated by traits including color, ethnicity, gender, religion, and sexual orientation, facilitating the difference between hate speech and non-hate speech material. The results of the poll show that Twitter is the most popular dataset for hate speech identification (Table 2).

6 Machine Learning-Based Approaches

A significant advancement in this field involved the application of machine learning techniques by researchers and practitioners to build adaptable hate speech detection models. Hate speech detection systems based on machine learning showed promise but encountered difficulties in understanding subtle language nuances and addressing imbalances in dataset categories, leveraging essential components such as:

6.1 Data Preprocessing

Cleaning and preparing textual data, including tasks such as tokenization, stemming, and removing stop words.

6.2 Feature Extraction

Converting textual data into numerical representations suitable for machine learning algorithms.

6.3 Classification Algorithms

Utilizing algorithms like Naive Bayes, Support Vector Machines (SVM), Random Forest, and Gradient Boosting to classify text as hate speech or non-hate speech.

6.4 Ensemble Methods

Combining multiple classifiers to improve performance and robustness.

6.5 Cross-Validation

Employing techniques like k-fold cross-validation to evaluate model performance.

7 Deep Learning-Based Approaches

By recognizing complex patterns and nuanced contextual information within text data, deep learning algorithms, specifically neural networks, have brought about a significant transformation in the field of hate speech detection. This investigation explores the utilization of deep learning models for hate speech detection, highlighting their effectiveness in handling context-dependent hate speech and evolving language styles. It also outlines their characteristics and potential biases, delving into key aspects of deep learning methodologies include:

7.1 Convolutional Neural Networks (CNNs)

Leveraging CNNs for text classification tasks by applying Convolutional layers to capture local features in text.

7.2 Recurrent Neural Networks (RNNs)

Utilizing RNNs, such as Long Short-Term Memory (LSTM) and Gated Recurrent Unit (GRU), to model sequential dependencies in text.

7.3 Transformers

Utilizing Transformer-based frameworks like BERT (Bidirectional Encoder Representations from Transformers) and GPT (Generative Pre-trained Transformer) to enhance contextual understanding and achieve precise hate speech detection (Table 3).

8 Evaluation Metrics

Hate speech detection models undergo evaluation using a range of metrics, selected based on their particular objectives and needs. Certain metrics hold greater significance in specific scenarios, such as the importance of minimizing false positives in content moderation or emphasizing recall for legal purposes. It's essential for researchers and practitioners to opt for metrics that align with the intended application and interpret the outcomes within their specific context. The metrics commonly employed include Accuracy (A), Precision (P), Recall (R), and F1-Score (F). Table 4 provides a summary of the principal evaluation metrics utilized in this study.

9 Result and Discussion

In this part, we look at how various algorithms performed when measurements were added to the study dataset. The outcomes are presented in Table 5 below (Fig. 1).

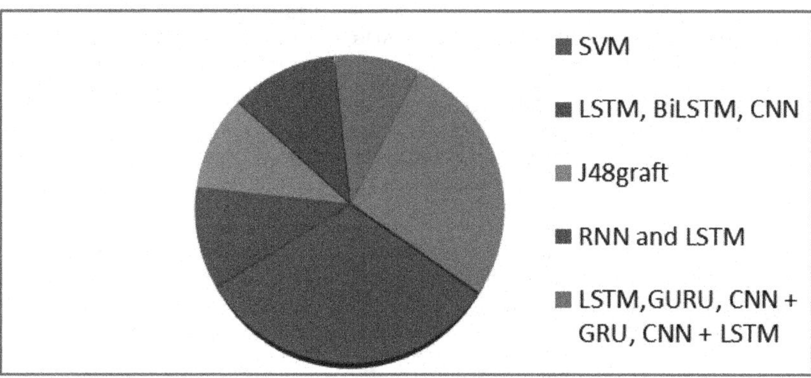

Fig. 1. Precision Of Algorithm based on different datasets.

By employing a variety of datasets from various social media platforms, this research conducts a comparative analysis of the Support Vector Machine (SVM) method in relation to other machine learning techniques for hate speech

Table 2. Overview of Acquired Datasets

Dataset	Paper	Size	Diversity	Description	Source
HS and Offensive Language	[12]	Over 16,000 labeled tweets	Focuses primarily on Twitter data	A Twitter-specific dataset called HateSonar contains abusive words and hate speech	HateSonar Datasets
HS Twitter Dataset	[13]	Over 24,000 labeled tweets	Covers multiple languages	HateEval is a multilingual dataset with hate speech annotations for tweets	HateEval Dataset
Offensive Language Identification Dataset	[14]	Over 14,000 labeled tweets	Addresses different types of offenses	The OLID dataset contains tweets labeled for three tasks: offense detection, target identification, and categorization into different offense types	OLID dataset
Wikipedia Talk Pages	[15]	Hundreds of thousands of comments	Represents diverse discussions	This dataset includes Wikipedia talk page comments labeled for toxicity and aggression	Wikipedia Talk Pages
Gab HS	[16]	Thousands of labeled samples	Likely contains extreme hate speech	A dataset organized from Gab social media platform, known for its controversial content	Gab Hate Speech Dataset
Waseem-Hovy HS Dataset	[17]	10,574	Focused on Sexism/Racism	The English tweets in this dataset are classified as either hate speech, vulgar language, or neither. It is frequently employed in studies on the recognition of hate speech	Waseem-Hovy Dataset
Multimodal HS Dataset	[18]	Tens of thousands of memes and caption	Provides multimodal data	HateXplain includes not only text but also images with explanations to detect and explain hate speech. It addresses the multimodal nature of online hate speech	HateXplain Dataset
Datasets from Kaggle and GitHub	[19]	9,973	Hate Speech (Directed, Generalized),Relevance (0,1), STANCE (Support, Opposition, Neither)	On websites like Kaggle and GitHub, other smaller-scale hate speech detection datasets may be accessed. These datasets can include segments or subgenres of hate speech	Kaggle Datasets
Twitter HS Detection Dataset	[20]	80,000	Abusive, Hateful, Normal, Spam	a collection of tweets with labels for hate speech, vulgar language, and other inappropriate stuff	Twitter Hate Speech
Online HS Dataset	[21]	22,324	Incorporates multiple modalities , Hate, Not hate	This dataset includes examples of foul language and hate speech from various web sources	OHSD
Founta HSTwitter Dataset	[22]	Varied (depends on subset)	Represents offensive tweets	The dataset consists of a selection of tweets that have been labelled as either hate speech, offensive language, or neither	Founta
Stormfront HS Corpus	[23]	Thousands of labeled samples	-	This dataset, which has been used in studies on the identification of hate speech, comprises postings from the white nationalist forum Storm front	Stormfront Hate Speech Corpus

Table 3. Comparison of all algorithms

Algorithm	Pros	Cons	Use Cases
Naive Bayes	Simple and interpretable	Assumes independence between features	Quick baseline model for small datasets
Logistic Regression	Simple and interpretable	Limited to linear separability	Binary classification tasks
Support Vector Machines (SVM)	Effective for high-dimensional data	Requires tuning of hyperparameters	Text classification, binary or multiclass problems
Random Forest	Robust to overfitting	May not capture complex linguistic nuances	Binary/multiclass classification, feature selection
Gradient Boosting (XGBoost, LightGBM)	High accuracy, good for feature selection	Requires careful hyperparameter tuning	Text classification, structured datasets
Deep Learning Models (LSTM, CNN, BERT)	Can capture complex linguistic patterns	Requires large data,computationally expensive	Complex text classification tasks, sequential data
Hybrid Models	Combine strengths of multiple algorithms	More complex to implement and tune	High-performance applications
Ensemble Methods	Improve overall performance and robustness	Increased complexity, may require more resources	High-performance applications

Table 4. Summary of Evaluation Metric

Metric	Description	Formula
A	It evaluates the proportion of correctly identified occurrences in a dataset that include both hate speech and non-hate speech. However, when working with unbalanced datasets, it could produce false findings	(TP + TN) / (TP + TN + FP + FN)
P	Indicating the model's capacity to reduce false positives, it calculates the proportion of correctly predicted positive occurrences, such as instances of hate speech, among all anticipated positives.It gauges the model's success in recognising hate speech by comparing the predicted positive cases of hate speech to the actual positive instances in a dataset	TP / (TP + FP)
R	It gauges the model's success in recognising hate speech by comparing the predicted positive cases of hate speech to the actual positive instances in a dataset	TP / (TP + FN)
F	It is a statistic that strikes a compromise between recall and accuracy by giving a single numerical number that takes both false positives and false negatives into account	2 * (P * R) / (P+ R)

identification. The findings reveal that the SVM algorithm achieves the highest precision score, followed by the Convolutional Neural Network (CNN), Naive Bayes, Decision Tree, Random Forest, and Multilayer Perceptron in descending order. Additionally, the study underscores the utilization of limited sample sizes and various mathematical criteria, including accuracy, sensitivity, recall, and precision.

Table 5. Comparison Results Based on Algorithms and Metrics

Cite	Platform	Category	ML Technique	Highlighting Facts	Methods Used	P	R	F1
[24]	Twitter, UseNet, Wiki	Abuse	Supervised	Word embedding, linguistics, and lexicon	SVM	0.82	0.8	0.81
[25]	Form-spring	Internet harassment	Supervised	BOW	M-NB and Stochastic Gradient Descent	-	-	0.9
[26]	Twitter	Hate speech Word2Vec	Supervised	Word2Vec	LSTM, BiLSTM, CNN	0.83	0.78	0.8
[16]	Twitter	offensive, hateful	Supervised	Semantic, sentiment-based, and unigram	J48graft	0.79	0.78	0.78
[27]	Twitter	Hate, offensive	Supervised	Word clusters, N-grams, Skip-grams, and hierarchical	RBF kernel, SVM	0.78	0.8	0.79
[28]	Twitter	Sexual harassment or prejudice	Supervised	the frequency of words, and vector optimization	RNN and LSTM	0.9	0.87	0.88
[29]	Twitter	Reformism	Supervised	Meaningful Context	SVM	0.85	0.84	0.85
[30]	Twitter	Disability, sexuality, gender identity, and religious	Supervised	BOW	LR, biLSTM	-	-	94
[31]	Twitter	Racism, Sexism	Supervised	Word embedding	CNN + GRU	-	-	0.94
[32]	Twitter	Hate, Racism, Sexism	Supervised	incorporating keras phrases	LSTM,GURU, CNN + GRU, CNN + LSTM	0.72	0.75	0.73
[33]	Twitter	Abusive, Hate	Supervised	-	CNN and BiLSTMCNN	0.74	-	-
[34]	Twitter	Hate speech	Supervised	Word2Vec, Aravec	CNN + LSTM	0.65	0.79	0.71
[35]	Twitter	Hateful, abuse, sexism, prejudice, religious discrimination	Supervised	SG, CNN, CBOW	CNN, CNN-LSTM, and BiLSTM-CNN	0.74	-	-

10 Conclusion

Several approaches have contributed to the advancement of hate speech detection systems. However, challenges such as contextual understanding, fairness, privacy concerns, and interpretability persist. To enhance accuracy, researchers should prioritize areas like contextual awareness, data integration, bias assessment, privacy safeguards, metric selection, addressing cross-lingual and low-resource languages, creating dynamic systems, and collaborating with stakeholders.

Detecting hate speech in the digital age presents a significant challenge that demands innovative solutions. Deep learning and machine learning techniques have proven effective in developing automated detection systems. Conventional rule-based systems have improved accuracy, while feature engineering and text representation techniques provide valuable insights. It's crucial to address ethical considerations, including fairness, privacy, transparency, and responsible data collection in this context.

References

1. Alkomah, F., Ma, X.: A literature review of textual hate speech detection methods and datasets. Information **13**(6), 273 (2022)
2. Jahan, M.S., Oussalah, M.: A systematic review of hate speech automatic detection using natural language processing. Neurocomputing **546**, 126232 (2023)
3. Pereira-Kohatsu, J.C., Quijano-Sánchez, L., Liberatore, F., Camacho-Collados, M.: Detecting and monitoring hate speech in Twitter. Sensors **19**(21), 4654 (2019)
4. Ayo, F.E., Folorunso, O., Ibharalu, F.T., Osinuga, I.A.: Machine learning techniques for hate speech classification of Twitter data: state-of-the-art, future challenges and research directions. Comput. Sci. Rev. **38**, 100311 (2020)
5. Al-Hassan, A., Al-Dossari, H.: Detection of hate speech in social networks: a survey on multilingual corpus. In: 6th International Conference on Computer Science and Information Technology, vol. 10. ACM (2019). https://doi.org/10.5121/csit.2019.90208
6. Poletto, F., Basile, V., Sanguinetti, M., Bosco, C., Patti, V.: Resources and benchmark corpora for hate speech detection: a systematic review. Lang. Resour. Eval. **55**, 477–523 (2021)
7. Matamoros-Fernández, A., Farkas, J.: Racism, hate speech, and social media: a systematic review and critique. Telev. New Med. **22**(2), 205–224 (2021)
8. Paz, M.A., Montero-Díaz, J., Moreno-Delgado, A.: Hate speech: a systematized review. Sage Open **10**(4), 2158244020973022 (2020)
9. Salminen, J., Hopf, M., Chowdhury, S.A., Jung, S.G., Almerekhi, H., Jansen, B.J.: Developing an online hate classifier for multiple social media platforms. Hum. Centric Comput. Inf. Sci. **10**, 1–34 (2020)
10. Cao, R., Lee, R.K.W, Hoang, T.A.: DeepHate: hate speech detection via multi-faceted text representations. In: Proceedings of the 12th ACM Conference on Web Science, pp. 11–20 (2020)
11. Kovács, G., Alonso, P., Saini, R.: Challenges of hate speech detection in social media: data scarcity, and leveraging external resources. SN Comput. Sci. **2**(2), 95 (2021)
12. Waseem, Z., Hovy, D.: Hateful symbols or hateful people? Predictive features for hate speech detection on Twitter. In: Proceedings of the NAACL Student Research Workshop, pp. 88–93 (2016)
13. Fortuna, P., Nunes, S.: A survey on automatic detection of hate speech in text. ACM Comput. Surv. (CSUR) **51**(4), 1–30 (2018)
14. Zampieri, M., Malmasi, S., Nakov, P., Rosenthal, S., Farra, N., Kumar, R.: SemEval-2019 task 6: identifying and categorizing offensive language in social media (OffensEval). arXiv preprint arXiv:1903.08983 (2019)
15. Wulczyn, E., Thain, N., Dixon, L.: Ex Machina: personal attacks seen at scale. In: Proceedings of the 26th International Conference on World Wide Web, pp. 1391–1399 (2017)
16. Watanabe, H., Bouazizi, M., Ohtsuki, T.: Hate speech on Twitter: a pragmatic approach to collect hateful and offensive expressions and perform hate speech detection. IEEE Access **6**, 13825–13835 (2018)
17. Peterson, D., Boyd-Graber, J., Palmer, M., Kawahara, D.: Leveraging VerbNet to build corpus-specific verb clusters. In: Proceedings of the Fifth Joint Conference on Lexical and Computational Semantics, pp. 102–107 (2016)
18. Gomez, R., Gibert, J., Gomez, L., Karatzas, D.: Exploring hate speech detection in multimodal publications. In: Proceedings of the IEEE/CVF Winter Conference on Applications of Computer Vision, pp. 1470–1478 (2020)

19. Gomez, R., Gibert, J., Gomez, L., Karatzas, D.: Exploring hate speech detection in multimodal publications. In: Proceedings of the IEEE/CVF Winter Conference on Applications of Computer Vision, pp. 1470–1478, (2020)
20. Davidson, T., Warmsley, D., Macy, M., Weber, I.: Automated hate speech detection and the problem of offensive language. In: Proceedings of the International AAAI Conference on Web and Social Media, vol. 11, pp. 512–515 (2017)
21. Mathew, B., Saha, P., Yimam, S.M., Biemann, C., Goyal, P., Mukherjee, A.: HateXplain: a benchmark dataset for explainable hate speech detection. In: Proceedings of the AAAI Conference on Artificial Intelligence, vol. 35, pp. 14867–14875 (2021)
22. Brassard-Gourdeau, E., Khoury, R.: Subversive toxicity detection using sentiment information. In: Proceedings of the Third Workshop on Abusive Language Online, pp. 1–10 (2019)
23. De Gibert, O., Perez, N., García-Pablos, A., Cuadros, M.: Hate speech dataset from a white supremacy forum. arXiv preprint arXiv:1809.04444 (2018)
24. Wiegand, M., Ruppenhofer, J., Schmidt, A., Greenberg, C.: Inducing a lexicon of abusive words–a feature-based approach. In: Proceedings of the 2018 Conference of the North American Chapter of the Association for Computational Linguistics: Human Language Technologies, Volume 1 (Long Papers), pp. 1046–1056 (2018)
25. Pawar, R., Agrawal, Y., Joshi, A., Gorrepati, R., Raje, R.R.: Cyberbullying detection system with multiple server configurations. In: 2018 IEEE International Conference on Electro Information Technology (EIT), pp. 0090–0095. IEEE (2018)
26. Kamble, S., Joshi, A.: Hate speech detection from code-mixed Hindi-English tweets using deep learning models. arXiv preprint arXiv:1811.05145 (2018)
27. Malmasi, S., Zampieri, M.: Challenges in discriminating profanity from hate speech. J. Exp. Theor. Artif. Intell. **30**(2), 187–202 (2018)
28. Pitsilis, G.K., Ramampiaro, H., Langseth, H.: Effective hate-speech detection in Twitter data using recurrent neural networks. Appl. Intell. **48**(12), 4730–4742 (2018)
29. Fernandez, M., Alani, H.: Contextual semantics for radicalisation detection on Twitter (2018)
30. Ousidhoum, N., Lin, Z., Zhang, H., Song, Y., Yeung, D.Y.: Multilingual and multi-aspect hate speech analysis. arXiv preprint arXiv:1908.11049 (2019)
31. Zhang, Z., Luo, L.: Hate speech detection: a solved problem? The challenging case of long tail on Twitter. Semant. Web **10**(5), 925–945 (2019)
32. Al-Hassan, A., Al-Dossari, H.: Detection of hate speech in Arabic tweets using deep learning. Multimedia Syst. **28**(6), 1963–1974 (2022)
33. Mulki, H., Haddad, H., Ali, C.B., Alshabani, H.: L-HSAB: a Levantine Twitter dataset for hate speech and abusive language. In: Proceedings of the Third Workshop on Abusive Language Online, pp. 111–118 (2019)
34. Faris, H., Aljarah, I., Habib, M., Castillo, P.A.: Hate speech detection using word embedding and deep learning in the Arabic language context. In: ICPRAM, pp. 453–460 (2020)
35. Duwairi, R., Hayajneh, A., Quwaider, M.: A deep learning framework for automatic detection of hate speech embedded in Arabic tweets. Arab. J. Sci. Eng. **46**, 4001–4014 (2021)

Phishing Detection Using 1D-CNN and FF-CNN Models Based on URL of the Website

Chandra Kumar Mete and C. D. Jaidhar(✉)

National Institute of Technology Karnataka, Surathkal 575025, Karnataka, India
jaidharcd@nitk.edu.in

Abstract. Web browsing has become an integral part of our daily lives, with most modern computer devices supporting easy access to online services and information. However, this convenience comes with a significant risk to user security. Web users are exposed to various types of cyberattacks, such as Phishing, malware, profiling, etc. These hazards have the potential to compromise individuals or organizations and deny lists. The traditional Phishing defense is no longer effective in shielding users from the constantly evolving nature of Phishing Uniform Resource Locators (URLs). To address this issue, this work proposes a One-Dimensional Convolutional Neural Networks (1D-CNN) and Feed-Forward Convolutional Neural Network (FF-CNN)-based Phishing URL detection approach. The proposed approach is trained with three different datasets: a URL-based feature dataset, an embedded feature-based dataset, and a combination of both feature datasets. Experiments show that the proposed 1D-CNN-based approach achieved detection accuracy of 98.83%, 98.09%, and 98.91% on the URL-based features dataset, embedded features dataset, and combined features dataset, respectively. Furthermore, the proposed FF-CNN-based approach achieved an accuracy of 98.87%, 97.18%, and 98.78% on the same datasets. This research provides an effective approach to combating the growing threat of web-based attacks and safeguarding the security of web users.

Keywords: Convolutional Neural Networks · Cyberattacks · Cybersecurity · Phishing · Uniform Resource Locator

1 Introduction

Social media platforms have become virtual meeting places for the public recently. People can be targeted by Phishing attacks when using social networks to communicate. The act of Phishing endangers privacy, incites virus attacks, and frequently results in the theft of sensitive information. Phishing attacks can happen through various methods, like instant chats, fake Uniform Resource Locators (URLs), fraudulent emails, and spoofed websites. Phishing aims to get private information in order to commit identity theft or gain money. Attacks

N. Chauhan et al. (Eds.): MIND 2023, CCIS 2128, pp. 125–139, 2024.
https://doi.org/10.1007/978-3-031-62217-5_11

using Phishing are ruining businesses all over the world. Most Phishing attacks primarily target web mail and financial or payment institutions.

A web Phishing attack involves altering the website's appearance and contents. For example, a gang of hackers using the alias "anonymous" attacked the website of the Rach Gia airport in 2017. Every day, hundreds of websites are hacked worldwide. The main reason for website vandalism is security weaknesses that allow transferring files to servers that are still reachable by hackers. For website proprietors, the effects of defacement assaults are extremely concerning. Attacks also stop a website from functioning. Due to the disruptions caused by the intruders, data loss occurs, and the website's owner's reputation is questioned.

Websites used for Phishing sometimes look pretty similar to legitimate websites. Phishing websites have relatively specific topologies. Unlike legal websites, which require more time to design, Phishing websites may be created and distributed quickly. The framework of a Phishing website is more complex and challenging to integrate than a regular website. The remaining topological structure is disregarded in the Phishing detection system, which focuses on a single web page's features.

Whitelist and blacklist techniques, Deep Learning (DL)-based methods, Machine Learning (ML) based methods, and heuristic-based methods are the four different categories of Phishing website detection methods. The black-and-whitelist Phishing website detection technique has a relatively quick detection rate. Although it is not immune to zero-day attacks, the detection rate does depend on the number of websites on the blacklist and whitelist. Heuristic detection was created to detect Phishing websites by gathering data from numerous online pages and third-party services, such as website ratings, network traffic monitoring, and WHOIS information, to circumvent issues with blacklist tactics. The extraction of third-party service features is challenging, making detection time-consuming and inaccurate. ML-based techniques are used to identify manually derived Phishing URL features while detecting Phishing websites. This tactic could improve the effectiveness of detection.

Supervised learning is used to create predictive or classification models. The model is trained and evaluated using labeled historical data collected from websites. To identify Phishing attempts, web browsers' built-in models can be employed. Most of the ML methods depend on feature extraction, which exhibits high accuracy in Phishing attack detection. However, the size of a classifier grows due to the more number of features, and over-fitting issues may arise. Another difficulty of the classical ML-based approach is selecting the best features. The extraction of features can also be used to train ML-based classification algorithms. However, specialists with various levels of knowledge and judgment can manually determine the features of URLs and HTML content. DL-based models are more effective than conventional classification methods.

The rest of the manuscript is structured as follows: A review of anti-Phishing methods is covered in Sect. 2. In Sect. 3, the proposed approach is explained. Section 4 describes the dataset used, feature extraction, and pre-processing.

Section 5 summarizes experimental results. Finally, the paper is concluded in Sect. 6.

2 Literature Survey

2.1 Whitelist-Based Techniques

In whitelist-based URL, similarity checks are used to identify Phishing sites from legitimate ones. To prevent Domain Name System (DNS) pharming attacks-a technique is employed to compare the query with the DNS [7]. Cao et al. [2] suggested an automatic whitelist method, in which system recalls a user's prior login and notifies them of unauthorized access. The number of reliable websites that can be viewed online is constrained, despite the fact that whitelist-based Phishing identification techniques appear to be sufficient. To build a reliable device with great accuracy, a full inventory of reliable websites is required; else, false-positive rates increase as a result of a lack of knowledge about websites that are white-listed, which is practically difficult to gather for all permitted websites internationally.

2.2 Blacklist-Based Techniques

To address the common issues connected with maintaining a current list, a blacklist generation technique published [10]. However, it uses other websites (like Google) to compare top results for domain name searches. Additionally, blacklist strategies experience a serious problem of zero-hour Phishing efforts as newly made Phishing sites are not included in the list.

2.3 Content-Based Techniques

A. K. Jain et al. [5] proposed an approach in which they used a searching mechanism that compared the website's domain name under study with the websites that showed up as an output of our search query. They included characteristics in the search query, such as the site name and keywords made up of the data's header, metadata, and body text. First, they applied conventional TF-IDF and then a weighted heuristic method to identify the website as Phishing and legitimate. The outcomes demonstrate that weighted TF-IDF beats conventional TF-IDF.

U Ozker and O. K. Sahingoz [9] proposed a Phishing website detection technique using the website content. Authours tested eight ML algorithms such as Naïve Bayes (NB), Random Forest (RF), Support Vector Machine (SVM), Logistic Regression (LR), K Nearest Neighbors (KNN), Decision Tree (DT), Multilayer Perceptron (MLP), and XGBoost. Results showed that the authors proposed approaches provide better detection accuracy.

A technique with two phases - a prefiltering phase and a classification phase-was suggested [3]. First, online sites whose URLs and contents don't match are screened. The remaining websites are then classified by various metrics, including mental similarity and heuristic ratings derived from the URL. The experiment's findings show that the precision is 98%.

M. Moghimi, and A. Y. Varjani [8] suggested work consists of two feature sets with four characteristics. The first feature set evaluates the web page's resource identification, and the components of the web page's components' access protocols are identified by the second feature set. Search engines, blacklists, and whitelists, among other third-party services, are kept separate from these features. These two feature groups will be taken from the page Document Object Model and Online Page Contents. The SVM categorizes websites using the web page feature vector. This work's main objective is to create innovative characteristics that improve the efficacy of Phishing detection techniques. The trial shows that 99.14% of the suggested model is accurate.

2.4 URL-Based Techniques

A novel lightweight Phishing website detection technique presented by Zouina and Outtaj [15] is based on URL features such as the URL's length, the number of dots and hyphens, the number of numerical characters, a variable indicating whether an IP address is contained in the URL, and the similarity score. The technique produces a recognition rate of 95.80%.

S. C. Jeeva and E. B. Rajsingh [6] focused on the best feature selection to differentiate legal websites from Phishing websites. After feature selection, several classification algorithms were applied, and performance was evaluated. They achieved considerable accuracy in detecting Phishing URLs.

Bahnsen et al. [1] used URLs as input for the ML model. They extracted the statistical characteristics of URLs and classified them using Long Short Term Memory (LSTM). The obtained experimental result shows that LSTM is better than RF and achieved 98.7% accuracy.

Phishing detection using RCNN, a quick technique for detecting Phishing websites that only need the website's address, was suggested by Wang et al. [12]. A DL neural network categorizes the actual URL after the URL's content is encoded into a two-dimensional tensor. They first capture global and local characteristics of the URL using a bidirectional LSTM network then they use CNN.

A two-step technique for multidimensional feature Phishing identification was devised by Yang et al. [13]. LSTM-CNN is used in the first stage to derive character sequence features from the provided URL and classify the data. The second stage involves the creation of multidimensional features from the statistical characteristics of URLs, website content features, and deep learning categorization outcomes.

To acquire the URL vector representations, Yuan et al. [14] created a technique that blends word embedding with the structures of URLs. They divide the URLs into 5 components: URL route, URL path protocol, domain name, domain extension, and sub-domain name. Existing categorization algorithms teach the vector representations of URLs to recognize Phishing URLs.

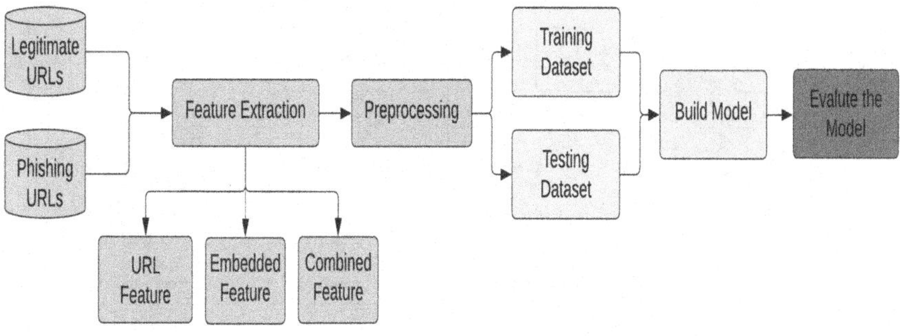

Fig. 1. Generic Steps of Phishing URLs Detection

3 Proposed Work

The technique for identifying Phishing URLs is detailed in this section. The generic steps that are followed in this work are shown in Fig. 1. First, URLs were collected from various sources, such as Kaggle, Phish Storm, and PhishTank, for creating the dataset. From the collected datasets, three different types of features were extracted, i.e., URL-based features, embedded features, and combination of both the features. Extracted features are then preprocessed to create a training dataset and a testing dataset as shown in Fig. 2. After that, the proposed approach was trained and evaluated.

3.1 1D Convolutional Neural Network (1D-CNN)

CNN may be used for one-dimensional data, even though it is most frequently employed with multidimensional data and has been successful in image and video analysis problems. For more information about ID-CNN, refer [11]. The input data's dimensionality and the way the filter traverses the data are the main differences between a 1D, 2D, and 3D CNN. When shorter segments of the entire dataset are expected to yield interesting features and the feature's position within the segment may be more critical, a 1D-CNN is highly successful.

1D-CNN can forecast the items from datasets using vectorised data. To derive more exclusionary feature depictions, the 1D-CNN could be used that describe any underlying patterns or correlations within the vector segments defining each element in the dataset. The classifier (such as a fully connected neural network layer) receives these new features and uses them along with the derived features to determine the classification. Convolutional layers can be thought of as feature extractors because they do not require feature ranking or selection.

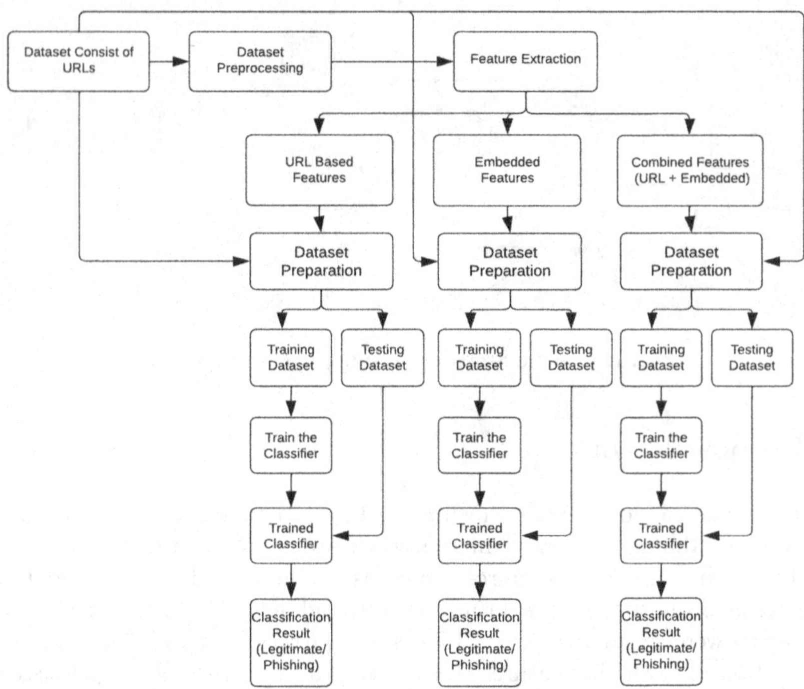

Fig. 2. Block Diagram of the Proposed Approach

3.2 FeedForward-Convolutional Neural Network (FF-CNN)

A DL network called a FF-CNN is used to classify and recognize images. There are several levels in the network, including an input layer, hidden layers, and an output layer. The hidden layers are layers where the network performs the bulk of its computation, using convolutional and non-linear activation layers to extract features from the input and produce a class prediction. The feed-forward aspect of the network refers to the flow of data through the network, which goes from the input layer to the output layer, without looping back. Every layer takes data from layers below it, performs its computation, and passes its result to the next layer. The network's biases and weights are learned during training so that it can map the input picture to the appropriate class.

Object identification, face recognition, and scene labeling are just a few of the computer vision applications that FF-CNNs have proven effective. They have also been used in other fields, including time-series analysis, natural language processing, and voice detection. The ability of FF-CNNs to automatically learn hierarchical representations of the input data, which can capture both local and global features of the image, is one of their key strengths. This allows the network to model complex visual patterns effectively and make accurate class predictions, even with limited training data.

FF-CNN upscales input columns to 144 outputs and restructures the information into a 2D grid for CNN using the Feed Forward Neural Network-1. The result is then reshaped using a reshape filter into a 12 × 12 grid. The input features are then thoroughly mined using a 2-dimensional CNN. Two convolution layers of 3 ×3 × 5 and 3 × 3×10 were used in turn. A 1 × 640 vector was produced from the flattened CNN output feature maps. The Feed Forward Neural Network-2 reduces the CNN output to one output. The output layer of the FF-CNN employs a Sigmoid activation function, while the hidden levels use a ReLU activation function. The architecture of FF-CNN is given in Fig. 3.

4 Dataset and Pre-processing

The datasets were gathered from a variety of sources, including Kaggle, Phish Storm, and PhishTank. Legitimate URLs were obtained from Kaggle and Phish-Strom, while Phishing URLs were acquired from PhishTank. The total number of legitimate URLs in the dataset is 53,723, and there are 64,475 Phishing URLs. To extract features from these URLs, Algorithm 1 was employed, which extracted 124 NLP and statistical features. These features were grouped into several categories, including entire URL features, URL domain features, URL directory features, URL file features, and URL parameter features. Each category contains features such as the number of dots, the number of hyphens, and the number of question marks.

After feature extraction, preprocessing was employed to remove any rows or columns with identical values. This step is described in Algorithm 2. Additionally, character-label embedding was used to extract embedded features from the URLs. This involved in converting the entire URL to a one-hot encoded vector and then using embedding to create 128-dimensional embedded features. Algorithm 3 outlines the embedding steps.

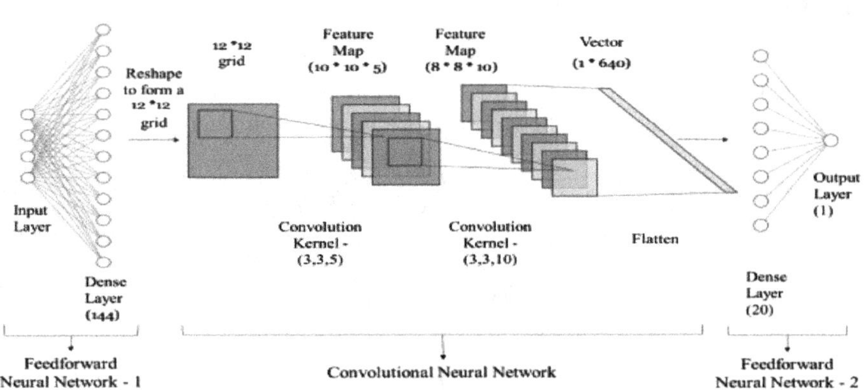

Fig. 3. Architecture of FF-CNN [4]

Algorithm 1. Feature Extraction

Require: List of URLs
Ensure: Dataset.csv

$i \Leftarrow 1$
$totalURLs \Leftarrow length(URLs)$
while $i \leq totalURLs$ **do**
  $url \Leftarrow URLs(i)$
  $f1 \Leftarrow getURLFtr(url)$ ▷ return statistical and NLP features of entire URL
  $f2 \Leftarrow getDomainFtr(url)$ ▷ return statistical and NLP features of Domain of URL
  $f3 \Leftarrow getDirFtr(url)$ ▷ return statistical and NLP features of Directory of URL
  $f4 \Leftarrow getFileFtr(url)$ ▷ return statistical and NLP features of File path of URL
  $f5 \Leftarrow getParamFtr(url)$ ▷ return statistical and NLP features of Parameter of URL
  toCsv(f1, f2, f3, f4, f5) ▷ combined all features and store into CSV file
  $i \Leftarrow i + 1$
end while

Algorithm 2. Pre-Processing

Require: Dataset.csv
Ensure: Processed_Dataset.csv

$df \Leftarrow read(dataset.csv)$
$df \Leftarrow deleteRow(df)$ ▷ delete row if entire row have same value
$df \Leftarrow deleteCol(df)$ ▷ delete col if entire col have same value
toCsv(df) ▷ store df to CSV file

5 Experimentation and Results

5.1 Performance Measures

To evaluate the proposed approach, widely used performance measures like Accuracy (Acc), Precision (Pre), Recall (Rec), and F1-score (F) were used. These metrics were calculated as follows (for more information refer [1]):

$$Acc = \frac{TP + TN}{TP + TN + FP + FN} \tag{1}$$

$$Pre = \frac{TP}{TP + FP} \tag{2}$$

$$Rec = \frac{TP}{TP + FN} \tag{3}$$

$$F = 2 \times \frac{Rec \times Pre}{Rec + Pre} \tag{4}$$

Algorithm 3. Embedding

Require: List of URLs
Ensure: Embedded_Dataset.csv

```
i ⇐ 1
totalURLs ⇐ length(URLs)
while i ≤ totalURLs do
    url ⇐ URLs(i)
    v ⇐ char_to_vector(url)                 ▷ converst URL to vector
    v_list.append(v)                        ▷ append vector v to list
    i ⇐ i + 1
end while
e ⇐ embedding(v_list)                       ▷ list of vector to be embedded
toCsv(e)                                    ▷ store embedded features to CSV file
```

5.2 Experiment 1: Comparison of Performance of Proposed 1D-CNN-based Approach on Different Datasets

In this experiment, three different datasets were used for model training. Manually extracted features (URL features), embedding features, and a combination of both were used for model training. 20% of the data was utilized for testing, while the remaining 80% was used for training.

In this experiment, 1D-CNN functionality was assessed after it was trained. Three different dataset types were used: manually derived features from URLs, embedding features, and a combination of both. 20% of the data was used for testing, while the remaining 80% was used for training. Table 1 shows the experimental results of the proposed 1D-CNN-based approach in terms of precision, recall, and F1-score. Figure 4 presents the accuracy of the classifier on three different datasets. Experimental results indicates that the proposed 1D-CNN-based approach trained on the combined features achieved the highest accuracy, outperforming the models trained on URL features and embedding features. This suggests that combining manually extracted features and embedding features can improve the 1D-CNN-based approach performance.

Table 1. Experimental results of 1D-CNN on different datasets

Dataset	Precision	Recall	F1-score
URLs features	0.9883	0.9882	0.9882
Embedded	0.9808	0.9806	0.9807
Combined	**0.9891**	**0.989**	**0.989**

5.3 Experiment 2: Comparison of the Performance of Proposed 1D-CNN-based Approach with PCA and Without PCA

In this experiment, we investigated the impact of Principal Component Analysis (PCA) dimensionality reduction on the dataset that we used in this experimental work. We compared the performance of the ID-CNN with and without PCA on different datasets, including manually extracted features, embedding features, and a combination of both. The testing results are presented in Table 2, and the accuracy is visualized in Fig. 5. Experimental results show that the use of PCA led to an increase in accuracy on the manually extracted feature dataset. However, a small drop in accuracy was observed on the embedded features and combined feature datasets when PCA was applied. This suggests that the effectiveness of PCA may depend on the nature of the dataset and the features used. In summary, our findings indicate that PCA can be a valuable technique for improving the 1D-CNN-based approach performance on certain types of datasets.

5.4 Experiment 3: Comparison of Performance of the proposed FF-CNN-based Approach on Different Datasets

In this experiment, we assessed how well a FF-CNN performed after being trained on three different datasets: manually extracted features (URL features), embedding features, and a mixture of both. For training, we used 80% of the data, and for testing, 20%. The precision, recall, and F1-score outcomes of the FF-CNN are shown in Table 4. Figure 6 displays the model's accuracy for the different datasets. Our findings show that the FF-CNN trained on manually extracted features outperformed models trained on embedding features and combined features in terms of accuracy. This implies that the manually derived URL features include valuable data for forecasting the target variable. In summary, the experimental results obtained demonstrate that FF-CNN is a good model for predicting the target variable on various dataset types, with manually derived features proving to be especially helpful. Exploring the potential of FF-CNN

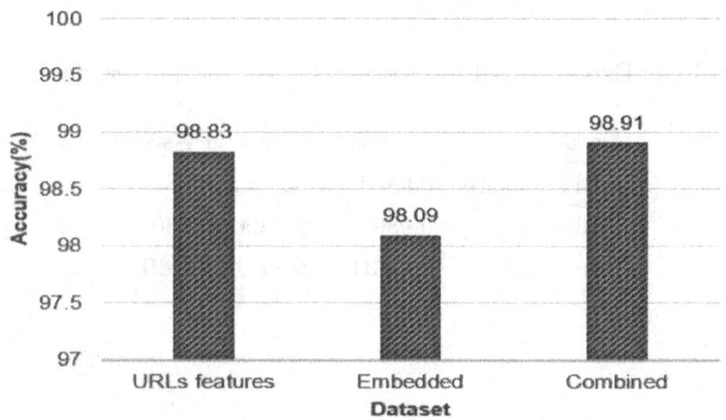

Fig. 4. Accuracy of 1D-CNN on different dataset

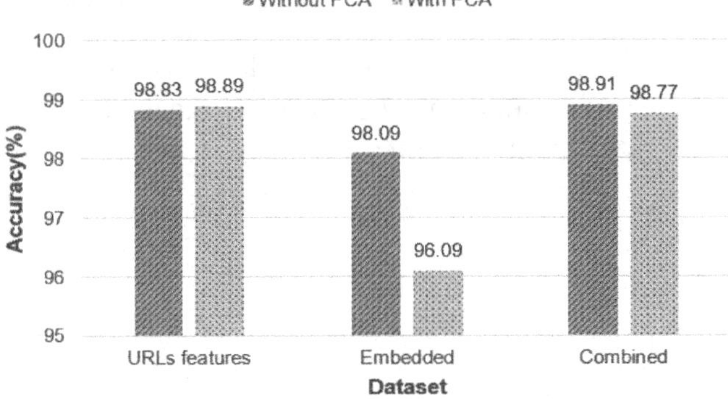

Fig. 5. Accuracy of 1D-CNN with PCA and without PCA

Table 2. Experimental results of 1D-CNN with PCA and without PCA

Dataset		Precision	Recall	F1-score
URLs features	Without PCA	0.9883	0.9882	0.9882
	With PCA	0.9889	0.9887	0.9888
Embedded	Without PCA	0.9808	0.9806	0.9807
	With PCA	0.9638	0.9609	0.9622
Combined	Without PCA	0.9891	0.989	0.989
	With PCA	0.9875	0.9877	0.9876

Table 3. Experimental result of 1D-CNN and FF-CNN

Dataset	Model	Precision	Recall	F1-score
URLs features	1D-CNN	0.9883	0.9882	0.9882
	FF-CNN	0.9902	0.9892	0.9206
Embedded	1D-CNN	0.9808	0.9806	0.9807
	FF-CNN	0.9763	0.9715	0.7365
Combined	1D-CNN	0.9891	0.989	0.989
	FF-CNN	0.9873	0.9903	0.7073

in combination with several types of features and datasets will require more research.

5.5 Experiment 4: Comparison of Performance of the Proposed 1D-CNN-based Approach and FF-CNN-based Approach

In this experiment, the performance of Proposed 1D-CNN-based and FF-CNN-based approach was compared on three different datasets: manually extracted features (URL features), embedding features, and a combination of both, as

Table 4. Experimental results of FF-CNN on different datasets

Dataset	Precision	Recall	F1-score
URLs features	**0.9902**	0.9892	**0.9206**
Embedded	0.9763	0.9715	0.7365
Combined	0.9873	**0.9903**	0.7073

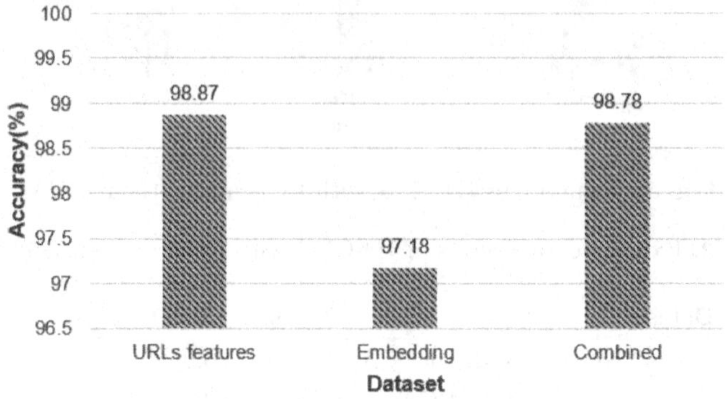

Fig. 6. Accuracy of FF-CNN on different dataset

presented in Table 3. The obtained experimental results, displayed in Fig. 7, show that FF-CNN outperformed 1D-CNN in accuracy on the manually extracted feature dataset. However, 1D-CNN achieved higher accuracy than FF-CNN on the embedding features and the combined feature datasets. The choice of the model architecture should depend on the nature of the dataset and the features used. While FF-CNN may perform better on datasets with manually extracted features, 1D-CNN may be more effective on datasets with embedded features or a combination of both. Overall, the experimental results obtained demonstrate

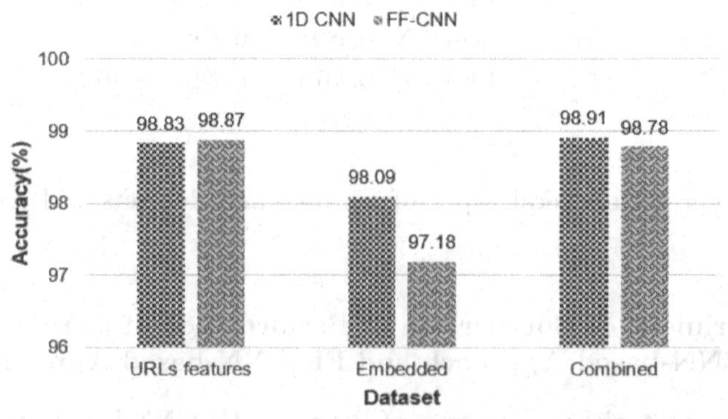

Fig. 7. Accuracy of 1D-CNN and FF-CNN

that 1D-CNN and FF-CNN are effective for predicting the target variable on different datasets. Further investigation is needed to identify the optimal model architecture for specific datasets and features.

5.6 Comparison Proposed 1D-CNN-based Approach and FF-CNN-based Approach with Other ML Models

Table 5. Comparison of proposed model with other ML models

Dataset	Model	Accuracy(%)	Precision	Recall	F1-score
URLfeatures	Naïve Bayes	96.03	0.9631	0.9577	0.9598
	SVM	98.31	0.9836	0.9825	0.983
	1D-CNN	98.83	0.9883	0.9882	0.9882
	FF-CNN	98.87	0.9902	0.9892	0.9206
Embedded	Naïve Bayes	86.61	0.877	0.8749	0.8661
	SVM	92.84	0.9343	0.9236	0.927
	1D-CNN	98.09	0.9808	0.9806	0.9807
	FF-CNN	97.18	0.9763	0.9715	0.7365
Combined	Naïve Bayes	95.82	0.9579	0.9579	0.9579
	SVM	98.37	0.9841	0.983	0.9835
	1D-CNN	98.91	0.9891	0.989	0.989
	FF-CNN	98.78	0.9873	0.9903	0.7073

In Table 5, we present the comparative performance of 1D-CNN and FF-CNN with other popular machine learning classifiers, including Naïve Bayes and SVM. Table shows that our DL models outperformed the traditional ML classifiers on all the datasets. In particular, FF-CNN achieved the highest accuracy, precision, and recall on the URL features dataset, followed by 1D-CNN, SVM, and Naïve Bayes, while 1D-CNN achieved the highest F1-score, followed by SVM, Naïve Bayes, and FF-CNN. On the embedded features dataset, 1D-CNN outperformed other classifiers with the highest accuracy, precision, recall, and F1-score. On the combined features dataset, 1D-CNN achieved the highest accuracy, precision, and F1-score, while FF-CNN had the highest recall. These results demonstrate the effectiveness of our proposed deep learning models in detecting Phishing websites and their superiority over traditional machine learning classifiers in terms of accuracy, precision, recall, and F1-score.

6 Conclusion

This study demonstrates how DL models can be used to detect Phishing URLs, offering a promising solution to this problem. This work proposes a Phishing website detection approach using 1D-CNN and FF-CNN, which were trained and evaluated with three datasets. NLP and statistics were used to create the datasets, as well as embedding or a combination of both. The experimental results revealed that both achieved high accuracy rates on all three datasets. Moreover, the use of PCA dimensionality reduction led to improved accuracy for the URL-based feature dataset while decreasing accuracy for the other two datasets. Despite this, the suggested approach attained a higher accuracy of 98.91% on the combined feature dataset. The results of the experiment indicate that the proposed method can accurately identify Phishing websites based on URL features, reducing the dangers of Phishing attacks. In order to increase the models' detection ability, future studies may look into the usage of more intricate features or various DL models. This study provides valuable insights into using DL to detect Phishing websites and emphasizes the need for cybersecurity investment to safeguard individuals and businesses against cyber threats.

References

1. Bahnsen, A.C., Bohorquez, E.C., Villegas, S., Vargas, J., González, F.A.: Classifying phishing URLs using recurrent neural networks. In: 2017 APWG Symposium on Electronic Crime Research (eCrime), pp. 1–8 (2017). https://doi.org/10.1109/ECRIME.2017.7945048
2. Cao, Y., Han, W., Le, Y.: Anti-phishing based on automated individual white-list, pp. 51–60 (10 2008). https://doi.org/10.1145/1456424.1456434
3. Chen, Y.S., Yu, Y.H., Liu, H.S., Wang, P.C.: Detect phishing by checking content consistency. In: Proceedings of the 2014 IEEE 15th International Conference on Information Reuse and Integration (IEEE IRI 2014). pp. 109–119 (2014). https://doi.org/10.1109/IRI.2014.7051880
4. Ilango, H.S., Ma, M., Su, R.: A feedforward-convolutional neural network to detect low-rate dos in IoT. Eng. Appl. Artif. Intell. **114**, 105059 (2022). https://doi.org/10.1016/j.engappai.2022.105059
5. Jain, A.K., Parashar, S., Katare, P., Sharma, I.: Phishskape: A content based approach to escape phishing attacks. Proc. Comput. Sci. **171**, 1102–1109 (2020). https://doi.org/10.1016/j.procs.2020.04.118, third International Conference on Computing and Network Communications (CoCoNet'19)
6. Jeeva, S.C., Rajsingh, E.B.: Phishing URL detection-based feature selection to classifiers. Int. J. Electron. Secur. Digit. Forensics **9**(2), 116–131 (2017)
7. Kang, J., Lee, D.: Advanced white list approach for preventing access to phishing sites. In: International Conference on Convergence Information Technology (ICCIT 2007), pp. 491–496 (2007). https://doi.org/10.1109/ICCIT.2007.50
8. Moghimi, M., Varjani, A.Y.: New rule-based phishing detection method. Expert Syst. Appl. **53**, 231–242 (2016). https://doi.org/10.1016/j.eswa.2016.01.028
9. Ozker, U., Sahingoz, O.K.: Content based phishing detection with machine learning. In: 2020 International Conference on Electrical Engineering (ICEE), pp. 1–6 (2020). https://doi.org/10.1109/ICEE49691.2020.9249892
10. Sharifi, M., Siadati, H.: A phishing sites blacklist generator, pp. 840 – 843 (03 2008). https://doi.org/10.1109/AICCSA.2008.4493625
11. Shenfield, A., Howarth, M.: A novel deep learning model for the detection and identification of rolling element-bearing faults. Sensors (Basel, Switzerland) **20** (09 2020). https://doi.org/10.3390/s20185112

12. Wang, W., Zhang, F., Luo, X., Zhang, S.: PDRCNN: Precise phishing detection with recurrent convolutional neural networks. Security Commun. Netw. **2019**, 1–15 (10 2019). https://doi.org/10.1155/2019/2595794
13. Yang, P., Zhao, G., Zeng, P.: Phishing website detection based on multidimensional features driven by deep learning. IEEE Access **PP**, 1–1 (01 2019). https://doi.org/10.1109/ACCESS.2019.2892066
14. Yuan, H., Yang, Z., Chen, X., Li, Y., Liu, W.: URL2Vec: URL modeling with character embeddings for fast and accurate phishing website detection. In: 2018 IEEE International Conference on Parallel & Distributed Processing with Applications, Ubiquitous Computing & Communications, Big Data & Cloud Computing, Social Computing & Networking, Sustainable Computing & Communications (ISPA/IUCC/BDCloud/SocialCom/SustainCom), pp. 265–272 (2018). https://doi.org/10.1109/BDCloud.2018.00050
15. Zouina, M., Outtaj, B.: A novel lightweight URL phishing detection system using SVM and similarity index. Human-Centric Comput. Inform. Sci. **7**(1), 1–13 (2017). https://doi.org/10.1186/s13673-017-0098-1

Diabetes Prediction Using Machine Learning Classifiers

Dharna Choudhary, Pradeep Gupta, and Sonam Gupta(✉)

Ajay Kumar Garg Engineering College Ghaziabad, Ghaziabad, India
Guptasonam6@gmail.com

Abstract. Diabetes Mellitus is an endocrine disorder that arises when your blood glucose or blood sugar is too high. Your body either does not create enough insulin or does not use the insulin that it does produces adequately. Insulin is a hormonal substance that regulates glucose levels in blood. Hyperglycaemia refers to high blood sugar levels, commonly known as blood glucose. It can lead to serious health consequences in diabetics over time. This condition can lead to substantial and progressive harm across various bodily systems, with a notable impact on neurons and blood vessels. Diabetes affects 537 million people worldwide, making it the deadliest and most frequent non-communicable disease. Diabetes takes the lives of approximately 2–5 million people each year. In the year 2014, diabetes affected 8.5% of individuals aged 18 and older. In 2019, diabetes directly led to 1.5 million deaths with almost half of these occurring before the age of 65. Additionally, diabetes led to 560 000 deaths linked to chronic kidney disease and elevated blood glucose was a factor in around 20% of cardiovascular-related deaths. Diabetes increased age-specific death rates by 5% between 1999 and 2020. Diabetes related fatalities rose by 14% in low-and middle-income nations. The death rate due to diabetes is said to be increased to 629 million by 2045.

Keywords: Diabetes · Healthcare · Accuracy · Machine Learning

1 Introduction

The condition known as Diabetes mellitus is an endocrine illness related with carbohydrates that is defined by a decrease in the body's ability to generate or react to the hormone insulin. Diabetes is a dominant source of sickness and fatalities, ignoring the fact that these end results are brought on by the disorder's immediate effect. Diabetes, if untreated, leads to a wide range of health problems. Diabetes is generally of three types: Type1, Type2 and Gestational. Type1 diabetes develops when a person's body cannot produce enough insulin. Type2 diabetes affects around 90% of the patients and is caused by the person's body inability to make or utilize insulin properly. Gestational diabetes generally fades up soon after birth[1]. Diabetes kills around 1.5 million people each year if it is not treated or controlled properly. Diabetes has no cure, but it may be controlled by healthy diet and regular exercise. If physical activity and diet are insufficient, insulin therapy is required. Diabetes is characterized

N. Chauhan et al. (Eds.): MIND 2023, CCIS 2128, pp. 140–148, 2024.
https://doi.org/10.1007/978-3-031-62217-5_12

by excessive urination, dehydration, and starvation. Diabetes identification at early stage is a critical medical problem [2]. The majority of diabetes cases have no widely accepted cure. Insulin replacement therapy (insulin injections) is the most regularly utilized T1 Diabetes. Anti-diabetic medicines such as Metformin and Acarbose, as well as, lifestyle adjustments can help prevent or treat T2 Diabetes. Periodic examinations and blood testing with a physician are the most effective way to detect diabetes early. T2D diabetes symptoms might be minor. It could take years for them to be revealed. The signs are typically milder than in type 1diabetes. Consequently, the illness may not be identified until years later, once complications have arisen. Type 2 diabetes was formerly only found in adults, but it is gradually becoming more common in children. Impaired glucose tolerance (IGT) and Impaired fasting glycerin (IFG) are conditions that fall between normal and diabetic. Current medical research and experts agree that the chances of healing are better if the condition is detected early. With technological advancements, ML algorithms are effective for early illness identification and disease illness [3]. Various machine learning algorithms deliver efficient results for knowledge collection by creating multiple classification and ensemble models from obtained datasets. Various machine learning techniques are capable for diabetes prediction; nevertheless, choosing the optimum technology is difficult. Patients with IGT or IFG should be a key target population for diabetes prevention because of their elevated risk of developing the diabetes. The WHO'S seeks to encourage and promote the enforcement of effective diabetes tracking, prevention, and control measures particularly in nations with poor and middle-incomes. World Diabetes Day (WDD) is an important healthcare event held on November 14th each year to highlight the rising prevalence of diabetes and its consequences, as well as to educate people about diabetes prevention. After reviewing other research articles, the author came across some of the research questions stated below:

RQ1: Which Machine learning model outperforms all other algorithms?

RQ2: Why Machine learning is better than deep learning method?

The main body of this paper is structured as follows: A literature review is included in Sect. 2. Section 3 described the dataset that would be used on ML and DL algorithms. Section 4 discusses the results. Finally the final section briefly summarizes potential research directions.

2 Literature Review

The author of this study [1] suggested web-based personalized diabetes monitoring system and an analytical prediction model based on ML techniques to forecast type 2 diabetes. By collecting a patient's data and preparing it for further analysis using machine learning models, The crucial information of the users is continually monitored. This system is intended to address several issues in diabetic health care. Big Data and IOT predictive strategies for diabetes data analysis have been proposed. Using the most crucial features, many prediction models are explored for the prediction of diabetes such as Logistic Regression, K-Nearest Neighbor, Naïve-Bayes, Support Vector Classifier, Random Forest, Decision Tree Classifier, Gradient Boosting, Multi Layer Perceptron and Artificial Neural Network.7691 occurrences in an SD dataset were used to evaluate the effectiveness of categorization methods. According to the proposed model the results showed that DT and GB outperforms other algorithms with accuracy of 87.36% and 87.49% respectively.

The prediction model in this study [2] was created using the R programming language, according to the author's post. In this paper, a platform for data analytics is used to help clinicians and researchers identify links between a patient's physiological symptoms and diabetes related issue. In addition to multi-tiered classification of T2D associated complication risk prediction, to a specific course of medications, the analytics suite also offers preliminary, forecasting, and visual data analysis. The insights provided in this research look into complex data analysis techniques, that could be used as decision-making aids by doctors to improve T2D management. Visual analytics simplifies the outcome for physicians as well as patients. The information provided has the ability to help physicians in developing strategies for treatment of T2D patients. The information provided has the ability to help doctors in making treatment strategies for diabetes patients. This provides a significant benefit that was previously unavailable for a more individualized strategy to cure diabetes that will be more secure and favorable for the patient because it will avoid unwanted adverse complications and provide quicker, better therapy. It will also benefit the healthcare system financially.

According to the author in this paper [3], the study should also look at the enhancement in performance over previous studies in terms of reliability, specificity, sensitivity, and Area Under Curve scores. With a 95.94% accuracy rate in determining whether an individual would acquire T2DM in 7–8 years, the suggested ML technique is the first time in the field. While developing and testing the suggested framework, a number of challenges were found. There is no other openly accessible OGTT dataset that can be used to evaluate the utility of our generated features for T2DM prediction. The model scored 82.02% precision,79.8% sensitivity, 82.46% specificity, and an AUC score of 86.7% for the top five characteristics. The top-30 traits performed best, with an accuracy of 95.94%, a sensitivity of 100%, a specificity of 91.5%, and an AUC score of 96.3%. When assessing the model with all characteristics, the accuracy reduced to 84.46%. Although machine learning algorithms have been used to diagnose illnesses, there has been a minimal study on age long disease forecasting, notably type 2 diabetes. In addition, identifying distinguishing traits or indicators of risk for the emergence of diabetes in future is crucial. In this research, we present two unique methods for extracting features for identifying the optimal risk variables, which is followed by the application of a pipeline for machine learning pipeline for long-term diabetes type 2 forecasting.

Based on the following considerations, in this study [4], a research was undertaken using Machine Learning (ML) methods to investigate the influence of dietary components on Blood Glucose Levels (BGLs) forecasting in the short and intermediate term. In Type 1 Diabetes patients on AP systems, an ML model capable of predicting BGLs after 10, 20, 40, and 60 min following the meal based on the insulin dosages, BGs, and dietary parameters was adopted. To study the influence of nutritional variables on model predictions, a FFNN was introduced with various BGL, insulin, and nutritional factor dispositions. The concept was validated using both open and self-produced data. In this paper, an ML-based system for post-meal blood sugar prediction at different PHs in Type 1 Diabetes patients is proposed using FFNN.

This study [5] proposes a unique data mining/deep learning architecture to improve established risk assessment approaches of mortality in the hospital of diabetic ICU patients by adding patient care flows from earlier admissions to hospitals. In addition, the paper describes how to convert electronic medical histories to a care flow format suited for process analysis, as well as how this data may be utilised to forecast patient outcomes. This work provides two contributions. First, a process mining/deep learning architecture for transforming care flows encoded in EHRs into log files suited for process mining is suggested. Second, by improving traditional risk score approaches, the proposed architecture has been proven to successfully enhance mortality prediction in the hospital of diabetic ICU patients by upgrading conventional risk score methodologies. The paper underlines the need of simulating prior patient care flows for predicting outcomes and process mining as a viable set of tools for future studies. Diabetes patients having at least three hospital visits, one of which included an ICU stay, are eligible for review. Furthermore, previous to the most recent hospitalization, all patients were found to have a blood glucose level(HbA1c) value above or equivalent to 6.5%. One of the first data mining-based techniques for modeling past healthcare data of hyperglycemia ICU patients in tandem with severity levels to forecast fatality while hospitalized was presented in this work. In this approach, established procedures are paired with the benefits of adding historical data, resulting in a more comprehensive assessment of the patients' illnesses.

The author of this research report [6], proposed a decision level fusion based machine learning based diabetes assistance model. The SVM and ANN models comprise the actual framework. These algorithms examine the dataset to forecast if a diabetes result is positive or negative. This study's dataset is split 70:30 between training and testing data. For future use the fused models are saved in the cloud. The suggested fuzzy decision system has a higher prediction accuracy of 94.87 than the other existing systems. Furthermore, diabetes death rates can be diminished if the disease is detected soon and preventative interventions are implemented. We used a dataset with 520 instances and 17 characteristics based on diabetes symptoms to put the proposed framework into action.

The author of this research report [6], proposed a decision level fusion based machine learning based diabetes assistance model. The SVM and ANN models comprise the actual framework. These algorithms examine the dataset to forecast if a diabetes result is positive or negative. This study's dataset is split 70:30 between training and testing data. For future use the fused models are saved in the cloud. The suggested fuzzy decision system has a higher prediction accuracy of 94.87 than the other existing systems. Furthermore, diabetes death rates can be diminished if the disease is detected soon and preventative interventions are implemented. We used a dataset with 520 instances and 17 characteristics based on diabetes symptoms to put the proposed framework into action.

The author of this study [7], proposed in this post that the purpose of this effort is to develop a model that is efficient in properly forecasting the likelihood of developing diabetes in individuals. To diagnose diabetes in early stage, three M.L classification algorithms namely Decision Tree, Supervised Machine Learning, and Naïve Bayes, are used in this model. Experiments are carried out using the Pima Indians Diabetes Database (PIDD), which is obtained from the UCI machine learning repository. Multiple indicators including Precision, accuracy, F-measure and recall are used to assess the performance of the three approaches. The number of cases appropriately and wrongly classified determines accuracy. The results shows that NB outperform other algorithms with the maximum precision of 76.3%. We might infer that the Naive Bayes classification method outperforms other algorithms in comparison.

In this study [8], the author proposed a model that can predict the likelihood that an individual has diabetes. Various measures are used to compare three ML algorithms: Logistic Regression, Naïve Bayes and K-Nearest Neighbour. Experiments are being conducted on the Pima Indian Diabetes (PIDD) dataset We attained 94%, 79%, and 69% accuracy using the Logistic Regression (LR), Naive Bayes (NB), and K-nearest Neighbor (KNN) methods, respectively. In comparison to other algorithms, the results demonstrate that LR is more effective at predicting diabetes. The results showed that LR was more effective than other classifiers in predicting diabetes since it has a greater precision of 94%.

In this study [9], in this post the author proposed that Six machine learning algorithms were utilized in this experimental investigation. The algorithms are NB,RF,SVM,LR,DT and KNN. On the PIMA Indian dataset, all of these algorithms are applied. The results were acquired after testing all six algorithms on the same dataset with Enthought Canaopy. The prediction accuracy was the primary evaluation parameter. The accuracy of the algorithm is its total success rate. SVM, KNN, LR, DT, RF, and NB are among the methods used. Diabetes predictions were developed using a 768-record PIMA Indian dataset. The prediction model was trained and tested using 8 characteristics. In accordance with the trial data, SVM and KNN have the best diabetes prediction accuracy for predicting diabetes. Both of these methods yield 77% accuracy, which is the highest of the four algorithms examined in this article. However, it can be inferred that SVM and KNN are appropriate for forecasting diabetic illness.

In this study [10], the author of this work suggested using categorization methods including DT, ANN, NB and SVM algorithms while creating models. For Decision Tree, Naïve Bayes, and Support Vector Machine, respectively, the models have precisions of 85%, 77% and 77.3%. Text images and tree data are examples of unstructured and semi-structured data that the SVM approach does well with. The SVM method drawback is that a lot of important key features need to be precisely incubated in order to generate the most effective classification results for each specific circumstance. The decision tree: It is easily understandable and easy to use. Instability resides in the decision tree, huge changes can be observed by making minor changes to the data structure of the optimal decision tree. They are usually incorrect ANN: Provides accurate results and is simple to deploy. Dealing with massive data with a complicated model is difficult. Time-consuming to process. The Accuracies of different algorithms are: Decision tree, Accuracy is 74% for class 0 and for class 1 is 49%, Support Vector Classifier, Accuracy is 82% for class 0 and for class 1 is 0%, Gaussian Naïve Bayes, Accuracy is 80% for class 0 and for class 1 is 58%, Artificial Neural Network, Accuracy is 82% for class 0 and for class 1 is 0% (Table 1).

Table 1. Shows the comparison table of different models and approaches used by different researchers

S. No.	Author	Algorithm Used or Model	Result			
			Accuracy	Sensitivity	Specificity	AUC
1	RADWA MARZOUK [4]	Logistic Regression, Naïve Bayes, Random Forest, KNN, Decision Tree, SVM, GB, MLP, ANN	DTC and GB predict high accuracy. DTC = 87.47% GB = 87.49%	–	–	–
2	MD. Shafiqul Islam [6]	Ensemble Learning, Polynomial SVM	95.94%	100%	91.5%	96.3%
3	Usama Ahmed [9]	Fused Machine Learning	94.87%	–	–	–
4	Deepti Sisodia[10]	Decision Tree, SVM, Naïve Bayes	NB = 76.30%	–	–	–
5	Fayroza Alaa Khaleel[11]	Logistic Regression, Naïve Bayes, KNN	LR = 94%	–	–	–
6	Muhammad Azeem Sarwar[12]	SVM,KNN, LR, DT, RF, NB	SVM and KNN = 77%	–	–	–
7	Priyanka Sonar[13]	Decision Tree, SVM, NB, ANN	NB = 85%	–	–	–

3 Dataset

Various datasets have been used to analyze the system model proposed by different researchers. The dataset's goal is to use specific diagnostics metrics included in the information to diagnostically forecast whether or not a patient has diabetes. Data is preprocessed from many platforms to remove unnecessary data and information. Preprocessed data is utilized in feature extraction. For extracting features from preprocessed data, feature extraction methods are utilized. Researchers gather data from various platforms and evaluate it to make predictions. Table 2 provides a list of the datasets examined in the study (Table 2).

Table 2. Datasets used by different researchers to analyze the model

S. No	Links	DataSet
4,5,6	diabetes/https://www.andreagrandi.it/2018/04/14/ machine-learning-pima-indians-diabetes	PIMA diabetes
3	https://www.kaggle.com/johndasilva/diabetes	Diabetes
7,2,1	https://archive.ics.uci.edu/dataset/529/ early+stage+diabetes+risk+prediction+dataset	UCI Machine Learning Repository

4 Results and Discussions

Diabetes prediction typically involves using machine learning algorithms to analyze various health-related data of an individual and anticipate the likelihood of them evolving diabetes in the future. The process usually includes the following steps: Data Collection: Gather relevant data about the individual, including personal information (age, gender, family history), lifestyle factors (diet, exercise, smoking habits), and medical history (blood pressure, cholesterol levels, previous medical conditions). Data Preprocessing: Clean and prepare the data for analysis, analyzing missing information, dealing with anomalies, and reshaping the data into an applicable format for the use of ML algorithms. Feature Selection: Choose the feature variables that are most likely to affect diabetes prediction from the available features. The process aids in simplifying the model and enhancing its correctness. Model Selection: Choose an appropriate ML algorithm (e.g., LR, SVM, DT, and neural networks) for diabetes prediction based on the category of data and the description of the problem. Model Training: Use the accumulated and pre-treated data to train the selected machine learning model. The system discovers relationships and trends in the data during training that can be utilized to generate suggestions. Model Evaluation: Use evaluation metrics like precision, accuracy, recall and F1 score to gauge how well the trained model is doing. This step helps determine how well the model can predict diabetes based on the given data. Diabetes Prediction: Apply the trained model to new, unseen data to predict the probability of diabetes in an individual. It's important to remember that the accuracy of the prediction model is determined by the standard and amount of data available for training, the features picked, and the machine learning method used. These algorithm are used in diabetes prediction LR, DT, RF, SVM, Neural Networks, NB, GBM, LightGBM, Logistic Model Tree, Gaussian Processes.

RQ1. Which Model performs best from all other algorithm?

Ans. Ensemble model is best model from all other model whose accuracy is 95.94% since two unique methods for extracting features for identifying the optimal risk variables, which is followed by the application of a pipeline for machine learning pipeline for long term diabetes type 2 forecasting (Fig. 1).

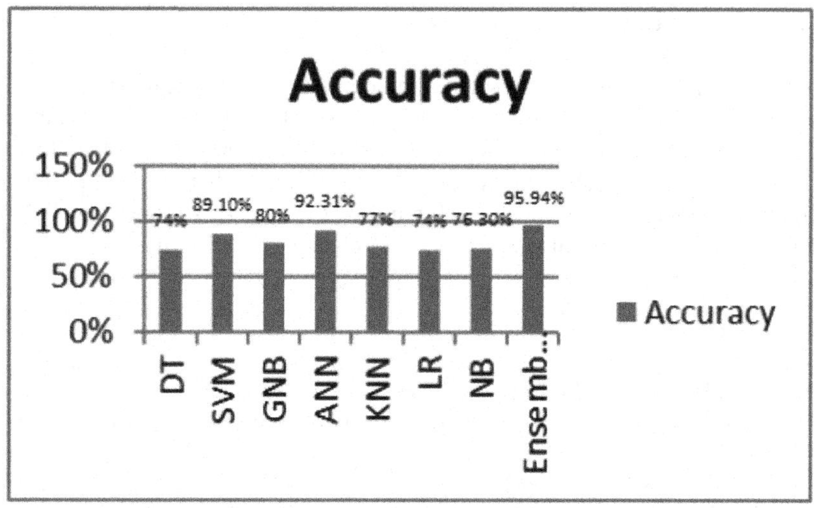

Fig. 1. Shows the performance of various ML algorithms on Diabetes Prediction

RQ2: Why is Machine Learning preferred over Deep Learning Methods in Diabetes Prediction?

Ans. The Machine learning algorithms are considered to analyze data more accurately and solve problems or tasks automatically than Deep Learning models since deep learning models work well on image datasets so, image must be better. Machine learning with its advanced prediction and categorization models, plays a critical role in achieving early predictions.

5 Conclusion

Diabetes prediction using machine learning provides great promise in assisting healthcare providers and individuals in proactive disease management and prevention. It can assist in recognizing people at higher chance of developing diabetes, allowing early arbitration and lifestyle modifications that may help improve overall health outcomes. However, it is essential to remember that machine learning models are not a replacement for medical cure and expert advice. They should be seen as a supportive tool to complement the expertise of healthcare professionals in making informed decisions and providing personalized care. Diabetes prediction is a crucial area of research and application in the healthcare domain. Machine learning algorithms have demonstrated encouraging results in predicting the possibility of individual developing diabetes based on various risk factors and health-related data.

6 Future Work

Diabetes prediction should focus on advancing the state-of-the-art by incorporating new data sources, improving model interpretability and uncertainty estimation, and striving for personalized and dynamic risk profiling. Ultimately, the goal is to develop accurate, transparent, and ethical predictive models that can assist healthcare professionals in better understanding and managing diabetes, leading to improved patient outcomes and better population health.

References

1. Marzouk, R., Alluhaidan, A.S., El_Rahman, S.A.: An analytical predictive models and secure web-based personalized diabetes monitoring system. IEEE Access **10**, 105657–105673 (2022)
2. Philip, N.Y., Razaak, M., Chang, J., O'Kane, M., Pierscionek, B.K., et al.: A data analytics suite for exploratory predictive, and visual analysis of type 2 diabetes. IEEE Access **10**, 13460–13471 (2022)
3. Islam, M.S., Qaraqe, M.K., Belhaouari, S.B., Abdul-Ghani, M.A.: Advanced techniques for predicting the future progression of type 2 diabetes. IEEE access **8**, 120537–120547 (2020)
4. Annuzzi, G., et al.: Impact of nutritional factors in blood glucose prediction in type 1 diabetes through machine learning. IEEE Access **11**, 17104–17115 (2023)
5. Theis, J., Galanter, W.L., Boyd, A.D., Darabi, H.: Improving the in-hospital mortality prediction of diabetes ICU patients using a process mining/deep learning architecture. IEEE J. Biomed. Health Inform. **26**(1), 388–399 (2021)
6. Ahmed, U., et al.: Prediction of diabetes empowered with fused machine learning. IEEE Access **10**, 8529–8538 (2022)
7. Ahmed, U., et al.: Prediction of diabetes empowered with fused machine learning. IEEE Access **10**, 8529–8538 (2022)
8. Khaleel,F.A., Al-Bakry, A.M.: Diagnosis of diabetes using machine learning algorithms. Materials Today: Proc. **80**, 3200–3203 (2023)
9. Sarwar, M.A., Kamal, N., Hamid, W., Shah, M.A.: Prediction of diabetes using machine learning algorithms in healthcare. In: 2018 24th International Conference on Automation and Computing (ICAC), pp. 1–6. IEEE (2018)
10. Sonar, P., Malini, K.J.: Diabetes prediction using different machine learning approaches. In: 2019 3rd International Conference on Computing Methodologies and Communication (ICCMC), pp. 367–371. IEEE (2019)

A Deep Learning Method for Obfuscated Android Malware Detection

Nitin Benjamin Dasiah, Ritu Gain, V. Sabarisrinivas, and K. Sitara(✉)

Department of Computer Science and Engineering, National Institute of Technology Tiruchirappalli, Tiruchirappalli 620015, India
sitara@nitt.edu

Abstract. With smartphones becoming increasingly prevalent and irreplaceable parts of modern society and individual life, it opens new windows for cybercriminals into our everyday life. Mobile devices are now at risk of being attacked by adversaries ranging from small-time crooks hoping to make a quick profit scamming people to authoritarian nation-states trying to attack and target journalists and human rights activists Malware programs are codes that are written by these adversaries to perform malicious tasks on the victim's devices. These tasks can be spying on victims, encrypting all their files and extorting money, or using the computational power of a victim‘s device for illegal purposes. Many anti-malware solutions that exist for Android Smartphones rely on manual analysis and signatures to detect malware. However, most modern malware relies on polymorphic tendencies to change the signatures. Another major way of detecting malware is by using Machine Learning and Deep Learning models for detection and classification. One of the major issues faced by most detectors is Adversarial evasion, where an adversary modifies the malware using various techniques to intentionally induce a misclassification by the detectors to evade it. Another major issue in this area is the selection of features from a large pool. Selecting a large number of features and not selecting enough can both be detrimental to the model's performance. In this project, we propose a novel robust malware detection mechanism based on Deep Learning for Android devices that solves both of the aforementioned challenges and thus creating a secure Android ecosystem.

Keywords: Malware · Android · Adversarial Evasion · Deep Learning · Classifiers · Auto-Encoders

1 Introduction

Malware analysis and detection are one of the most pervasive fields of computer science as malware causes massive damage to individuals, organizations, and countries. As we enter a new era where wars are fought on computers, it is imperative to focus on defences. As the access to the internet, computers and smartphones are becoming prevalent across the world, malware is becoming

N. Chauhan et al. (Eds.): MIND 2023, CCIS 2128, pp. 149–164, 2024.
https://doi.org/10.1007/978-3-031-62217-5_13

more sophisticated to cause more damage. It is therefore imperative to build a detection system that is robust and efficient in detecting malware. In this work, we are exploring a novel method of detecting malware in android systems, which has the largest market share for mobile phone operating systems.

Malware are programs that are designed to execute a nefarious task usually targetin a specific type of system like a desktop computer, industrial workstation, web server, or mobile phone. Traditionally Malware Detectors use a hashed signature of a file to detect malware. Even today this is one of the common ways to detect malware. However, most modern malware are polymorphic, meaning they are able to change their codes, content and thus the signature at the run-time. As such it is easy for them to change signatures. Hence this method of detection will not help identify such malware.

Most of the recent works in the literature employ machine learning based supervised/unsupervised models to detect malware using various features. This method is often mired with two major issues. Firstly, the malware authors start modifying their malware to be resilient towards the malware detectors by employing various methods of obfuscation. Obfuscation consists of a set of techniques that involve changing the components of the code to evade detection and make the analysis process difficult. This creates an adversarial game between the malware developers and the malware detectors to constantly evade and detect various types of malware. The second challenge on the detection side is the selection of features from a large pool of features to use as a basis for decision-making. Selecting too many features from the sample can create an overfitting issue and not having enough features can cause underfitting issues. As we observe in the literature survey, most of the Android malware detectors that use machine learning methods (including the ones that use deep neural networks) are often overfitted with the training model and cannot perform well with a real-life sample.

The existing methods of detecting malware which is obfuscated include methods such as finding the digital signature or hash of an application and comparing it with already existing digital signatures of known malware and checking for a match. These methods can easily be bypassed as small changes to the bytecode will bring changes to the digital signature and prevent the malware from being detected. Malware authors can make use of obfuscation techniques to prevent their malware from being detected and analysed.

In this work our objective is to build a fast and more accurate deep learning engine to detect Android Malware at scale with some level of resilience towards adversarial evasion. We also plan to build a web application like Virustotal for Android applications that use deep neural networks to detect malware instead of a database of signatures.

2 Literature Survey

The paper by Aboaoja et al 2022 [2] discusses the various types of malware detection and the issues faced by each method. It also tries to classify the different types of detection. Odusami, Modupe and Abayomi-Alli Et-al, 2018 [6] discuss various different methods of malware analysis in Android systems. These methods can be used for analysing a file and to come to a conclusion on whether a particular file is malware or benign (safe) software. Our focus is on deep learning based detection methods, which are commonly used in conjunction with static and dynamic analysis to detect malicious software.

A paper by Su, X., Zhang, et al 2016 [8] introduces the concept of using deep learning for malware detection. They use a layered and hybrid approach containing features from both static analysis (permissions, API calls) and dynamic analysis (behaviour of the program) and use a Deep Belief Network and Support Vector Machine to identify malware with 92.4–99.5% accuracy. A paper by Yi Zhang et al 2018 [11] extracts static manifest information from the Android app and converts it into a series of vectors through embeddings and then uses these vectors on a CNN with 97.4% accuracy. A paper by Zhongru et al 2020 [7] uses the opcode from the .dex file encoded in an image and passed through a custom CNN and RNN architecture for an accuracy of 93.6 percent and 94.4%. A paper by Pooja et al 2022 [9] worked on implementing a dex-based model similar to the previous paper but on a standard Efficientnet architecture.

In the paper by Dhanya et al 2023, [1], the authors evaluate a novel method of creating adversarial samples and use it in the training process to train a CNN model to detect malware.

Most of the deep learning based models designed for malware detection purpose are binary classifiers classifying whether a given program is malware or benign (safe) software. However, in any practical scenario, there is a need for a multiclass classifier to detect the type of malware as the response to a ransomware infection will be different to the response to a trojan infection. Most of the papers suffer from overfitting issues, selection and engineering of features are done manually, As a result, there are either too many features and thus there is overfitting in the training process or not enough features for generalisation.

3 Proposed Work

Figure 1 shows various components of our proposed methodology. Initially, a dataset is created from publicly available datasets to introduce obfuscation in it for adversarial training. These samples are called adversarial samples. This dataset is used to train an autoencoder model. Using the encoded representation of the autoencoder model a classifier model is created to classify an APK file into one of the six categories:- Adware, Banking Trojan, Benign (Safe) Software, Ransomware, Scareware, and SMS Trojan. The trained model is transfered into a flask-based web application which acts as a frontend to the malware detector. We tried LSTM and image based autoencoders. The problem with the former is discussed in Subsect. 4.2.

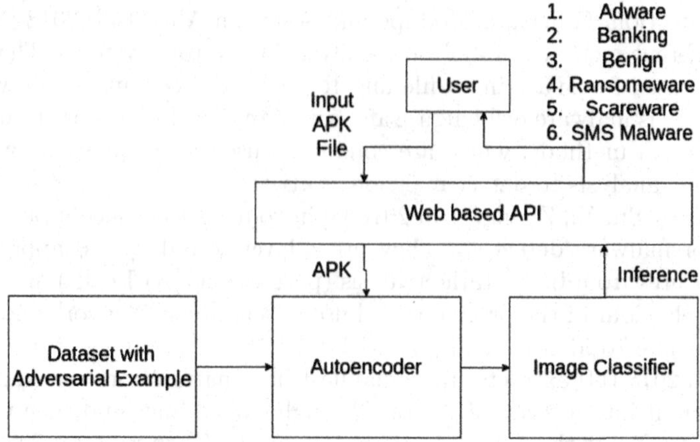

Fig. 1. Block Diagram of the Proposed Methodolgy

3.1 Adversarial Sample Generation

We randomly chose 10% of the APK files from each of six the classes. An integer is randomly generated using the bash $RANDOM internal function. This is a pseudorandom function that generates a number between 0 - 32767. By using this function with a modulo operator, a variable that contains a random number from 0–7 is created. A black box tool Obfuscapk [3] is used to select one of the following methods given in Fig. 2 chosen based on the random value K generated in the previous step to randomly obfuscate each file.

The degree of randomness is introduced to maintain experimental integrity.

3.2 Autoencoder

Malware varies in size based on the type of malware and how obfuscated it is. When malware is obfuscated, only a small part of the bytecode contains the harmful code and the rest is irrelevant or padded data. The entire bytecode is, therefore, not relevant to detecting the type of malware. It should be possible to use an encoder to get a smaller encoded representation that can better detect the type of malware and improve the generalizability of the neural network.

If an autoencoder is able to compress bytecode into an encoded representation that can summarize the bytecode, we can use the smaller encoded representation for classification instead of the entire bytecode, therefore improving upon the speed of the neural network and the generalizability of the neural network.

We must test each encoder with various sizes of encoded representation to ensure the encoded representation contains all the information required for classification.

K	Method	Technique
0	Advanced Reflection	Uses reflection to invoke dangerous APIs of the Android Framework.
1	Arithmetic Branch	Insert junk code. In this case, the junk code is composed by arithmetic computations and a branch instruction depending on the result of these computations, crafted in such a way that the branch is never taken.
2	Call Indirection	This technique modifies the control-flow graph without impacting the code semantics
3	Debug Removal	Remove debug information.
4	Goto	It modifies the control-flow graph by adding two new nodes by inserting arbitrary go to to and fro from different subroutines.
5	Method Overload	It exploits the overloading feature of the Java programming language to assign the same name to different methods but using different arguments.
6	Reflection	A suitable method invocation (i.e., no constructor methods, public visibility, enough free registers etc.) is redirected to a custom method that will invoke the original method using the Reflection APIs.
7	Reorder Code	This technique consists of changing the order of basic blocks in the code

Fig. 2. Techniques for Adversarial Evasion

3.3 LSTM Autoencoder

Data Preprocessing. Each of the APK files was unpacked and the binary dex files were extracted and converted the hex stream of the bytecode of the binary file into integers. Each of the integers ranges from 0 to 255. These were batched into batches of 2048 and these batches were passed one at a time into the LSTM as the sequence of input data.

Model. The encoder part of the LSTM takes in the input data of the bytecode in a sequence and produces a single output. This output is then passed onto the decoder which takes in the single output from the encoder and attempts to recreate the sequence of input data containing the bytecode.

By training the model, we force the encoder to summarize important features from the input data into a single representation and force the decoder to learn the features from the single representation and rebuild the input data. We train the autoencoder until the loss converges and transfer the encoder part of the autoencoder to the classifier.

The classifier contains a feed-forward neural network, that takes in the output from the encoder and attempts to classify the input sample into its class. We do not freeze the weights of the encoder as it might still relearn which features it summarizes to the output. We train the classifier until the loss converges and accuracy is at its highest.

Workflow of the Model.

1. **Training the Autoencoder**
   The LSTM encoder took inputs of size 2048, with varying sequence lengths for each data sample. The LSTM encoder had a hidden state size of 512. The

last row of the LSTM encoder output was taken as the encoded representation, which was a single vector of size 2048. The LSTM decoder took the encoded representation and tried to recreate outputs of size 2048, with the same sequence length as the input. The LSTM decoder had a hidden state of size 512. For each output from the decoder, the hidden state and cell states from the previous output are passed as input to the LSTM along with the encoded representation. The loss function used for the autoencoder was mean squared error loss. The autoencoder training was optimized using the ADAM optimizer. The autoencoder had 75,540,480 trainable parameters.

2. **Training the Classifier**
The encoder part of the autoencoder is taken and a neural network classifier is added on top of the encoder. The classifier takes in the output from the encoder, which is a single vector of size 2048. The classifier contained three layers. The first layer took in the encoded representation of size 2048 and output a vector of size 512. The second layer took the input of 512 and output a vector of 512. The third layer took the input of 512 and output a vector of size of 6, corresponding to the 6 classes. The loss function used for the classifier was the cross-entropy loss. The classifier training was optimized using the ADAM optimizer. The encoder and classifier together had 68,456,454 trainable parameters.

3.4 Image Based Autoencoder

Data Preprocessing. Our code unpacked each of the APK files and then extracted the binary dex file. The hex stream of the bytecode of the binary file were converted into integers. Each of the integers ranges from 0 to 255, which can be used to represent the intensities of pixels. The integers are arranged into a matrix, and this matrix is converted into an image. These images are then resized to 256×256 and used as input to the neural network. Samples of encoded software are given in the Figs. 3(a) and 3(b).

Model. An image autoencoder as shown in Fig. 4, where the encoder takes in an image of size 256×256×3. It undergoes convolution to reduce the size of the representation. This encoded representation is reduced to a smaller percent of the original size and tested for accuracy. This encoded representation is passed to the decoder where it undergoes convolution transpose operations, where it increases in size until it reaches back to 256×256×3. The classifier takes in the input from the encoder and flattens it, and uses a feed-forward neural network consisting of dense layers and dropouts until it produces an output of size 6, corresponding to the number of possible classes.

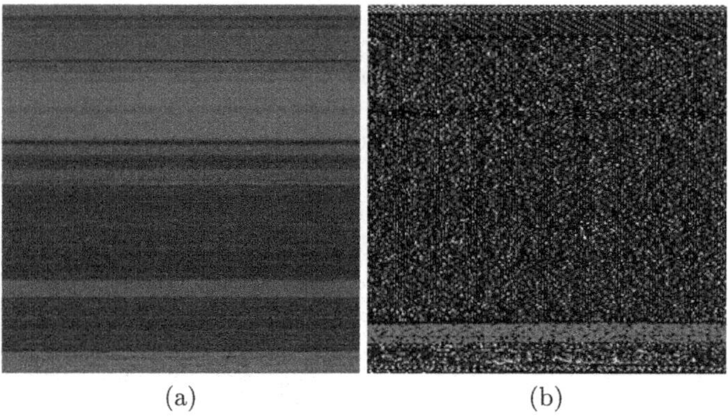

Fig. 3. (a) Benign Software Encoded as an Image and (b) Ransomware Software Encoded as an Image

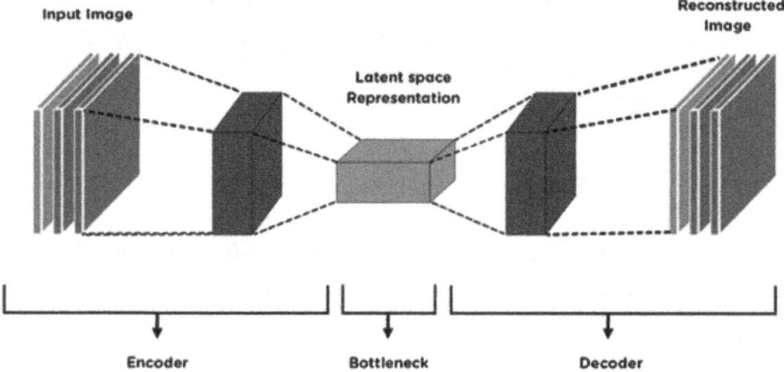

Fig. 4. Image Autoencoder

Workflow of the Model

1. **Training the Autoencoder** The image encoder takes an image input of 256×256×3 and convolves the data to smaller sizes. The image decoder takes the input from the encoder and applies convolution transposition to get back the original size. The loss function used to train the autoencoder was mean squared error loss. The autoencoder training was optimized using the ADAM optimizer.
2. **Training the Classifier** The encoder from the autoencoder is copied to the classifier. The image encoder takes an image input of 256×256×3 and convolves the data to smaller sizes. The classifier takes the input from the encoder and flattens it and adds a feed-forward neural network consisting of dense layers and dropouts to classify the input. The classifier produces an output of size 6, corresponding to the number of classes in the dataset. The loss function used to train the classifier was the cross-entropy loss. The classifier training was optimized using the ADAM optimizer.

3.5 Web Application

A web app was built to interface with the user and collect an APK file to detect whether the given APK is malware and to detect its particular class. The frontend of the website is basic HTML, and CSS and the backend is written in Flask Framework and Python. TensorFlow and Keras Transfer Learning libraries are used for prediction purposes. After training our aforementioned model we generated the H5 file of our model and transferred it into our flask web - application through these libraries.

4 Results and Discussions

4.1 Dataset Description

A combination of two datasets **CICMalAnal2017** and **Maldroid 2020** is used for our project. Both of them are developed by the Canadian Institute of Cybersecurity, University of New Brunswick [4,5]. Each of the datasets contains raw APK files across the 6 following categories: Adware, Banking Trojan, Benign (Safe) Software, Ransomware, Scareware, and SMS Trojan. The following Table 1 shows the data split for each class in our dataset.

Table 1. Data Split across Each Class

Class	Non-Obfuscated Data Samples	Obfuscated Data Samples
Adware	1512	147
Banking	2470	235
Benign	600	56
Ransomeware	100	7
Scareware	112	8
SMS	4822	476
Total	9618	929

For training each model, we will use 60% of the data for training and the remaining 40% for testing. Non-Adversarial Training refers to training only on the non-obfuscated data samples. Adversarial Training refers to training on both non-obfuscated and obfuscated data samples.

4.2 LSTM Based Autoencoder

Learnings. The main purpose of trying an LSTM-based autoencoder was to avoid arbitrarily resizing data to input it into a neural network. We expected that an LSTM-based autoencoder could build an encoder that can resize data based on the important features the data contained instead of resizing the data arbitrarily. After multiple attempts, a few drawbacks were observed.

- The size of the data was too large for even the LSTM to be able to understand long-distance dependencies and features, as the number of time steps was very large, often reaching eight hundred time steps or more. Due to the large number of time steps, the LSTM did not have enough memory in the hidden and cell states to learn all the long-range features properly. This also increased the memory requirements and time requirements for training as the values of each time step were stored for backpropagation.
- The number of parameters in the autoencoder model was over 75 million parameters, and the number of parameters in the encoder and classifier model was over 68 million. Increasing the size of the neural network meant increasing the memory requirement at each time step, therefore making the memory requirements high and, usually being unable to load the data on the GPU.
- Due to the previous factors, there was little control over the architecture of the LSTM as small changes either increased the time taken to train or increased the memory required by the neural network.
- GPUs were unable to meet the memory requirements with batch sizes greater than one, making the training longer and more prone to noise.
- The size of the encoded representation was too small to summarize all the important features of the data, but increasing the size of the encoded representation caused GPUs to run out of memory.
- Training a large network of that size over multiple time steps takes large amounts of time and energy. Hence it was not able to train the neural network to trian for more than one epoch.

Results. The time taken to train the autoencoder was 2736 min and 3 s per epoch. The training and testing loss for each sample was on average over 3000 using mean squared error loss. The time taken to train the classifier was 1886 min and 38 s per epoch. The training and testing accuracy were 0.5008 and 0.4955 respectively. We were unable to test for convergence as the model took too long to train and the GPUs were overheating and unable to handle the load.

The coding language used was Python 3.7.16. Pytorch version 1.12.1 is used as the library for creating and training the neural network. The cudatoolkit version used to run on Nvidia RTX3050 Notebook GPU was 11.2.

4.3 Image-Based Autoencoder

Learnings. As the LSTM model was too large and inefficient, we decided to train an autoencoder using images, as image-based classification reached high accuracy. While this takes away from our original idea to not summarize data arbitrarily, we were still able to test out the effects of encoding an image and the difference it makes while training on adversarial data. The Figs. 5, 6, 7 show the sizes we used for the image encoder, decoder, and classifier parts of our initial model. The encoder takes an input of size $256\times256\times3$ and convolves it to size $128\times128\times16$ and then $64\times64\times8$ as the final encoded representation. The encoded representation is 16% of the size of the original image.

```
Model: "sequential_17"
_________________________________________________________________
 Layer (type)                Output Shape              Param #
=================================================================
 conv2d_35 (Conv2D)          (None, 128, 128, 16)      448

 conv2d_36 (Conv2D)          (None, 64, 64, 8)         1160

=================================================================
Total params: 1,608
Trainable params: 1,608
Non-trainable params: 0
_________________________________________________________________
```

Fig. 5. Size of Image-Based Encoder

The decoder takes an input of size 64×64×8 (same as the size of the output of the encoder) and applies convolution transposition to size it to 128×128×16, then 256×256×16, and finally outputs a 256×256×3 image after convolution. This is equal to the original size of the image.

```
Model: "sequential_18"
_________________________________________________________________
 Layer (type)                Output Shape              Param #
=================================================================
 conv2d_transpose_14 (Conv2D  (None, 128, 128, 8)      584
 Transpose)

 conv2d_transpose_15 (Conv2D  (None, 256, 256, 16)     1168
 Transpose)

 conv2d_37 (Conv2D)          (None, 256, 256, 3)       435

=================================================================
Total params: 2,187
Trainable params: 2,187
Non-trainable params: 0
```

Fig. 6. Size of Image-Based Decoder

The classifier takes an input of size 64×64×8 (same as the size of the output of the encoder) and applies convolution to size it to 64×64×4, then flattens it to 16384. It is followed by a dense layer of size 128, with a dropout of 30%. This

```
Model: "sequential_25"
_________________________________________________________________
 Layer (type)                Output Shape              Param #
=================================================================
 conv2d_45 (Conv2D)          (None, 64, 64, 4)         292

 flatten_11 (Flatten)        (None, 16384)             0

 dense_22 (Dense)            (None, 128)               2097280

 dropout_2 (Dropout)         (None, 128)               0

 dense_23 (Dense)            (None, 6)                 774

=================================================================
Total params: 2,098,346
Trainable params: 2,098,346
Non-trainable params: 0
```

Fig. 7. Size of Image-Based Classifier

is followed by a final dense layer of 6, which is equal to the number of classes in the dataset.

Results The image-based autoencoder was trained on data without adversarial evasion samples. The training and the testing accuracy with respect to epochs is shown in Fig. 8.(a). The time taken to train the autoencoder is on average 240 s per epoch.The autoencoder converges at epoch 6 with a validation loss of 90 for the batch size of 32 using mean squared error loss. The time taken to train the classifier is on average 37 s per epoch. The training and testing accuracy were 0.8528 and 0.8631. The validation set accuracy converged 3 epochs into training.

When Image based autoencoder was trained on data with adversarial evasion samples. The training and the testing accuracy with respect to epochs is shown in Fig. 8.(b). The time taken to train the autoencoder is on average 194 s per epoch. The autoencoder converges at epoch 16 with a validation loss of 251 for the batch size of 32 using mean squared error loss. The time taken to train the classifier is on average 34 s per epoch. The training and testing accuracy were 0.8344 and 0.8361. The validation set accuracy converged 16 epochs into training.

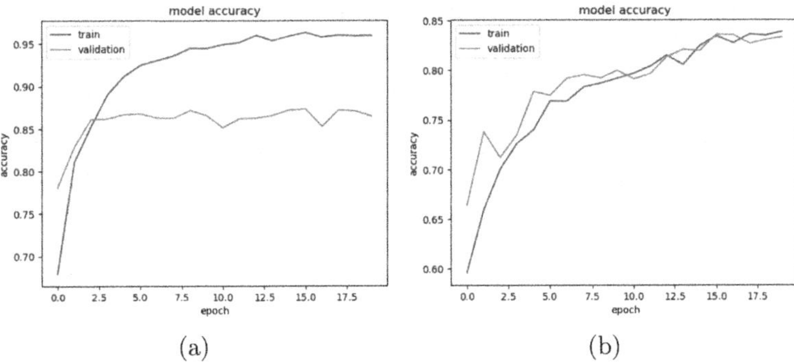

Fig. 8. Accuracy of the Image Autoencoder Model on (a) Non Adversarial Data (b) Adversial Data

It is noticed from Fig. 8 (b) that the testing dataset has higher accuracy than the training dataset for multiple epochs. This shows us that while the accuracy of the autoencoder model might be lower than the base model, the generalizability of the autoencoder model is higher than the base model [10].

Further Testing. As the initial autoencoder model performs well, we further test the possible improvements by increasing and decreasing the size of the encoder model and the encoded representation.

Larger Encoded Representation. The size of the autoencoder and the encoded representation is increased and tested on the adversarial dataset. The encoded representation is a 50% increase over the size of the previous encoded representation.

In the encoder, the network takes in an image of size 256×256×3, applies convolution transposition to expand it to 512×512×64, then convolves it back to 128×128×3, which is 25% the size of the original image. The number of trainable parameters are 25315.

In the decoder, the network takes in an input of size 128×128×3(same as the size of the larger encoder's output), applies convolution transposition to expand it to 512×512×3, then convolves it back to 256×256×3, which is the size of the original image. The number of trainable parameters are 1827.

The classifier, the network takes in an input of size 128×128×3(same as the size of the larger encoder's output), applies convolution transposition to expand it to 128×128×4, then flattens it to a size of 65,536, followed by a dense layer of 128, and finally a dense layer of 6, which corresponds to the number of classes in the dataset. The total number of parameters are 8,389,622.

The autoencoder training time took an average of 177 s per epoch and converged to a loss of 78. The training time for the classifier took an average of 132 s per epoch. The accuracy of the model increases from 83% to 85%, but it starts to overfit the data and loses its generalizability property.

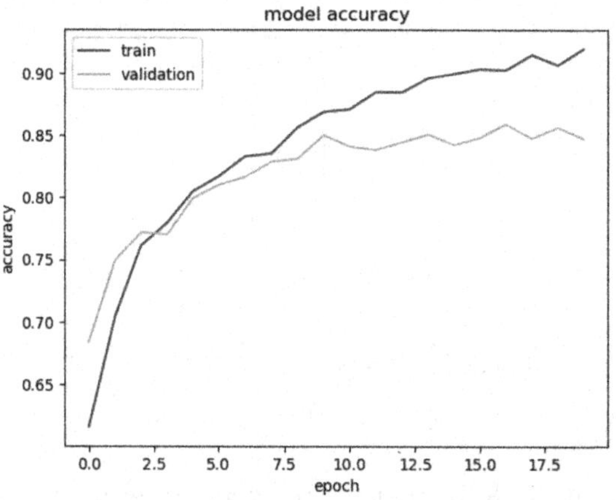

Fig. 9. Accuracy of the Large Autoencoder

Moreover, the increase in memory requirements and training time does not justify the small increase in accuracy.

Smaller Encoded Representation. The size of the autoencoder is increased and encoder representation is decreased and then tested on the adversarial dataset. The encoded representation is 50% of the size of the previously encoded representation.

In encoder, the network takes in an image of size 256×256×3, applies convolution transposition to expand it to 512×512×64, then convolves it to 64×64×4, which is 8% the size of the original image. The number of trainable parameters are 26332.

In the decoder, the network takes in an input of 64×64×4 (same as the size of the smaller encoded representation), applies convolution transposition to expand it to 512×512×32, then convolves it to 256×256×3, which is the size of the original image. The number of trainable parameters are 6971.

In the classifier, the network takes in an input of size 64*64*4 (same as the size of the smaller encoded representation), then flattens it to a size of 16,384, followed by a dense layer of 128, and finally a dense layer of 6, which corresponds to the number of classes in the dataset. The number of trainable parameters are 2,098,202.

The autoencoder training time took an average of 214 s per epoch and converged to a loss of 504. The training time for the classifier took an average of 135 s per epoch. The accuracy of the model increases from 83% to 85%, but it starts to overfit the data and loses its generalizability property.

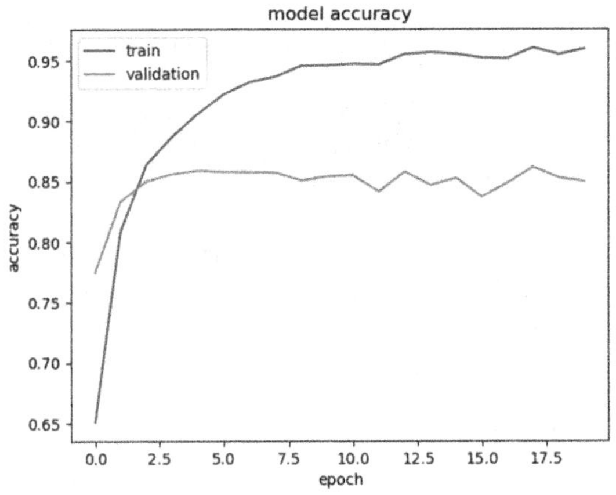

Fig. 10. (b) Accuracy for Smaller Encoded Representation

Moreover, the increase in memory requirements and training time does not justify the small increase in accuracy.

The coding language used was Python 3.7.12. The library used for creating and training the neural network was Tensorflow version 2.11.0. The cudatoolkit version used to run on GPU T4 × 2 was 11.3.

5 Result Comparisons

5.1 Non-adversarial Training

The performance of the proposed methods are compared with EfficientNet models [10] and is shown in Table 2. The proposed image encoder based model has lesser overfitting and better generalization for half the parameters and training time as required by EfficientNet. The LSTM model has the highest accuracy for the first epoch, but the number of parameters and training time make it infeasible as a commercial product.

5.2 Adversarial Training

The performance of the proposed methods are compared with EfficientNet models [10] and is shown in Table 3. The initial image autoencoder has the fastest training and testing time for the classifier, and has the ability to generalize the most. EfficientNet has the highest accuracy but has a large number of parameters and overfits the training data a little. The smaller encoded representation of the image produced the highest accuracy among the image encoder models, but it has the highest overfitting amongst all the models.

Table 2. Accuracy of the Models for Non-Adversarial Data

Model	Training Time of Auto Encoder	Training Time of Classifier	Accuracy of Training Set	Accuracy of Testing Set	Number of Parameters
EfficientNetB0	-	63 s	0.9437	0.9066	4M
LSTM Based Model	2736 m	1886 m	0.5008	0.4955	68M
Image Based Model	240 s	37 s	0.8528	0.8631	2M

Table 3. Accuracy of the Models for Adversarial Data

Model	Training Time of Auto Encoder	Training Time of Classifier	Accuracy of Training Set	Accuracy of Testing Set	Number of Parameters
EfficientNetB0	-	63 s	0.9093	0.8824	4M
LSTM Based Model	–	–	–	–	–
Image Based Model	194 s	34 s	0.8344	0.8361	2M
Larger Image Model	177 s	132 s	0.8689	0.8501	8M
Smaller Image Model	213 s	132 s	0.8866	0.8556	2M

6 Conclusion

We researched and learnt about the different methods to detect malware that exist currently. We developed multiple models to test the use of encoding in malware detection so we can improve the existing detection methods. The initial concept of using an LSTM to summarize the bytecode into a fixed-size representation, that can be used to classify the software turned out to be an inefficient method with large training times and low accuracy. The image-based autoencoder has slightly lower accuracy than the exsisting model. Running the code multiple times showed that the image-based autoencoder was affected by the random values the parameters are initialized with. It is noticed that increasing the size of the encoded representation and the size of the autoencoder does not affect the accuracy of the classifier by a large margin. The increase in accuracy was usually followed by an overfit. We also notice that the testing data has higher accuracy than the training data for multiple epochs in the initial model and training happens at one-third the time it takes for the base model with half the number of parameters as the base model. Image Autoencoders seem to be one of the better solutions for light-weight malware detectors that have the ability to better generalize and predict malware.

We notice that for half the parameters and a third of the training time, autoencoders are able to classify software almost as accurately as the base model. And although we lose accuracy, we can notice that the testing data has higher accuracy than the training data in the autoencoder model for multiple epochs. This goes on to show that while the accuracy of classification of the testing dataset is a side-effect of learning to classify the training data in the base model, in our model, learning the patterns and features and generalizing it takes a higher priority. Therefore after each epoch, the testing dataset immediately shows better accuracy as compared to the training data.

As neural networks cannot decrypt data or recognize patterns in encrypted data, we need to take a hybrid approach. We need to remove the packing and padding from the data and run it in a sandboxed environment with checkpoints to prevent the code from complete running but also taking peeks at the code after it gets decrypted at run-time to check it for malware.

References

1. Dhanya K. A.: Obfuscated malware detection in iot android applications using markov images and cnn. IEEE Syst. J., 1–11 (2023). https://doi.org/10.1109/JSYST.2023.3238678
2. Aboaoja, F., Zainal, A., Ghaleb, F., Al-rimy, B., Eisa, T., Elnour, A.: Malware detection issues, challenges, and future directions: a survey. Appli. Sci. **12**, 8482 (08 2022). https://doi.org/10.3390/app12178482
3. Aonzo, S., Georgiu, G.C., Verderame, L., Merlo, A.: Obfuscapk: an open-source black-box obfuscation tool for android apps. SoftwareX **11**, 100403 (2020). https://doi.org/10.1016/j.softx.2020.100403, https://www.sciencedirect.com/science/article/pii/S2352711019302791

4. Mahdavifar, S., Abdul kadir, A.F., Fatemi, R., Alhadidi, D., Ghorbani, A.: Dynamic android malware category classification using semi-supervised deep learning, pp. 515–522 (Aug 2020). https://doi.org/10.1109/DASC-PICom-CBDCom-CyberSciTech49142.2020.00094
5. Mahdavifar, S., Alhadidi, D., Ghorbani, A.: Effective and efficient hybrid android malware classification using pseudo-label stacked auto-encoder. J. Netw. Syst. Manag. **30** (2022). https://doi.org/10.1007/s10922-021-09634-4
6. Odusami, M., Abayomi-Alli, O., Misra, S., Shobayo, O., Damaševičius, R., Maskeliunas, R.: Android malware detection: A survey (Oct 2018). https://doi.org/10.1007/978-3-030-01535-0_19
7. Ren, Z., Wu, H., Ning, Q., Hussain, I., Chen, B.: End-to-end malware detection for android iot devices using deep learning. Ad Hoc Netw. **101**, 102098 (2020). https://doi.org/10.1016/j.adhoc.2020.102098, https://www.sciencedirect.com/science/article/pii/S1570870519310984
8. Su, X., Zhang, D., Li, W., Zhao, K.: A deep learning approach to android malware feature learning and detection. In: 2016 IEEE Trustcom/BigDataSE/ISPA, pp. 244–251 (2016). https://doi.org/10.1109/TrustCom.2016.0070
9. Yadav, P., Menon, N., Ravi, V., Vishvanathan, S., Pham, T.: A two-stage deep learning framework for image-based android malware detection and variant classification. Comput. Intell. **38** (05 2022). https://doi.org/10.1111/coin.12532
10. Yadav, P., Menon, N., Ravi, V., Vishvanathan, S., Pham, T.D.: Efficientnet convolutional neural networks-based android malware detection. Comput. Sec. **115**, 102622 (2022). https://doi.org/10.1016/j.cose.2022.102622, https://www.sciencedirect.com/science/article/pii/S0167404822000219
11. Zhang, Y., Yang, Y., Wang, X.: A novel android malware detection approach based on convolutional neural network. In: Proceedings of the 2nd International Conference on Cryptography, Security and Privacy, ICCSP 2018, pp. 144-149. Association for Computing Machinery, New York (2018). https://doi.org/10.1145/3199478.3199492

Code-Mixed Language Understanding Using BiLSTM-BERT Multi-attention Fusion Mechanism

Mayur Wankhade(✉), Nehal Jain, and Annavarapu Chandra Sekhara Rao

Department of Computer Science and Engineering, Institute of Technology, Dhanbad, India
wankhademayurk@gmail.com

Abstract. Code-mixed language, characterized by the seamless blending of multiple languages, presents a formidable challenge for natural language understanding systems. In our work, we have propose a novel approach to address the complexities of code-mixed text comprehension by combining BiLSTM-BERT models with a multi-attention fusion mechanism. This paper proposes a novel approach for Code-mixed language joint intent classification and slot filling (JIC-SF) using a BiLSTM-BERT multi-attention model. The proposed model employs multi-attention mechanisms, including self-attention and cross-attention, to dynamically weigh the importance of different parts of the input text for JIC-SF. We evaluated our model on benchmark datasets: ATIS, SNIPs and Hind-English Code-mixed (HiEn-CMD) datasets. The results demonstrate that our approach outperforms the state-of-the-art models on benchmark datasets. Specifically, our model achieved an intent accuracy of 97.87% and a slot F1-score of 95.97% on the ATIS dataset, an intent accuracy of 98.86% and a slot F1-score of 96.25% on the SNIPs dataset, and intent accuracy of 84.24% and a slot F1-score of 82.68% on the HiEn-CMD dataset. Our proposed BiLSTM-BERT multi-attention model for JIC-SF provides a promising solution to improve the accuracy and efficiency of natural language understanding (NLU) systems, which can benefit various applications such as virtual assistants, chatbots, and customer service systems.

Keywords: Intent Classification · Slot Filling · Deep Learning · Natural Language Understanding

1 Introduction

Voice AI has gained popularity with the emergence of smart speakers and personal voice assistants like Alexa, Siri, Bixby, Google Home, and Cortana. These devices facilitate goal-directed conversations, making NLU a critical aspect. NLU involves identifying the user's intent, retrieving the necessary information or "slots" and engaging in a conversation with the user. JIC-SF are two crucial responsibilities of an NLU system. Intent classification recognizes the user's aim or request, while slot filling extracts precise information from user input to fulfil the intent. Though earlier research focused on these tasks separately, they

N. Chauhan et al. (Eds.): MIND 2023, CCIS 2128, pp. 165–172, 2024.
https://doi.org/10.1007/978-3-031-62217-5_14

are interrelated and essential for a conversational AI system to comprehend and respond to user input. Bilingual code-mixed language understanding, which involves understanding both the intent and specific slots in a mixed-language utterance, is a challenging task in natural language processing (NLP). JIC-SF aim to simultaneously identify the intent or purpose of a user's utterance and extract relevant slots or entities. However, the presence of code-mixing adds complexity due to linguistic variations, word-level ambiguity, and the need to handle multiple languages within a single utterance. This research focuses on developing techniques and models to enable effective JIC-SF in bilingual code-mixed language understanding.

Despite making substantial advancements in improving accuracy and efficiency, the previously mentioned models are only constrained to the English language and hence are regarded as monolingual. Recently, multilingualism and code-mixing have become increasingly prevalent in various communication channels, including social media, online forums, and messaging platforms. Code-mixing refers to the practice of alternating between two or more languages within a single conversation or text. This phenomenon poses significant challenges for NLP tasks, including language understanding and machine translation, as the traditional language models are primarily trained on monolingual data. Consequently, researchers have focused on developing techniques and models to address the complexities associated with understanding multilingual code-mixed language. In a country like India, which is a linguistically diverse country, people often use a blend of languages in their everyday conversations, which is called "code-mixing". Code-mixing, the phenomenon of using multiple languages in a single conversation, poses significant challenges for NLU tasks such as JIC-SF. To address these challenges, we have proposed deep BiLSTM-BERT ensemble mechanisms for Bi-lingual code-mixed JIC-SF. Our focus in this study will primarily be on the Hinglish Bilingual language, which is a mixture of English and Hindi, two of the most widely spoken languages.

1.1 Contributions

- Our proposed approach provides a promising solution for JIC-SF that is applicable across different datasets and domains.
- The BiLSTM component captures the sequential information of the input text, while the BERT component provides pre-trained contextualized embeddings that capture the broader context of the input text. In addition, our model supports bilingual Hinglish code-mixed language which has accomplished by fine-tuning mBERT, contributing to the advancement of the field.
- Our model employs self-attention and cross-attention mechanisms to dynamically weigh the importance of different parts of the input text for both JIC-SF.
- Our proposed model achieved higher accuracy and slot F1 score compared to previous state-of-the-art models.

2 Related Work

The preliminary research conducted on JIC-SF was carried out independently and in conjunction with each other. In the field of intent classification, there are two traditional methods for determining the intention of an utterance: rule-based and statistical. Hashemi [11] suggests that rule-based systems rely on predetermined rules created by experts to match new utterances to their intended meanings, while statistical models such as CRF [2] extract key characteristics from input datasets.

Recent advancements in deep learning techniques have led researchers to incorporate various deep neural networks into intent classification tasks, as demonstrated in [23], deep belief networks (DBN) to extract features from a large set of unlabelled data and then used support vector machines (SVM) for classification. To address scalability issues with DBNs, [5] proposed deep convex networks (DCN). [11] used a convolutions neural network (CNN) to identify important features of input text and classify it into different intent categories, facilitating the identification of semantically related searches through vector space embedding [24,25]. Similarly, incorporated contextual information from previous utterances into present ones using RNN. To address the vanishing gradient problem, [21] employed RNN-LSTM-based models. For slot-filling tasks prior to the introduction of deep learning methods, the most sophisticated models were the maximum entropy markov models [16] and the CRF.

The joint task of intent classification and slot-filling has been addressed by several techniques proposed in the literature. [26] proposed a CNN-based model for sequence tagging, followed by a globally normalized triangular CRF model (TriCRF). In [9] suggested an RNN model for simultaneously performing domain, intent, and slot-filling tasks. For instance, [19] used a code-mixed dataset from social media and developed an LSTM model for sentiment classification. Numerous studies have examined the content of code-mixed languages, such as in works by [20] which uses pre-trained word embeddings and which uses a code-switching ELMo model. In recent years, transformer-based multilingual models like mBERT [6] and XLM-R [3] have demonstrated remarkable effectiveness in various multilingual tasks.

3 Proposed Model

Our proposed model contain hybrid BiLSTM-mBERT multi-head query attention mechanism. The proposed model to detect complex dependencies between words and comprehend the relationship between words in a sentence, ultimately facilitating the identification of intent and relevant slots.

3.1 Problem Definition

The tasks of JIC-SF are characterized as multi-class classification tasks at the sentence level and token level. Given a user sentence $u = (w_1, w_2, ..., w_n)$ consisting of n tokens and $\forall u \in U$ where U denotes the whole set of user utterances, we predict an Intent label $\hat{I}$ from a set of pre-defined intents I.

$$\hat{I}_i = \underset{i \in n}{argmax}\, P(I_i/u), \forall u \in U \tag{1}$$

and a sequence of slot labels $S = (s_1, s_2, .., s_n)$, one for every word or token in a sentence, such that,

$$\hat{S}_i = \underset{S_i}{argmax}\, P(S_i/u), \forall u \in U \tag{2}$$

We have considered the Intent classification and Slot-filling tasks for monolinguals and bilingual (combination of English-Hindi) code-mix language understanding support model.

3.2 BiLSTM Attention Mechanism for Code-Mixed Intent Classification and Slot Filling

The BiLSTM which processes allowing uses the information from both directions. The BiLSTM encoder consists of three gates (input, output, and forget) that regulate the flow of information into and out of the cells.

$$fr_t = \Theta(W^{(f)} [x_t\; h_{t-1}]^T + b^{(f)}_{t-1}) \tag{3}$$

$$in_t = \Theta(W^{(i)} [x_t\; h_{t-1}]^T + b^{(i)}_{t-1}) \tag{4}$$

$$ou_t = \Theta(W^{(o)} [x_t\; h_{t-1}]^T + b^{(o)}{}_{t-1}) \tag{5}$$

$$c_t = \Theta(fr_t \bullet c_{t-1}) + in_t \bullet tanh(W^c [x_t\; h_{t-1}]^T + b^{(c_t)}_{t-1}) \tag{6}$$

$$h_t = ou_t \bullet tanh(c_t) \tag{7}$$

where W and b denote the input weight and bias. All small letters shows vector, x_t is input ($x_t \in R$), t represents time. Θ represents the sigmoid function, $\bullet$ represents element-wise product of vectors, c_t represents the current cell state, fr_t, in_t, ou_t denotes forget, input and output gate respectively, and the produced hidden state is represented by h_t. The hidden state calculated combined to produce context-sensitive hidden states 8.

$$h_t = [\overrightarrow{h_t} \oplus \overleftarrow{h_t}] \tag{8}$$

3.3 mBERT Code-Mixed Domain Knowledge Adaption

The mBERT is based on a bidirectional transformer encoder that allows it to extract multilingual representations from input sentences. This allows us to leverage the power of multilingual language models to generate high-quality contextualized representations for text inputs in multiple languages, without the need for language-specific models or data. mBERT adopted from [6] which receives an input sentence from the user, consisting of a sequence of words denoted with a special token as mentioned below.

$$u = ([CLS]w_1, w_2, ..., w_n, [SEP]) \tag{9}$$

Next, the pre-trained encoder produces a sequence of contextualized representations $H = (h_{[CLS]}, h_1, s_2, ..., h_n, h_{[SEP]})$ for the input sequence.

3.4 Multi-head Query Attention Mechanism

The multi-head query attention mechanism is applied to the BiLSTM layer outputs to capture the contextual relationships between the input tokens and their surrounding context. This mechanism facilitates the identification of intent and relevant slots by encoding comprehensive contextual information about the input tokens. Finally, the JIC-SF are accomplished using a softmax layer based on the outputs of the attention layer.

$$\hat{I}_i = softmax(W^{(i)} h_{CLS} + b^{(i)}) \tag{10}$$

$$\hat{S}_j = softmax(W^{(s)} h_j + b^{(s)}) \tag{11}$$

where $\forall i, j \in [1, .., n]$, W is the weight vector matrix and b is the bias.

4 Result Analysis

In this study, we proposed a BiLSTM-BERT multi-attention model for JIC-SF, which achieved state-of-the-art performance on two benchmark datasets: ATIS [12] and Snips [4] and HiEn-CMD [17] dataset. The highest result obtained are indicated in blue colour in Table 1. In particular, on the ATIS dataset, our model achieved an intent accuracy of 97.87% and a slot F1-score of 95.97%, representing a significant improvement over the previous state-of-the-art model's results, respectively. On the Snips dataset, our model achieved an intent accuracy of 98.86% and a slot F1-score of 96.25%. We have validated our proposed approach on an English and bilingual (Hindi-English) code-mixed dataset for JIC-SF. Our architecture has been compared to the baseline model, which achieves 84.24% accuracy on the HiEn-CMD dataset. The accuracy obtained by the proposed model on domain-specific code-mixed JIC-SF on bilingual features is beneficial for low-resource learning. The proposed BiLSTM-BERT multi-attention model combines the strengths of BiLSTM and BERT to effectively capture the input text's contextual information while using multi-attention mechanisms to dynamically weigh the importance of different parts of the input text for both JIC-SF. The BiLSTM component captures the sequential information of the input text, while the BERT component provides pre-trained contextualized embeddings that capture the broader context of the input text. The multi-attention mechanisms enable the model to focus on relevant parts of the input text for each task, leading to improved intent classification and slot-filling performance. One interesting finding from our experiments is that the model performance is susceptible to the size of the training dataset. This finding suggests that our proposed model is beneficial when training data is limited. Our proposed BiLSTM-BERT multi-attention model provides a promising approach to JIC-SF in NLU.

4.1 Baseline Methods

The baseline state-of-the-art models as explained below

- **Joint Seq.** [8] proposed a model approach that integrates domain categorization, intent, and slot filling into a bi-directional RNN-LSTM architecture.
- **Attention-based method** joint learning method was presented by [7,14]) for obtaining better-combined tasks by learning the correlation between intent and slots.
- **Self-attentive** [13] proposed an enhanced self-attentive model with an improved gate mechanism for intent by leveraging the semantic relationship between slots and intent.
- **Slotted-Gated** [7] proposed model comprises of main components: a bidirectional LSTM operating at the word level and a slot-gated mechanism.
- **Interrelated** [18] proposed an iterative technique to strengthen the connections between slots and intents along with a bi-directional interrelated system for joint tasks.
- **Bi-model** [22] coupled bidirectional LSTM, a Bi-model based RNN semantic frame parsing network structure has developed to manage the JIC-SF.
- **BERT-Joint** overcome the limited generalisation capacity of conventional NLU models, BERT-Joint was introduced by [1].
- **RoBERTa-Joint** [15] RoBERTa is a pre-trained transformer-based language model that has been fine-tuned for performing joint tasks.
- **Capsule NLU** [27] suggested a capsule-based neural network model, which are small groupings of neurons organised in layers.
- **Transformer-NLU:BERT** performed joint tasks using Transformer-NLU [10] suggested an enhanced pre-trained language model.

Table 1. The proposed model comparison with state-of-the-art models performance on ATIS, SNIPS, and HiEn-CMD datasets.

Model	ATIS			SNIPS			HiEn-CMD		
	Intent (Acc.)	Sent. (Acc.)	Slot (F1)	Intent (Acc.)	Sent. (Acc.)	Slot (F1)	Intent (Acc.)	Sent. (Acc.)	Slot (F1)
Joint Seq	92.60	80.70	94.30	96.90	73.20	87.30	76.90	71.20	77.13
Attention-Based	91.10	78.90	94.20	96.70	74.10	87.80	74.01	70.21	78.41
Sloted-Gated	95.41	83.73	95.42	96.86	76.43	89.27	77.19	74.12	77.33
Capsule-NLU	95.00	83.40	95.20	97.30	80.90	91.80	78.01	74.43	78.08
Interrelated SF-First	97.76	86.79	95.75	97.43	80.57	91.43	79.06	74.54	78.30
Interrelated ID-First	97.09	86.90	95.80	97.29	80.43	92.23	79.90	75.62	79.09
BERT-Joint	97.42	87.57	95.74	98.71	91.57	96.27	80.19	75.64	80.53
RoBERTa-Joint	97.42	87.23	95.32	98.71	90.71	95.85	80.96	76.68	81.02
Transformer-NLU:BERT	97.87	88.69	96.25	98.86	91.86	**96.57**	80.19	76.88	81.54
Transformer-NLU:RoBERTa	97.76	87.91	95.65	**98.86**	92.14	96.35	80.19	75.64	80.53
Our Models	97.87	88.35	95.97	98.86	91.57	96.25	84.24	80.54	82.68

5 Conclusion

Multilingual code-mixed language understanding poses significant challenges due to linguistic variations, word-level ambiguity, and intricacies associated with code-mixed text. In this study, we proposed a novel approach to joint JIC-SF using a BiLSTM-BERT multi-attention model. Our model integrated the strengths of BiLSTM and BERT to effectively capture the input text's contextual information while employing multi-attention mechanisms to dynamically weigh the importance of different parts of the input text for both intent classification and slot filling. Specifically, our model achieved high intent accuracy and slot F1-score on the ATIS, Snips and HiEn-CMD datasets. The proposed approach support for English and bilingual code-mixed language understanding. The proposed approach offers a promising solution to enhance the precision and efficacy of natural language understanding systems. This advancement has the potential to yield substantial benefits across a spectrum of applications, including virtual assistants, chatbots, and customer service systems. This research contributes to the advancement of code-mixed language processing, shedding light on a path toward more accurate and robust natural language understanding systems for multilingual and multicultural societies. Furthermore, the proposed multi-attention fusion mechanism has the potential to be extended to other NLP tasks in diverse linguistic environments.

References

1. Chen, Q., Zhuo, Z., Wang, W.: Bert for joint intent classification and slot filling. arXiv preprint arXiv:1902.10909 (2019)
2. Chen, Z., Yang, R., Zhao, Z., Cai, D., He, X.: Dialogue act recognition via CRF-attentive structured network. In: The 41st International ACM SIGIR Conference on Research & Development in Information Retrieval, pp. 225–234 (2018)
3. Conneau, A., et al..: Unsupervised cross-lingual representation learning at scale. arXiv preprint arXiv:1911.02116 (2019)
4. Coucke, A., et al.: Snips voice platform: an embedded spoken language understanding system for private-by-design voice interfaces. arXiv preprint arXiv:1805.10190 (2018)
5. Deng, L., Yu, D.: Deep convex net: a scalable architecture for speech pattern classification. In: Twelfth Annual Conference of the International Speech Communication Association (2011)
6. Devlin, J., Chang, M.W., Lee, K., Toutanova, K.: BERT: pre-training of deep bidirectional transformers for language understanding. arXiv preprint arXiv:1810.04805 (2018)
7. Goo, C.W., et al..: Slot-gated modeling for joint slot filling and intent prediction. In: Proceedings of the 2018 Conference of the North American Chapter of the Association for Computational Linguistics: Human Language Technologies, vol. 2 (Short Papers), pp. 753–757 (2018)
8. Hakkani-Tür, D., Tür, G., Celikyilmaz, A., Chen, Y.N., Gao, J., Deng, L., Wang, Y.Y.: Multi-domain joint semantic frame parsing using bi-directional RNN-LSTM. In: Interspeech, pp. 715–719 (2016)
9. Hakkani-Tur, D.Z., et al.: Multi-domain joint semantic frame parsing (Dec 28 2017), uS Patent App. 15/228,990
10. Hardalov, M., Koychev, I., Nakov, P.: Enriched pre-trained transformers for joint slot filling and intent detection. arXiv preprint arXiv:2004.14848 (2020)
11. Hashemi, H.B., Asiaee, A., Kraft, R.: Query intent detection using convolutional neural networks. In: International Conference on Web Search and Data Mining, Workshop on Query Understanding (2016)

12. Hemphill, C.T., Godfrey, J.J., Doddington, G.R.: The ATIS spoken language systems pilot corpus. In: Speech and Natural Language: Proceedings of a Workshop Held at Hidden Valley, Pennsylvania, June 24-27, 1990 (1990)
13. Li, C., Li, L., Qi, J.: A self-attentive model with gate mechanism for spoken language understanding. In: Proceedings of the 2018 Conference on Empirical Methods in Natural Language Processing, pp. 3824–3833 (2018)
14. Liu, B., Lane, I.: Attention-based recurrent neural network models for joint intent detection and slot filling. arXiv preprint arXiv:1609.01454 (2016)
15. Liu, Y., et al.: RoBERTa: a robustly optimized BERT pretraining approach. arXiv preprint arXiv:1907.11692 (2019)
16. McCallum, A., Freitag, D., Pereira, F.C.: Maximum entropy Markov models for information extraction and segmentation. In: ICML, vol. 17, pp. 591–598 (2000)
17. Mukherjee, S., Nediyanchath, A., Singh, A., Prasan, V., Gogoi, D.V., Parmar, S.P.S.: Intent classification from code mixed input for virtual assistants. In: 2021 IEEE 15th International Conference on Semantic Computing (ICSC), pp. 108–111. IEEE (2021)
18. Niu, P., Chen, Z., Song, M., et al.: A novel bi-directional interrelated model for joint intent detection and slot filling. arXiv preprint arXiv:1907.00390 (2019)
19. Prabhu, A., Joshi, A., Shrivastava, M., Varma, V.: Towards sub-word level compositions for sentiment analysis of Hindi-English code mixed text. arXiv preprint arXiv:1611.00472 (2016)
20. Pratapa, A., Choudhury, M., Sitaram, S.: Word embeddings for code-mixed language processing. In: Proceedings of the 2018 Conference on Empirical Methods in Natural Language Processing, pp. 3067–3072 (2018)
21. Ravuri, S., Stolcke, A.: Recurrent neural network and LSTM models for lexical utterance classification. In: Sixteenth Annual Conference of the International Speech Communication Association (2015)
22. Wang, Y., Shen, Y., Jin, H.: A bi-model based RNN semantic frame parsing model for intent detection and slot filling. arXiv preprint arXiv:1812.10235 (2018)
23. Wankhade, M., Annavarapu, C.S.R., Abraham, A.: CBMAFM: CNN-BiLSTM multi-attention fusion mechanism for sentiment classification. Multimed. Tools Appl. **83**, 1–32 (2023). https://doi.org/10.1007/s11042-023-17437-9
24. Wankhade, M., Annavarapu, C.S.R., Abraham, A.: MAPA BiLSTM-BERT: multi-aspects position aware attention for aspect level sentiment analysis. J. Supercomput. **79**(10), 11452–11477 (2023). https://doi.org/10.1007/s11227-023-05112-7
25. Wankhade, M., Rao, A.C.S.: Opinion analysis and aspect understanding during COVID-19 pandemic using BERT-Bi-LSTM ensemble method. Sci. Rep. **12**(1), 17095 (2022)
26. Xu, P., Sarikaya, R.: Convolutional neural network based triangular Crf for joint intent detection and slot filling. In: 2013 Ieee Workshop on Automatic Speech Recognition and Understanding, pp. 78–83. IEEE (2013)
27. Zhang, C., Li, Y., Du, N., Fan, W., Yu, P.S.: Joint slot filling and intent detection via capsule neural networks. arXiv preprint arXiv:1812.09471 (2018)

The Potential of 1D-CNN for EEG Mental Attention State Detection

NandaKiran Velaga(✉) and Deepak Singh

Department of Computer Science and Engineering, National Institute of Technology Raipur, Raipur, CG, India
nandakiranvelaga09@gmail.com, dsingh.cs@nitrr.ac.in

Abstract. In cognitive neuroscience, attention detection via electroencephalogram (EEG) signals is a crucial task, especially when looking into brain-computer interfaces (BCIs). However, the current biggest challenge in BCI research is the accurate classification of EEG signals. The old methods, such as visual assessment, were neither standardised or statistically analysed. Because of these limitations, many techniques have been created to quantify and extract meaningful data from EEG signals. It has been shown that machine learning algorithms can reliably classify attention states using EEG data. Support Vector Machine (SVM) and k-Nearest Neighbors (KNN) are two examples of such methods. However, more study is required to ensure these algorithms are as precise and reliable as possible. In light of the challenges presented by EEG signal classification, we have employed state-of-the-art deep learning algorithms to enhance the identification of mental attention states. Specifically, we have used a sophisticated deep learning model that integrates spatial dependency analysis, namely 1D Convolutional Neural Networks (CNN). By leveraging the power of 1D CNN, our approach is able to capture intricate spatial patterns within EEG signals, allowing for robust feature extraction and improved classification accuracy. Our model has undergone rigorous training on a diverse dataset comprising 34 EEG signals from 5 participants across different conditions. The model successfully differentiates between distinct mental states (focused, unfocused, drowsy) by analysing EEG data gathered in the experimental setting, with an impressive accuracy of 98.47% and a loss of 0.0144. This study underscores the importance of leveraging advanced computational approaches to unlock the valuable information contained within EEG signals.

Keywords: Mental Attention State · Electroencephalogram (EEG) · Brain-Computer Interface (BCI) · Convolutional Neural Network (CNN)

1 Introduction

The human brain, an extraordinary organ responsible for processing information, controlling body functions, and generating complex cognitive processes, has

N. Chauhan et al. (Eds.): MIND 2023, CCIS 2128, pp. 173–185, 2024.
https://doi.org/10.1007/978-3-031-62217-5_15

been a subject of fascination and scientific inquiry for a long time [1]. Understanding its intricate workings and cognitive functions has led to the emergence of research focused on techniques such as Brain-Computer Interfaces (BCI) that utilize Electroencephalography (EEG) to gain valuable insights into the underlying processes and mental attention states [2,3]. EEG records the brain's electrical activity through electrodes on the scalp, providing valuable insights into various cognitive functions [4,5]. Researchers have developed algorithms to classify and interpret EEG signals associated with different mental states [6].

Accurate EEG signal classification is a primary challenge in BCI research. In earlier approaches, such as visual inspection, there were limitations due to the lack of standardization and statistical analysis methods. These shortcomings hindered the progress of EEG signal analysis. Overcoming the limitations mentioned, researchers have developed various techniques to quantify and extract relevant information from EEG signals. These techniques include the application of traditional machine learning algorithms like Support Vector Machine (SVM) and k-Nearest Neighbors (KNN) which have shown promise in accurately classifying attention states based on EEG signals [7]. However, further research is still necessary to enhance the accuracy and reliability of these algorithms. Through the refinement and optimization of machine learning models, advancements are made to improve the classification performance and overcome challenges like inter-subject variability and noise interference in EEG data.

In an effort to improve the accuracy and dependability of existing algorithms for classifying mental attention states based on EEG signals, we have adopted a complex architecture known as 1D Convolutional Neural Networks (CNN). By harnessing the power of 1D CNN, our approach aims to capture intricate spatial patterns present in EEG signals, facilitating robust feature extraction and ultimately leading to improvements in the overall classification accuracy [8]. Traditionally, accurately classifying EEG signals and detecting mental attention states have been challenging due to the complex relationships and dependencies present in the spatial distribution of EEG data. However, by utilizing 1D CNN, we can effectively exploit the inherent structure of EEG signals and model spatial dependencies more efficiently. One of the key advantages of our approach lies in the automatic learning capabilities of deep learning models [9]. Through training, the 1D CNN learns to extract informative features directly from the raw EEG data, eliminating the need for manual feature engineering. This not only improves classification accuracy but also reduces the reliance on prior expertise. The summary of the originality of the proposed method is as follows:

- This study introduces a novel 1D CNN deep learning model that accurately detects mental attention states in EEG data, outperforming traditional machine learning methods and enhancing precision.
- The proposed approach leverages the 1D CNN to effectively capture spatial dependencies in EEG signals, enhancing the classification accuracy of mental attention states.

- These findings have significant implications for the development of brain-computer interfaces, enhancing usability and enabling personalized treatments.

Section 2 reviews mental state detection research. Section 3 discusses dataset selection, preprocessing, and machine learning model deployment. Section 4 discusses the results. Section 5 provides the conclusion.

2 Literature Review

Brain Computer Interface (BCI) systems have emerged as devices designed to enable individuals with motor disabilities to communicate with computers using brain signals [10]. The purpose of these systems is to decode mental processes into digital instructions for use with computers. The effective extraction of characteristics from EEG data and their subsequent classification is a major difficulty in contemporary BCI research [11]. The analysis of EEG signals is an integral part of brain-computer interfaces. EEG signal analysis is crucial in the realm of BCI devices because it allows for the interpretation of brain activity. Visual inspection was used in the past, but this method was not standardised and couldn't be analysed statistically. To isolate specific characteristics or patterns from the brain signals, feature extraction methods are used. EEG signals are extremely informative about a person's mental state in the context of attention monitoring. Various attention states, such as focused, unfocused, and drowsy, can be detected and categorised by analysing the patterns and frequencies found in EEG data [7]. Attention-related EEG activity has been linked to specific frequency bands, including theta, alpha, and beta waves [12]. When applied to the study of EEG signals, BCI systems have the potential to revolutionise several fields. In the classroom, BCI technology can be used to gauge a student's focus and motivate them to learn more [13]. Furthermore, BCI technology can help enhance HCI by enabling people to operate devices with their brain signals [7]. Furthermore, BCI systems may be useful in medical applications, particularly for the purpose of providing patients with motor limitations with additional means of communicating with the outside world. The evaluated publications use a variety of processing methods and algorithms to decode EEG signals and identify corresponding attention states. Support Vector Machine (SVM) and k-Nearest Neighbors (KNN) are two examples of machine learning algorithms that have shown promise in recent studies for accurately classifying attention states based on EEG signals [7,12]. In addition, wavelet filtering methods have been shown to improve attention state detection by isolating the important frequency components from EEG signals [12]. The interpretation of brain activity for computer interaction is made possible by the use of EEG signal processing, which plays a pivotal role in BCI systems. The detection and classification of attention states is facilitated by extracting characteristics from EEG signals and using machine learning methods. Education, cognitive studies, and HCI can all benefit greatly from BCI systems because of the novel ways they provide of measuring users' attention and improving their interactions with computers.

3 Proposed Methodology

Our proposed methodology for EEG-based mental attention state detection consists of three key steps: dataset selection and description, pre-processing, and the application of machine learning models. Figure 1 shows the flowchart of our methodology:

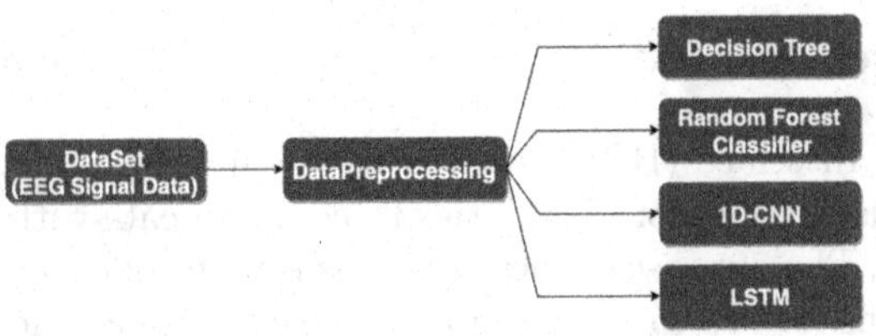

Fig. 1. Flowchart of Proposed Methodology

3.1 Dataset Selection and Description

The study utilized a diverse dataset, comprising 34 EEG signals from 5 subjects, sourced from Kaggle [14]. These EEG recordings, collected non-invasively from 14 scalp channels, each spanned approximately 54 min, enabling long-term cognitive process examination. Importantly, the dataset includes three distinct mental attention states: focused, unfocused, and drowsy, intentionally induced during experimental sessions. Figure 2 shows EEG waveforms from 3 channels of the 7th signal.

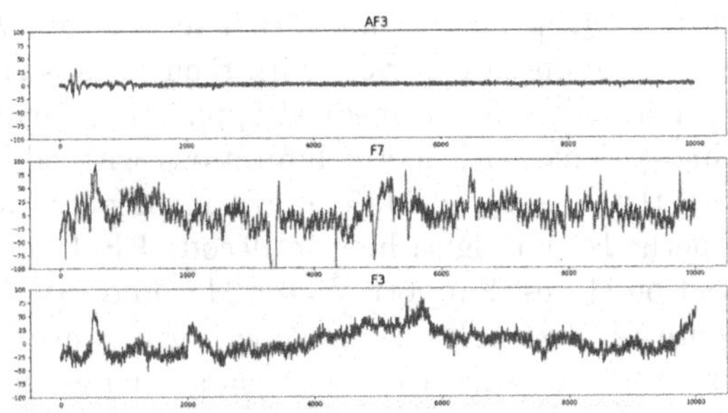

Fig. 2. EEG waveforms of few channels of a signal from the Dataset.

3.2 Pre-processing

In the preprocessing phase, we carefully selected channels with essential information from an initial dataset of 14 channels recorded using a specific headset configuration. Modifications were made based on empirical observations and domain expertise. To ensure data quality and reliability, a DC offset removal procedure was applied, eliminating potential biases or irregularities in the recorded signals and aligning the EEG signal amplitudes with expected values in the range of -100 to 100 microvolts. A visual inspection identified channels with flat lines, indicating possible technical issues or electrode misplacement, and these less informative channels were excluded. We retained channels displaying distinct neural activity patterns, specifically F7, F3, P7, O1, O2, P8, and AF4, for further analysis.

After the Channel Selection and Quality Control we have performed the following preprocessing steps:

Data Segmentation. Data segmentation divided EEG signals into focused, unfocused, and drowsy states by calculating marker points based on the sampling rate. Focused state data ranged from 0–10 mins, unfocused from 10–20 min, and drowsy from 20–30 min.

High-Pass Filtering. High-pass filters removed low-frequency noise and artifacts from the EEG data, enhancing the representation of brain activity. We applied a Butterworth filter with specific parameters: a cutoff frequency of 0.16 Hz, a sampling rate of 128 Hz, and a filter order of 5. Formula for the Butterworth filter:

$$y(t) = \frac{A}{1 + \left(\frac{\omega_c}{\omega}\right)^n} \tag{1}$$

where y(t) is the output signal after filtering. A is a gain-modifying parameter used in filtering. ω_c is the high-pass filter's cutoff frequency. ω is the frequency variable. n is the filter order, which determines the filter's cutoff sharpness.

Figure 3 compares the raw EEG signal and the high-pass filtered signal of the 33rd EEG signal in the dataset.

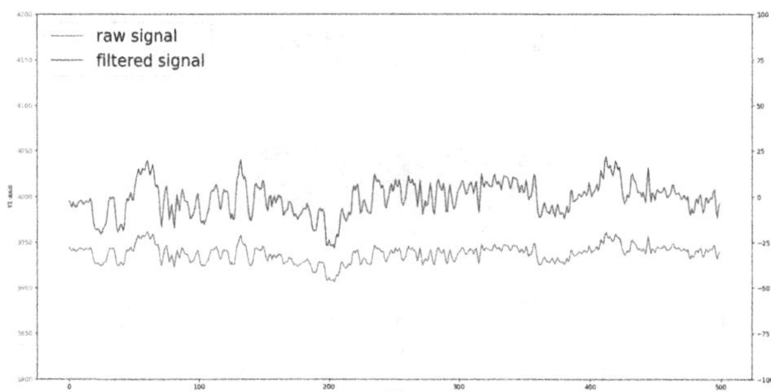

Fig. 3. Comparison between before and after filtered signal.

Time-Varying Power Spectrum Analysis Using Short-Time Fourier Transform (STFT). We employed the Short-Time Fourier Transform (STFT) with a one-second time step to analyze time-varying features in the EEG data [15]. The following Blackman window function was used with 128 samples for STFT calculation:

$$\text{window\_blackman}(t_{\text{win}}, M) = 0.42 \quad -0.5\cos\left(\frac{2\pi t_{\text{win}}}{M-1}\right) + 0.08\cos\left(\frac{4\pi t_{\text{win}}}{M-1}\right) \tag{2}$$

where t_{win} is the number of the time in the window. M is the window's length (128 in this study).

The power spectrum obtained from STFT was used to describe the relative strength of different frequencies in the EEG signal. It revealed frequency-specific power fluctuations across different cognitive states. Figure 4 shows the spectrum of 18th EEG signal depicted using STFT.

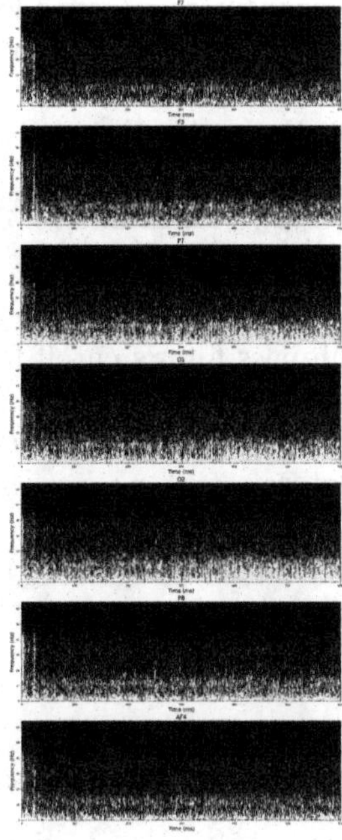

Fig. 4. Power Spectrum of one of the EEG Signal.

Frequency Binning and Range Selection. To improve data utility, we grouped the power values determined by STFT into 0.5 Hz bins and focused on the 0–18 Hz frequency range. This procedure enhanced data resolution by decreasing frequency resolution.

Averaging over a 15-Second Running Window. To capture neural activity dynamics and improve temporal resolution, we averaged the binned power values over a 15-second running window. This approach provided a smoother representation of EEG signals and reduced the impact of short-term fluctuations. And the power spectrum of the 18th EEG signal, averaged across the 15-second time frame, is shown in Fig. 5.

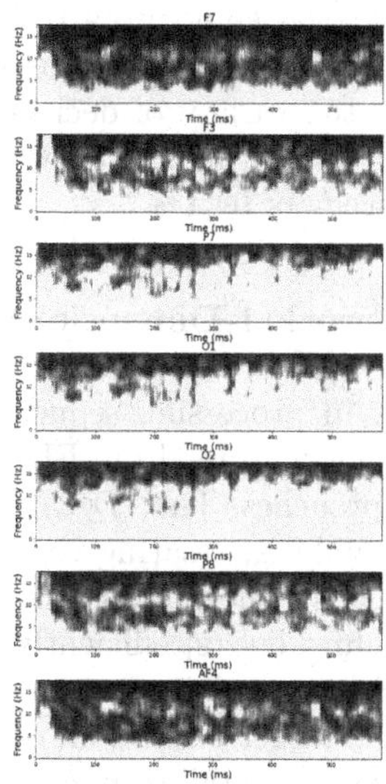

Fig. 5. Average Power Spectrum of one of the EEG Signal.

3.3 The Application of Machine Learning Models

In this study, a variety of machine learning models were used to detect mental attention states based on EEG signals, with a particular emphasis on the 1D CNN model. Filtration, feature extraction, and noise reduction were among the preprocessing steps of the dataset. Decision tree and random forest algorithms were utilised in the context of traditional methods. In the context of deep learning, we employed 1D Convolutional Neural Networks (CNN) and Long Short Term Memory Networks (LSTM) as part of our methodology [16]. Each model's performance was evaluated using an independent test set, with metrics including accuracy, precision, recall, and F1 score considered.

Decision Tree Classifier. The Decision Tree classifier was employed for determining mental attention states based on EEG data in this study. This supervised learning approach is effective for EEG signals, capturing complex relationships [17]. A pre-processed dataset from 5 participants was divided into a training and test set. The Decision Tree model, with a capped depth of 16, successfully classified mental attention states, achieving 89.96% accuracy.

Random Forest Classifier. The Random Forest classifier was used as a robust machine learning model in this study on the EEG detection of mental attention states. To improve prediction accuracy, the proposed ensemble learning system uses several decision trees to effectively capture complex correlations within the EEG signals [18]. The data set was split into a training set and a test set. The training data was then used to instantiate a Random Forest classifier, which was then trained. Leveraging the variety of decision trees and random feature subsets improved the classifier's performance. We were able to classify the mental attention states with an accuracy of 94.1%.

Convolutional Neural Network(1-Dimension). The study employed a 1D Convolutional Neural Network (1D CNN) optimized for EEG mental attention state detection, which excels in processing sequential data. This architecture automatically extracts pertinent features from EEG recordings, surpassing traditional machine learning approaches. The 1D CNN consisted of various layers tailored for sequential data analysis, treating each channel separately to capture channel-specific information. These layers, including convolutional layers, activation functions, and pooling layers, efficiently extracted local patterns as feature maps. Subsequently, fully connected layers learned intricate relationships between these features and the target classes, all of which are outlined in detail in Table 1. And Fig. 6 contains the detailed architecture of our 1D-CNN model.

Table 1. Layers, Parameters, and Activation Functions of the 1D CNN Model

Layer	Parameters	Activation
Conv1D_1	Filters: 32, Kernel: 3	ReLU
MaxPooling1D_1	Pool Size: 2	-
Conv1D_2	Filters: 64, Kernel: 3	ReLU
MaxPooling1D_2	Pool Size: 2	-
Flatten	-	-
Dense_1	Units: 64	ReLU
Dense_2	Units: 3 (3 output classes)	Softmax

The Keras library, a high-level neural network API in Python, was utilized to develop, compile, and train a 1D-CNN model for EEG mental attention state detection. This model was trained using data from all participants over 53 epochs, with a batch size of 32 and a validation split of 0.2, achieving an impressive accuracy of 98.47%. Additionally, individualized 1D CNN models were trained for EEG mental attention state detection using data from each

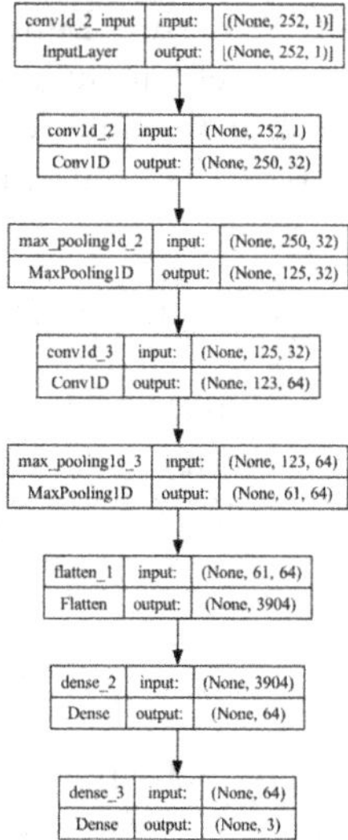

Fig. 6. Architecture of 1D-CNN.

subject. Each model underwent 30 epochs of training, achieving a remarkable record-high accuracy of 99.39%.

Long Short Term Memory Networks(LSTM). For EEG mental attention state detection, we utilised Long Short-Term Memory (LSTM), a form of recurrent neural network (RNN) architecture [19]. It processed sequence data, capturing temporal dependencies, and used TensorFlow and Keras for model construction. The LSTM model was compiled with sparse categorical cross-entropy loss and the Adam optimizer. It was trained for 60 epochs with a batch size of 32, achieving a classification accuracy of 91.07%. LSTM proved effective in analyzing EEG data and classifying mental attention states, contributing to advancements in state-of-the-art mental attention state detection systems.

4 Results Discussion

The research explored the effectiveness of 1D Convolutional Neural Networks (CNN) in analyzing spatial correlations and the performance of various machine learning (ML) models for EEG mental attention state detection. The findings offer a comparative assessment of the efficiency of these models, derived from comprehensive experimentation and evaluation using train and test datasets. These insights illuminate the strengths and weaknesses of each model, aiding in the selection of appropriate methods for EEG analysis in mental attention state detection studies.

Performance Comparison of Machine Learning Models. Initially, traditional machine learning (ML) models, including Decision Tree and Random Forest, were employed to establish a baseline for EEG mental attention state detection. The summarized results are presented in Table 2.

Table 2. Performance Comparison of Traditional Machine Learning Models

Model	Accuracy (%)	Precision (%)	Recall (%)	F1 Score (%)
Decision Tree	89.96	89.96	89.96	89.96
Random Forest	94.10	94.10	94.10	94.10

Performance Comparison of Deep Learning Models. In addition to traditional ML models, the study also explored the effectiveness of deep learning models, specifically 1D CNN and LSTM, for detecting mental attention states in EEG signals. These models were trained on preprocessed dataset and optimized using validation sets. The performance of these models is displayed in Table 3.

Table 3. Performance of Deep Learning Models

Model	Accuracy (%)	Precision (%)	Recall (%)	AUC(%)	F1 Score (%)
1D CNN	**98.46**	**98.47**	**98.46**	**99.85**	**98.46**
LSTM	91.07	91.10	91.07	98.00	91.06

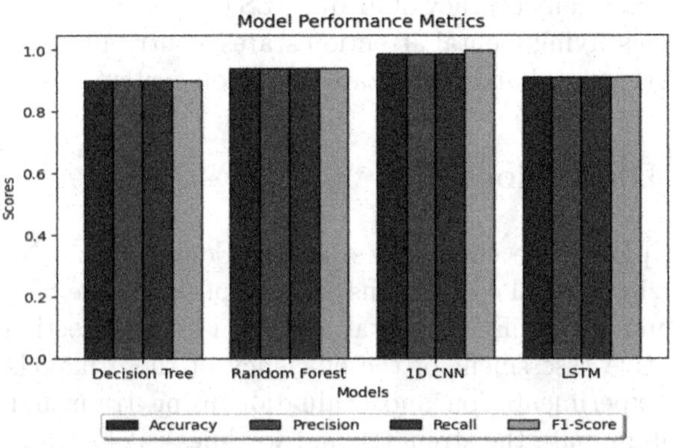

Fig. 7. Performance of Machine Learning Models

Table 4. Performance Metrics of the Model

Subject	Accuracy (%)	Precision (%)	Recall (%)	AUC(%)	F1 Score (%)
1	**99.39**	99.39	99.39	99.97	99.39
2	**99.54**	99.54	99.54	100.00	99.54
3	**97.87**	97.99	97.87	99.92	97.89
4	**99.91**	99.91	99.91	100.00	99.91
5	**98.10**	98.18	98.10	99.95	98.11

Table 4 presents a comprehensive evaluation of the 1D CNN model's performance for each subject.

Our study underscores the effectiveness of both traditional machine learning models and advanced deep learning models for EEG mental attention state detection. Decision Tree and Random Forest models demonstrated good performance, showcasing their ability to capture complex relationships within EEG signals. However, the 1D CNN model outperformed traditional models in terms of accuracy and other metrics, as depicted in Fig. 7. The exceptional performance of the 1D CNN model can be attributed to its architecture, allowing for the extraction of local and global spatial dependencies in EEG signals. By incorporating multiple convolutional layers, pooling layers, and dense layers, the 1D CNN model effectively captures informative features and patterns in the EEG data, leading to precise mental attention state classification.

5 Conclusions

In conclusion, our study introduced an innovative approach to EEG-based mental attention state detection, leveraging state-of-the-art deep learning models. Comparing traditional machine learning and other deep learning models, the 1D CNN model emerged as the most effective in consistently identifying mental states from EEG data. Its success is attributed to its ability to capture both local and global spatial dependencies, facilitating robust feature extraction. These results underscore the potential of deep learning models, particularly the 1D CNN [20], in EEG signal analysis and mental state recognition, with implications for brain-computer interfaces, neurological disorder diagnosis, and mental health monitoring. The integration of deep learning techniques facilitates real-time analysis and personalized interventions. While the exceptional performance of the 1D CNN underscores the significance of advanced computational methods in EEG mental state recognition, further research is warranted for validation, including broader datasets, interpretability of deep learning models, and deeper insights into cognitive processes and neurological conditions.

Acknowledgment. This work has been supported by the National Institute of Technology, Raipur, under the Seed Grant Project No. NITRR/Seed Grant/2021-22/47.

References

1. Liu, N.H., Chiang, C.Y., Chu, H.C.: Recognizing the degree of human attention using EEG signals from mobile sensors. Sensors (Switzerland) **13**, 10273–10286 (2013)
2. Bin. H.: ACM digital library., ACM special interest group on computer-human interaction., ACM SIGMOBILE., and ACM special interest group on spatial information. In: Proceedings of 2011 International Workshop on Ubiquitous Affective Awareness and Intelligent Interaction. ACM (2011)
3. Belo, J., Clerc, M., Schön, D.: EEG-based auditory attention detection and its possible future applications for passive BCI. Front. Comput. Sci. **3**, 4 (2021)
4. Sridhar, S., Manian, V.: EEG and deep learning based brain cognitive function classification. Computers **9**, 1–18 (2020)
5. Souza, R.H.C.E., Naves, E.L.M.: Attention detection in virtual environments using EEG signals: a scoping review. Front. Physiol. **12**, 727840 (2021)
6. Mohamed, Z., El Halaby, M., Said, T., Shawky, D., Badawi, A.: Characterizing focused attention and working memory using EEG. Sensors (Switzerland), **18**(11), 3743 (2018)
7. Acı, Ç.İ., Kaya, M., Mishchenko, Y.: Distinguishing mental attention states of humans via an EEG-based passive BCI using machine learning methods. Expert Syst. Appl. **134** 153–166, (2019)
8. Kiranyaz, S., Avci, O., Abdeljaber, O., Ince, T., Gabbouj, M., Inman, D.J.: 1d convolutional neural networks and applications: a survey (2019)
9. Kiranyaz, S., Avci, O., Abdeljaber, O., Ince, T., Gabbouj, M., Inman, D.J.: 1d convolutional neural networks and applications: a survey. Mech. Syst. Signal Process. **151**, 107398 (2021)
10. Dānishgāh i Ṣanʻatī-i Amīr Kabīr, Institute of Electrical, Electronics Engineers, and Iran) International Iranian Conference on Biomedical Engineering (2nd : 2017 : Tehran. In: 2017 24th Iranian Conference on Biomedical Engineering and 2017 2nd International Iranian Conference on Biomedical Engineering (ICBME)
11. Vaid, S., Singh, P., Kaur, C.: EEG signal analysis for BCI interface: a review. vol. 2015-April, pp. 143–147. Institute of Electrical and Electronics Engineers Inc., 4 (2015)
12. Djamal, E.C., Pangestu, D.P., Dewi, D.A.: Dewi. EEG-based recognition of attention state using wavelet and support vector machine, pp. 139–144. Institute of Electrical and Electronics Engineers Inc., 1 (2017)
13. Al-Nafjan, A., Aldayel, M.: Predict students' attention in online learning using EEG data. Sustainability (Switzerland) **14**(11), 6553 (2022)
14. Mishchenko, Y., Acı, C.I., Kaya, M.: EEG data for mental attention state detection (2019). https://www.kaggle.com/datasets/inancigdem/eeg-data-for-mental-attention-state-detection
15. Jaganathan, K., Eldar, Y.C., Hassibi, B.: STFT phase retrieval: Uniqueness guarantees and recovery algorithms. IEEE J. Selected Topics Signal Process. **10**(4), 770–781 (2016)
16. Toa, C.K., Sim, K.S., Tan, S.C.: Electroencephalogram-based attention level classification using convolution attention memory neural network. IEEE Access **9**, 58870–58881 (2021)
17. Fürnkranz, J.: Decision Tree. In: Sammut, C., Webb, G.I. (eds.) Encyclopedia of Machine Learning, pp. 263–267. Springer US, Boston, MA (2010). https://doi.org/10.1007/978-0-387-30164-8_204

18. Breiman, L.: Random forests. Mach. Learn. **45**(1), 5–32 (2001)
19. Hochreiter, S., Schmidhuber, J.: Long short-term memory. Neural Comput. **9**(8), 1735–1780 (1997)
20. Sibilano, E., et al.: An attention-based deep learning approach for the classification of subjective cognitive decline and mild cognitive impairment using resting-state eeg. J. Neural Eng. **20**, 2 (2023)

Potato Leaf Disease Classification Using Deep Learning Model

Raj Kumar(✉), Tushar Agrawal, Vinayak Dhar Dwivedi, and Harsh Khatter

KIET Group of Institutions, Delhi-NCR, Ghaziabad, India
raj0697@gmail.com, harsh.khatter@kiet.edu

Abstract. India's primary industry is agriculture, which suffers an annual loss of 35% agricultural yield due to plant diseases. Illness-related harvest losses are a serious issue for both major farming operations and rural communities. Subsequently, the detection of plant diseases is crucial to agriculture. If adequate care is not taken in this area, it could have a significant negative influence on plants by lowering the productivity, quality, and quantity of the corresponding good or service. Automatic disease detection not only reduces labor costs associated with maintaining vast fields of crops, but also picks up symptoms as soon as they appear on plant leaves. The majority of plant illnesses may be identified from the symptoms that occur on the leaves; however, due to the wide variety of diseases, recognizing and classifying diseases with the naked eye is not only laborious and time-consuming, but also prone to inaccuracy with a high error rate. In this study, authors proposed a sequential deep learning model where in each convolution layer is followed by a max pool layer in order to extract most relevant features form the input images. For experimental validation of proposed deep learning model, study uses 2152 potato leaves images from Plant Village Dataset out of which 1000 are of early blight and 1000 are of late blight the remaining 152 images are of healthy leaves. Authors have divided this dataset into 32 different batches and trained the model using multiple subsequent 2-Dimensional convolutional layers and 2-Dimensional Max pooling layer with Rectified Linear Unit (RELU) as the activation function. With ADAM optimizer and 50 epochs, authors achieved a maximum accuracy of 98.83% and a loss of only 4.47%.

Keywords: AI in agriculture · Neural Network · Deep Learning · Plant Leaf Disease Classification

1 Introduction

Demand of plant-based products. Consequently, protecting crops from plant diseases is crucial to meeting the growing demand for food, both in terms of quantity and quality. Agriculture productivity is a significant economic factor. Economically speaking, plant diseases have an annual cost to the global economy of roughly US$220 billion. Thus, plant diseases are considered as a severe threat to

N. Chauhan et al. (Eds.): MIND 2023, CCIS 2128, pp. 186–200, 2024.
https://doi.org/10.1007/978-3-031-62217-5_16

the economy and food security. Therefore, the diagnosis of ailments in plants is crucial to agriculture. If adequate care is not taken in this area, it could have a significant negative influence on plants by lowering the productivity, quality, or quantity of the corresponding good or service. Plant leaf diseases have grown to be a major issue in recent years, necessitating precise research and quick deep learning applications in the classification of plant diseases. The incorporation of latest technologies such as AI, DL etc. in agriculture has solved or reduced the problems of farmers to a large extent. These technologies provide a very efficient and cost-effective solution to problems of farmers.

This study aims to predict and classify the diseases in plants using images of leaves as the leaves show first sign of any disease in a plant. This helps in knowing the problem at a very early stage and thus required prevention can be done. The project involves creation of a dataset of classified plant leaves with and without diseases if any. This data set is used to train a Convolutional Neural Network build using TensorFlow. Data augmentation is also to make the model more robust. The backend server is designed using tf serving and fast API and front end is developed using React JS and React Native. Rest of the work is organized as follows: In Sect. 2, authors outlined the motivation behind study. Section 3 briefly summarized the recent work in the domain of plant disease classification. In Sect. 4, authors mentioned about the problem statement of the study. Methodology and architecture being adopted are discussed in Sects. 5 and 6 respectively. Results and discussion is carried out in Sect. 7 and work finally concluded in Sect. 8.

2 Motivation

The need of creating autonomous plant disease diagnosis models based on discernible symptoms on leaves has recently been shown by developments in Deep Learning models. Computer vision and CNN (Convolutional Neural Network) can be used to predict plant diseases quickly and at an extremely early stage. Therefore, incorporating cutting-edge technology like Deep Learning and Machine Learning into agriculture for disease detection and categorization to improve production offers farmers a financially viable alternative.

3 Literature Review

According to the article, "Plant health and food security", published by Food and Agriculture Organization of the United Nations, more than 80% of a person's diet is made up of plants. They are therefore essential to guaranteeing food security, which is the ongoing accessibility of enough inexpensive, safe, and nutrient-rich food for all of us to living active, healthy lives. Plant pests and diseases can affect crops, reducing the amount of food that is accessible and affordable while increasing the price of food. This poses a threat to food security. Plant parasites and illnesses may also have a negative impact on food flavor, changing people's traditional eating choices. Over the years, outbreaks of plant pests and diseases have led to severe food shortages and famines. A catastrophic Brown spot fungus outbreak (Bipolarism Oryza, also known as Helminthophobia Oryza) that struck India in 1942-1943 resulted in the destruction of up to 90% of the country's rice crops in Bengal region, which lead to the death of around 2 million people. Over a million people perished in the great Irish famine of 1845, which also forced 1.5 million people to leave their birthplace, was brought on by the potato late blight disease that is brought on by the pest known as Phytophthora infesters, which is thought to be native to Central America. Food security is now more at risk from plant diseases and pests than ever before as a result of expanding international trade and a changing climate. Growing trade makes it more likely that these pests will leave their natural habitats, and shifting climatic patterns bring new opportunities for plant pests and illnesses. Due to these reasons, 20% to 40% of global food production is destroyed which affects the world economy about $220 Billion.

Authors have gone through a lot of research papers related to the field of our research and project and have tried to come with a better understanding and solution to the problem. During the research, authors came to know various problems faced during early solutions and models of the Plant Disease Classification Models and Algorithms but the recent developments in AI and ML algorithms over the past few years have led to improved and consistent solutions to the problem. Highly enhanced and latest algorithms at the backend integrated with modern computing hand held devices such as smartphones prove to be a very optimal and highly efficient solution to the problem of plant disease prediction and classification [1]. Smartphones in particular provide particularly special methods to assist in the detection of diseases because of their powerful computational capabilities, sharp displays, and full accessory sets that are already incorporated into them, such as potent HD cameras.

CNNs are the foundation stone of Deep Learning in graphics and images data. With time, a single technique in particular-the convolutional neural network-has been created and refined, leading to the improvements in computer vision with deep learning. Convolutional Neural Networks (ConvNets) are typically developed with a set resource budget, and if more resources are available, the accuracy can be scaled up. The ConvNet models can be scaled, and its network depth, width and resolution can be balanced in order to improve its performance. This is done according to the requirements and the resources available for the project. Based on the number and types of layers and activation functions there are various CNN architecture available such as AlexNet, LeNet, ResNet, Inception (GoogleNet), EfficientNet, MobileNet etc.

Two of the most crucial methods for proper training and model resilience are data segmentation and data augmentation. These two methods will enable us to create a highly accurate and effective model. The technique of image segmentation involves dividing a picture into regions, subregions, or objects with similar features. The two primary factors utilized to process image segmentation are discontinuity and similarity. These characteristics are used to categorize the picture segmentation into edge-based segmentation and region-based segmentation. Paul

DAYANG and Armandine Sorel KOUYIM MELI [2] in their research have compared various segmentation techniques and algorithms in order to find the best Image Segmentation Techniques. They have compared K-means clustering, K-nearest neighbors and canny edge algorithms to segment and classify the three of the most grown crops around the world wiz. Potato, Corn and Tomato. Results obtained show that this algorithm is ineffective and inefficient for Solanaceae plant family, which includes potatoes. Due to the difficulties of selecting the k-value, the performance of the k-nearest neighbor method is very bad. Finally, all of the selected plants may be predicted with high accuracy thanks to the k-means algorithm. Small datasets force the model to overfit, which results in subpar performance when dealing with real-world data. Image augmentation provides fresh data can be utilized for model training by altering the already-existing data. To put it another way, it refers to the process of improving the dataset that is made accessible for deep learning model training. Image augmentation uses a variety of techniques, including cropping, rotating, flipping, noise reduction, and blurring.

Leaf GAN is one popular image augmentation mechanism used to create augmented images of plant leaves. Leaf GAN converts healthy photos into a variety of diseased images as a data augmentation method to improve the accuracy of plant disease detection. In a study Quan Huu Cap et al. [3] have proposed the use of Leaf GAN for plant leaf image augmentation to classify 5 different cucumber diseases. When Leaf Gan's performance was compared to that of vanilla Cycle GAN, it was shown that the generalization could not be improved by vanilla Cycle GAN. It only improved performance by 0.7% from the baseline, however utilizing Leaf GAN, it improved performance by up to 7.4%. In addition, the images produced by Leaf GAN were of higher quality than those produced by vanilla CycleGAN. The EfficientNet is one of the most recent advancements in CNN. By utilizing a method known as Compound Coefficient, EfficientNet scales up models in a straightforward yet efficient manner. It uses a pre-set scaling factors rather that randomly changing dimensions such as width, depth, resolution etc. Using the scaling method and AutoML, 7 different models in various dimensions were developed. They outperformed CNN's most recent accuracy standards.

Many researches have been conducted to predict and classify Plant Diseases with high accuracy using EfficientNet CNN [4,5]. Muhammad E. H. Chowdhury et al. [4] have proposed the use of a CNN architecture based on EfficientNet to classify various tomato diseases. With a 20-kilogram annual per capita consumption and 15% of all vegetable consumption, tomatoes are a significant food crop throughout the world. According to a recent study North America consumes about 42 kg of tomatoes per person annually on the other hand the consumption is 31 kg of tomatoes per person annually in Europe. In the model, they have used about eighteen thousand segmented and simple tomato leaf images for the characterization of diseases in tomatoes. In this project, U-net and Modified U-net models were used as segmentation models for the binary classification, 6-class classification and 10-class classification of tomato diseases. EfficientNet B-4 and

B-7 were used. In the study, it was concluded that the models perform better when trained with Deeper Network and segmented images. B-7 model gave an accuracy of 99.95% in binary and 99.12% in 6 class classification. EfficientNet-t B4's classification accuracy was 99.89% for ten-class classification using segmented pictures. Similar to this study Ümit Atila et al. [5] in their study have proposed to use EfficientNet model for the classification of plant diseases. Very popular Plant Village dataset having 38 classes and 53503 images of fourteen different plants. Out of all 38 classes, 12 are classified as healthy and the remaining 26 are diseased. B4 and B5 EfficientNet models were utilized for disease classification. Their training was done by Transfer Learning approach. The study compares the performance of EfficientNet(B4 and B4) with other popular CNN models. The test dataset findings revealed that EfficientNet architecture's B5 model gave an accuracy score of 99.91% and the B-4 model gave an accuracy score of 99.97% which was better than many other DL models.

Students at Pakistan's HITEC University [6] conducted research on fruit health monitoring and early disease classification using Correlation Coefficient and Deep Features (CCDF). How closely two or more variables' measurements are similar across a dataset is indicated by the correlation coefficient. The proposed method includes two key steps: first, the detection of infected regions, and second, feature extraction and categorization. In the first step, the input image's contrast is first increased using a hybrid technique, and then a proposed correlation coefficient-based segmentation technique that separates the diseased areas from the background is applied. The feature extraction of specific diseases is carried out in the second stage using 2 pre-trained models (VGG16, caffe AlexNet). Prior to the max-pooling stage, a parallel features fusion step is incorporated to combine the extracted features. This technique gave classification accuracy of about 98.60%. According to S. Ashwinkumar, S. Rajagopal, V. Manimaran, B. Jegajothi [7] automated plant disease detection methods are useful for detecting disease symptoms when they first emerge on plant leaves, which helps to lessen the onerous process of monitoring big crop farms. They have created a model for predicting and classifying plant disease using Optimal Mobile Network-Based Convolutional Neural Network (OMNCNN). The proposed OMNCNN model utilizes pre-processing, segmentation, feature extraction, and classification as its primary operational steps. To pinpoint the areas of the leaf picture that are impacted, bilateral filtering and Kapur's thresholding are used. Moreover, MobileNet model is used for feature extraction and Emperor Penguin Optimizer (EPO) is used to optimize the working of MobileNet. This technique has shown promising results. It gives accuracy of 98.7% and maximum precision of 0.985.

Nowadays Extreme Learning Machines (ELM) Deep Learning algorithms is also used for the prediction and classification of plant diseases. ELM is a training algorithm for Single Layer Feedforward Neural Network (SLFN). Anshul Bhatia et al. [8] have used this model for the classification of Tomato Diseases. They have used Tomato Powdery Mildew Disease (TPMD) dataset which is very imbalanced hence various resampling techniques viz. SMOTE, ROS, RUS, and IMPS have been used. This study concludes that the ELM model provides best accuracy with Importance Sampling (IMPS) with 89.8% of Classification Accuracy [9].

4 Problem Statement

Plant disease in agriculture is one of the biggest issues for a nation like India where it is the primary occupation. Plant diseases are to blame for 35% of India's crop yield losses. Illness-related harvest losses are a serious issue for both major farming operations and rural communities [10]. If proper precautions are not taken in this regard, it could have a significant negative impact on plants by lowering the productivity, quality, or output of the corresponding good or service. The leaves of the plant are the first to display these symptoms of any plant disease. Thus, detecting and treating plant diseases through their leaves at an early stage can stop harvests from suffering catastrophic damage [11]. The incorporation of Deep Learning in agriculture has brought a reform in the field of agriculture and provides a very cost-effective solution to problems of farmers [12]. This study uses highly accurate CNN architecture to create a model which can classify diseases in plant using images of the leaves of the plant. A dataset of potato plant leaves, pre classified with diseases if any, is used to train the model.

5 Methodology

For creating a solution to the problem, authors have used TensorFlow and TensorFlow Lite to develop a Convolutional Neural Network (CNN). The approach and steps that have been followed are shown in Figs. 3 and 8. Authors have used potato leaves dataset to train deep learning model. In next section, details of dataset and different processing steps are discussed.

5.1 Dataset

Authors have used the "Plant Village" dataset rom Kaggle for this research. This collection includes a total of 2152 photos for identifying potato diseases as well as ones for identifying tomatoes and peppers. But the Potato dataset will be our major emphasis. Three groups of photos make up this dataset of potatoes. It comprises of 46.46% images of early and late blight each and the remaining 7% of the images are that of healthy plant leaves. The dataset contains just 256 by 256 pixels photos. These photographs were downloaded into the tf.data.dataset using the TensorFlow dataset. Authors are able to get photos in groups using tf.data.dataset. If user reads the photos in batches, user can do impressive things like ". filter," ". map," and much more. Authors read the photographs into batches of 32 images for this project. Thus, the dataset will have a length of 68.

Data Acquisition See (Figs. 1 and 2)

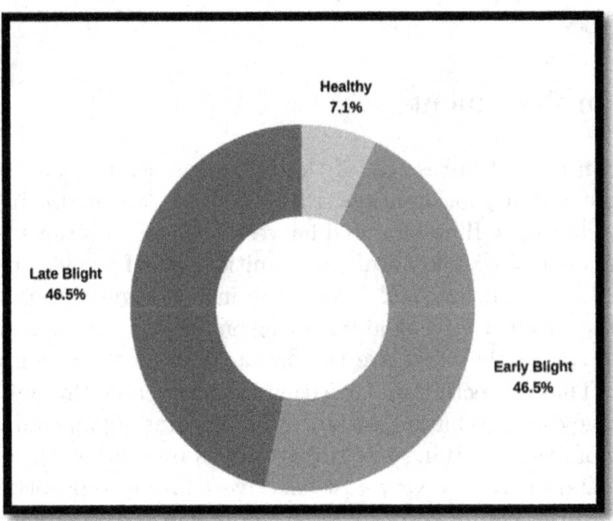

Fig. 1. Dataset Composition.

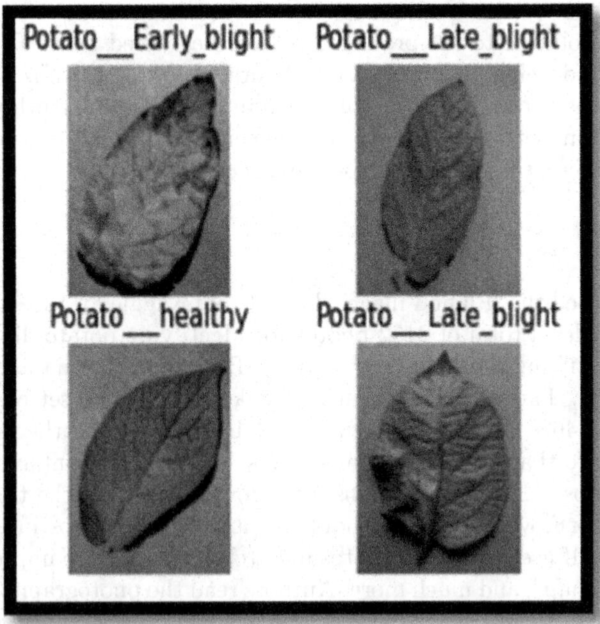

Fig. 2. Sample images from plant village dataset.

5.2 Data Splitting

When splitting dataset, authors have maintained around 80% of it as training data and divided the other 20% into two halves. 10% have been split for validation, and 10% will be used for testing. The training procedure will make use of the validation set. Authors shall validate this 10% of the data after each epoch. Authors utilized 10% test data when have completed all of the epochs to gauge how accurate our model is. For splitting purpose, it used take () method [13].

Shuffling of Data. Before training the ML model, it is crucial that the dataset is thoroughly shuffled to remove any bias or patterns in the split datasets. The photographs kept in three different directories have been randomly shuffled using a separate function that we created. TensorFlow dataset will be passed to this method. Prior to dividing the data into three parts, this data shuffle is performed.

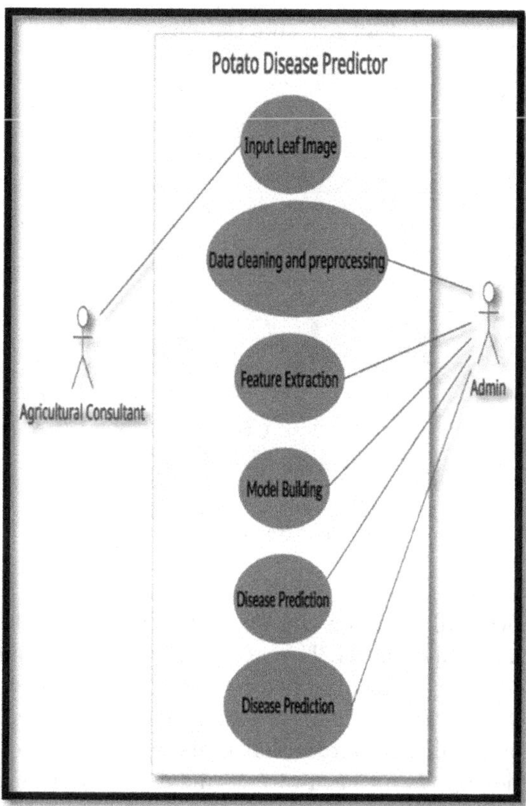

Fig. 3. Use case diagram for plant disease detection system.

Caching and Shuffling. When we need the same image on a subsequent iteration, caching keeps the image in memory rather than reading it from the disc. By cutting down on the processing time required for a specific image; this enhances the pipeline's performance (Figs. 4 and 5).

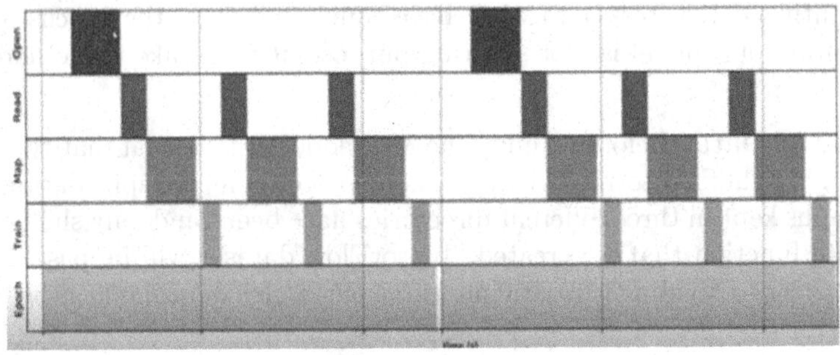

Fig. 4. Before Caching.

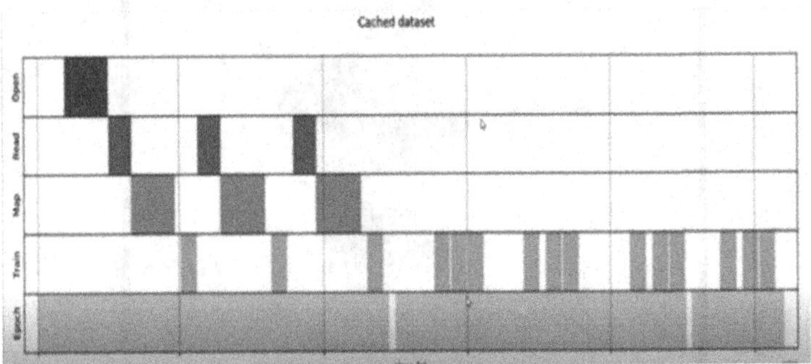

Fig. 5. After Caching.

The performance will be improved if the prefetching loads the subsequent batch from the disc while the GPU or CPU is actively training. Prefetching is the process of loading a resource before it is needed in order to reduce the amount of time spent waiting for it. Caching operations frequently employ a cache. It enables preloading resources that users will require before they request them, which enables apps and hardware to maximize performance and reduce wait times (Figs. 6 and 7).

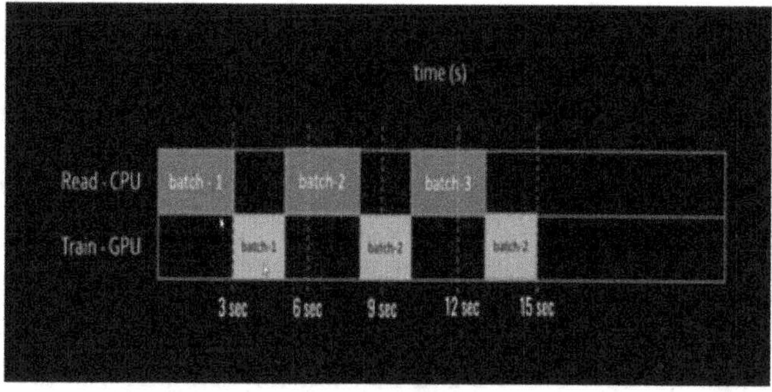

Fig. 6. Before Prefetching.

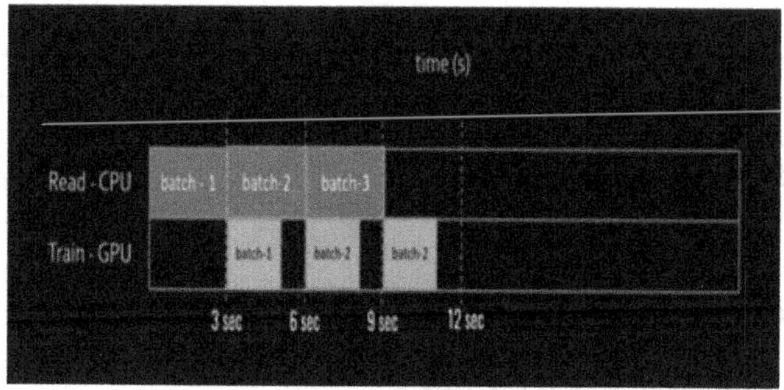

Fig. 7. After Prefetching.

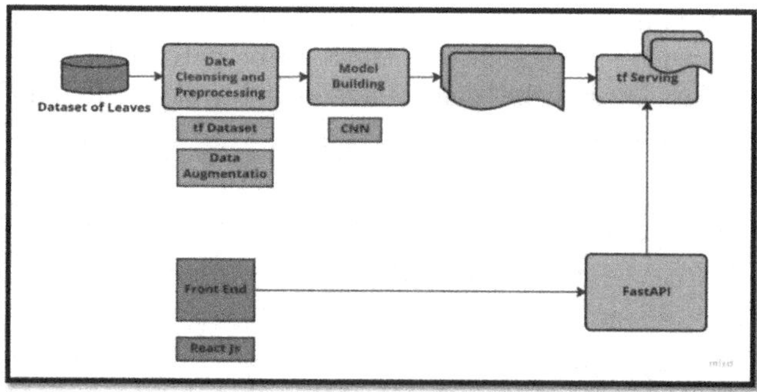

Fig. 8. Methodology used for Plant leaf disease classification.

Data Preprocessing

- **Resizing** Image scaling is a vital step in the pre-processing images. Deep learning models are typically easier and faster to train on small images. A larger input image requires the neural network to learn from four times as many pixels, which extends the training period for the design. We execute this action because it will handle resizing in the event that we provide a prediction with an image that is not 256 by 256 pixels [14].
- **Scaling** Data sets having dissimilar data points and feature values require more time for training and the accuracy of the model is also low. On the other hand, if the values of features are more similar then the model may train well and quickly. Scaling is a method for bringing distant data points closer together, hence it can be used in any circumstance where there are distant data points. Scaling is used to generalise data points, or to put it another way, to reduce the distance between them.
- **Augmentation** In our approach, "RandomFlip" is implemented, which is similar to rotating an image by 180 degrees, flipping it horizontally, and then conducting "Random Rotation" to produce the augmented images. It's crucial to remember that after rotation, image dimensions might not be preserved. If your image is square, right-angle rotation will keep the image's dimensions constant. A 180° rotation would preserve the shape's dimensions if it were a rectangle. As the image is rotated at lower degrees, the final image size will change.

6 Model Architecture

6.1 Convolutional Neural Network

To create the proposed CNN model, authors created a "resize and rescale" layer that will resize all of the input photos to 255 by 255 before rescaling them by dividing them by 255. The "augmentation" layer is the next layer. Then, six pairs of "Conv2D" and "MaxPooling2D" layers are used. The number of layer pairings was determined through trial and error to improve accuracy. Once all of these layers have been stacked, they must all be flattened to create an array of neurons. The last layer is the "dense" layer which will classify all three groups and forecast the outcome (Fig. 9).

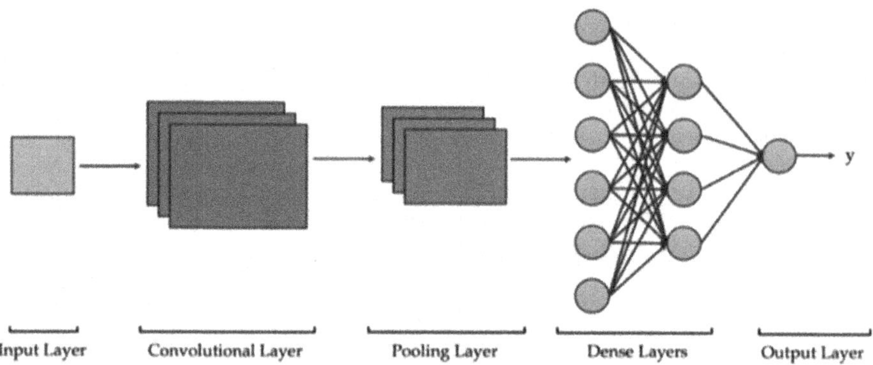

Fig. 9. Deep learning model Architecture

7 Results and Discussion

Compilation is a task carried out before training begins and following the writing of the model's statements. It also defines the metrics, optimizer or learning rate, loss function, and checks for format issues. Authors use the "Adam optimizer," a replacement optimization method for stochastic gradient descent, to train deep learning models. By fusing the most advantageous aspects of the AdaGrad and RMSProp algorithms, Adam develops an optimization technique that can handle sparse gradients in noisy environments. For this purpose, authors have used a system with Intel i5 8th Gen processor with 8 GB main memory having 1.6 GHz as its base frequency and 3.9 GHz as its maximum frequency. Compilation must be followed by model fitting.

7.1 Model Evaluation

Authors have evaluated our model using the test dataset after training it using 50 epochs. Because our model hasn't seen this dataset, it is utilised to assess how well it is working by applying it to a test dataset. The accuracy is 98.83% with a loss of only 4.47%. Each time, data is trained, and this accuracy could change a little. Through trial and error to improve accuracy. Once all of these layers have been stacked, they must all be flattened to create an array of neurons. The last layer is the "dense" layer which will classify all three groups and forecast the outcome (Fig. 10).

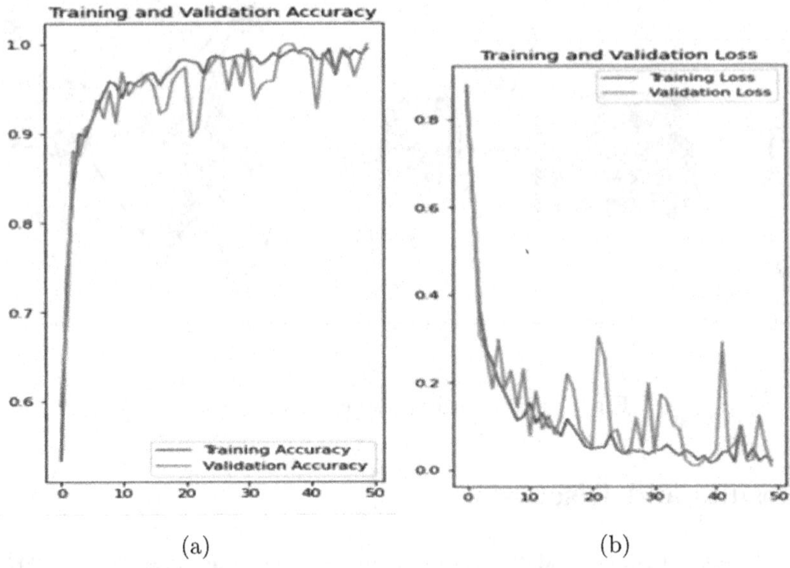

(a) (b)

Fig. 10. (a) Classification accuracy plot for deep learning model used, (b) Loss function plot for deep learning model used.

7.2 Model Predictions

See (Fig. 11)

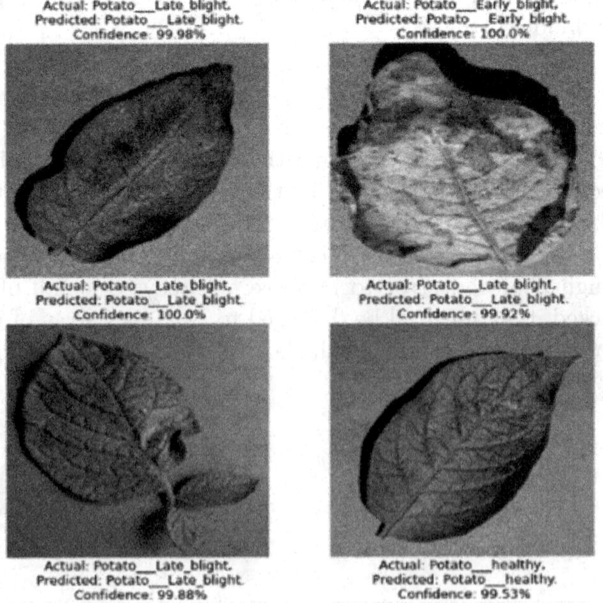

Fig. 11. Sample predicted results by deep learning model.

8 Conclusion

In this study, authors have proposed the use of CNN with a layer of resizing and rescaling and 6 pairs of Conv2D and MaxPooling layers to detect and classify potato leaves for three categories namely "Early Blight", "Late Blight" and "Healthy" using the Potato leaves images of the Plant Village Dataset. Authors have used image segmentation and image augmentation to make our model more accurate and robust in real life conditions. Authors have used shuffling, prefetching and caching to make our model more efficient and faster. The complete dataset is divided into 32 different batches, and authors have used 50 epochs to train our model on a local computer system with i5 8th Gen processor and 8 GB of RAM. Authors have used Rectified Linear Unit (RELU) as the activation function for the convolutional layers and Softmax as the activation function for the last dense layer by using these combinations, model have achieved a maximum accuracy of 98.83% and with a loss of only 4.47%.

References

1. Verma, A., et al.: Plantosphere: next generation adaptive and smart agriculture system. J. Sensors **2022**, 1–10 (2022)
2. Dayang, P., Meli, A.S.K.: Evaluation of image segmentation algorithms for plant disease detection. Int. J. Image Graph. Signal Process **13**, 14–26 (2021)
3. Cap, Q.H., Uga, H., Kagiwada, S., Iyatomi, H.: LeafGAN: an effective data augmentation method for practical plant disease diagnosis. IEEE Trans. Autom. Sci. Eng. **19**(2), 1258–1267 (2020)
4. Chowdhury, M.E.H., et al.: Automatic and reliable leaf disease detection using deep learning techniques. AgriEngineering **3**(2), 294–312 (2021)
5. Atila, Ü., Uçar, M., Akyol, K., Uçar, E.: Plant leaf disease classification using EfficientNet deep learning model. Eco. Inform. **61**, 101182 (2021)
6. Gao, J., Westergaard, J.C., Riis Sundmark, E.H., Bagge, M., Liljeroth, E., Alexandersson, E.: Automatic late blight lesion recognition and severity quantification based on field imagery of diverse potato genotypes by deep learning. Knowl. Based Syst. **214**, 106723 (2021)
7. Ashwinkumar, S., Rajagopal, S., Manimaran, V., Jegajothi, B.: Automated plant leaf disease detection and classification using optimal MobileNet based convolutional neural networks. Mater. Today Proc. **51**, 480–487 (2022)
8. Bhatia, A., Chug, A., Singh, A.P.: Application of extreme learning machine in plant disease prediction for highly imbalanced dataset. J. Stat. Manage. Syst. **23**(6), 1059–1068 (2020)
9. Minhaz Hossain, S.M., Deb, K., Dhar, P.K., Koshiba, T.: Plant leaf disease recognition using depth-wise separable convolution-based models. Symmetry **13**(3), 511 (2021)
10. Kumar, R., Shukla, N., Princee: Plant disease detection and crop recommendation using CNN and machine learning. In: 2022 International Mobile and Embedded Technology Conference (MECON), pp. 168–172. IEEE (2022)
11. Dwivedi, P., Kumar, S., Vijh, S., Chaturvedi, Y.: Study of machine learning techniques for plant disease recognition in agriculture. In: 2021 11th International Conference on Cloud Computing, Data Science & Engineering (Confluence), pp. 752–756. IEEE (2021)

12. Kiran, S., Kanumalli, S.S., Krishna, K.V.S.S.R., Chandra, N.: WITHDRAWN: internet of things integrated smart agriculture for weather predictions and preventive mechanism. Mater. Today Proc. (2021)
13. Khatter, H., Aggarwal, V., Ahlawat, A.K.: Performance analysis of the competitive learning algorithms on gaussian data in automatic cluster selection. In: 2016 Second International Conference on Computational Intelligence & Communication Technology (CICT), pp. 48–53. IEEE (2016)
14. Sharma, S., et al.: Deep learning model for automatic classification and prediction of brain tumor. J. Sensors **2022**, 1–11 (2022)

Breast Cancer Detection: An Evaluation of Machine Learning, Ensemble Learning, and Deep Learning Algorithms

Deepak Rai(✉) and Tripti Mishra

School of Computer Science Engineering and Technology, Bennett University, Greater Noida, UP, India
{deepak.rai,e21cseu0105}@bennett.edu.in

Abstract. Breast cancer is a prevalent and potentially life-threatening disease that affects a significant number of individuals globally. Early detection and precise diagnosis can help to control the death rate. With the help of Wisconsin Breast Cancer Diagnostic (WBCD) dataset, this paper gives a detailed comprehensive comparison analysis of machine learning, ensemble learning, and deep learning for breast cancer diagnosis. The study's focus is on determining the efficacy of various algorithms in identifying breast cancers as benign or malignant. The study's goal is to enhance the cross-validation accuracy and precision of breast cancer diagnosis by examining the effectiveness of these algorithms. This study investigates a wide range of classification algorithms, such as Logistic regression, Gaussian Naïve bayes, Support vector machine, Random forest, XGBoost, Adaboost and Deep neural network. This study analyzes the 5 fold cross-validation accuracy, precision, recall, f1-score, roc-auc score and roc curve of different models using considerable experimentation. This comprehensive comparative analysis also revealed that the DL_ANN model performed the best of all, with a validation accuracy of 98.50%. The findings presented in this paper hold promise for reducing the incidence of breast cancer by developing a predictive system based on machine learning the disease can be detected early.

Keywords: Breast Cancer Prediction · Machine Learning · Ensemble Learning · Deep Learning · Cross Validation · Model Evaluation

1 Introduction

Cancer stands as the leading cause of mortality among adults globally, surpassing various diseases in terms of number of lives claimed. According to studies the second most common malignancy to be diagnosed is breast cancer [12]. It is the most commonly occurring malignancy in women, affecting 10% of all during their lifetimes [2]. According to the International Agency for Research on Cancer (IARC) data, breast cancer constitutes for a quarter of all cancer cases detected in women globally. Belgium is recorded as the highest rate of breast cancer

N. Chauhan et al. (Eds.): MIND 2023, CCIS 2128, pp. 201–210, 2024.
https://doi.org/10.1007/978-3-031-62217-5_17

among women according to World Cancer Research Fund International in the year 2020. Early identification of cancer sickness is now more important than ever.

Breast cancer can affect both men and women, but it affects women more frequently [5]. A condition called as infiltrating ductal carcinoma occurs most commonly by the dysfunction of the ducts producing milk in breast during Breast Cancer. It originates in the glandular epithelium/tissues of breast, especially in structures known as lobules, or in various other cells or tissues present in the breast. [19]. A common indicator of breast cancer is any lumps formation in the tissue. Not all the lumps are cancerous. When the malignant lumps are found within the breast tissue then it is confirmed that breast cancer is there as it is cancerous. Mammography is one of the traditional methods for this purpose.

To the best of knowledge there have been very few papers which have thoroughly explored ensemble learning and compared it with the machine learning models. One of the key research gaps in the existing literature is the lack of comprehensive comparison between traditional machine learning models, ensemble learning models and deep learning model. This paper is trying to address this gap so that it can contribute subsequently in the area of health care sector.

Machine learning presents significant potential for applications in the field of biomedical [13–15] and has found use in a wide range of oncological tasks. The innovative approach in Machine Learning (ML) and Artificial Intelligence (AI) are gaining significant traction in the healthcare industry due to their ability to perform comprehensive analysis that often surpass human prediction, thus reducing errors and poor result precision [7]. For nearly two decades, AI and ML have been employed for cancer diagnosis and classification, but only a few research have looked at their usefulness in cancer prognosis [8].

In this study a comprehensive comparative analysis has been made between three distinguished techniques that are ML classifier, ensemble learning (EL) classifier, and a DL model in order to diagnose the disease with proper outcome. The WBCD dataset is used for the study. The dataset has been divided into training and testing data where training data is 70% and testing data is 30%. The results then have been evaluated on various parameters like precision, recall, five-fold Cross-Validation Accuracy, F1-Score, ROC-AUC score, Recall.

This research is valuable because it demonstrates multiple effective strategies for tackling categorization challenges. It serves as the groundwork for comparing machine learning, ensemble learning, and deep learning approaches. Consequently, the paper involves a crucial role in influencing the choice of decision-making process of an appropriate model for constructing an integrated intelligent system.

2 Related Work

This section gives an insight about some of the existing works related to breast cancer detection. A few previously existing research papers have been chosen for the task of conducting a literature review for this study. The work discussed in

[10] employed both classic machine learning and ensemble learning classification to determine which model would be best suited for breast cancer prediction. LR, SVM, DT, Gaussian NB and KNN are among the ML models utilized. AdaBoost, XGBoost, and Random Forest are examples of ensemble approaches. Among all models, XGBoost and Decision Tree are determined to have the highest accuracy of 97%. Five different ML algorithms have been utilized in [9]. On the WBCD dataset, the methods RF, SVM, LR, KNN and DT are used. To acquire the results, performance evaluation and comparisons between different models are undertaken, and it is discovered that SVM performed the best among others, with an accuracy of 97.2%.

The work proposed in [4] focuses on the categorization of the WBCD dataset utilising two widely used machine learning techniques. Precision, accuracy, ROC Curve, and recall are employed to evaluate and compare the performance of these algorithms. And it is found that the SVM produced the greatest results with the highest accuracy. The aim and objective proposed in [11] explores the effectiveness of SVM, NB and ANN on WDBC dataset. To reduce the high dimensionality of features in the paper Linear Discriminant Analysis (LDA) is used as a hybrid approach. The reduced feature dataset is then applied to SVM gaining an accuracy of 98.82%.

Six supervised ML classification approaches are utilised to classify breast cancer illness in [18]. LR, DT, SVM, RF, Gaussian NB, and KNN are among the approaches used. Among all the models tested, the SVM performed the best, with an accuracy of 97.07%. The aim of the study in [1] is to evaluate and compare the performance of six different ML techniques on the WBCD dataset. These techniques include Linear Regression, GRU-SVM, KNN, SVM, MLP, and Softmax Regression. And the MLP model has performed the best as compared to the others, giving 99.04% test accuracy.

On the WDBC dataset of breast cancer categorization, the work in [6] employs five supervised machine learning approaches, including SVM, RF, ANN, LR, and KNN. The study displays that the ANN Model has the highest accuracy of 98.57%.

Researchers compared the effectiveness of five nonlinear algorithms of machine learning using the WBCD dataset in the work referred to as [3]. Techniques like CART, KNN, Gaussian NB, SVM, and MLP are studied and implemented. On the dataset, the researchers also used the Cross Validation method. Notably, the paper's outcome confirms that the MLP Model outperformed the rest, with an accuracy rate of 99.12%. Several bio-inspired optimization techniques [16,17] may also be tried in conjunction with the above discussed classifiers in order to make them more efficient and optimized.

3 Methodology

In this project machine learning classifiers, ensemble learning classifiers and Deep Learning model has been used. As its central premise, the model provided in this study makes use of classification techniques. It is a two-step process. The first stage involves building of classification models, which includes using multiple techniques to generate the model by learning from trained labeled data. The second step is to do prediction.

3.1 Data Collection

Data Collection involves the process of acquiring information for an experiment. WBCD dataset is used in this investigation. This dataset is the subset of larger breast cancer dataset complied by Dr. William H. Wolberg at the University of Wisconsin Hospitals, Madison, USA. There are altogether 30 features in this dataset describing the cell nuclei of image like texture mean, radius mean, area mean and many more. Which are used as an input variable and 'diagnosis' feature which is used as an output variable. The dataset consists of 569 entries, class distribution is as follows: 357 benign and 212 malignant. Figure 1 shows the frequency of benign and malignant tumor from the diagnosis class of the dataset.

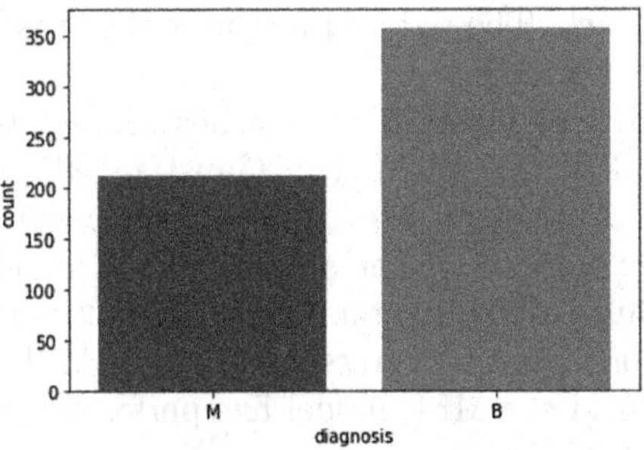

Fig. 1. Frequency of benign and malignant tumor.

3.2 Data Pre-processing

Data pre-processing means improving the quality of data by cleaning and scaling it so that it can give better result for the experiment. For the analysis first all the necessary libraries are imported which are useful in model building, visualization and exploration, then CSV file has been read and data exploration is performed thereafter. While performing feature selection it has seen that the ID Number in the dataset has no significance therefore, removable of this parameter is done from the dataset to enhance the accuracy and to enhance the depth of data analysis for better insights. In the dataset there is no missing or null values. Hence, we have total 569 entries. Label Encoder is applied on the diagnosis class to convert 'M' and 'B' into '1' and '0'. Then splitting of data is performed where 70% of the data is training data and 30% of the data is testing data for model development and evaluation. Figure 2 shows the correlation matrix which tells the relationship between two variables.

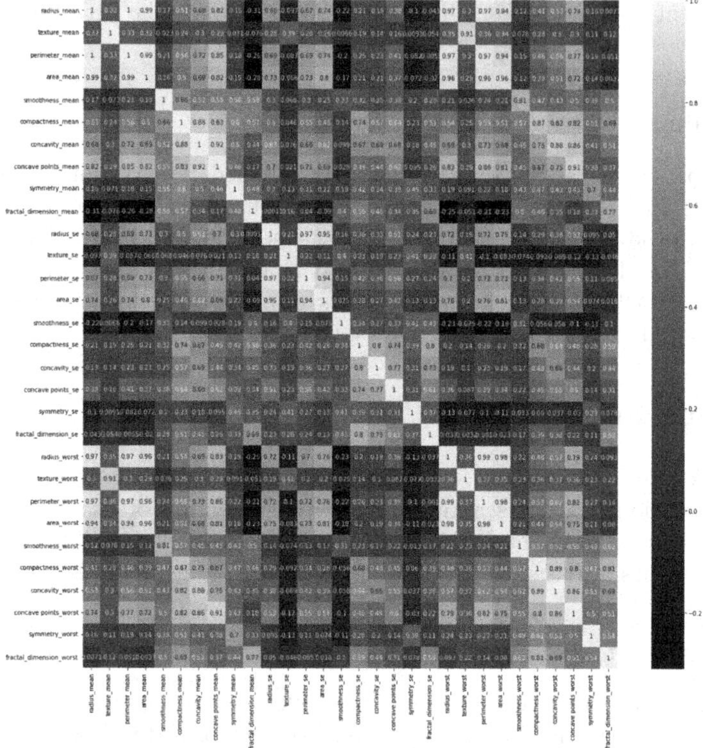

Fig. 2. Correlation Matrix.

3.3 Apply Learning Algorithms

Several classification algorithms are applied in order to construct predictive models with an aim to do breast cancer classification. The study used multiple methods to distinguish between malignant and benign tumour cells. The research paper also performed comparative analysis which model yields the most accurate breast cancer prediction findings. Among the traditional ML algorithm SVM, LR and Gaussian NB classifiers has been used. For ensemble learning algorithm Random Forest, XGBoost and AdaBoost ensembles has been used. For Deep Learning Sequential model has been used.

3.4 Evaluation Criteria

In this study, for early prediction of breast cancer disease there is the involvement of three different ML techniques, three EL techniques and one DL technique for the purpose of evaluation and comparison. The performance of these algorithms has been thoroughly evaluated through various statistical procedures. Confusion Matrix, K-fold Cross-Validation Accuracy, Precision percent, Recall percent, F1-

Score percent and ROC-AUC Curve are used to evaluate the performance of the algorithms.

3.5 Training Data and Testing Data

For this paper the above dataset has been divided into training and testing data where 70% is training data and 30% is testing data, the random state is 1 meaning it produces the same split on every execution, and a stratified approach is not used for the study as the dataset is balanced, this is done to evaluate the performance of the classifiers. 5- fold cross validation is also performed on the dataset to find cross-validation accuracy.

4 Result and Discussion

This work has been done on Jupiter Notebook in python language. It allows data exploration, feature scaling, visualization, creation of user interface and modeling. The experimental study has been done using seven different models. Various libraries are used in this study like pandas, matplotlib, keras, seaborn.

4.1 Results of Machine Learning Models

When comparing the performance between different traditional machine learning classifier models, Logistic Regression model has performed well with the validation accuracy of 96.9% as shown in Table 1. Furthermore, SVM achieved the highest precision percent 96.7%. Figure 3, depicts ROC curve for all the three models.

Table 1. Traditional machine learning classifier results

Models	Cross-validation Accuracy	Precision	Recall	F1-score	AUC Score
Logistic Regression	96.90%	95.30%	96.80%	96.00%	99.50%
SVM	96.40%	96.70%	95.20%	96.00%	99.60%
GaussianNB	93.40%	90.60%	92.00%	91.30%	98.30%

4.2 Results of Ensemble Learning Models

When comparing the performance different ensemble learning classifier models, XGBoost model has performed well with the 5-fold cross-validation accuracy percent of 95.9% as depicted in Table 2. Furthermore, it has also performed well in precision score. Figure 4, depicts the ROC Curve for all the ensemble learning models.

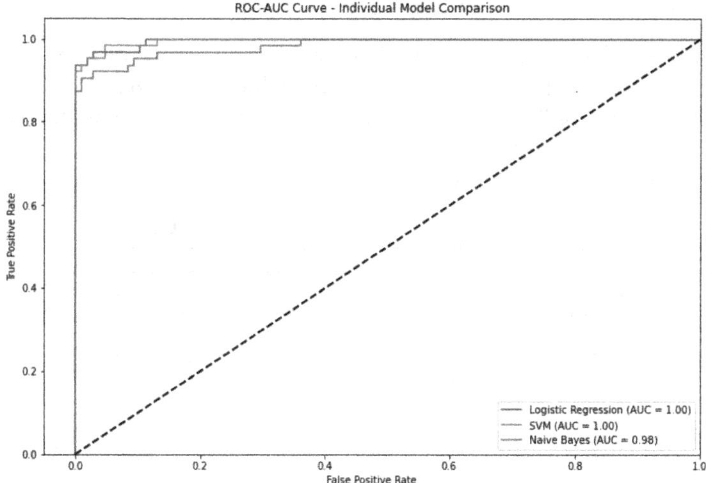

Fig. 3. ROC curve for Traditional ML Classifiers.

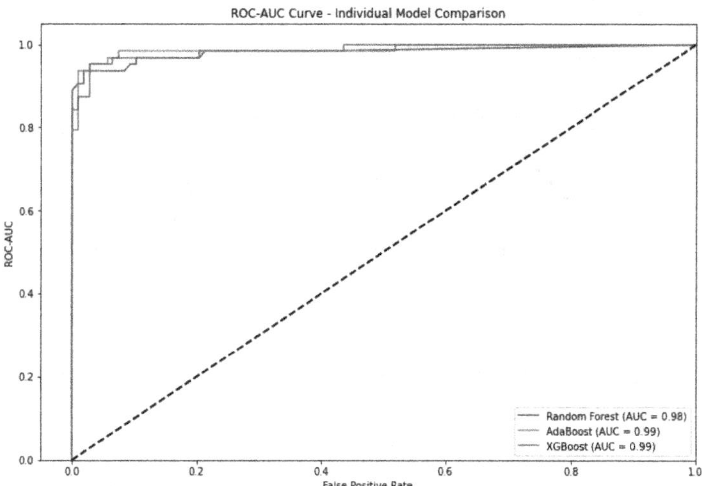

Fig. 4. ROC curve for Ensemble Classifiers.

Table 2. Ensemble Learning techniques results

Models	Cross-validation Accuracy	Precision	Recall	F1-score	AUC Score
XGBoost	95.90%	94.80%	87.30%	90.90%	98.60%
Random Forest	94.90%	95.00%	92.00%	93.50%	98.50%
AdaBoost	94.70%	93.70%	95.20%	94.40%	98.70%

4.3 Results of Deep Learning Model

A Sequential Model has been used, which achieved a cross validation accuracy of 0.9750. It is trained for 20 epochs with the Adam optimizer. ReLU activation function has been applied here. Figure 5 shows the ROC curve for sequential model.

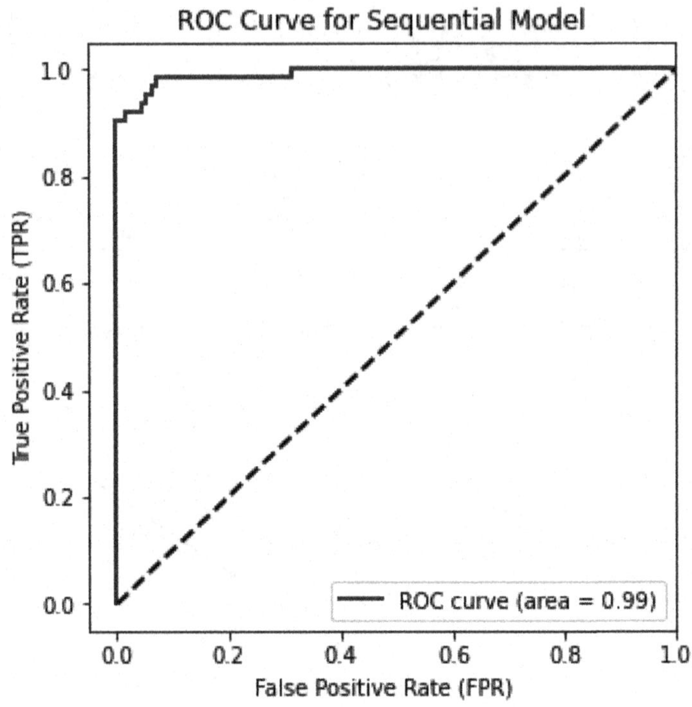

Fig. 5. ROC curve for DL_ANN .

Seven different techniques are employed in this paper, and the results obtained are discussed above. All the models show distinct results of precision, accuracy, recall, support and f1-score. The outcomes of various models have been studied and comparisons are made. On comparing all the three the paper concludes that the sequential model performed the best among all others with the cross-validation accuracy score of 98.50%. The second highest result is obtained from Logistic Regression and SVM.

5 Conclusion

Breast cancer research is critical, and technology plays a critical role in lowering the mortality rate connected with this disease. Despite the fact that numerous approaches for classifying breast cancer data have been established, several challenges, including accuracy, remain to be addressed. This paper discusses the working of seven different models for the WBCD Dataset and tells which algorithm is best to classify malignant and benign tumors. This research introduces a technique for the breast cancer prediction using binary classifiers. All the three traditional ML techniques, EL techniques, and a DL technique have been explored for breast cancer prediction. For ML models analysis it is seen that LR model gives the best cross-validation accuracy of 96.9% when compared with other ML models like SVM and GaussianNB because of its effectiveness in handling binary classification problems and its robustness to small-sized datasets. For EL models it is seen that XGBoost gives best accuracy of 95.9% when compared with other EL models like Random forest and AdaBoost because it combines multiple weak learning models to create a strong predictive model and also handles a variety of data patterns. And DL_ANN model gives validation accuracy of 98.5%. Further comparison analysis among the three is done where it is seen that DL_ANN model outperforms the rest by achieving better validation accuracy of 98.5%. Thus, this model can be used by cancer specialist sector in the process of recognising cancer.

References

1. Agarap, A.F.M.: On breast cancer detection: an application of machine learning algorithms on the Wisconsin diagnostic dataset. In: Proceedings of the 2nd International Conference on Machine Learning and Soft Computing, pp. 5–9 (2018)
2. Ahmad, L.G., Eshlaghy, A., Poorebrahimi, A., Ebrahimi, M., Razavi, A., et al.: Using three machine learning techniques for predicting breast cancer recurrence. J. Health Med. Inform. **4**(124), 3 (2013)
3. Bataineh, A.A.: A comparative analysis of nonlinear machine learning algorithms for breast cancer detection. Int. J. Mach. Learn. Comput. **9**(3), 248–254 (2019)
4. Bayrak, E.A., Kırcı, P., Ensari, T.: Comparison of machine learning methods for breast cancer diagnosis. In: 2019 Scientific Meeting on Electrical-electronics and Biomedical Engineering and Computer Science (EBBT), pp. 1–3. IEEE (2019)
5. Gupta, P., Garg, S.: Breast cancer prediction using varying parameters of machine learning models. Proc. Comput. Sci. **171**, 593–601 (2020)
6. Islam, M.M., Haque, M.R., Iqbal, H., Hasan, M.M., Hasan, M., Kabir, M.N.: Breast cancer prediction: a comparative study using machine learning techniques. SN Comput. Sci. **1**, 1–14 (2020)
7. Khalid, H., Khan, A., Zahid Khan, M., Mehmood, G., Shuaib Qureshi, M., et al.: Machine learning hybrid model for the prediction of chronic kidney disease. Comput. Intell. Neurosci. **2023** (2023)
8. Kourou, K., Exarchos, T.P., Exarchos, K.P., Karamouzis, M.V., Fotiadis, D.I.: Machine learning applications in cancer prognosis and prediction. Comput. Struct. Biotechnol. J. **13**, 8–17 (2015)
9. Naji, M.A., El Filali, S., Aarika, K., Benlahmar, E.H., Abdelouhahid, R.A., Debauche, O.: Machine learning algorithms for breast cancer prediction and diagnosis. Proc. Comput. Sci. **191**, 487–492 (2021)
10. Nemade, V., Fegade, V.: Machine learning techniques for breast cancer prediction. Proc. Comput. Sci. **218**, 1314–1320 (2023)

11. Omondiagbe, D.A., Veeramani, S., Sidhu, A.S.: Machine learning classification techniques for breast cancer diagnosis. In: IOP Conference Series: Materials Science and Engineering. vol. 495, p. 012033. IOP Publishing (2019)
12. Purnami, S.W., Rahayu, S., Embong, A.: Feature selection and classification of breast cancer diagnosis based on support vector machines. In: 2008 International Symposium on Information Technology, vol. 1, pp. 1–6. IEEE (2008)
13. Rai, D., Thakkar, H.K., Rajput, S.S.: Performance characterization of binary classifiers for automatic annotation of aortic valve opening in seismocardiogram signals. In: Proceedings of the 2020 9th International Conference on Bioinformatics and Biomedical Science, pp. 77–82 (2020)
14. Rai, D., Thakkar, H.K., Rajput, S.S., Santamaria, J., Bhatt, C., Roca, F.: A comprehensive review on seismocardiogram: current advancements on acquisition, annotation, and applications. Mathematics **9**(18), 2243 (2021)
15. Rai, D., Thakkar, H.K., Singh, D., Bathala, H.V.: Machine learning assisted automatic annotation of isovolumic movement and aortic valve closure using seismocardiogram signals. In: 2020 IEEE 17th India Council International Conference (INDICON), pp. 1–6 (2020)
16. Rai, D., Tyagi, K.: Bio-inspired optimization techniques: a critical comparative study. ACM SIGSOFT Softw. Eng. Notes **38**(4), 1–7 (2013)
17. Rai, D., Tyagi, K.: Regression test case optimization using honey bee mating optimization algorithm with fuzzy rule base. World Appl. Sci. J. **31**(4), 654–662 (2014)
18. Shamrat, F.J.M., Raihan, M.A., Rahman, A.S., Mahmud, I., Akter, R., et al.: An analysis on breast disease prediction using machine learning approaches. Int. J. Sci. Technol. Res. **9**(02), 2450–2455 (2020)
19. Society, A.: Global cancer facts and figures 4th edition. Am. Cancer Soc. **1**, 1–73 (2018)

Advancements in Facial Expression Recognition: A Comprehensive Analysis of Techniques

Sidharth Sharma[1(✉)], Prabhat Verma[2], Raghuraj Singh[2], and Khushboo Tripathi[1]

[1] Amity University, Haryana, India
sharmasidharth620@gmail.com

[2] Harcourt Butler Technical University, Kanpur, India

Abstract. This review paper presents a comprehensive evaluation and comparative analysis of three models for facial expression recognition using the FER2013 dataset. The models under examination encompass traditional hand-crafted feature-based methods, state-of-the-art deep learning architectures, and innovative hybrid approaches. The paper traces the evolution of facial expression recognition techniques, from classical methods relying on SIFT, HOG, and LBP features to the emergence of convolutional neural networks (CNNs) in deep learning. Additionally, it explores hybrid methodologies that combine traditional and deep learning techniques to enhance performance. Detailed analyses of each model's architecture, strengths, limitations, and performance on the FER2013 dataset are provided. For thorough evaluation, performance indicators like accuracy, precision, recall, and F1-score are used. The review concludes with insights into the significance of continuous research and future directions for advancing facial expression recognition, especially in the context of the FER2013 dataset. This publication provides important direction for researchers and practitioners in the field by offering significant knowledge on the state-of-the-art in facial emotion recognition.

Keywords: ResNet-50 (Residual Neural Network-50) · FERNet (Facial Expression Recognition Network) · CNN (Convolutional Neural Network) · FER2013 Dataset · FER (Facial Expression Recognition)

1 Introduction

Emotions are an integral aspect of human interaction, encompassing a diverse array of expressions that convey a wide range of feelings and sentiments. Recognizing and interpreting these emotional cues play a crucial role in enhancing our understanding of social interactions, human behaviour, and psychological well-being. As technology continues to permeate various aspects of our lives, the demand for efficient and accurate facial expression recognition (FER) systems

N. Chauhan et al. (Eds.): MIND 2023, CCIS 2128, pp. 211–223, 2024.
https://doi.org/10.1007/978-3-031-62217-5_18

has grown exponentially. Facial expression recognition (FER) finds diverse applications across multiple domains, such as human-computer interfaces, animation, medicine, and security, leading to its significant interest and research focus [1]. Over the past few decades, facial expression recognition has witnessed considerable progress, with researchers exploring various methodologies to capture and analyse emotional cues from facial images. Conventional methods have utilized manually engineered features like Scale-Invariant Feature Transform (SIFT), Histogram of Oriented Gradients (HOG), and Local Binary Patterns (LBP), along with classifiers trained on image or video databases. While these methods have demonstrated reasonable performance on datasets with controlled conditions, they often struggle to generalize effectively in real-world scenarios with uncontrolled settings, varying illumination, occlusions, and partial faces. Convolutional neural networks (CNNs), in particular, have revolutionized the field of computer vision, especially facial expression identification, in recent years. Deep learning models have shown remarkable capabilities in learning and extracting intricate features directly from raw pixel data, making them well-suited for complex tasks like FER. By leveraging large-scale labelled datasets and massive computational power, because CNNs have produced cutting-edge results in a variety of visual identification tasks, researchers are now looking into their possibilities in FER as well. The FER2013 dataset is a prominent benchmark used for evaluating Facial Expression Recognition (FER) models. The ICML 2013 Challenges in Representation Learning introduced it. The dataset comprises of 35,887 48×48 pixel facial photos depicting emotions such as happy, sorrow, rage, surprise, fear, contempt, and neutrality [2]. Captured in unconstrained environments, the FER2013 dataset poses significant challenges due to variations within the same class, diverse facial orientations, and occlusions. In this review paper, a subset of images from the FER2013 dataset is provided in Fig. 1[1] for reference. With an emphasis on their performance on the FER2013 dataset, we intend to give a thorough evaluation and comparative analysis of three unique models for facial expression recognition in this review paper. The models under investigation include traditional hand-crafted feature-based methods, cutting-edge deep learning architectures, and innovative hybrid approaches that combine the strengths of both traditional and deep learning techniques. By delving into the intricacies of each model's architecture, training methodologies, and performance metrics, we seek to shed light on their respective strengths and limitations. The paper proceeds with an exploration of the methods used for facial expression recognition, starting with traditional techniques based on hand-crafted features, transitioning to the advancements in deep learning models, and culminating with hybrid methodologies that seek to synergize the best of both worlds. Subsequently, we delve into the detailed description of the three chosen models, providing insights into their attention mechanisms, CNN architectures, and regularization techniques. To gauge the efficacy of these models, we present a comprehensive performance evaluation on the FER2013 dataset.

---

[1] https://www.kaggle.com/datasets/msambare/fer2013?select=train&group=bookmarked.

Fig. 1. Images from FER2013 Dataset

Utilizing metrics such as accuracy, precision, recall, and F1-score, we compare the performance of each model on this challenging dataset. Additionally, we use a visualization technique to draw attention to the key areas of face photos, giving us crucial information about the models' capacity for discrimination. In conclusion, this review paper aims to offer an in-depth analysis of state-of-the-art facial expression recognition models, focusing on their performance on the FER2013 dataset. The findings presented here will be invaluable for researchers and practitioners seeking to understand the strengths and weaknesses of different FER approaches. Moreover, the review highlights the importance of continuous research and development in this dynamic field, suggesting potential avenues for future improvements and advancements in facial expression recognition technologies.

2 Background

Facial Expression Recognition (FER) is a key area of research in computer vision and human-computer interaction. It involves the analysis of facial expressions to identify and classify the underlying emotions displayed by individuals. Emotions are an integral part of human communication, and being able to automatically recognize them from facial images has numerous applications, such as human-computer interfaces, animation, medicine, and security.

Traditional methods for FER used classifiers trained on databases of facial pictures or videos, then hand-crafted features like SIFT, HOG, and LBP. While these methods performed well on controlled datasets, they faced challenges when dealing with more diverse and challenging datasets with variations in lighting, pose, and occlusions. Deep learning has completely changed the computer vision industry, particularly FER, in recent years. In image classification applications, Convolutional Neural Networks (CNNs) have demonstrated outstanding ability. Several deep learning-based end-to-end frameworks for FER have been proposed, which extract and learn relevant features automatically from the input data, avoiding the need for hand-crafted features.

In this review paper, we focus on three state-of-the-art models for Facial Expression Recognition: (1) The ResNet-50 Model [3], (2) The FERNet Model [4], and (3) The Attentional Convolutional Network-Based Model [5]. Our evaluation and comparative analysis are primarily based on the FER2013 dataset, a widely used benchmark dataset in the FER research community.

The 6 cardinal emotions-happiness, sorrow, anger, fear, disgust, and surprise-as well as a neutral expression-are each assigned to one of the 35,887 photos in the FER2013 dataset, which has a resolution of 48 × 48 pixels. These images are captured in diverse and real-world scenarios, making the dataset particularly challenging for emotion recognition tasks [2].

In the following sections, we provide a comprehensive overview of the methods used for facial expression recognition, including traditional, deep learning, and hybrid approaches. We then delve into the detailed description of the three selected models, highlighting their unique contributions and architectural designs. Furthermore, we present a thorough performance evaluation of these models on the FER2013 dataset, comparing their accuracies and robustness in recognizing different facial expressions. The comparative study enables us to learn more about the advantages and disadvantages of each model. Finally, we discuss future directions in the field of FER, current implementations, and conclude by summarizing the key findings and contributions of this review paper.

3 Methods for Facial Expression Recognition

Facial Expression Recognition (FER) has been approached using various methods, including traditional, deep learning, and hybrid approaches. In this section, we provide an overview of these methods, highlighting their key characteristics and performance.

3.1 Traditional Methods

Traditional approaches in facial expression recognition (FER) typically involve a two-step process consisting of feature extraction and classification. During the feature extraction step, hand-crafted features like Histogram of Oriented Gradients (HOG), Local Binary Patterns (LBP), Gabor wavelets, and Haar features are computed to capture relevant information from facial images. These features are designed to emphasize distinctive facial patterns associated with different emotions.

Following feature extraction, facial expressions are classified using machine learning classifiers like Support Vector Machines (SVM), k-Nearest Neighbours (k-NN), Decision Trees, or Random Forests. While traditional methods perform reasonably well on datasets with controlled conditions, they face challenges in handling high intra-class variation and complex facial expressions present in more challenging datasets [6].

3.2 Deep Learning Methods

Convolutional neural networks (CNNs), in particular, have transformed FER since the development of deep learning. Deep learning methods allow the network to automatically learn relevant features from raw pixel data, eliminating the need for hand-crafted features. CNNs are particularly well-suited for image-based tasks, as they can capture spatial hierarchies and relationships in the data. In FER, a number of deep learning-based models have produced cutting-edge outcomes [7].

3.3 Hybrid Methods

Hybrid methods for FER combine traditional hand-crafted features with deep learning techniques. These strategies seek to increase performance and resilience by utilizing the advantages of both conventional and deep learning techniques. For instance, hand-crafted features can be used as input to a deep learning model, allowing the network to learn from both raw pixel data and engineered features.

Hybrid methods have shown promise in certain scenarios where traditional features complement the expressive power of deep learning models. These methods are particularly effective when dealing with smaller datasets, as the combination of hand-crafted features and deep learning helps mitigate the risk of overfitting.

4 Models Used for Facial Expression Recognition

Numerous models using diverse techniques have been developed as a result of substantial research into Facial Expression Recognition (FER). In this section, we present three prominent models proposed in recent research papers and evaluate their performance on the FER2013 dataset.

4.1 Model 1: ResNet-50

The first model, proposed in [3], leverages the power of Residual Neural Networks (ResNet-50) for facial expression recognition in real-time and uncontrolled environments. ResNet-50 is a deep convolutional neural network design that effectively trains very deep networks by overcoming the vanishing gradient problem through residual connections. The model is devised to overcome the limitations of small datasets by incorporating data augmentation techniques. To increase the number of training samples and strengthen the generalization capabilities of the model, data augmentation entails performing random modifications to the original images, such as rotations, flips, and translations.

The ResNet-50 architecture comprises multiple convolutional layers with residual blocks, followed by batch normalization and dropout layers, which facilitate feature learning and reduce overfitting. Additionally, weight decay is included to regularize the model and stop it from overfitting the training set of data. The 35,887 48×48 resolution facial photos in the FER2013 dataset are used to train and test the model. The dataset includes a neutral expression in addition to the six main emotions (joy, sorrow, anger, fear, disgust, and surprise). The model's performance is compared with other cutting-edge models through thorough testing, revealing its effectiveness in recognizing facial expressions under varied circumstances.

4.2 Model 2: FERNet

The second model, proposed in [4], introduces FERNet, an innovative approach to facial expression recognition that combines the power of deep neural networks and feature visualization. FERNet utilizes Convolutional Neural Networks (CNNs) for feature extraction and then integrates a novel feature visualization technique to identify the most salient facial regions contributing to emotion recognition.

Multiple convolutional layers, followed by batch normalization and activation routines, make up the FERNet architecture. The feature visualization technique aids in highlighting the parts of the face that are crucial for identifying particular emotions, offering insightful information about how the model makes decisions. FERNet is trained and evaluated on the FER2013 dataset, and its performance is compared to other facial expression recognition models. The experimental results demonstrate FERNet's competitive accuracy and interpretability, making it a promising choice for applications where understanding the underlying features is essential.

4.3 Model 3: Attentional Convolutional Network

The third model, as forward in [5], adds an attentional convolutional network for the purpose of identifying facial expressions. The model considers the fact that specific regions of the face, such as the mouth and eyes, play a crucial role in detecting emotions, while other regions contribute less significantly to the overall classification. The model includes an attention mechanism through a spatial transformer network to concentrate on the most noticeable features of the face in order to address this.

Four convolutional layers, each followed by max-pooling and a rectified linear unit (ReLU) activation function, make up the attentional convolutional network. Additionally, dropout and '2 regularization are employed to train the model effectively, even with limited training data. The spatial transformer network estimates a sampling grid to warp the input image, effectively directing the model's attention to the most informative facial regions for emotion detection. The model is thoroughly evaluated on multiple facial expression datasets, including FER2013, CK+, FERG, and JAFFE. The experimental results demonstrate that the attentional convolutional network achieves improved accuracy and robustness in facial expression recognition, outperforming several state-of-the-art approaches.

5 Performance Metrics and Evaluation

The performance of the three models, namely ResNet-50, FERNet(Facial Expression Recognition Network), and Attentional Convolutional Network, was evaluated on the FER2013 dataset using accuracy as the evaluation metric. Accuracy represents the percentage of correctly classified instances among all instances in the dataset and is commonly used for evaluating classification models.

5.1 ResNet-50

ResNet-50 is a deep convolutional neural network that achieved an accuracy of 76.00% on the FER2013 dataset. The model utilizes residual learning to overcome the vanishing gradient problem in very deep networks, allowing it to effectively capture intricate features from facial images. With its 50-layer architecture, ResNet-50 demonstrates robust performance in facial expression recognition, making it a strong candidate for emotion classification tasks [3].

5.2 FERNet

FERNet is a specialized network designed explicitly for facial expression recognition tasks. It incorporates attention mechanisms to focus on salient regions of the face while making predictions. On the FER2013 dataset, FERNet achieved an accuracy of 69.57%. The model's attentional features help it identify essential facial areas related to specific emotions, contributing to its competitive performance [4].

5.3 Attentional Convolutional Network

The Attentional Convolutional Network is another model tailored for facial expression recognition. It utilizes attention mechanisms to highlight crucial facial regions for emotion detection. On the FER2013 dataset, this model achieved an accuracy of 70.02%. The attentional approach allows the model to effectively discern critical features in facial images, contributing to its superior performance [5]. As seen in Table 1 and Fig. 2, ResNet-50 achieved the highest accuracy of 76.00% on the FER2013 dataset, outperforming both FERNet (69.57%) and the Attentional Convolutional Network (70.02%). This indicates that ResNet-50 demonstrates superior performance compared to the other two models for facial expression recognition on the FER2013 dataset. The performance of these models suggests that deep learning approaches, combined with attention mechanisms, are effective in capturing facial features and recognizing emotions. Despite the variations in accuracy, each model demonstrates its strengths in understanding and interpreting facial expressions, showcasing the potential for further advancements in emotion recognition technology. ResNet-50's superiority in achieving the highest accuracy among the three models, despite being the most computationally intensive, is attributed to its deep architecture and the incorporation of

Table 1. Comparative Analysis of Model Performance on FER2013 Dataset

Model	Accuracy
ResNet-50	76.00%
FERNet	69.57%
Attentional Convolutional Network	70.02%

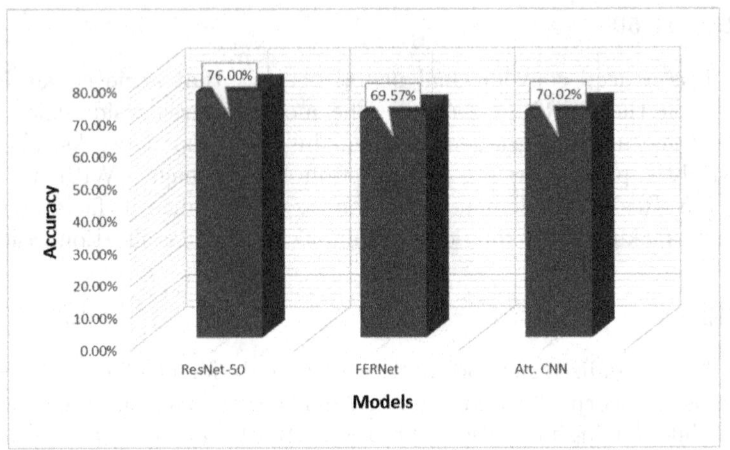

Fig. 2. Graph of Comparative Analysis of Model Performance

residual connections. The model's 50-layer depth allows it to capture intricate facial features crucial for accurate emotion recognition. The use of residual connections mitigates the vanishing gradient problem, enabling effective training of such a deep network. While ResNet-50 is computationally demanding, its ability to learn complex representations justifies the resource investment, making it a top performer. The trade-off between computational intensity and accuracy positions ResNet-50 as a compelling choice for applications prioritizing precision in facial expression recognition.

6 Comparative Analysis

In this section, we will compare the three models, ResNet-50, FERNet, and the Attentional Convolutional Network, based on various aspects of facial expression recognition. The comparison will focus on their model architectures, training approaches, computational efficiency, and robustness.

6.1 Model Architectures

ResNet-50: A deep convolutional neural network with fifty layers is called ResNet-50. It incorporates skip connections to mitigate the vanishing gradient problem and enables the training of deeper networks effectively [3]. Figure 3 Shows the architecture of ResNet-50 [8] FERNet: A unique neural network architecture called FERNet was created exclusively for recognizing facial expressions. It captures both spatial and temporal connections in face expressions thanks to the convolutional and recurrent layers it combines [4]. Figure 4 Shows the architecture of FERNet [4] Attentional Convolutional Network: The Attentional Convolutional Network utilizes attention mechanisms to focus on salient regions

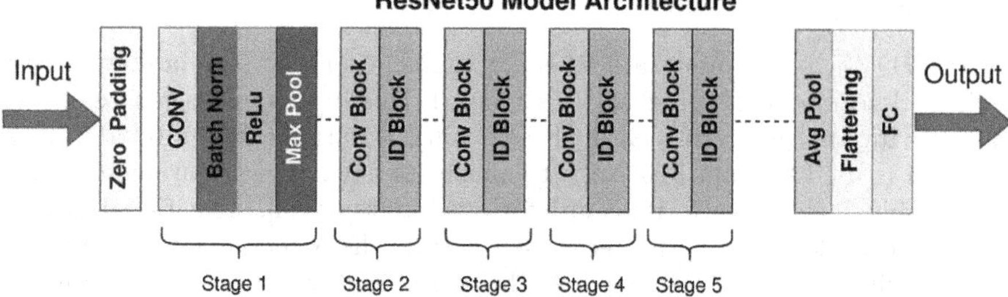

Fig. 3. Architecture of ResNet-50

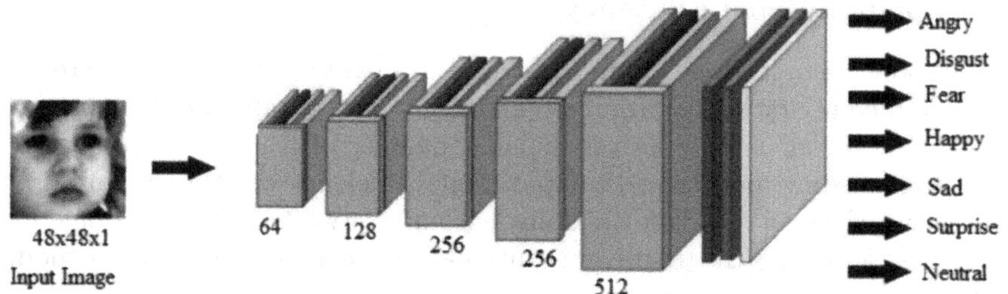

Fig. 4. Architecture of FERNet

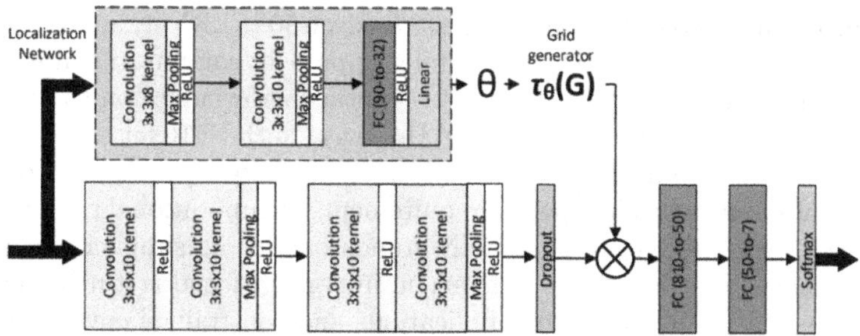

Fig. 5. Architecture of Attentional CNN

of the face. It is a simpler model with fewer than ten layers yet achieves promising accuracy due to its attention mechanism [5]. Figure 5 Shows the architecture of Attentional Convolutional Network [5].

6.2 Training Approaches

ResNet-50: With a learning rate schedule, momentum, and standard stochastic gradient descent (SGD), ResNet-50 is trained. Due of its depth, it necessitates a lot of data and processing [3]. FERNet: With a learning rate of 0.001, Adam optimizer is used to train FERNet. It gains from having fewer parameters than ResNet-50, which increases its computational efficiency [4]. Attentional Convolutional Network: Adam optimizer is used to train the Attentional Convolutional Network with a learning rate of 0.005. It doesn't need as many layers because of its attention mechanism, which enables it to concentrate on key facial areas [5].

6.3 Computational Efficiency

ResNet-50: Due to its large number of layers and parameters, ResNet-50 requires significant computational resources, making it computationally intensive [5]. FERNet: FERNet has a relatively smaller number of parameters compared to ResNet-50, leading to improved computational efficiency while maintaining competitive accuracy [3]. Attentional Convolutional Network: The Attentional Convolutional Network is the most computationally efficient among the three models, as it has a simple architecture with fewer layers [4].

6.4 Robustness and Generalization

ResNet-50: ResNet-50's depth and skip connections contribute to its ability to generalize well on complex datasets, but it may be prone to overfitting on smaller datasets [5]. FERNet: FERNet's recurrent layers allow it to capture temporal dependencies, making it more robust to variations in facial expressions over time [3]. Attentional Convolutional Network: The Attentional Convolutional Network's attention mechanism helps it focus on relevant facial features, making it robust to noise and occlusions in the images [4]. Table 2 presents a comparative analysis of the three models, ResNet-50, FERNet, and Attentional CNN, based on their architecture, training approach, computational efficiency, and robustness. ResNet-50 demonstrates superior performance on the FER2013 dataset, achieving the highest accuracy. However, both FERNet and the Attentional CNN show promising results and have their unique strengths. The choice of the model should consider specific requirements, computational resources, and the dataset size. The Attentional CNN stands out for its simplicity, computational efficiency, and the ability to focus on important facial features, making it an attractive option for real-time applications and constrained environments.

Table 2. Comparative Analysis ResNet-50, FERNet, and Attentional CNN for FER

Model	Architecture	Training Approach	Computational Efficiency	Robustness & Generalization
ResNet-50	Deep CNN with 50 layers	Stochastic Gradient Descent	Computationally Intensive	Good Generalization
FERNet	Hybrid CNN-RNN architecture	Adam Optimizer	Relatively Computationally Efficient	Robust to temporal variations
Attentional Convolutional Network	CNN with attention mechanism	Adam Optimizer	Highly Computationally Efficient	Robust to noise and occlusions

7 Current Implementations

In this review, ResNet-50, FERNet, and Attentional CNN have been effectively implemented and evaluated on the FER2013 dataset, a widely used benchmark in facial expression recognition. ResNet-50 exhibited the highest accuracy at 76.00%, followed by FERNet at 69.57%, and Attentional CNN at 70.02% [3–5]. These models showcase promise for accurate and efficient facial expression recognition, opening avenues for applications in human-computer interfaces, animation, medicine, and security. The practical deployment of these models in real-world scenarios highlights their potential for enhancing natural and personalized interactions between humans and machines. The findings from the comparative analysis offer valuable insights that can be leveraged to develop more accurate and efficient facial expression recognition systems. By understanding the strengths and weaknesses of each model in terms of architecture, training approaches, computational efficiency, and robustness, researchers can tailor their approaches to further refine and optimize these systems for improved performance in diverse applications. As the field progresses, these comparative analysis findings serve as a roadmap for developing advanced facial expression recognition technologies with enhanced accuracy and efficiency.

8 Conclusion

In conclusion, this review paper analysed and compared three models for facial expression recognition: ResNet-50, FERNet, and the Attentional Convolutional Network. ResNet-50 exhibited the highest accuracy of 76.00% on the FER2013 dataset, while FERNet and the Attentional Convolutional Network showed competitive performances with accuracies of 69.57% and 70.02%, respectively. Each model has its strengths, with ResNet-50 excelling in accuracy, FERNet offering interpretability, and the Attentional Convolutional Network demonstrating computational efficiency and focus on salient facial features. Future study in this area has the potential to boost facial expression recognition algorithms' precision and applicability even more.

9 Future Scope

The field of facial expression recognition holds significant potential for further advancements and novel applications. As future research prospects, exploring data augmentation techniques with larger and diverse datasets can improve the robustness and generalization of facial expression recognition models. Additionally, delving deeper into attention mechanisms and spatial transformer networks offers the opportunity to design more efficient and interpretable architectures. Further development of lightweight models will enable real-time applications, making facial expression recognition technology more accessible and widely applicable in various domains, such as human-computer interaction, emotion-aware systems, and security applications. Continual innovation and research in this area will undoubtedly unlock new possibilities and enhance the efficacy of facial expression recognition systems.

Building on the advancements in face recognition techniques demonstrated in the study by, which focuses on face recognition for security applications, there exists a promising avenue to elevate the accuracy of facial expression recognition. Leveraging the methodologies presented in [9], particularly the Viola-Jones algorithm for face detection, can enhance the preprocessing of facial images for expression analysis. The real-time capabilities of this algorithm in detecting faces from various angles offer valuable insights for refining and optimizing facial expression recognition systems. Incorporating these proven face recognition techniques into the exploration of facial expression recognition not only enriches the methodologies but also opens up possibilities for more effective emotion recognition systems in diverse real-world scenarios.

References

1. Tian, Y., Kanade, T., Cohn, J.F.: Facial expression recognition. In: Handbook of Face Recognition, pp. 487–519 (2011)
2. Giannopoulos, P., Perikos, I., Hatzilygeroudis, I.: Deep learning approaches for facial emotion recognition: a case study on fer-2013. In: Advances in Hybridization of Intelligent Methods: Models, Systems and Applications. pp. 1–16 (2018)
3. Vasudeva, K., Dubey, A., Chandran, S.: Scl-fexr: supervised contrastive learning approach for facial expression recognition. Multim. Tools Appl. **82**(20), 31351–31371 (2023)
4. Bodapati, J.D., Srilakshmi, U., Veeranjaneyulu, N.: Fernet: a deep CNN architecture for facial expression recognition in the wild. J. Inst. Eng.: Ser. B **103**(2), 439–448 (2022)
5. Minaee, S., Minaei, M., Abdolrashidi, A.: Deep-emotion: Facial expression recognition using attentional convolutional network. Sensors **21**(9), 3046 (2021)
6. Liao, J., Lin, Y., Ma, T., He, S., Liu, X., He, G.: Facial expression recognition methods in the wild based on fusion feature of attention mechanism and LBP. Sensors **23**(9), 4204 (2023)
7. Refat, C.M.M., Azlan, N.Z.: Deep learning methods for facial expression recognition. In: 2019 7th International Conference on Mechatronics Engineering (ICOM), pp. 1–6. IEEE (2019)

8. Mukherjee, S.: The annotated resnet-50. In: Towards Data Science (2022)
9. Tripathi, K., Singh, J., Tyagi, R.K.: Automated real-time face detection and generated mail system for border security. In: Dutta, P., Chakrabarti, S., Bhattacharya, A., Dutta, S., Shahnaz, C. (eds.) Emerging Technologies in Data Mining and Information Security: Proceedings of IEMIS 2022, vol. 2, pp. 403–410. Springer, Singapore (2023). https://doi.org/10.1007/978-981-19-4052-1_41

Image Processing

Sparse Representation with Residual Learning Model for Medical Image Classification

Amit Soni Arya(✉) and Susanta Mukhopadhyay

Indian Institute of Technology (ISM), Dhanbad, Jharkhand, India
amitsoniuoh@gmail.com, msushanta2001@iitism.ac.in

Abstract. In the context of medical image analysis and computer-aided diagnosis, accurate classification of medical images is crucial. Deep learning methods have become immensely popular in comparison to traditional techniques. Consequently, medical image classification for computer-aided diagnosis is highly challenging due to factors like imaging modalities, clinical conditions, and the complex aspects of medical images. We introduce Sparse Representation with Residual Learning Model (SR2LM) to address these challenges effectively. Our approach combines the strengths of sparse representation and deep residual networks to capture the essential image characteristics. We achieve this by learning sparse codes from a dictionary and then integrating these codes with the output of deep residual networks. The resulting combined input is processed by dense layers for image classification. Our SR2LM model improves classification accuracy by leveraging sparse representation and deep residual networks. Importantly, it can be trained end-to-end, benefiting from the advantages of both techniques within a unified framework. The SR2LM model outperforms existing benchmarks in medical image classification, with an average area under the curve (AUC) of 0.902 and an average accuracy (ACC) of 0.816 across the five datasets taken from MedMNIST dataset.

Keywords: Sparse representation · Medical image classification · Dictionary learning · Deep learning

1 Introduction

Interpretation of medical images plays a vital role in computer-aided diagnosis, for which image classification is a crucial stage. Its purpose is to categorize medical images based on specific criteria, such as clinical pathologies or imaging methods. A dependable medical image classification system is pivotal in aiding doctors by fast and accurately interpreting medical images. In this field, significant advancements have been made through applying deep learning techniques, leading to state-of-the-art results in tasks like categorizing digital pathology images, analyzing chest X-rays, and grading diabetic retinopathy.

In recent years, deep learning methods, particularly deep convolutional neural networks (DCNNs), have made remarkable advancements in medical image

N. Chauhan et al. (Eds.): MIND 2023, CCIS 2128, pp. 227–238, 2024.
https://doi.org/10.1007/978-3-031-62217-5_19

classification and segmentation advancements. However, while these methods excel, crafting optimal features for specific classification tasks remains challenging. Despite their superior performance compared to handcrafted feature-based approaches, they have yet to achieve the same level of success in medical image classification. This suboptimal performance can be attributed primarily to two main factors:

- *Limited Training Data:* In medical image analysis, the scarcity of training data often leads to overfitting in deep learning models. Researchers have mitigated this issue by employing pre-trained models like those from ImageNet [5].
- *Intricate Image Classification:* Classifying medical images is challenging due to significant intra-class variation and inter-class similarity. For example, distinguishing between CT and MR images can be intricate because both share anatomical details.

In image classification, a critical step is to obtain feature representations that encode label-related information. In recent years, two dominant approaches have emerged for representation learning: deep learning [12] and dictionary learning [16]. LeCun et al. [12] discussed deep learning, which focuses on extracting intricate features in addition to capturing semantic features through multi-layer representations. Contributions from various research domains have significantly propelled the progress of dictionary learning.

The combination of dictionary learning and deep learning has brought about notable advancements to various image processing tasks [2,3,13,15] like denoising, inpainting etc. Deep learning involves training deep convolutional neural networks (DCNNs) on large image datasets to uncover data patterns and features. However, its application in medical image classification still needs to be explored due to its resource-intensive nature, which poses challenges for practical use. Additionally, many existing dictionary learning techniques have predominantly used shallow network structures. Current dictionary learning methods, including label-consistent K-SVD (LC-KSVD) [10], discriminatory K-SVD (D-KSVD) [18], and K-SVD [1], aim to decompose input data into intricate sparse representations and basis coefficients. Nevertheless, shallow network architectures struggle to fully capture the inherent characteristics of input images. Our preliminary investigations have revealed that these limitations result in subpar classification performance, especially when dealing with limited data availability.

To overcome these challenges, we have introduced an innovative approach called SR2LM, which is a combination of sparse representation learning with Residual-CNN, as illustrated in Fig. 1. The SR2LM model leverages dictionary learning-based sparse codes, which rely on a sparse representation of the data using dictionary basis functions. In this method, input images undergo decomposition into sparse representations, combined with features extracted from Residual-CNN. This combined information is then used to train a deep neural network (DNN) of classification. This approach enables efficient utilization of data and computational resources while achieving exceptional accuracy in image classification tasks. The primary contributions of this research are as follows:

- We introduce SR2LM for medical image classification to harness the advantages of both dictionary and deep learning techniques.
- We use sparse representation from dictionary learning to extract coarse features from input images. This reduces the need for adding excessive number of convolutional layers in deep learning, thus lowering computational overhead.
- Our approach combines the features extracted through sparse representation with those from a Residual-CNN network, resulting in more refined features for medical image classification.
- We conduct an ablation study to assess the individual and combined effects of the proposed module.
- Extensive testing across diverse datasets demonstrates that our approach surpasses state-of-the-art methods, yielding competitive results.

2 Related Work

In this section, we present concise descriptions of existing methods used to describe this article for image classification.

2.1 Dictionary Learning

Dictionary learning [1,7,16] is a technique that iteratively refines a set of basis functions to efficiently represent complex data in a sparse manner, finding applications in diverse fields such as image processing, natural language processing, and signal analysis. This dictionary consists of linearly combined basis functions or atoms, aiming to approximate the original data. The objective is to identify a sparse set of coefficients, such that when these coefficients are multiplied by the dictionary atoms, they reconstruct the original data. In the realm of audio, images, and video signals, the process of transforming them into compact representations-whether through uniform or structured approaches guided by the intrinsic complexity of the original data, as elucidated by Elad et al. [7]. These comprehensive dictionaries shed light on the underlying data characteristics.

2.2 ResNet

In the field of neural networks, He et al. [9] introduced the Residual Networks (ResNet) architecture, which has gained significant recognition in the literature. Prior to the development of ResNets, deep neural network structures encountered specific limitations [14]. Notably, very deep neural networks suffered from vanishing gradients, which hindered their performance. Moreover, simply adding more layers did not consistently lead to performance improvements. The objective was to enhance performance by expanding network depth inspite of the adverse factors mentioned above. To address this challenge and minimize data loss, the authors introduced Skip/Residual connections as a pivotal innovation in their architecture.

In this study, we conducted our analysis on a medical image dataset utilizing the Residual-CNN model. The subsequent sections comprehensively explain the architectural details and pre-trained weight structure of ResNet50. In fact, Residual-CNN is a CNN model with 50 layers. It employs bottleneck residual blocks that reduce parameters and matrix operations using 1×1 convolutions, improving training speed. Unlike the usual two-layer structure, Residual-CNN features a stack of five layers per block.

3 The Proposed Method

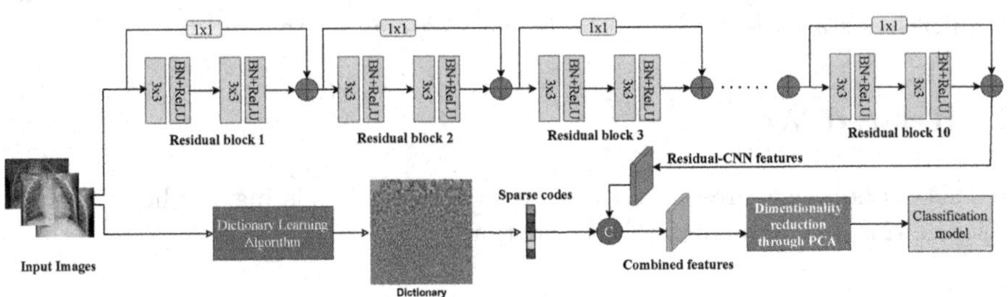

Fig. 1. Overview of the proposed Sparse Representation with Residual Learning Model for Medical Image Classification.

As depicted in Fig. 1, the proposed method combines features from sparse representation and residual network subsequently to improve image analysis.

- *Dictionary Learning and Sparse Representation:* Initially, we explicitly learn a dictionary from input images. This learned dictionary is then utilized to create sparse representations, a process where the image is represented using a subset of dictionary atoms. This step enhances feature extraction.
- *Residual-CNN Features:* Features extracted from a residual network are introduced for further processing. These features capture essential information from the images.
- *Combination of Features:* The features obtained from sparse representation and the residual network are integrated to harness their complementary strengths, forming a more comprehensive image representation. However, this fusion may introduce redundancies.
- *Dimensionality Reduction with PCA:* The combined features may contain the redundant features that should undergo dimensionality reduction using principal component analysis (PCA). This step refines the feature set by eliminating unnecessary redundancies while retaining important information.
- *DNN-Based Classification:* The refined features, now reduced in dimensionality, are input into a DNN classifier. This DNN facilitates the final image classification with minimal computational overhead.

This innovative model intelligently merges the capabilities of residual network and dictionary learning techniques. It harnesses the effectiveness of sparse coding, a fundamental element within dictionary learning that efficiently selects a subset of atoms for data representation. In the following sections, we provide a detailed exploration of each component within this approach: sparse representation using dictionary learning, feature extraction via the residual network, dimensionality reduction through PCA, and the architecture of the DNN designed for medical image classification.

3.1 Dictionary Learning and Sparse Representation

Sparse representation, a mathematical method, optimizes memory and processing efficiently by emphasizing the essential data elements. It finds extensive applications in diverse fields, including machine learning and signal processing. Donoho [6] underscores the pivotal role of sparse representations in simplifying complex signals for straightforward classifiers, such as linear models. Additionally, the effectiveness of sparse representation and sparse-inducing regularization in capturing crucial signal components are exemplified by Zhang et al. [19]. Recent advancements in deep learning have elevated the significance of dictionary learning, enabling the extraction of robust and distinctive feature representations from raw, unprocessed input data.

Given a set of N n-dimensional input signals, represented as $\boldsymbol{X} = [\boldsymbol{x}_1, \boldsymbol{x}_2, \cdots, \boldsymbol{x}_N] \in \mathcal{R}^{n \times N}$, the process of learning the reconstructive dictionary $\boldsymbol{\mathcal{D}}$ and sparse codes $\boldsymbol{\alpha}$ for $\boldsymbol{X}$ involves solving the optimization problem expressed as follows:

$$\langle \boldsymbol{\mathcal{D}}, \boldsymbol{\alpha} \rangle = argmin_{\boldsymbol{\mathcal{D}}, \boldsymbol{\alpha}} \|\boldsymbol{X} - \boldsymbol{\mathcal{D}}\boldsymbol{\alpha}\|_F^2 = \sum_{i=1}^{N} \|\boldsymbol{x}_i - \boldsymbol{\mathcal{D}}\boldsymbol{\alpha}_i\|_2^2 \quad s.t. \quad \|\boldsymbol{\alpha}_i\|_0 < s \tag{1}$$

Here, ($\boldsymbol{\mathcal{D}} = [\boldsymbol{d}_1, \boldsymbol{d}_2, \cdots, \boldsymbol{d}_K] \in \mathcal{R}^{n \times K}$) represents the dictionary with K atoms (where K is the dictionary size, and having $K > n$ results in an overcomplete dictionary), and $\boldsymbol{\alpha} = [\boldsymbol{\alpha}_1, \boldsymbol{\alpha}_2, \cdots, \boldsymbol{\alpha}_N] \in \mathcal{R}^{K \times N}$denotes the sparse codes of input signals $\boldsymbol{X}$ over the dictionary $\boldsymbol{\mathcal{D}}$.

3.2 Residual-CNN Network Features

In our approach, we harnessed the capabilities of Residual-CNN for feature extraction from input images. This process utilizes the residual network blocks that are pretrained on the ImageNet dataset [5]. To adapt these blocks for our specific task, we conducted a fine-tuning process using our available training images. It is important to note that we omitted the pooling and softmax layers, as our primary objective was feature extraction through the Residual-CNN. These extracted features play a pivotal role in subsequent classification tasks.

3.3 Dimensionality Reduction with PCA

Our approach begins by extracting features employing the modules discussed above. The features extracted from the two modules are then combined into a unified set. To optimize the dimensionality of this combined feature set, we employ PCA, a powerful tool for reducing feature dimensionality effectively. It is important to note that the combined feature set may contain redundant features. To enhance the efficiency of our classifier and streamline its performance, we implement a filtering process to eliminate these redundancies. The resulting refined feature set is subsequently used to further enhance and fine-tune the overall performance of our proposed model. This sequential process ensures that our model benefits from comprehensive feature extraction and efficient dimensionality reduction.

3.4 Deep Neural Network (DNN) for Classification

In our approach, we have introduced a DNN framework for classification, utilizing features extracted from sparse code and Residual-CNN, as illustrated in Fig. 1. The architecture of the DNN model is shown in Table 1 which comprises five densely connected layers, with 1024, 512, 256, 128, and 7 neurons, respectively. The first four layers employ the rectified linear unit (ReLU) activation function, followed by dropout and batch normalization layers. The final dense layer of the DNN is equipped with a softmax activation function. The inclusion of the softmax function holds particular significance in the context of multi-class classification tasks. It serves crucial role of transforming the output values of the final layer into a probability distribution across the potential classes. Consequently, when presented with an input, the class with the highest probability within this distribution is identified as the ultimate prediction class. This approach ensures our model delivers robust and accurate predictions for multi-class classification scenarios.

Table 1. Classification model architecture.

Layer type	Output shape	Activation function	Regularization	Dropout rate
Dense 1	1024	ReLU	L2 (0.01)	0.5
Dense 2	512	ReLU	L2 (0.01)	0.5
Dense 3	256	ReLU	L2 (0.01)	0.5
Dense 4	128	ReLU	L2 (0.01)	0.5
Dense 5	7	Softmax	–	–

4 Experimental Results

4.1 Description of Datasets

In our study, we assess the performance of the SR2LM model using the well-established MedMNIST dataset [17]. This dataset encompasses various modalities, offering a diverse range of medical data for evaluation purposes. We subject each dataset to identical evaluation criteria to ensure a fair and meaningful comparison with prior research. For a comprehensive understanding of these datasets, we provide an overview in Table 2.

Table 2. Table presents a detailed overview of the datasets utilized for evaluating the proposed model.

MedMNIST2D	Data Modality	Tasks(# Classes)	# Samples	# Training/Validation/Test
DermaMNIST	Dermatoscope	Multi-Class (7)	10,015	7,007/1,003/2,005
PneumoniaMNIST	Chest X-Ray	Binary-Class (2)	5,856	4,708/524/624
RetinaMNIST	Fundus Camera	Ordinal Regression (5)	1,600	1,080/120/400
BreastMNIST	Breast Ultrasound	Binary-Class (2)	780	546/78/156
BloodMNIST	Blood Cell Microscope	Multi-Class (8)	17,092	11,959/1,712/3,421

4.2 System Implementation

The proposed method has been employing python framework, utilizing libraries like TensorFlow and the scikit-learn on a Windows 10 platform. The system configuration included a 64-bit operating system, 16 GB of RAM, and an Intel i7-10750H 2.60 GHz CPU. In terms of experimental parameters: In the dictionary learning stage, the number of dictionary components (atoms) is 200. Sparse representation is accomplished using the orthogonal matching pursuit optimization technique [4]. Dictionary learning underwent a maximum of 500 iterations. The DNN training was carried out using the Adam optimizer and the sparse categorical cross-entropy loss function. DNN performance was evaluated based on accuracy. The experimentation spanned a total of 200 epochs.

4.3 Results and Analysis

Our research experiments comprehensively evaluated classification accuracy (ACC) and the area under the curve (AUC) across multiple datasets, including those mentioned previously. The comparative analysis given for five datasets from the MedMNIST dataset collection [17] and detailed information about these datasets can be found in Table 2. To assess the effectiveness of our proposed method, we compared its performance with that of established state-of-the-art techniques, including ResNet-18(28) [9], ResNet-18(224) [9], ResNet-50(28) [9], ResNet-50(224) [9], Auto-sklearn [8], and AutoKeras [11]. The results of this comparative analysis, including ACC and AUC values, are presented in Table 3. The SR2LM model surpasses existing benchmarks in medical image classification, achieving an average a AUC of 0.902 and an average ACC of 0.816 across the five datasets sourced from the MedMNIST dataset shown in the Table 3.

This evaluation is a crucial measure of our proposed method's performance against well-established benchmarks, providing a robust assessment of its effectiveness within the datasets mentioned above.

In Fig. 2, we meticulously tracked the training and validation accuracy of the proposed model across multiple datasets, each represent distinct medical imaging challenges. These datasets encompassed in Fig.2 (a) the PneumoniaMNIST dataset, (b) the DermaMNIST dataset, and (c) the BreastMNIST dataset.

In Fig. 2(a), the PneumoniaMNIST dataset presented specific challenges. Tracking training and validation accuracy allowed us to assess the model's adapt-

Table 3. Comparison table of accuracy (ACC) and area under the curve (AUC) for the proposed method to the other methods

Methods	BloodMNIST		PneumoniaMNIST		RetinaMNIST		BreastMNIST		DermaMNIST		Average	
	AUC	ACC	AUC	ACC	AUC	ACC	AUC	ACC	AUC	ACC	AUC	ACC
ResNet-18 (28)	**0.998**	0.958	0.944	0.854	0.717	0.524	0.901	0.863	0.917	0.735	0.895	0.786
ResNet-18 (224)	**0.998**	**0.963**	0.956	0.864	0.710	0.493	0.891	0.833	**0.920**	0.754	0.895	0.781
ResNet-50 (28)	0.997	0.956	0.948	0.854	0.726	0.528	0.857	0.812	0.913	0.735	0.888	0.777
ResNet-50 (224)	0.997	0.950	0.962	0.884	0.716	0.511	0.866	0.842	0.912	0.731	0.890	0.783
Auto-sklearn	0.984	0.878	0.942	0.855	0.690	0.515	0.836	0.803	0.902	0.719	0.870	0.754
AutoKeras	**0.998**	0.961	0.947	0.878	0.719	0.503	0.871	0.831	0.915	0.749	0.890	0.784
{Proposed}	0.994	0.959	**0.968**	**0.972**	**0.728**	**0.530**	**0.905**	**0.863**	0.916	**0.760**	**0.902**	**0.816**

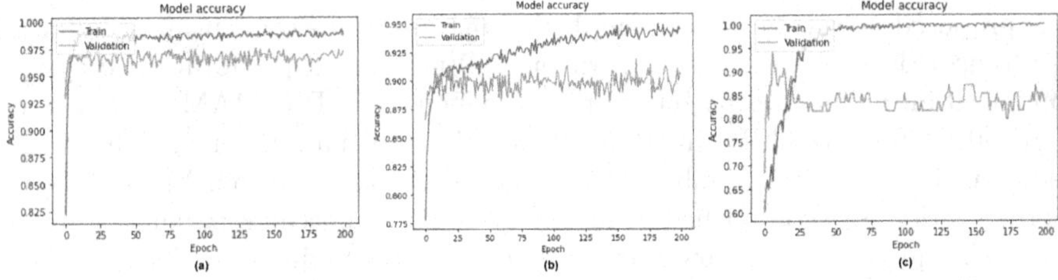

Fig. 2. Proposed model epoch wise train and validation accuracy (a) For PneumoniaMNIST dataset (b) For DermaMNIST dataset (c) For BreastMNIST dataset(*Please zoom the figure for better visualization*)

ability to diagnosing pneumonia. In Fig. 2(b) the DermaMNIST dataset featuring dermatology images, accuracy measurements were crucial for evaluating the model's ability to identify essential dermatoscopic features and patterns. In Fig. 2(c) for the BreastMNIST dataset, epoch-wise accuracy records helped us gauge the model's proficiency in recognizing intricate structures and anomalies.

These epoch-wise accuracy records provided insights into the model's learning dynamics and served as a basis for evaluating its effectiveness in handling diverse medical imaging datasets. Such detailed analyses are vital in ensuring the reliability and applicability of the proposed model in real-world medical scenarios.

The losses during training and validation of the proposed model were tracked across multiple epochs, focusing on three distinct datasets: PneumoniaMNIST, DermaMNIST, and BreastMNIST. The evolution of the model's performance during the training process is visually captured in Figs. 3(a), 3(b), and 3(c), corresponding to each dataset, respectively.

Figure 3(a), showing corresponding to the PneumoniaMNIST dataset, we observed how the model's training and validation losses evolved with each epoch. It provided insights into the model's performance in learning pneumonia-related patterns. Moving on to Fig. 3(b), associated with the DermaMNIST dataset, we scrutinized the model's adaptation to dermatological images by tracking its epoch-wise training and validation loss trends. In Fig. 3(c), which corresponds to

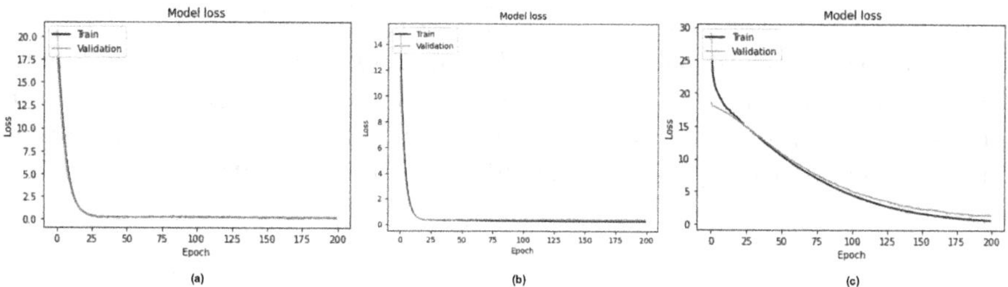

Fig. 3. Proposed model epoch wise train and validation loss (a) For PneumoniaMNIST dataset (b) For DermaMNIST dataset (c) For BreastMNIST dataset (*Please zoom the figure for better visualization*)

the BreastMNIST dataset, we focused on the model's behaviour during training on breast-related data.

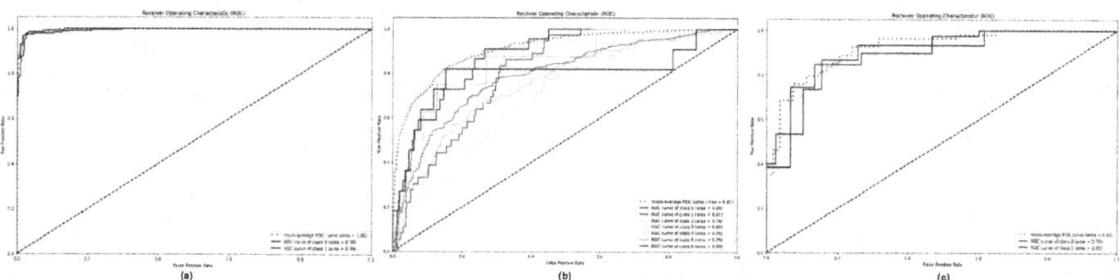

Fig. 4. Proposed model epoch wise AUC with different classes (a) For PneumoniaMNIST dataset (b) For DermaMNIST dataset (c) For BreastMNIST dataset (*Please zoom the figure for better visualization*)

The performance evaluation of our proposed model is presented in terms of epoch-wise AUC for different classes across three distinct datasets: (a) PneumoniaMNIST dataset, (b) DermaMNIST dataset, and (c) BreastMNIST dataset.

In Fig. 4(a), we meticulously tracked the epoch-wise AUC scores for binary classification tasks on the PneumoniaMNIST dataset. The binary nature of this classification, distinguishing between pneumonia and non-pneumonia cases, provides a foundational assessment of the model's discriminating ability. Figure 4(b) focuses on the DermaMNIST dataset, a more challenging multi-class scenario involving five distinct classes. The DermaMNIST dataset plays a pivotal role in dermoscopic disease diagnosis and analysis tasks. The presence of multiple classes adds complexity to the evaluation, making it a rigorous test of the model's discriminatory power. Lastly, Fig. 4(c) showcases epoch-wise AUC trends for binary classification on the BreastMNIST dataset, distinguishing between benign and malignant cases. This analysis offers insights into the model's adaptability to varying classification complexities in medical image analysis.

Taking into account these details, we observe that while Fig. 4(a) and Fig. 4(c) involve binary classification tasks, Fig. 4(b) presents a more challenging multi-class classification scenario with five distinct classes. This dynamic evaluation approach provides insights into the model's ability to evolve and adapt to different classification complexities, particularly in the context of medical image analysis tasks.

5 Ablation Study

The ablation study conducted in Table 4 aims to provide a comprehensive analysis of the performance differences between two critical approaches: one without dictionary learning (utilizing Residual-CNN) and the other incorporating dictionary learning (our proposed method). In this study, we meticulously assess the performance of these two approaches, dissecting their respective strengths and weaknesses. By comparing the outcomes achieved through these distinct methodologies, we gain a deeper understanding of the impact of dictionary learning on the overall effectiveness of our proposed model. This evaluation demonstrated the contributions of dictionary learning and highlighted the significance of our proposed approach in enhancing the outcomes, offering valuable insights into its potential for various applications.

Table 4. Ablation study for the shows the without dictionary (Residual-CNN) learning and with dictionary learning (Proposed) performance

Dataset	Ablated varient			
	Residual-CNN		**Proposed**	
	AUC	ACC	AUC	ACC
PneumoniaMNIST	0.962	0.884	**0.968**	**0.972**
RetinaMNIST	0.716	0.511	**0.728**	**0.530**
BreastMNIST	0.866	0.842	**0.905**	**0.863**
DermaMNIST	0.912	0.731	**0.916**	**0.760**
BloodMNIST	**0.997**	0.950	0.994	**0.959**

6 Conclusion

In summary, this article introduces SR2LM, an innovative approach that leverages the strengths of both deep learning models and dictionary learning. Our method incorporates novel dictionary learning and sparse representation techniques by seamlessly integrating them with residual-CNN features to facilitate the extraction of intricate features from input images. Additionally, we employ PCA to account for redundant features within this refined feature set, which is subsequently used as input to a DNN classifier. Despite limited training data, the performance evaluation of SR2LM on five publicly available datasets showcases its remarkable capabilities. Notably, SR2LM surpasses leading dictionary learning methods and achieves results comparable to state-of-the-art CNN-based models. It underscores the enhanced effectiveness of deep representation learning achieved by SR2LM. In the future, we plan to explore SR2LM's applications across various domains and assess its performance on larger datasets. SR2LM holds significant promise in advancing machine learning and deep representation techniques.

References

1. Aharon, M., Elad, M., Bruckstein, A.: K-svd: an algorithm for designing overcomplete dictionaries for sparse representation. IEEE Trans. Signal Process. **54**(11), 4311–4322 (2006)
2. Arya, A.S., Mukhopadhyay, S.: Adaptive sparse modeling in spectral and spatial domain for compressed image restoration. Signal Process. **213**, 109191 (2023)
3. Arya, A.S., Saha, A., Mukhopadhyay, S.: ADMM optimizer for integrating wavelet-patch and group-based sparse representation for image inpainting. In: The Visual Computer, pp. 1–28 (2023)
4. Cai, T.T., Wang, L.: Orthogonal matching pursuit for sparse signal recovery with noise. IEEE Trans. Inf. Theory **57**(7), 4680–4688 (2011)
5. Deng, J., Dong, W., Socher, R., Li, L.J., Li, K., Fei-Fei, L.: Imagenet: a large-scale hierarchical image database. In: 2009 IEEE Conference on Computer Vision and Pattern Recognition, pp. 248–255. IEEE (2009)
6. Donoho, D.L.: Compressed sensing. IEEE Trans. Inf. Theory **52**(4), 1289–1306 (2006)
7. Elad, M.: Sparse and Redundant Representations: From Theory to Applications in Signal and Image Processing. Springer, New York (2010). https://doi.org/10.1007/978-1-4419-7011-4
8. Feurer, M., Klein, A., Eggensperger, K., Springenberg, J., Blum, M., Hutter, F.: Efficient and robust automated machine learning. Adv. Neural Inf. Process. Syst. **28** (2015)
9. He, K., Zhang, X., Ren, S., Sun, J.: Deep residual learning for image recognition. In: Proceedings of the IEEE Conference on Computer Vision and Pattern Recognition, pp. 770–778 (2016)
10. Jiang, Z., Lin, Z., Davis, L.S.: Learning a discriminative dictionary for sparse coding via label consistent k-svd. In: CVPR 2011, pp. 1697–1704. IEEE (2011)
11. Jin, H., Song, Q., Hu, X.: Auto-keras: an efficient neural architecture search system. In: Proceedings of the 25th ACM SIGKDD International Conference on Knowledge Discovery and Data Mining, pp. 1946–1956 (2019)
12. LeCun, Y., Bengio, Y., Hinton, G.: Deep learning. Nature **521**(7553), 436–444 (2015)
13. Mahdizadehaghdam, S., Panahi, A., Krim, H., Dai, L.: Deep dictionary learning: a parametric network approach. IEEE Trans. Image Process. **28**(10), 4790–4802 (2019)
14. Miotto, R., Wang, F., Wang, S., Jiang, X., Dudley, J.T.: Deep learning for healthcare: review, opportunities and challenges. Brief. Bioinform. **19**(6), 1236–1246 (2018)

15. Song, J., Xie, X., Shi, G., Dong, W.: Multi-layer discriminative dictionary learning with locality constraint for image classification. Pattern Recogn. **91**, 135–146 (2019)
16. Wright, J., Yang, A.Y., Ganesh, A., Sastry, S.S., Ma, Y.: Robust face recognition via sparse representation. IEEE Trans. Pattern Anal. Mach. Intell. **31**(2), 210–227 (2008)
17. Yang, J., et al.: Medmnist v2-a large-scale lightweight benchmark for 2d and 3d biomedical image classification. Scientific Data **10**(1), 41 (2023)
18. Zhang, Q., Li, B.: Discriminative k-svd for dictionary learning in face recognition. In: 2010 IEEE Computer Society Conference on Computer Vision and Pattern Recognition, pp. 2691–2698. IEEE (2010)
19. Zhang, S., Wang, J., Tao, X., Gong, Y., Zheng, N.: Constructing deep sparse coding network for image classification. Pattern Recogn. **64**, 130–140 (2017)

COVID-19 Detection from Chest X-Ray Images Using GBM with Comparative Analysis

Abisek Dahal(✉), Abu Motaleb Rony, and Soumen Moulik

Department of CSE, National Institute of Technology, Shillong, Meghalaya, India
abiseknitskm@gmail.com

Abstract. Effective disease management and control depend on the quick and precise diagnosis of COVID-19. Chest X-ray(CXR) imaging has gained prominence as a convenient and accessible diagnostic tool. This study presents a Gradient Boosting Machines(GBM) and Convolutional Neural Networks (CNNs)-based model of COVID-19 detection, along with a comprehensive comparative analysis of the performances of various other machine learning (ML) algorithms. We compiled collected and pre-processed datasets comprising CXR of healthy people and those with COVID-19 positive. The model was trained with diverse CNN architectures and hyperparameter tuning optimized their performance. Algorithm effectiveness was assessed using evaluation metrics including accuracy, precision, recall and F1-score. Experimental results revealed the strengths and weaknesses of each algorithm in COVID-19 detection and the benefit of using these algorithms. The CNN and GBM model successfully differentiate between COVID-19-positive cases and healthy people with a remarkable accuracy rate of 97.4% but GBM take less computation time as compared to CNN.

Keywords: COVID-19 Detection · Convolutional Neural Networks · Chest X-Ray · Machine Learning

1 Introduction

Effective disease management and control depend heavily on the timely and precise diagnosis of diseases. CXR imaging has become one of the more practical and accessible diagnostic methods in many cases. We give a thorough comparison analysis of COVID-19 detection using machine learning algorithms with CXR in this paper. To carry out this study we meticulously collected and pre-processed datasets comprising CXR images from COVID-19-positive patients as well as healthy individuals. Ten machine learning algorithms were subsequently put into practise, including Support Vector Machines (SVM), K-Nearest Neighbours (K-NN), AdaBoost, Decision Tree, Gradient Boosting Machine, Logistic Regression, Naive Bayes, Random Forest, Recurrent Neural Network (RNN) and XG Boost (eXtreme Gradient Boosting). These algorithms were trained using

N. Chauhan et al. (Eds.): MIND 2023, CCIS 2128, pp. 239–247, 2024.
https://doi.org/10.1007/978-3-031-62217-5_20

various architectures and their performance was optimized through hyperparameter tuning. To evaluate the effectiveness of the algorithms a range of evaluation metrics such as accuracy, precision, recall and F1 score were employed. The experimental results of our study provided insights into the strengths and weaknesses of each algorithm in the detection of COVID-19. Through a comparative analysis against benchmark models, we gained a deeper understanding of their relative performance.

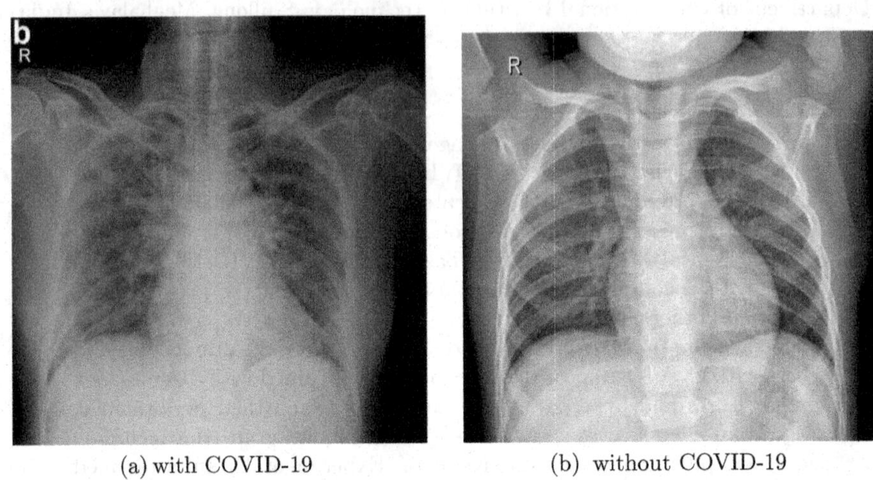

(a) with COVID-19 (b) without COVID-19

Fig. 1. Chest X-ray of an individuals

The Fig. 1a presents a CXR of an individual infected with COVID-19. This image exhibits specific characteristics associated with the disease, such as ground-glass opacities, bilateral infiltrates and consolidation. These radiographic findings are often observed in COVID-19 patients and indicate the presence of pneumonia caused by the virus. The abnormal opacities can vary in size, shape and distribution reflecting the severity and stage of the infection. In contrast Fig. 1b displays a CXR image of a patient without COVID-19.

A comparative analysis of this image with the COVID-19-infected CXR provides a visual contrast that allows us to identify the distinct features characteristic of COVID-19. Furthermore we employed visual interpretation techniques, including visualization and analysis to shed light on the decision-making processes of the models. The results of our study show that the CNN and GBM algorithm performed better than the other algorithms that were compared, displaying great precision and specificity. This shows that it may have the ability to detect COVID-19 accurately from CXR images. The GBM and CNN model successfully distinguished between COVID-19-positive cases and healthy people with a remarkable accuracy rate of 97.41%.

2 Related Works

Several studies have been conducted to evaluate the performance of machine learning algorithms for COVID-19 detection from CXR images. One study proposed an automatic deep learning(DL) classification method using CNN [1]. The authors in [2] proposed a amalgamation of deep learning and transfer learning. They came to the conclusion that the accuracy could be improved by two image pre-processing processes and the creation of pseudo-color images. To investigate the possibility of a DL decision-tree based model was proposed in [3].

The author in [4] proposed an automated system for COVID-19 using a DL algorithm using limited training data sets. They achieved an accuracy of 91.3% and demonstrated the potential of DL for COVID-19 diagnosis. An intelligent deep CNN-based COVID-19 detection algorithm was proposed in [5] which achieved an accuracy of 96.5% and demonstrated the potential of it for COVID-19 diagnosis. They used a two-step clustering techniques incorporating bootstrap aggregation with a number of NN methodologies to improve diagnostic sensitivity and lower error rates.

The author in [6] introduce classification framework called SLIPR that tackles the problem of inaccurate labels which can hinder the performance classification. Moreover to replicate a noisy environment they just use random noise. The author in [7] proposed a deep-learning method that achieved an accuracy of 96.5%. A systematic review of machine learning to ascertain and predict for COVID-19 using CXR as well as CT scans was conducted [8]. X-rays can act as an essential visual assistance and diagnostics framework for visualization tests and illness diagnosis in clinical process [10]. The author in [12] presents a two-phase approach for real-time COVID-19 detection using CXR combining a D-CNN and ELMs for classification. The author in [13] proposed a 'DeepChest' to learn desirable features from images. In comparison to earlier methods, "DeepChest" requires a far smaller number of max-pooling layers, fewer convolutional layers and fewer training iterations to execute. As a result, its performance overall and capacity for forecasting will suffer.

3 Proposed Model

3.1 Data Collection

Data collection involved the compilation of a diverse dataset consisting of CXR images from both positive and negative cases. Standard reprocessing techniques namely resizing, normalization and noise reduction is used to enhance the quality of the dataset. The dataset underwent rigorous review ensuring precise labeling with bounding boxes or segmentation masks. We have used CXR images image to evaluate the proposed architecture. Due to the high sensitivity of medical data, we have utilized a combination of publicly available dataset sourced from Kaggle (https://www.kaggle.com/datasets/tawsifurrahman/covid19-radiography-database) to conduct this research. To ensure transparency and replicability, we followed an 80% training and 20%

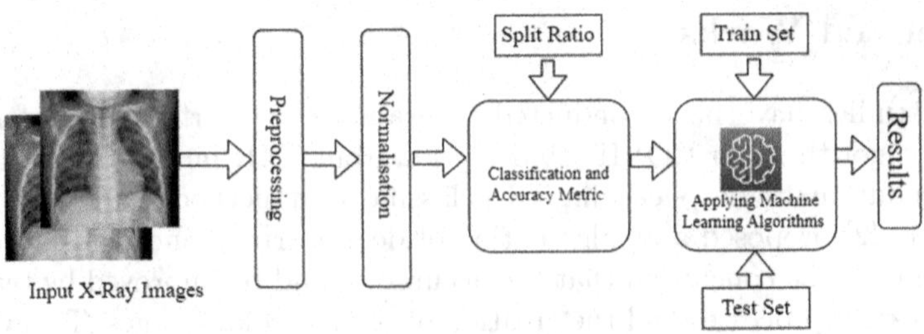

Fig. 2. Architecture of Proposed System

testing data split which will ensures extensive learning from a large portion of data. Followed by an unbiased evaluation of model performance on unseen data balancing effective training with accurate validation. The dataset encompasses 2905 chest X-ray images, encompassing 219 COVID-19 cases, 1341 normal cases and 1345 viral pneumonia cases.

3.2 Preprocessing

The resultant dataset comprises of X-ray images with diverse shapes and resolutions. To standardize the input dataset and ensure consistency throughout, we resized all images to a fixed dimension of 224×224 pixels. This standardization is essential for training Machine Learning models.

3.3 Normalisation

Furthermore, we implemented data augmentation techniques to augment the number and diversity of chest scans. Utilizing a large-scale dataset is crucial for training respective machine learning models and achieving satisfactory results. By employing data augmentation, we introduced variations to the initial images, including rotations, zooms, horizontal flips and shifts. Min-Max normalization and Z-score normalization is used to standardize the X-ray images. Min-Max normalization uniformly scales the pixel values while Z-score normalization ensures they conform to a normalized distribution. It is crucial for preparing the images for accurate and consistent analysis by machine learning algorithm. These techniques significantly increased the size and diversity of our dataset contributing to the overall goal of enhancing the model's performance.

3.4 Evaluation Metrics

We evaluate the performance of each algorithm by using normal evaluation technique used to evaluate machine learning model. The *Precision (P)* is calculated by dividing the number of true positives by the sum of true positives (TP) and false positives (FP). Mathematically,

$$P = \frac{\text{TP}}{\text{TP} + \text{FP}} \tag{1}$$

Recall (R) is calculated as ratio of true positives to the sum of true positives and false negatives (FN), quantifying the ability of a model to correctly identify positive instances. Mathematically,

$$R = \frac{\mathrm{TP}}{\mathrm{TP} + \mathrm{FN}} \tag{2}$$

A statistic called Mean Average Precision (mAP) is used to assess how well item detection and recognition systems perform. A thorough evaluation of the model's accuracy in detecting and localising objects in distinct categories is provided by calculating average precision for each individual class and then taking the mean across all provided classes.

$$mAP = \frac{1}{n} \sum_{i=1}^{n} AP_i \tag{3}$$

where n is the number of classes and $AP_i$is an average precision for class i. Average Precision (AP) is a performance metric used in object detection and information retrieval tasks to measure the quality of ranked predictions. Mathematically,

$$AP = \frac{1}{TP} \sum_{TP} IR \tag{4}$$

where TP represents true positives at each interpolated recall (IR) level.

F1-score (F1) is an evaluation metric which uses both precision as well as recall and calculated as harmonic mean of the two, providing a balanced measure of a model's accuracy. Mathematically,

$$F1 = \frac{2 \times \mathrm{P} \times \mathrm{R}}{\mathrm{P} + \mathrm{R}} \tag{5}$$

Sensitivity (Sen) is an unit that measures a machine learning model's ability to accurately detect positive instances. It represents the proportion of true positives that the model correctly identifies.

$$Sen = \frac{TP}{TP + FP} \tag{6}$$

Specificity (S) is a measure of a machine learning model's ability to precisely identify negative instances. It indicates the proportion of true negatives that the model accurately recognizes. Mathematically,

$$S = \frac{TN}{TN + FP} \tag{7}$$

Accuracy (A) is the ratio of correctly classified class to the total number of class, reflecting the overall correctness of a model's predictions. Mathematically,

$$A = \frac{TP + TN}{TP + TN + FP + FN} \tag{8}$$

3.5 Algorithms Used in Experiment

To conduct this experiment, we applied machine learning algorithms on proposed architecture in Fig. 2 both the original and normalised dataset. Our objective is to determine the algorithm that achieves the highest accuracy in detecting Covid-19 cases.

The algorithms used in our experiment are as follows:

1. CNN - Convolutional Neural Network
2. LR - Logistic Regression
3. DT- Decision Tree
4. NB - Naive Bayes
5. RF - Random Forest
6. K-NN - K-Nearest Neighbors
7. RNN - Recurrent Neural Network
8. AdaBoost
9. XGBoost
10. GBM - Gradient Boosting Machine
11. SVM - Support Vector Machine

We will compare the performance of these algorithms based on their accuracy.

Table 1. Comparison of Algorithms

Algorithm	P	R	F1	S	A
CNN	1	0.375	0.545	1	0.974
SVM	0.5	0.625	0.555	0.972	0.958
K-NN	0.8	0.5	0.615	0.994	0.974
Decision Tree	0.166	0.375	0.23	0.918	0.896
Naive Bayes	0.161	0.625	0.256	0.859	0.849
Logistic Regressi on	0.444	0.5	0.47	0.972	0.953
Random Forest	1	0.25	0.4	1	0.968
RNN	0.98	0.378	0.6	1	0.958
AdaBoot	0.5	0.25	0.333	0.989	0.958
XGBoost	1	0.25	0.4	1	0.968
GBM	1	0.370	0.540	1	0.974

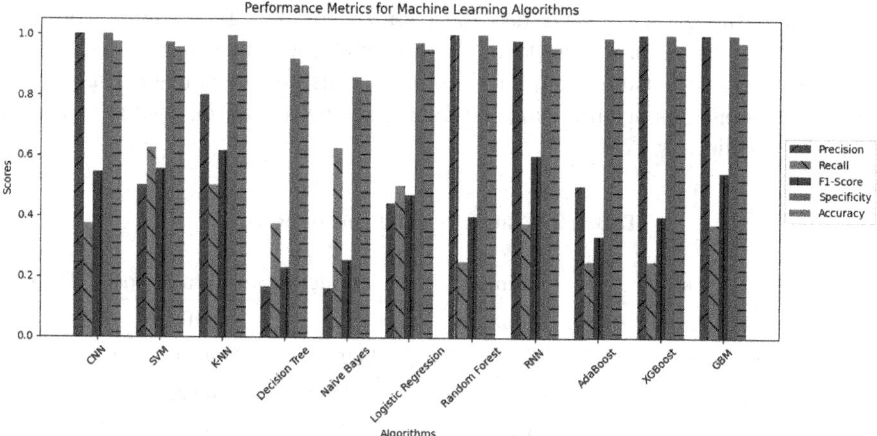

Fig. 3. Performance metric for Machine Learning Algorithms

4 Result and Simulation

The experiment was conducted using TensorFlow a popular framework for machine and deep learning model development and deployment. Additional libraries employed included Keras, SK-Learn and Scipy enhancing the experimentation process. The experiment necessitated a dedicated GPU on a computer server in google colab with the GPU with 15 GB GDDR5 VRAM for computational capabilities to facilitate efficient computations.

From Table 1 and Fig. 3 it is clear that GBM and CNN achieved the highest precision (P) among all the algorithms indicating a low false positive rate. This means that the CNN was able to correctly classify a large proportion of COVID-19 cases. SVM (Support Vector Machine) had the highest recall(R) of 0.625, suggesting a relatively lower false negative rate. SVM performed well in identifying true positive COVID-19 cases, although it had a slightly higher false positive rate compared to CNN. K-NN exhibited a high specificity(S) value 0.994, indicating a low false positive rate. This suggests that K-NN was effective in correctly classifying non-COVID-19 cases. DT, NB, LR, RF, RNN (Recurrent Neural Network), AdaBoost, XGBoost, and showed relatively lower evaluation metrics compared to GBM, CNN, SVM, and K-NN.

However, all demonstrated performance depends on the application's unique requirements. Overall the results suggest that GBM and CNN performed the best among the evaluated algorithms with high precision and specificity indicating its potential for accurate detection of COVID-19 with X-ray. We subsequently assessed the computational durations of all the algorithms listed in Table 2. We used the python time package to compute the training and testing times. The training time refers to the duration required for a particular model or machine learning algorithm to learn from the provided data. Conversely the testing time pertains to the duration needed for evaluating the results obtain by validating with new data against the trained data for the model. To estimate the total computation time (C_t), we employed the following formula: $C_t^i = T_t^i + T_s^i$, where T_t and T_s denote the time taken for training and testing the dataset respectively. This process ensures accurate measurements of the overall computational time for each classifier.

Table 2. Computation Time(In Sec.)

Algorithm	Training Time	Testing Time	Total Time
CNN	980.25	60.23	1040.48
SVM	870.49	20.95	891.44
KNN	70.85	12.18	83.03
Decision Tree	33.12	12.32	45.44
Naive Bayes	71.161	13.25	84.411
Logistic Regression	55.4	12.31	67.71
Random Forest	43.11	12.2	55.31
RNN	204.94	18.78	223.72
AdaBoot	16.32	7.25	23.57
XGBoost	32.89	8.25	41.14
GBM	420.12	32.12	452.24

5 Conclusion

Experimental results revealed the strengths and weaknesses of each algorithm in COVID-19 detection. Comparative analysis against benchmark models provided insights into relative performance. The GBM and CNN model stood out as the most effective in detecton COVID-19 using X-ray, achieving a remarkable accuracy rate of 97.41%. It displayed high Recall, F1 score and Precision indicating its ability to accurately identify positive cases. The GBM model's superior performance suggests its potential for clinical use in COVID-19 diagnosis due to less computation time. Further research and validation are necessary to confirm the general suitability and robustness of the GBM model across diverse patient populations and healthcare settings. Based on our computational analysis it seems that GBMs have an edge over CNNs when it comes to computational time making them a more convenient choice in certain situations. However, it is important to remember that CNNs offer their own unique advantages over GBMs. CNNs have a simpler architecture and training process which can make them more approachable and easier to work with. On the other hand, GBMs are an interesting technique that combines multiple weak models, usually decision trees, to create a more robust model. Ultimately, the decision between GBMs and CNNs depends on the specific needs and characteristics of the task you are tackling. It is crucial to take into account additional elements like computing complexity, scalability and interpretability when choosing an efficient algorithm for practical implementation. In future research we will focus on refining and validating these models for real-world clinical use.

References

1. Akter, S., Shamrat, F.M.J.M., Chakraborty, S., Karim, A., Azam, S.: COVID-19 detection using deep learning algorithm on chest X-ray images. Biology **10**(11), 1174 (2021). https://doi.org/10.3390/biology10111174. ISSN 0959-6526
2. Akter, S., Shamrat, F.J.M., Chakraborty, S., Karim, A., Azam, S.: COVID-19 detection using deep learning algorithm on chest X-ray images. Biology **10**(11), 1174 (2021)
3. Yoo, S.H., et al.: Deep learning-based decision-tree classifier for COVID-19 diagnosis from chest X-ray imaging. Front. Med. **7**, 427 (2020)
4. Mohammad-Rahimi, H., Nadimi, M., Ghalyanchi-Langeroudi, A., Taheri, M., Ghafouri-Fard, S.: Application of machine learning in diagnosis of COVID-19 through X-ray and CT images: a scoping review. Front. Cardiovasc. Med. **8**, 638011 (2021)
5. Alshahrni, M.M., Ahmad, M.A., Abdullah, M., Omer, N., Aziz, M.: An intelligent deep convolutional network based COVID-19 detection from chest X-rays. Alexandria Eng. J. **64**, 399–417 (2023). https://doi.org/10.1016/j.aej.2022.09.016. ISSN 1110-0168
6. Ying, X., Liu, H., Huang, R.: COVID-19 chest X-ray image classification in the presence of noisy labels. Displays **77**, 102370 (2023). https://doi.org/10.1016/j.displa.2023.10237. ISSN 0141-9382
7. Brunese, L., Martinelli, F., Mercaldo, F., Santone, A.: Machine learning for coronavirus covid-19 detection from chest x-rays. Procedia Comput. Sci. **176**, 2212–2221 (2020). https://doi.org/10.1016/j.procs.2020.09.258. ISSN 1877-0509
8. Roberts, M., Driggs, D., Thorpe, M., et al.: Common pitfalls and recommendations for using machine learning to detect and prognosticate for COVID-19 using chest radiographs and CT scans. Nat. Mach. Intell. **3**, 199–217 (2021). https://doi.org/10.1038/s42256-021-00307-0
9. Arias-Garzón, D., et al.: COVID-19 detection in X-ray images using convolutional neural networks, Mach. Learn. Appl. **6**, 100138 (2021). https://doi.org/10.1016/j.mlwa.2021.100138. ISSN 2666-8270
10. Qi, A., et al.: Directional mutation and crossover boosted ant colony optimization with application to COVID-19 X-ray image segmentation. Comput. Biol. Med. **148**, 105810 (2022). https://doi.org/10.1016/j.compbiomed.2022.105810. ISSN 0010-4825
11. Vayá, M.D.L.I., et al.: BIMCV COVID-19+: a large annotated dataset of RX and CT images from COVID-19 patients. arXiv preprint arXiv:2006.01174 (2020)
12. Hu, T., et al.: Real-time COVID-19 diagnosis from X-ray images using deep CNN and extreme learning machines stabilized by chimp optimization algorithm. Biomed. Signal Process. Control **68**, 102764 (2021). https://doi.org/10.1016/j.bspc.2021.102764. ISSN 1746-8094
13. Musallam, A.S., Sherif, A.S., Hussein, M.K.: Efficient framework for detecting COVID-19 and pneumonia from chest X-ray using deep convolutional network. Egypt. Inf. J. **23**(2), 247–257 (2022). https://doi.org/10.1016/j.eij.2022.01.002. ISSN 1110-8665

Violence Detection in Indoor Domestic Environment Using Multimodal Information

R. Aravinth, T. Shashwat, V. Yeshwanth, and K. Sitara(✉)

Department of Computer Science and Engineering, National Institute of Technology Tiruchirappalli, Tiruchirappalli 620015, Tamil Nadu, India
sitara@nitt.edu

Abstract. The recognition of violent activities has emerged as a prominent topic within the realm of computer vision research. This issue is of paramount importance within indoor domestic environments, given the heightened vulnerability of individuals residing in such conditions to potential attacks. Consequently, there exists a substantial imperative for the development of intelligent surveillance systems capable of autonomously monitoring individuals and identifying instances of violent behavior. While numerous techniques grounded in handcrafted and deep learning features have been proposed to address this challenge, it is noteworthy that many of these methodologies primarily focus on video data and often disregard the potential insights offered by audio information. In light of this, this paper presents a fusion model for violence detection, which integrates audio and video features to provide a comprehensive and nuanced assessment of potentially violent incidents. Our proposed approach leverages inflated 3D networks and pretrained models from the Visual Geometry Group to extract video and audio features, respectively. Subsequently, these extracted feature vectors are combined utilizing a joint cross-attention fusion model. The results of our proposed model are promising, with an achieved accuracy rate of 73.3%, coupled with a processing speed of 25 frames per second. This research contribution is instrumental in advancing violence detection technology, particularly within indoor domestic environments, where the safety and well-being of individuals are paramount concerns.

Keywords: I3D · VGGish model · Violence detection · Deep Learning

1 Introduction

Public video surveillance systems are widespread worldwide and offer a wealth of accurate information for various security applications. In contexts such as crime prevention and violence deterrence, the ability to make rapid decisions is paramount. However, this crucial capability is often hampered by the laborious task of sifting through hours of video footage. Automated violence identification

N. Chauhan et al. (Eds.): MIND 2023, CCIS 2128, pp. 248–259, 2024.
https://doi.org/10.1007/978-3-031-62217-5_21

presents a valuable avenue of exploration, with potential applications ranging from intelligent surveillance to analyzing videos uploaded via mobile applications and assisting prison guard robots. Manual detection, due to its limitations, is only feasible for a small fraction of the video material.

The motivation behind this project is to develop an automated violent action detector that can alleviate the burden on authorities tasked with monitoring extensive video content to identify events that may last mere seconds, thereby reducing potential casualties.

Domestic violence remains a deeply concerning issue in our society. It encompasses acts such as robbery and acts of revenge, which may involve physical harm or the use of weapons. People are particularly vulnerable to domestic violence because, in many cases, they are unaware of the situations they may be in.

Utilizing video surveillance systems offers a means to detect and prevent such activities, as fully manual detection is often impractical. To address this challenge, we propose an automatic violence detector designed to ingest surveillance video streams. This system processes visual and audio features separately before constructing a fusion model that combines both video and audio feature vectors to produce a comprehensive result.

The main focus of the model is to detect violence that occurs in indoor or work environments. For example: eldercare, offices, hospitals, and so on. The model should trigger an alarm immediately after a violent action of any kind is detected in the given video. First, to extract information from the video frames, we use an extractor based on the I3D classification model [1]. Then, for the audio information, we use the VGGish extractor [2]. Finally, our fusion model (Joint cross attention model) merges the extracted vectors to produce a comprehensive result. The major drawback of the existing models is that audio information is not taken into account for recognizing violent actions or behaviours in videos.

2 Related Works

The approach to violence detection has evolved from using standard machine learning algorithms like the Support Vector Machine (SVM) to using deep learning techniques. We did our literature survey on deep-learning models since it is the state-of-the-art technique.

In [3], a method from learning anomalies in videos using both normal and anomalous videos is proposed. Annotating anomalous segments in training videos is a time-consuming task, so the proposed approach leverages weakly labelled training videos with video-level labels. The approach treats normal and anomalous videos as bags and video segments as instances in multiple-instance learning. To improve anomaly localization during training, the ranking loss function incorporates sparsity and temporal smoothness constraints. Visual features are extracted from the C3D model [4].

The method in [5] is based on the analysis of visual characteristics and its auditory features and combining them to recognise the broader concept of violence. Visual features are extracted with a combination of Conv3D [4] and Long

Short-Term Memory (LSTM) [6]. Audio is processed with spectral contrast, a Fourier transform, and shallow NN. The fusion network is concatenating all the k-sub concept representations.

In [7], a novel method to process a video clip for action recognition that aims to address redundancy at both clip-levels and video-levels is proposed. At the clip level, it takes just the first frame of the clip and tries to preserve the spatial information in the clip as much as possible, while the audio segment contains temporal information. To address video-level redundancy, an attention-based LSTM network is designed to select the most useful image-audio pairs.

In [8], the authors focused on multimodal, weakly supervised violence detection. It uses multiple instance learning (MIL), where frame-level annotations are learned from video-level annotations. To capture long-range dependencies by using similarity priors among snippets, they propose a holistic and localised network (HL-Net), where the holistic branch models short-range interactions within a local neighbourhood, and the localised branch explicitly exploits relationships between snippets. The video and audio features are extracted from a pretrained I3D model and a VGGish model, respectively.

In [9] which is based on multimodal weakly supervised violence detection, the fusion process, which is based on fusing the video (RGB and Optical Flow) features extracted from the pre-trained I3D model and audio features extracted from the VGGish model. In [10] which is also based on multimodal, weakly supervised violence detection, the early fusion process is based upon cross-attention as well as local arousal. The video (RGB and Optical Flow) features extracted from the trained I3D model and audio features extracted from the VGGish model are used as the input for the cross-attention module, where the dimensions of audio and video features are different, a global mapping of the audio over the video is done, and the local arousal module is used to establish importance to sequences that are closer to each other.

In [11–13], the primary drawbacks are that the scope and size of the datasets (around 200–300 videos) is very limited. While the accuracy of these methods on custom built dataset might be more, it is more likely to be a case of overfitting. They do not feature audio representations, which is a major drawback because it has been found that audio representations have a strong correlation with visual representations. In [3], we have drastic improvements regarding the size and scope of the dataset, again they did not consider features from audio representations. In [5], we have the first model that included audio features in its classification model, but the division of violence into sub-concepts has limitations in scope and thus the model has high chances of overfitting. Also if the model is trained on large datasets, it might lead to computational isssues due to late-fusion. All the concepts referred are of extreme violence which are unlikely to happen in real-time situations. In [7], we have action recognition done by a computationally efficient model. In clip-level annotation, only the first frame in the image is taken along with the complete audio representation of the clip, valuable information is lost (the first frame might not contain the contextual temporal information). In [8], we have the largest dataset available (XD-Violence). The drawback here is that the authors simply concatenates the input rather than fusing the visual and audio representations.

A multi-encoder framework to encode features from video and audio modalities in a separate way to focus on particular task [14]. The work [15] address multimodal data and ignore the implicit alignment of multimodal features.

3 Proposed Framework

The proposed approach is outlined in Fig. 1. Initially, the data (RGB video containing audio) is fed into the pre-trained models, which act as feature extractors, and the video (RGB and Optical Flow) features and audio features are extracted.

The extracted features are then to be fused, since from [8–10], it has been found that multi-modal fusion performs better. For example, in a violent video, when an attacker attacks the victim, the video captures the moment the attack takes place, as well as the sound the victim makes, which is strongly related as he makes a particular sound when he performs an action. So the features are sent into the multi-modal fusion module, and the output is sent to a classifier to classify whether it is violent or not. While training on the data, validation is done by calculating the precision-recall score on a frame-level annotated validation dataset.

The trained model is then fed by real-time test samples, which predict if the footage is violent or non-violent. The footage is then collected, and the process continues. In summary, it is a multimodal approach which is based on previous results, fuses video and audio features to improve the prediction of a violent event.

VGGish and I3D Models are used to extract features from the audio and video parts respectively. The I3D (inflated 3D networks) network is a popular 3D video classification network. It learns spatiotemporal information directly from videos using 3D convolution. Training 3D networks for video classification is quite feasible and produces far better results. This I3D model is used to extract RGB and optical flow from the video. We utilise two mainstream networks as our visual features: extractors F and V, namely, the C3D and I3D networks. FC6 features are extracted from C3D that is pretrained on the Sports-1M dataset. Global pool features are extracted from I3D which is pre-trained on the Kinetics-400 dataset. I3D is a two-stream model; So, there are two versions of visual features: RGB and optical flow.

VGGish is a 128-dimensional audio embedding approach based by VGGNet [16] and pre-trained on a huge YouTube 8M dataset [17] including over 2 million human-labeled 10 s YouTube video soundtracks with over 600 audio event classes. VGGNet's original goal is to do large-scale image classification tasks, whereas VGGish's goal is to extract acoustic features from audio waveforms. The VGGish audio embedding approach employs 2D convolutional layers and 2D max-pooling layers, to generate a single 128-dimension feature output vector. The VGGish feature extractor transforms audio input features into a semantically meaningful 128-D embedding that can be fed into a downstream classification model. As VGGish embeddings are more semantically compact than raw acoustic characteristics, the downstream model can be shallower than normal.

3.1 Multi Modal Feature Fusion

Multimodal feature fusion (MMFF) is a commonly used approach in data analysis and machine learning that involves combining information from multiple sources, each with different types of data, into a single and comprehensive representation.

Fusion techniques are classified into two types: early fusion and late fusion. The early fusion technique involves the process of combining data by concatenating either the original or transformed features at the input level before feeding them into a unified model that can process all the information. The late fusion model architecture utilises decision-level aggregation of predictions. Here, early fusion is used to fuse the video and audio features since late fusion is computationally intensive and the extracted features are taken from state-of-the-art models. Figure 1 shows the proposed fusion model which consists of establishing correlations between the audio and the joint feature representations and between the video and the joint feature representations.

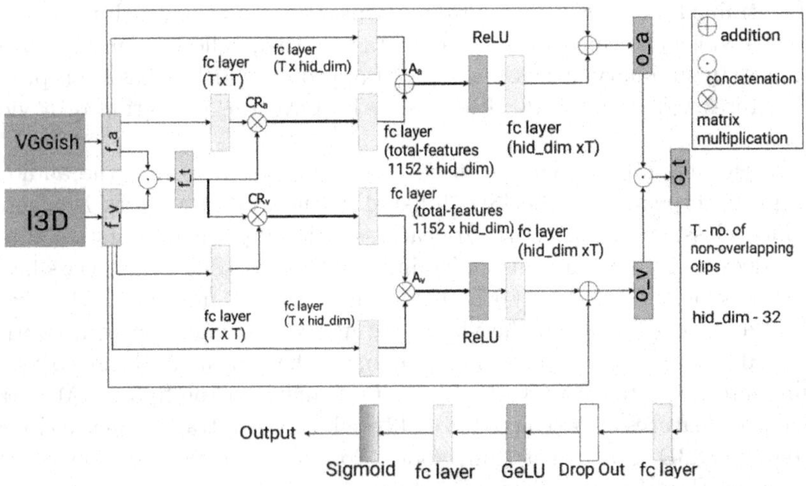

Fig. 1. Architecture of Proposed Fusion Model.

Let F_a and F_v represents the feature vector extracted for the Audio and Visual modalities where $F_a = \{f_a^1, f_a^2, ..f_a^T\} \in R^{d_a * T}$ and $F_v = \{f_v^1, f_v^2, ..f_v^T\} \in R^{d_v * T}$, where T is the number of non-overlapping fixed-size clips taken uniformly from a video, d_a and d_v represent the dimensions of the audio features and the visual features. The joint feature representation is obtained by concatenating the audio and visual features.

$$J = [F_a; F_v] \in R^{d_t * T} \tag{1}$$

where $d_t = d_a + d_v$, the total number of feature representations.

The concatenated joint feature representation is used to form correlations with audio and visual feature representations. The Joint correlation matrix CR_a across the Audio feature representations F_a, and the Joint feature representations J are given by:

$$CR_a = tanh((F_a^T W_{ja} J)/\sqrt{d_t}) \tag{2}$$

where $W_{ja} \in R^{T*T}$ represents the learnable weight matrix between the Audio features and the Joint features. Similarly the Joint correlation matrix CR_v across the Visual feature representations is given by

$$CR_v = tanh((F_v^T W_{jv} J)/\sqrt{d_t}) \tag{3}$$

The joint correlation matrices establishes similarity measures in both within modality as well as cross modality. Higher values of CR_a and CR_v indicate strong similarities in semantic information between the Visual and Audio representations.

In order to calculate cross-attention weights for each modality, we need to take into account that the joint correlation matrices ($R^{d_a * d_t}$, $R^{d_v * d_t}$)and the features of each modality($R^{d_a * T}$, $R^{d_v * T}$) have different dimensions. To address this issue, we utilize individual weight matrices that can be learned for each modality's features and its corresponding joint correlation matrix. To calculate the cross-attention weights for the Audio modality, we combine the joint correlation matrix CR_a and the Audio features F_a using learnable weight matrices W_{ca} and W_a, respectively. The resulting cross-attention weights for the Audio modality are given by :

$$A_a = ReLu(W_{aa} F_a + W_{ca} CR_a^T) \tag{4}$$

where $W_{ca} \in R^{k*d_t}$, $W_a \in R^{k*T}$ and A_a is the cross-attention map corresponding to audio modality. Similarly cross attention map for the Visual modality,

$$A_v = ReLu(W_v F_v + W_{cv} CR_v^T) \tag{5}$$

where $W_{cv} \in R^{k*d_t}$, $W_v \in R^{k*T}$, k is the hidden layer size.
Finally attention maps are used to calculate enhanced audio and visual features given by

$$F_{att,a} = W_{aa} A_a + F_a \tag{6}$$

$$F_{att,v} = W_{av} A_v + F_v \tag{7}$$

where $W_{aa} \in R^{k*T}$ and $W_{av} \in R^{k*T}$. The final audio-visual representation is given by

$$F = [F_{att,a}; F_{att,v}] \in R^{d_t * T} \tag{8}$$

Which is then fed into a classification network consisting of two fully connected layers, a GeLU activation layer and a dropout layer. The output of the fully connected layers is then passed to the sigmoid function to obtain the confidence score for the given input.

The Binary Cross-Entropy loss (BCEloss) function is used as the loss function since it is a two-class classification problem. MIL is used here, where frame-level annotation is learned from video-level annotations. From [3,8,10], we use the average of the k-max predictions in the video bag as the violence score, where k is given by, $k = [T/q + 1]$. The k-max predictions in the positive bag are most likely to contain violence, while the k-max predictions in the negative bag are usually hard samples, which may lead to false alarm. Therefore, our BCE loss function is expressed as

$$L_{cls} = -\frac{1}{N}\sum t_i \log p_i + (1 - t_i)\log(1 - p_i) \tag{9}$$

where t_i is the video-level annotation and p_i is the mean of the k-max predicted values.

For the final predictor to test on a video-level whether the given video is violent or not, we decided to choose the top-k frames having the most confidence score (meaning the k most violent frames) and computed mean of these values. If the value is greater than 0.5 we classify the video as violent. The value of k is computed based on [3,8,10], where $k = [T/q + 1]$.

3.2 Layers and Activation Functions Used

Linear layer. The linear layers are used as the learnable weight matrices in our model.

Tanh layer. The tanh layer is used to introduce non-linearity in the model. Non-Linearity introduces wide range of possible values for the given input.

ReLU layer. The ReLU layer is used because not all neurons are activated at the same time. Accordingly, a neuron is only rendered inactive if the output of a linear transformation is less than 0, whether it is nonlinear or effectively computed. In addition, it resolves the gradient issue.

GeLU layer. The GeLU layer is used in between the fully connected layers because it avoids the dying ReLU problem (outputs getting to 0 and unable to change weights).

Sigmoid layer. The sigmoid layer is used because we need our final score to be between 0(non-violent) to 1(violent) and the scope of sigmoid is (0,1). It is the standard for two class classification.

4 Results and Discussion

4.1 Dataset Used

The dataset used here is the XD-Violence dataset [8]. This is the first large-scale dataset created for violence detection. Due to computational costs and since our aim is to detect indoor violence, we decided to take the videos that felt relevant to our cause. Refer Table 1 for the details.

Dataset Preprocessing. The main task in the preprocessing phase of the video dataset is video annotation. We adapted the traditional single-image video annotation method that extracts each frame from the video and annotates the frames one by one. Annotating videos using the single image method is exceptionally time consuming, which increases the cost of the project by causing misclassification errors, missed deadlines, and annotation errors. Considering these, we decided to annotate frames within a range altogether instead of annotating each frame by frame of a video. It is summarized in Table 1.

Table 1. Number of videos in the original and truncated dateset, grouped for training and testing.

Dataset	Train/Test	Category	No. of videos
Original Dataset	Training	Violence	2472
		Non-Violence	1482
	Testing	Violence	500
		Non-Violence	300
Truncated Dataset	Training	Violence	1440
		Non-Violence	1440
	Testing	Violence	180
		Non-Violence	180

4.2 Parameter Tuning

Model training using different parameter values are performed to find the best parameter setting. The parameter comparison charts are plotted for the model (RGB+Audio modality) having the best accuracy during training. We tune the non-overlapping fixed number of clips to obtain maximum accuracy for the model. It is the most important to tune, as the model layers directly depend on its value, and once fixed, it cannot be varied during testing of the other parameters. From Fig. 2 (a), we observe that the best accuracy is at T = 200.

Further, we tune the following parameters to obtain maximum accuracy: dff, hidden_dim and batch size. The dff layer is the size of output of the fusion module's subsequent first fully connected layer. The hidden dimension layer is the layer used after the joint correlation matrix. The amount of samples that will be transmitted via the network is determined by the batch size. The change in batch size affects the accuracy and performance of the model as the loss back propagated depends on it. From Fig. 2 (b), (c) and (d), we observe the best accuracy to be at dff = 32, hidden_dim = 32 and batch size = 128 respectively.

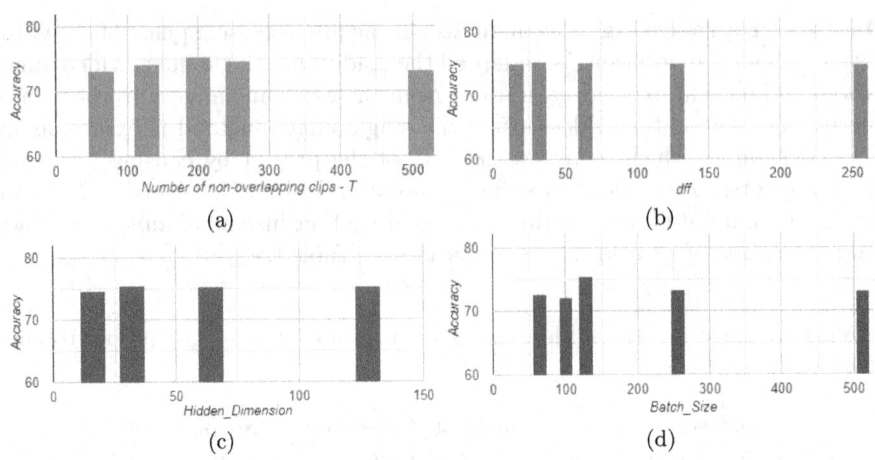

Fig. 2. Accuracy obtained on various parameters (a) Number of non overlapping clips (b) DFF (c) Hidden dimension (d) Batch Size

4.3 Performance Evaluation

Model accuracy and loss on various epochs in the training stage are shown in Fig. 3. X-axis is the number of epochs in all the graphs. The Y-axis is accuracy for (a), (b) and (c) while it is loss for (d), (e) and (f). A loss value indicates how well or poorly a particular model performs after each iteration of optimization. Ideally, we would expect the loss to decrease with each iteration. In the Fig. 3, the CLS-loss, apart from a few points, gradually decreases as the model adjusts its weights to minimise and learn from the losses.

The proposed method is tested on the testing dataset which was taken from the reduced XD-Violence dataset and results obtained is shown in Table 2. We performed testing using our best trained models for the respective modalities and we found out the accuracy for the testing data to be 73.26% for the RGB+Audio model while the RGB-only model turned out to give an accuracy of 68.43%. This shows an improvement of 4.78% over the RGB-only features. The accuracy for Flow+Audio modality turned out to be 72.15% while the Flow-only model turned out to have 67.74% accuracy giving a 4.33% improvement. The RGB+Flow+Audio model turned out to give an accuracy of 72.82%. Compared with [9], the testing accuracy decreases by 1.31% for the best model. [9] uses audio to recalibrate visual features and enhance it while we try to find both intra-modal and inter-modal correlations to enhance both audio and visual features.

The real-time situation of violence detection is shown in Fig. 4. The model predictor predicts the video in Fig. 4 (a) as violent since the confidence score (0.9916) is greater than 0.5. Figure 4 (b) is predicted as non-violent since the confidence score (0.4418) is lesser than 0.5.

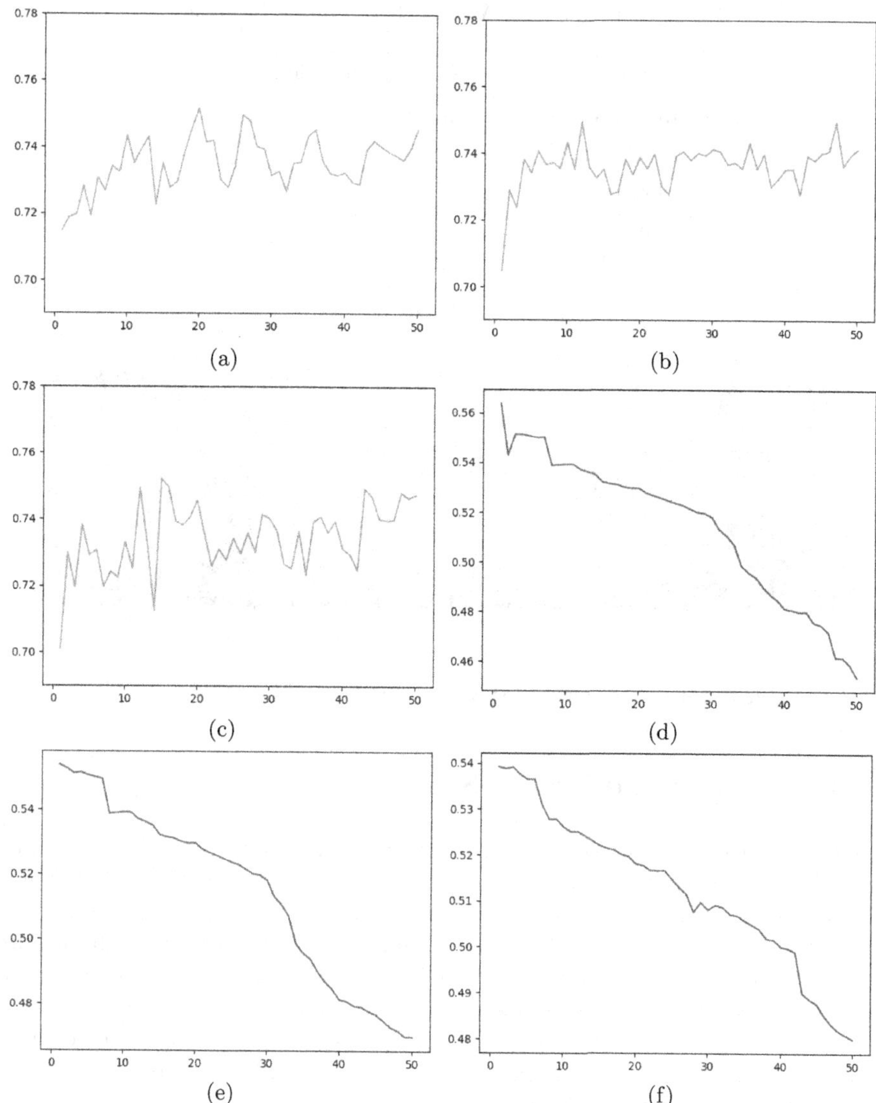

Fig. 3. Training accuracy and loss obtained on various epochs (a) Accuracy for (RGB+Audio) modality (b) Accuracy for (Flow+Audio) modality (c) Accuracy for (RGB+Flow+Audio) modality (d) Loss for (RGB+Audio) modality (e) Loss for (Flow+Audio) modality and (f) Loss for (RGB+Flow+Audio) modality.

Table 2. Frame level Average Precision performance.

Method	Average Precision (AP)
RGB-only	68.43
RGB+Audio	73.26
Flow-only	67.74
Flow+Audio	72.15
RGB+Flow+Audio	72.82
[9]	74.57

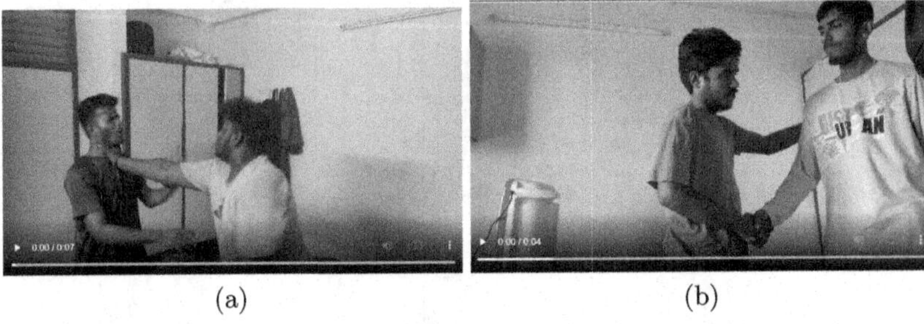

(a) (b)

Fig. 4. Sample scenarios. (a) Violent image (b) Non-violent image

5 Conclusion and Future Scope

A method for detecting violent activity using features from the video and audio part of indoor surveillance videos is proposed. The major obstacle we faced while training the data was computational power, which led to using only 75% of the dataset available. Searching through relevant violent videos was tough because the dataset consists of approximately 4000 videos. Our model was heavily dependent on the number of non-overlapping clips. Since they vary differently for each video, choosing a fixed value was tough. The proposed approach attained comparable results with existing methods and can be deployed for real-time application as the processing speed is 25 fps.

There is plenty of room for advancement in the field of automatic violence recognition models, as we aim to overcome the computational demands to improve on the model such as not skipping any of the video frames and making sure each frame of the video is processed by the model.

References

1. Carreira, J., Zisserman, A.: Quo vadis, action recognition? a new model and the kinetics dataset (2018)
2. Hershey, S., et al.: CNN architectures for large-scale audio classification (2017)

3. Chen, C., Sultani, W., Shah, M.: Real-world anomaly detection in surveillance videos. In: Conference on Computer Vision and Pattern Recognition (2018)
4. Tran, D., Bourdev, L., Fergus, R., Torresani, L., Paluri, M.: Learning spatiotemporal features with 3d convolutional networks (2015)
5. Bestagini, P., Dias, Z., Peixoto, B., Lavi, B., Rocha, A.: Multimodal violence detection in videos. In: International Conference on Acoustics, Speech, and Signal Processing (ICASSP) (2020)
6. Hochreiter, S., Schmidhuber, J.: Long short-term memory. Neural Comput. **9**(8), 1735–1780 (1997)
7. Grauman, K., Gao, R., Oh, T.-H.: Torresani, L.: Listen to look: action recognition by previewing audio. In: Conference on Computer Vision and Pattern Recognition (CVPR) (2020)
8. Shi, Y. et al.: Not only look, but also listen: learning multimodal violence detection under weak supervision. In: European Conference on Computer Vision (2020)
9. Hu, Y.-J., Li, Y.-X., Pang, W.-F., He, Q.-H.: Violence detection in videos based on fusing visual and audio information. In: International Conference on Acoustics, Speech, and Signal Processing (ICASSP) (2021)
10. Wu, X., Pu, Y.: Audio-guided attention network for weakly supervised violence detection. In: 2nd International Conference on Consumer Electronics and Computer Engineering (ICCECE) (2022)
11. Sudhakaran, S.K., Lanz, O.: Learning to detect violent videos using convolutional long short-term memory. In: 14th IEEE International Conference on Advanced Video and Signal Based Surveillance (AVSS) (2017)
12. Al-Tuma, R.F., Abdali, A.-M.R.: Robust real-time violence detection in video using CNN and LSTM. In: 2nd Scientific Conference of Computer Sciences (SCCS). University of Technology, Iraq (2019)
13. Jahlan, H.M.B., Elrefaei, L.A.: Detecting violence in video based on deep features fusion technique. In: The IIXth International Workshop on Representation, Analysis and Recognition of Shape and Motion for Imaging Data (2019)
14. Yang, L., Zhenjie, W., Hong, J., Long, J.: MCL: a contrastive learning method for multimodal data fusion in violence detection. IEEE Signal Process. Lett. **30**, 408–412 (2023)
15. Wei, D., Liu, Y., Zhu, X., Liu, J., Zeng, X.: MSAF: multimodal supervise-attention enhanced fusion for video anomaly detection. IEEE Signal Process. Lett. **29**, 2178–2182 (2022)
16. Simonyan, K., Zisserman, A.: Very deep convolutional networks for large-scale image recognition (2015)
17. Abu-El-Haija, S., et al.: Youtube-8m: a large-scale video classification benchmark (2016)

Real-Time Hand Gesture Recognition for American Sign Language Using CNN, Mediapipe and Convexity Approach

Vikas Bhatt(✉) and Ratnakar Dash

National Institute of Technology, Rourkela 769010, Odisha, India
{521CS1002,ratnakar}@nitrkl.ac.in, vikashbhat061@gmail.com

Abstract. Hand gesture recognition is crucial to computer vision and human-computer interaction(HCI), enabling natural and intuitive interactions between humans and machines. Sign language is essential for communication between deaf-mute and other people. In this research paper, we proposed an advanced deep learning-based methodology for real-time sign language detection designed to address communication disparities between individuals with normal hearing and the deaf community. The inception of our study involved the creation of a dataset comprising 37 unique sign language gestures. This dataset underwent preprocessing procedures to optimize its relevance for subsequent training of a customised Convolutional Neural Network (CNN) model. The trained CNN model demonstrated proficiency in recognizing and interpreting real-time sign language expressions, thereby contributing to the mitigation of communication barriers in this context. The implementation of two alternative methodologies was executed in parallel with the proposed approach. Specifically, real-time detection of American Sign Language (ASL) employed MediaPipe and Teachable Machine, while the second method illustrates the real-time detection of hand gestures utilizing a convexity-based approach. In this study, the proposed customised CNN model achieved an accuracy of 99.46% and, precision of 99 %, whereas the model trained with the teachable machine achieved 94.54% accuracy, and the method using the convexity approach achieved 84.44% accuracy.

Keywords: Hand gesture · CNN · HCI · media pipe · ASL · HSV color model · sign language recognition · real-time recognition

1 Introduction

Hand gesture recognition is a computer vision task that involves recognizing hand movements and gestures from video or image data. It has a wide range of applications, including human-computer interaction, virtual reality, and augmented reality. Modern technology has made it possible to record human gestures using video cameras on everyday gadgets like smartphones, tablets, and laptops. Given

N. Chauhan et al. (Eds.): MIND 2023, CCIS 2128, pp. 260–271, 2024.
https://doi.org/10.1007/978-3-031-62217-5_22

the ubiquitous use of these devices, communicating with computational systems using gestures has become more popular than in past years. The importance of gestures as a vital method of interaction between humans and computers is further amplified by the ongoing improvements in computer hardware and software. Sign language is the primary mode of communication for the deaf and those who cannot speak. It varies by country, each having its own grammar and rules. To bridge communication gaps, there's a need for automatic and interactive interpreters, which we try to develop through this paper. Sign language detection is an innovative technology that converts hand motions into text, streamlining the communication process for the deaf and mute community [1]. Sign languages vary across the globe, with each being distinct due to its unique dialect and cultural influences. Some prominent examples of sign languages include:

Indian Sign Language (ISL): ISL, with a user base exceeding 15 million, stands as the predominant sign language in the Indian subcontinent, according to [2].

American Sign Language (ASL): ASL, employed by more than 500,000 individuals in the United States and Anglophone Canada, integrates manual and automatic elements for efficient communication [2].

German Sign Language (GSL):GSL, acknowledged as a complete sign language in 2002, is spoken by approximately 200,000 individuals [2].

Portuguese Sign Language (PSL):PSL is mostly used by the deaf community of Portugal and is influenced by Swedish Sign Language [2].

Arabic Sign Language (ArSL): Developed based on the Arabic language, ArSL stands out from other sign languages due to its distinctive word order and morphology [2].

By understanding and recognizing the diversity of sign languages, sign language detection technology plays a crucial role in fostering inclusive and accessible communication worldwide.

Based on their techniques and uses, gesture recognition systems can be divided into three types. The first category makes use of sensors worn by the user to capture gestures with great precision. This technology, however, is deemed invasive because it needs the user to wear these sensors, restricting its applicability outside of controlled conditions where the sensors are linked to computers [3]. Gesture recognition systems in the second category use a tracking mechanism to track the movement of a physical device on the screen. The tracked route represents the identified gesture [4]. Although this method provides a more simplified gesture description and lowers processing costs, the range of conceivable movements it may express is less substantial and precise when compared to other categories.

The third and final category utilizes video cameras to capture and identify gestures. This recognition process involves extracting various features such as movement, position, velocity, and colour from the captured images. Unlike the second category, this approach can describe more complex gestures and is not restricted to controlled environments. By incorporating computer vision techniques, this category of gesture recognition can be integrated into devices like smartphones, making it applicable for gesture recognition in various settings and locations.

Figure 1 shows the complete workflow of the proposed model in this paper. After capturing the image from the webcam, data preprocessing steps such as resizing, normalization, and noise reduction to standardize and enhance the quality of the input image have been applied. In the Hand detection part, we identify and locate the hand sign in the image. Then feature extraction part is done with the help of CNN layers architecture shown in Fig. 2. The customised deep neural network, encompassing convolutional and fully connected layers, processes input features, and the resulting model is saved. In real-time, OpenCV is employed to capture video frames and preprocess them, and the saved model predicts sign language gestures with high efficiency. In Sect. 2, we describe the related work and Sect. 3 explains methods used in this paper to detect gestures. Section 4 outlines the experimental setup, and Sect. 5 shares findings regarding ASL sign language recognition, concludes the paper and explores future research directions.

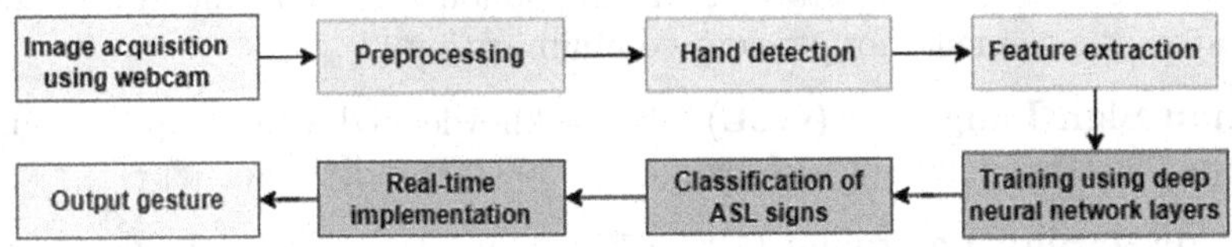

Fig. 1. hand gesture recognition system used for the ASL hand sign detection

2 Related Work

Barros et al. [5] developed a dynamic gesture and prediction system for new feature extraction based on a convexity method. In two independent modules, the system employs Hidden Markov Models and Dynamic Time Warping, and trials on the RPPDI Dynamic Gestures Dataset and Cambridge Hand Data show encouraging results for gesture recognition and prediction. Real-time gesture recognition stands as a vital component in gesture recognition systems, requiring the ability to anticipate and predict ongoing gestures before their completion, as emphasized by the findings of Xiao et al. [6]. This prediction aspect is essential as it allows the classifier to leverage the results to improve recognition accuracy and enables the system to function in real-time scenarios. The prediction process aims to identify a pattern that has not yet been fully manifested, ensuring efficient and timely gesture recognition. By effectively predicting gestures in real-time, the recognition system can respond swiftly and accurately to user input, enhancing its overall performance and user experience [5].

Mesbahi et al. [7] proposes an efficient hand gesture recognition method using convexity defect and background subtraction techniques. The approach extracts gesture-specific features, ensuring reliable recognition across different hand gestures with varying finger counts. Ivanska et al. [8] proposed a 3 stage approach that involves capturing images with a webcam, hand detection using the MediaPipe pipeline, and simple gesture classification. This system recognizes hand signs in real-time, which is beneficial for hearing or speech disorders. Alon et al. study proposed a hand gesture detection system using YOLOv3 to recognize American Sign-Language (ASL) letters, aiding individuals with hearing or speaking disabilities. Labelling hand gesture images with tools like LabelImg makes communication more accessible for deaf individuals and those unfamiliar with sign language [9]. Thongtawee et al. [10] proposed a straightforward and effective algorithm for feature extraction, enabling the recognition of American Sign Language alphabets from static and dynamic gestures. The algorithm combines four techniques: NwE (Number of white pixels at the edge), Fcen(Finger length from the centroid point), AngF (Angles between fingers), and delAng (Differences of angles between fingers of the first and last frame), and utilizes an Artificial Neural Network (ANN) for sign classification, achieving an impressive 95% recognition rate, surpassing other research in the field.

Saiful et al. [11] presents a pioneering deep learning solution for real-time sign language detection, leveraging a customized CNN model trained on a curated dataset of 11 sign words. Puchakayala et al. compared a CNN model and a YOLOv5 model and acquired an accuracy of 84.96% and 80.59%, respectively, for the ASL dataset [2]. Konwar et al. [12] presents an automated system for ASL, which employed the HSV colour model for skin colour detection and utilized edge detection techniques to identify the shape of the hand.

3 Methods Used

3.1 Proposed Convolutional Neural Network Architecture

Convolutional Neural Networks (CNNs) are specialized neural network architectures primarily developed for processing structured data, specifically for tasks like image analysis. CNNs have been widely adopted in computer vision and are the predominant technology for various visual applications, including tasks like image classification and object recognition. In Fig. 2, the CNN architecture has been proposed for ASL hand gesture recognition. In this model, we have given RGB input images with specified dimensions in a four-layer convolutional neural network (CNN) architecture. Each convolutional layer is followed by a max-pooling layer, which reduces input dimensionality. This design choice enhances our model's tolerance to small distortions and variations in the data, a critical aspect of our research. Each layer's dimensions and filter size are mentioned below the particular layer. We further compare our model with the existing convexity approach using contour and convex hull techniques and mediapipe using the teachable machine. The proposed customised CNN architecture for ASL recognition performs well in terms of accuracy and real-time scenarios compared to the other two models.

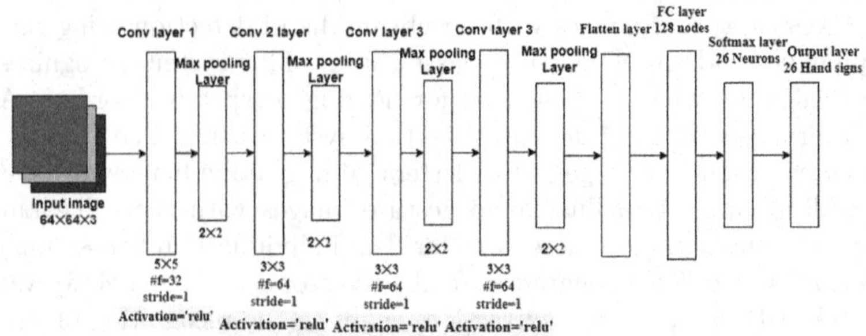

Fig. 2. CNN architecture used for ASL hand gesture recognition

3.2 ASL Recognition Using Convexity Approach, Convex Hull and Contour Detection

The Convexity Approach is a feature extraction method that uses dynamically chosen locations inside the hand contour to characterize hand gestures [5]. Each hand posture necessitates a minimal selection of points, resulting in a feature vector containing only the fundamental components required to describe the hand. This method works with a single image simultaneously, concentrating on photographs with the hand contour. The algorithm moves through three stages. First, by removing curves it lessens the geometric complexity of the hand model. Then, it determines the smallest group of points that can represent the condensed hand model. The process then calculates the separations between these spots and creates a feature vector that accurately captures the hand gesture [5].

Contours and Convex Hull: A succession of points that define the hand's perimeter pixels makes up the contour of the hand. After the contour has been obtained, the gesture and its shape can then be detected and identified using contour analysis. Figure 3 the contour part on the leftmost side with green color hand gesture's contour after using the Canny edge detection method [5].

In hand gesture analysis, the convex hull shown in Fig. 3 is computed based on the palm or hand form, capturing intricate shapes by forming a convex polygon along the green curve. Mesbahi et al. (2018) emphasize this method in their work on hand gesture recognition [7].

3.3 ASL Recognition Using Mediapipe and Teachable Machine

Mediapipe is a robust and versatile framework designed for real-time gesture recognition and human pose estimation. Mediapipe offers a flexible pipeline that allows researchers and developers to efficiently capture, process, and analyze human body movements and gestures using standard video camera inputs. The framework is built on deep learning techniques, making it a powerful tool for various applications in human-computer interaction, virtual reality, augmented

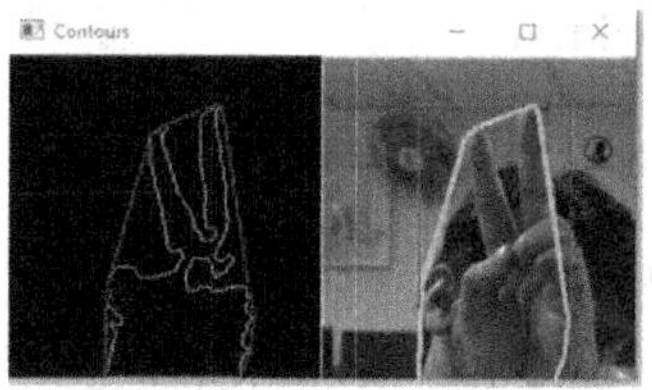

Fig. 3. Contour and convex hull

reality, and robotics. In this paper, we present the underlying architecture, key components, and performance evaluation of Mediapipe, demonstrating its effectiveness and potential impact in the field of computer vision and human-machine interaction. In Fig. 4 shows the keypoint localisation 21 hand-knuckle coordinates(each described from number 0 to 20) within the detected hand regions.

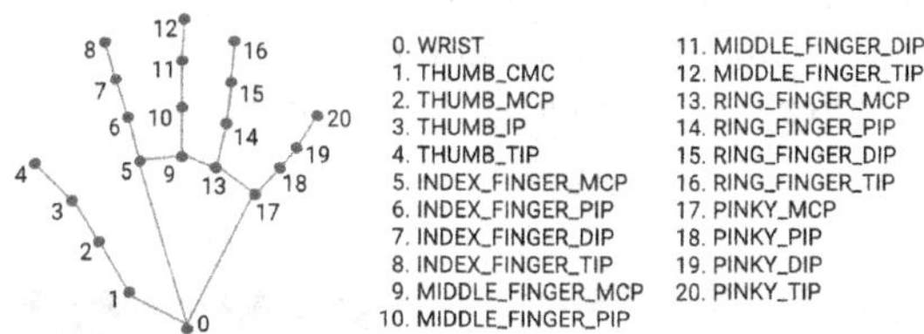

Fig. 4. hand landmarks [1]

Teachable Machine: Google designs a teachable machine to train a model using images. There are several hidden layers to train our model. The dataset collected with the help of a webcam is uploaded here, and then after training, the trained model have been saved in .h5 format and is used for sign language detection. Here, Transfer learning is used to execute our task for sign language detection. Figure 5 shows some of the collected images from the webcam and then used to train the model using the teachable machine.

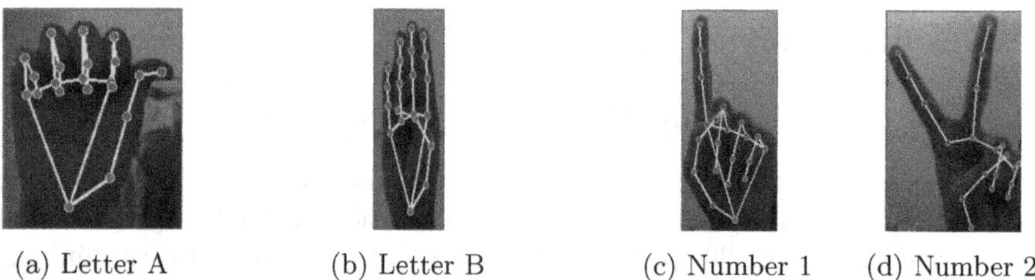

(a) Letter A (b) Letter B (c) Number 1 (d) Number 2

Fig. 5. Samples of self-constructed image dataset

4 Experimental Setup

4.1 Dataset Collection

The dataset has been collected with the help of a webcam. The ASl dataset has 26 letters and ten numbers from 0–9. We created our own dataset and also took reference from the Kaggle dataset of ASL hand sign detection. The dataset has been collected with the help of four subjects with complex backgrounds. The dataset consists of 26 letters from A to Z and numbers from 0–9 and also an empty or no gesture input. There are a total of 37 folders, with each folder containing 3000 images of a specific gesture.

4.2 American Sign Language Dataset

The American Sign Language (ASL) dataset is a visual data collection consisting of videos or images capturing hand gestures and signs used in American Sign Language communication. Figure 6 shows ASL sample dataset which consists of Twenty-six English alphabets and numbers from 0 to 9. In this paper, we recognise each character from the letter A to Z and numbers 0 to 9 in real-time.

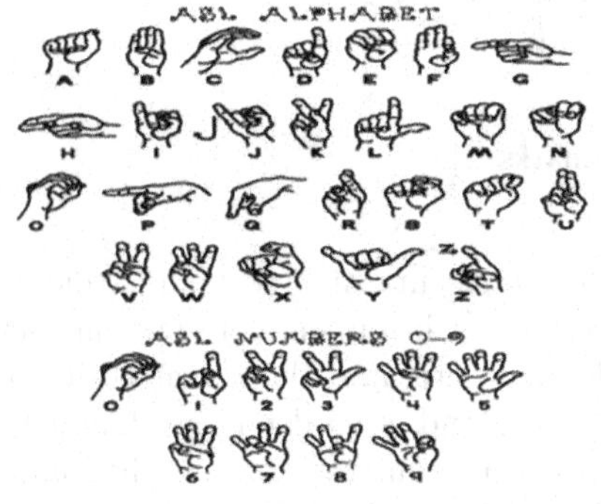

Fig. 6. ASL sample dataset [2]

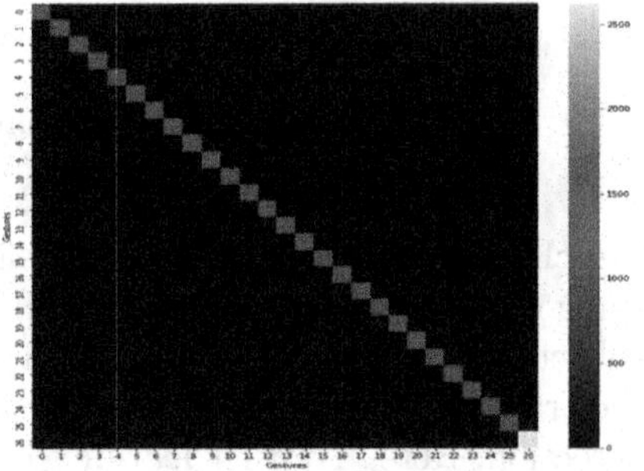

Fig. 7. Confusion matrix heatmap

5 Results Analysis

5.1 ASL Detection Using Customised CNN Layers Architecture

We extract images from the ASL dataset upon importing requisite libraries, resizing them to ensure uniform hand part recognition in the data preprocessing phase. we employ a 70–30 split, dedicating 70% of the dataset for training and reserving the remaining 30% for testing. After this, we apply one hot encoding method to represent categorical variables as numerical values for better results. The model used here consists of 4 convolutional layers followed by 4 max-pooling layers shown in Table 3. The flattened layer converts the 2D array to single inputs for dense layers. The model uses the softmax function for classification tasks. The model gets trained for 15 epochs cycle having 37 classes with a batch size of 64 and a learning rate of .001. The accuracy achieved is 99.46%, precision 99%. Precision and accuracy are calculated with the help of sklearn metrics using classification reports. Figure 9 shows the training and validation accuracy plot, having accuracy in the y-axis and epochs in the x-axis. Figure 7 shows the confusion matrix of gestures from A to Z and empty gestures having support from 0 to 2700 shown on the right side of the image. In Table 2, we can observe the classification report, which indicates the lowest precision values for the letters G and P, measuring at 0.94 and 0.95, respectively. The reason for the low precision of both the letters is that both actions are similar to the letter'H', which can be clearly observed from the ASL dataset. Figure 8 depicts the training dynamics of our hand gesture model, revealing insights into convergence and performance. The loss plot guides optimization strategies for enhancing model robustness.

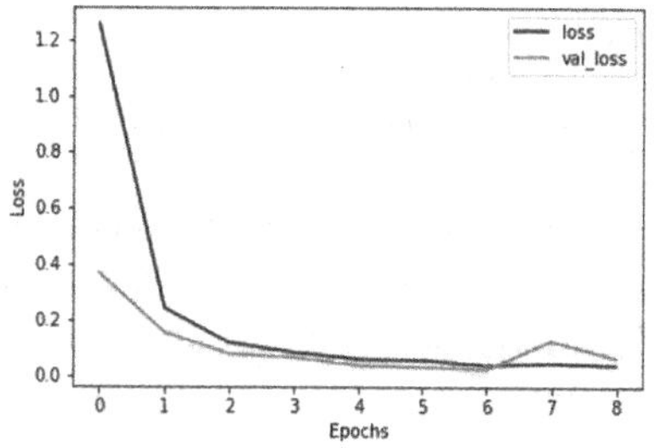

Fig. 8. Loss plot of CNN model for ASL dataset

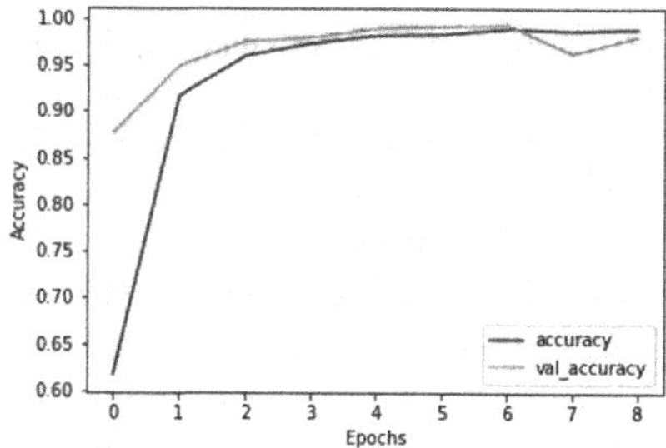

Fig. 9. Accuracy plot of CNN model for ASL dataset

5.2 Hand Sign Detection Using Mediapipe and Teachable Machine

In ASL recognition, An accuracy of 95.44% has been achieved. The model detects the hand gesture in real-time using a media pipe. The image has been taken with a webcam. The label files are saved corresponding to each letter and number. The letters are from A to Z, and the numbers are 0 to 9. This model performed on a teachable machine platform is trained on 50 epochs with a learning rate of .001. The model is trained on deep learning-based pre-trained models on the server side using a teachable machine interface and gives output in the format of keras_model.h5. It also provides label file names as labels.txt when we export the model after the training. The mediapipe is used to track the hands; the corresponding output is shown in Figs. 10 and 11. Several examples of detected gestures representing numbers 0–9 are illustrated in Fig. 10, while Fig. 11 displays the letters' outputs within the PyCharm software environment.

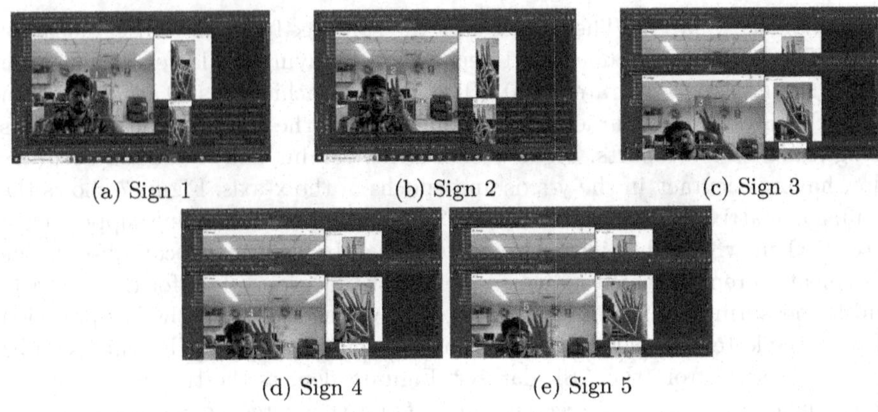

(a) Sign 1 (b) Sign 2 (c) Sign 3

(d) Sign 4 (e) Sign 5

Fig. 10. Hand gesture recognition of number signs 1, 2, 3, 4, and 5 in ASL

5.3 Convexity Approach Using Opencv

- Capture frames from the webcam within a defined rectangular sub-window to obtain hand data.
- Smooth and convert the image to the HSV color space using Gaussian blur to enhance image quality and enable binarization.
- Apply morphological transformations to filter out background noise, followed by another Gaussian blur for further refinement.
- Find the contour with the maximum area, creating a bounding box around the hand.
- Detect and mark fingertips by analyzing contours and using the cosine rule, adding a circle at far points with angles exceeding 90°.
- Display the finger count, visualized hand images with marked features, and exit the program upon pressing'q'.

  Figure 12 shows the output images after applying the above steps.

Table 1 shows the accuracy, precision and F1-measure of all three methods shown in the paper. The accuracy of the teachable machine using mediapipe and convexity approach is being calculated with standard accuracy, precision and F1 measure metric formula. Our proposed model clearly outperforms the other two existing approaches. In Eq. 1 all the TP,FP, FN and TN are manually observed for each symbol in real time. For the CNN method, it is calculated with sklearn metric formula, which is calculated by random samples and support generated by the program.

$$Accuracy = \frac{TP + TN}{TP + TN + FP + FN} \tag{1}$$

where TP= True Positive, TN = True Negative, FP = False positive, FN = False Negative.

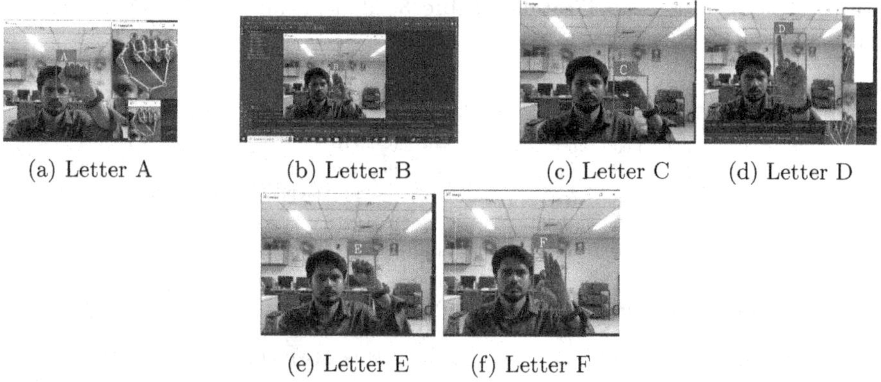

(a) Letter A (b) Letter B (c) Letter C (d) Letter D

(e) Letter E (f) Letter F

Fig. 11. Hand gesture recognition of Letters A, B, C, D, E, and F in ASL

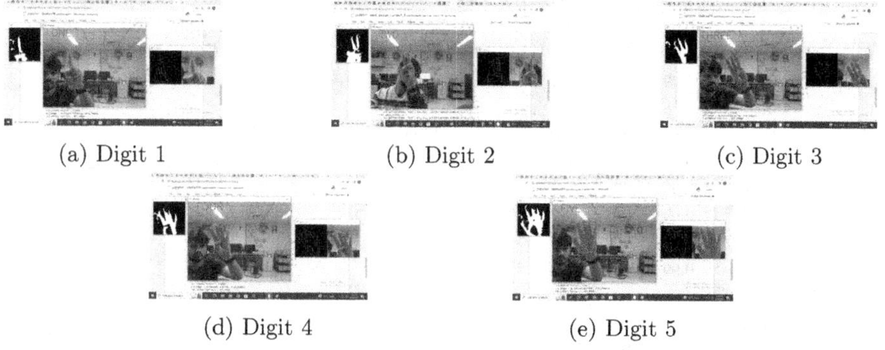

(a) Digit 1 (b) Digit 2 (c) Digit 3

(d) Digit 4 (e) Digit 5

Fig. 12. Hand gesture recognition of number sign 1, 2, 3, 4, and 5 using convexity approach

Table 1. Comparision between proposed customised CNN model, Mediapipe and Teachable machine, and convexity approach

Parameters	Proposed CNN model	Mediapipe and Teachable machine	Convexity approach
Accuracy(in %)	99.46	94.54	84.44
Precision(%)	99	93	84
F1 measure(%)	99	92.25	83.26

Table 2. Gestures classification report of model testing

	precision	recall	f1-score	support
0	1.00	0.98	0.99	900
1	1.00	1.00	1.00	900
2	1.00	1.00	1.00	900
3	1.00	1.00	1.00	900
4	0.99	0.96	0.98	900
5	1.00	0.99	0.99	900
6	0.94	1.00	0.97	900
7	1.00	1.00	1.00	900
8	1.00	0.99	0.99	900
9	0.98	0.99	0.99	900
10	1.00	0.96	0.98	900
11	1.00	1.00	1.00	900
12	0.99	0.99	0.99	900
13	0.99	1.00	0.99	900
14	0.99	0.99	0.99	900
15	0.95	1.00	0.97	900
16	0.99	0.99	0.99	900
17	0.99	0.98	0.99	900
18	1.00	0.98	0.99	900
19	1.00	0.99	0.99	900
20	0.98	0.99	0.99	900
21	0.97	0.99	0.98	900
22	0.99	0.99	0.99	900
23	0.97	0.99	0.98	900
24	0.96	1.00	0.98	900
25	1.00	0.99	1.00	900
26	1.00	0.97	0.99	2700
accuracy			0.99	26100
macro avg	0.99	0.99	0.99	26100
weighted avg	0.99	0.99	0.99	26100

Table 3. Model summary of CNN model used for ASL

Model: "sequential_4"		
Layer (type)	Output Shape	Param #
conv2d_16 (Conv2D)	(None, 60, 60, 32)	2432
activation_16 (Activation)	(None, 60, 60, 32)	0
max_pooling2d_16 (MaxPooling)	(None, 30, 30, 32)	0
conv2d_17 (Conv2D)	(None, 28, 28, 64)	18496
activation_17 (Activation)	(None, 28, 28, 64)	0
max_pooling2d_17 (MaxPooling)	(None, 14, 14, 64)	0
conv2d_18 (Conv2D)	(None, 12, 12, 64)	36928
activation_18 (Activation)	(None, 12, 12, 64)	0
max_pooling2d_18 (MaxPooling)	(None, 6, 6, 64)	0
conv2d_19 (Conv2D)	(None, 4, 4, 64)	36928
activation_19 (Activation)	(None, 4, 4, 64)	0
max_pooling2d_19 (MaxPooling)	(None, 2, 2, 64)	0
flatten_4 (Flatten)	(None, 256)	0
dense_8 (Dense)	(None, 128)	32896
dense_9 (Dense)	(None, 29)	3741
Total params: 131,421		
Trainable params: 131,421		
Non-trainable params: 0		

6 Conclusion

Advanced sign language recognition systems are at the forefront of research aimed at precisely deciphering the sign language of deaf people, thereby revolutionizing their communication. A substantial body of research is dedicated to advancing these critical endeavours. In this study, the model proposed helps deaf and hard-of-hearing people to communicate with others. The proposed CNN model achieves an accuracy of 99.46%, precision of 99% and F1 score of 0.99. The second approach using media pipe achieves an accuracy of 94.54%, while the convexity approach uses contour and convex hull techniques and achieves an accuracy of 84.44%. The CNN model under consideration is constructed with a stack of four convolutional layers, employing the Rectified Linear Unit (ReLU) activation function. Remarkably, this model outperforms the other two models in terms of accuracy. As part of future work, further advancements can be pursued to refine these methodologies, broadening their applicability and impact on sign language recognition. In the domain of pragmatic solutions, upcoming efforts can delve into avenues that amplify real-world usability. Incorporating mobile applications, wearable devices, or augmented reality interfaces could furnish convenient, on-the-go alternatives for users.

References

1. Anderson, R., Wiryana, F., Ariesta, M.C., Kusuma, G.P., et al.: Sign language recognition application systems for deaf-mute people: a review based on input-process-output. Procedia Comput. Sci. **116**, 441–448 (2017)
2. Puchakayala, A., Nalla, S., Pranathi, K.: American sign language recognition using deep learning. In: 2023 7th International Conference on Computing Methodologies and Communication (ICCMC), pp. 151–155. IEEE (2023)
3. Chu, X., Liu, J., Shimamoto, S.: A sensor-based hand gesture recognition system for japanese sign language. In: 2021 IEEE 3rd Global Conference on Life Sciences and Technologies (LifeTech), pp. 311–312. IEEE (2021)
4. Yuanyuan, S.H.I., Yunan, L.I., Xiaolong, F.U., Kaibin, M.I.A.O., Qiguang, M.I.A.O.: Review of dynamic gesture recognition. Virtual Reality Intell. Hardw. **3**(3), 183–206 (2021)
5. Barros, P., Maciel-Junior, N.T., Fernandes, B.J.T., Bezerra, B.L.D., Fernandes, S.M.M.: A dynamic gesture recognition and prediction system using the convexity approach. Comput. Vision Image Understand. **155**, 139–149 (2017)
6. Xiao, Y., Tong Liu, Y., Han, Y.L., Wang, Y.: Realtime recognition of dynamic hand gestures in practical applications. ACM Trans. Multimed. Comput. Commun. Appl. **20**(2), 1–17 (2023)
7. Mesbahi, S.C., Mahraz, M.A., Riffi, J., Tairi, H.: Hand gesture recognition based on convexity approach and background subtraction. In: 2018 International Conference on Intelligent Systems and Computer Vision (ISCV), pp. 1–5. IEEE (2018)
8. Ivanska, L., Korotyeyeva, T.: Mobile real-time gesture detection application for sign language learning. In: 2022 IEEE 17th International Conference on Computer Sciences and Information Technologies (CSIT), pp. 511–514. IEEE (2022)
9. Alon, H.D., Ligayo, M.A.D., Melegrito, M.P., Cunanan, C.F., Uy II, E.E.: Deep-hand: a deep inference vision approach of recognizing a hand sign language using american alphabet. In: 2021 International Conference on Computational Intelligence and Knowledge Economy (ICCIKE), pp. 373–377. IEEE (2021)
10. Thongtawee, A., Pinsanoh, O., Kitjaidure, Y.: A novel feature extraction for american sign language recognition using webcam. In: 2018 11th Biomedical Engineering International Conference (BMEiCON), pp. 1–5. IEEE (2018)
11. Saiful, M.N., et al.: Real-time sign language detection using CNN. In: 2022 International Conference on Data Analytics for Business and Industry (ICDABI), pp. 697–701. IEEE (2022)
12. Konwar, A.S., Borah, B.S., Tuithung, C.T.: An American sign language detection system using HSV color model and edge detection. In: 2014 International Conference on Communication and Signal Processing, pp. 743–747. IEEE (2014)

Compressors Using Modified Sorting and Parallel Counting

K. Harikrishna and S. K. Tripathy(✉)

Department of Electronics and Communication, National Institute of Technology Silchar, Assam 788010, India
sktripathy@ece.nits.ac.in

Abstract. Multiplier is an utmost important and key element in the area of digital signal processing units, mobile computing, and embedded systems. To obtain the multiplication result quickly it is necessary to design an efficient process to add all the partial products in less time. Therefore, in this paper, we have designed and developed a modified compressor to add partial products of multiplier. In order to achieve this, we have designed a new sorting circuit for 3-bit, and 4-bit, to reduce the delay. The (7,3) compressor is constructed using 3-bit and 4-bit sorting circuits and found that the proposed design is 8.46%, 15.64%, 24.77%, 22.78% and 31.16% better than other designs in delay, area, power, area delay product and power delay product, respectively. Further, (15,4) compressor is constructed using the two (7,3) compressor and it performs 48.92%, 42.92%, 45.54%, and 39.15% better than other designs in area, power, area delay product and power delay product, respectively. Similarly, (31,5) compressor is constructed using the two (15,4) compressors and observed that our design is 8.07%, 52.83%, 39.45%, 53.33%, and 40.09% better than other designs in delay, area, power, area delay product and power delay product, respectively.

Keywords: Multiplier · Partial Products · Compressor · Signal Processing

1 Introduction

The multiple operands summation is the most used task in digital signal processing units, mobile computing, and embedded systems. In the hardware Implementation of multiplier, the partial products are added using different algorithms. The most popular and used algorithms are the Dadda [1, 2], Wallace tree [3, 4], Toom-Cook [5], and Karatsuba [6]. These methods use full adders and half adders for summation of partial products and the output of these adders consists of two-bit. So based on the number of inputs and outputs the full adder can also be specified as a (3,2) compressor as it has three inputs and generates two outputs. High compression ratio compressors are needed for fast processing. Compressors using different methods has been proposed by various researchers [7–9]. The existing different methods used to develop compressors are logic gates [7], parallel counter [8], symmetric stacking [9], and sorting [10]. The sorting method used in [8] develops the better performance of the compressor. So, the

N. Chauhan et al. (Eds.): MIND 2023, CCIS 2128, pp. 272–280, 2024.
https://doi.org/10.1007/978-3-031-62217-5_23

(7,3) compressor using modified sorting circuit is proposed in this article. Further (15,4) compressor is constructed using two proposed (7,3) compressor and full adders. Similarly (31,5) compressor is constructed using two proposed (15,4) compressor and full adders.

2 Compressor Using Modified Sorting Circuit

To compress and count the number of ones in input we choose three steps as mentioned in [10]. Three steps are

1. Modified Sorting
2. One-Hot code generation
3. Output generation

2.1 Modified Sorting

The sorting circuit is used to sort all the inputs such that all 1's in the input sort to the top and all 0's shift to bottom, if exist. In [10] for 4 way sorting and 3 way sorting all the inputs are sorted using the two-bit sorter as shown in the Fig. 2 of Ref [10]. In this article, modified 4 way sorting and 3 way sorting circuits are proposed which effects the performance of compressor. The proposed 4-bit and 3-bit sorting circuits are shown in Figure 1 and 2, respectively. The 7 input bits of the (7,3) compressor is split into 4 and 3 bits, then they are fed to four way and three way sorting circuits, respectively.

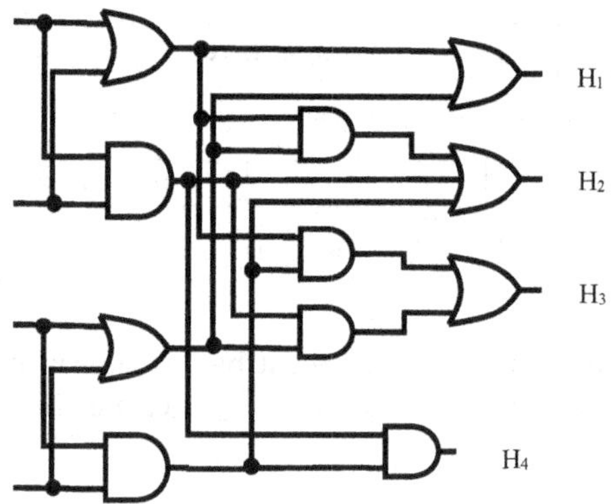

Fig. 1. Four-way sorting circuit

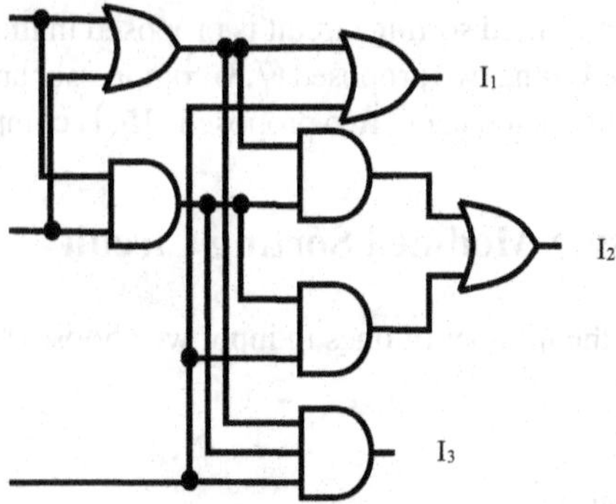

Fig. 2. Three-way sorting circuit

2.2 One-Hot Code Sequence Generation

One – Hot code sequence generation is used to find the position of (1,0) junction by which number 1's and number of 0's can be identified. After the process of sorting the input, the one-Hot code sequence generation step junction is to be found by which the count of 1's is known. In the process of One-Hot code generation a '1' is added at the top of the sorted sequence and named "fixed 1" and a '0' is added at the bottom of the sorted sequence and named "fixed 0". Figure 3 shows the addition of "fixed 0" and "fixed 1" to the reordered sequence.

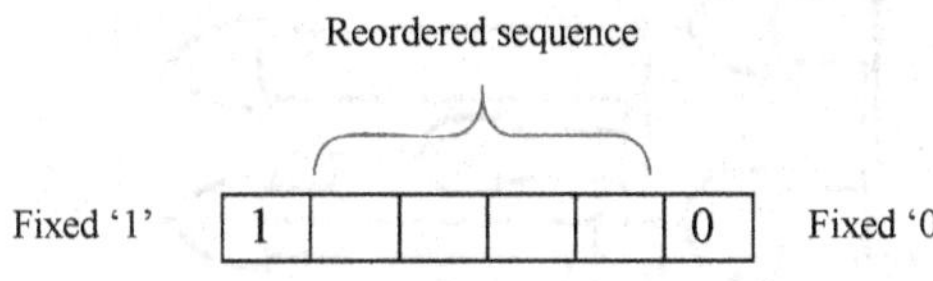

Fig. 3. One-Hot code generation

A $\overline{B}$ Gate is connected to all the adjacent bits as shown in Fig. 4. The possible combinations of adjacent bits in the reordered sequence are (1,1), (1,0), and (0,0).

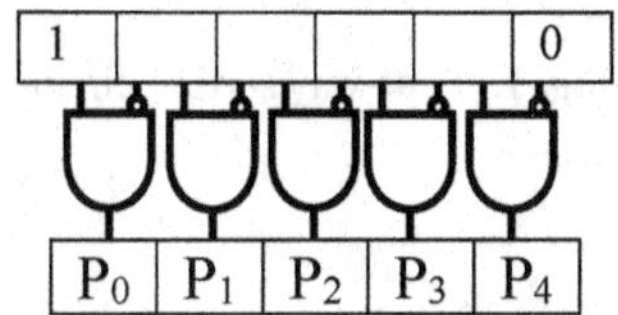

Fig. 4. One-Hot code sequence generation

After connecting the A $\overline{B}$ Gates to all the adjacent bits, of all the possible combinations the output of A $\overline{B}$ is '1' only at the (1,0) junction. The Outputs of all the A $\overline{B}$ Gates form a new sequence P_0–P_4.

Nature of One-Hot code sequence:
There is only one bit of value '1' in the one-Hot code sequence, so

$$P_0|P_1|P_2|P_3|P_4 = 1$$

If there are no '1's in the input sequence then $P_0 = 1$ and all other values of the output sequence are zero. If there is only one '1' in the input sequence then P_1=1 and all other values of the output sequence are zero. Similarly, if there are 'i' number of '1's in the input sequence then P_i=1 and all other values of the output sequence are zero.

2.3 Output Generation

2.3.1 (7,3) Compressor

The 7 input bits are split into 4 and 3 bits. The first 4 bits are sorted using the 4-way sorting circuit and the next 3 bits are sorted using the 3-way sorting circuit. The output of the 4-way sorting circuit is represented with sequence 'H' and the output of the 3-way sorting circuit is represented with the sequence 'I'. Then the two sequences are fed to the One-Hot code generation circuit. The output sequences of the One-Hot generation circuit which are formed by the 4-bit numbers and the 3-bit numbers are represented by the sequence 'P' and sequence 'Q' respectively as shown in Fig. 5.

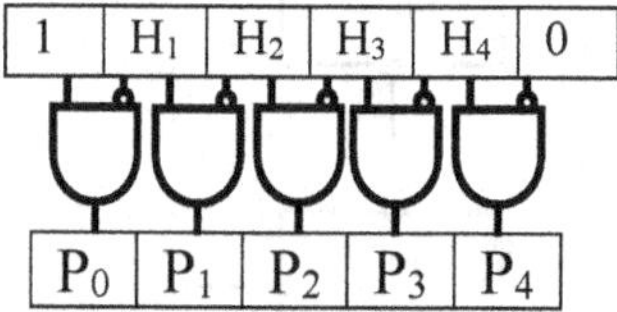

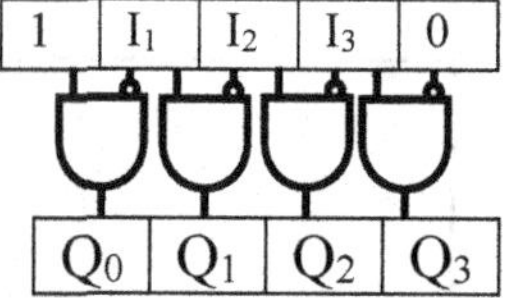

Fig. 5. One-Hot code generation for 4-bit and 3-bit numbers

Let's represent the outputs of the (7,3) compressor as C_2, C_1, and S. C_2 is the most significant bit and S is the least significant bit. Now we can get a relation between the number of '1's in the input and the output (C_2, C_1, S) i.e., number of 1's $= 2^2C_2 + 2^1C_1 + 2^0S$ and is shown in Table 1. From the Table 1, we can observe that for C_2 to be '1', there should be at least four '1's in the input sequence.

2.3.2 (15,4) Compressor

The proposed (15,4) compressor is generated by combining two (7,3) compressors as shown in the Fig. 6. The input 15 bits are split into two groups of 7 bits each and 1bit. Each group is fed to the (7,3) compressor separately. Each (7,3) compressor produces sum (S) and two carries (C_1, C_2). Two sum (S) generated by the two (7,3) compressors and 15th bit are added using full adder as shown in the Fig. 6. Two C_1 generated by two (7,3) compressors and the carry generated by first full adder are added using the second full adder. Similarly, two C_2 generated by two (7,3) compressors and the carry generated by the second full adder are added using the third full adder. The finally these full adder produces S_1, C_{11}, C_{12} and C_{13}.

Table 1. Truth table of (7,3) Compressor output

Number of '1's	C2	C1	S
0	0	0	0
1	0	0	1
2	0	1	0
3	0	1	1
4	1	0	0
5	1	0	1
6	1	1	0
7	1	1	1

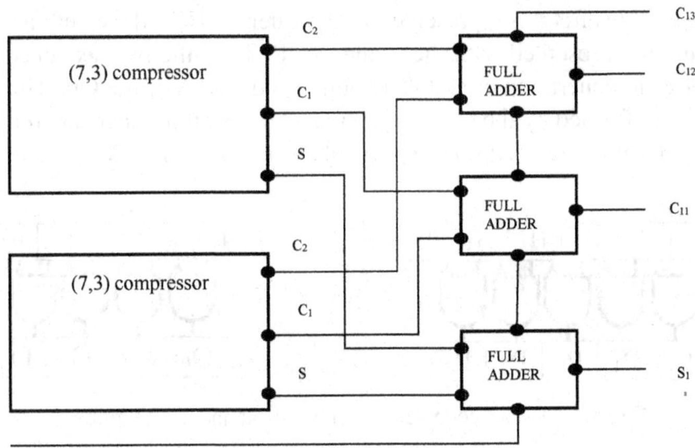

Fig. 6. Proposed design for (15,4) compressor

2.3.3 (31,5) Compressor

The proposed (31,5) compressor is generated by combining two (15,4) compressors as shown in the Fig. 7. The input 31 bits are split into two groups of 15 bits each and 1bit. Each group is fed to the (15,4) compressor separately. Each (15,4) compressor produces one sum (S) and three carries (C_1, C_2, C_3). Two sum (S) generated by the two (15,4) compressors and 15th bit are added using full adder as shown in the Fig. 7. Two C_1 generated by two (15,4) compressors and the carry generated by first full adder are added using the second full adder. Similarly, two C_2 generated by two (15,4) compressors and the carry generated by the second full adder are added using the third full adder. Similarly, two C_3 generated by two (15,4) compressors and the carry generated by the third full adder are added using the fourth full adder. The finally these full adder produces S_1, C_{11}, C_{12}, C_{13} and C_{14}.

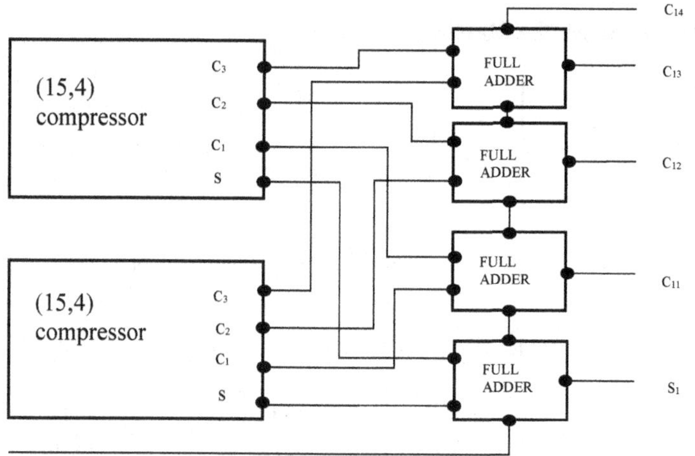

Fig. 7. Proposed design for (31,5) compressor

3 Results and Comparison

3.1 (7,3) Compressor

We constructed the (7,3) compressor in Verilog HDL to evaluate the designed circuit's delay, power, area, and performance. We compared the results with the best-reported designs in [10]. The (7,3) compressor is synthesized by the cadence genus with 90 nm process, and results are shown in Table 2. The proposed design has 11.2% less delay, 15.64% less area, and 25.87% less power compared with the design of [10]. The logic used for sorting in the design of [10] based on comparison of 2 bits whereas in this proposed design, sorting is done by using logic gates for finding the outputs for all the combinations of possible inputs. The total number of gates used for the proposed design is 26 and the total number of gates used to design [10] is 30. The total number of gates used in the proposed design is less compared to the design in [10]. Hence, from synthesis results it is observed that the proposed design has less delay, less area, and less power consumption. Further, the simulation results of (7,3) compressor is shown in the Fig. 8. We have checked for different type of inputs of all combinations of number of 1's in the inputs. In the figure we can observe that the number of 1's in the inputs is increased gradually and the output (C_2, C_1, S) are observed as expected.

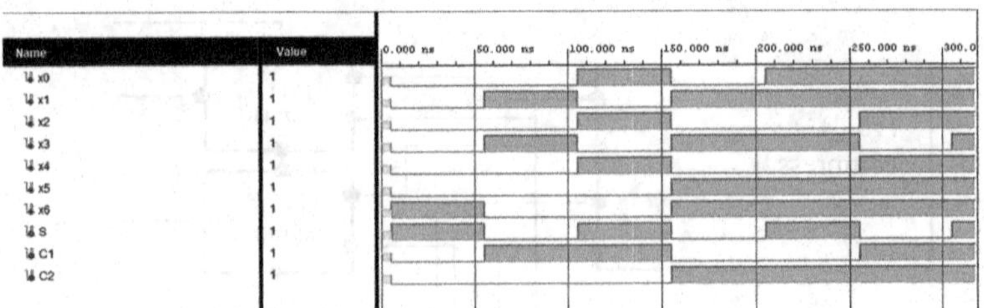

Fig. 8. Simulation results of (7,3) compressor

Table 2. Synthesis results of (7,3) compressor

Method	Proposed	[10]	Improve
Delay (ps)	670	732	8.46%
Area (μm^2)	114.292	135.485	15.64%
Power (μw)	3.37	4.48	24.77%
ADP (ns- μm^2)	76.575	99.175	22.78%
PDP (ns- μw)	2.257	3.279	31.16%

3.2 (15,4) Compressor

The simulation results of (15,4) compressor is shown in the Table 3. The proposed (15,4) compressor has more delay but consumes 48.92%, 42.92%, 45.54% and 39.15% less area, power, ADP and PDP respectively compared with earlier design. The proposed design is tested with some of the test cases and verified using the Xilinx tool and the simulation result of the proposed (15,4) compressor is shown in the Fig. 9.

Table 3. Synthesis results of (15,4) compressor

Method	Proposed	[10]	Improve
Delay (ps)	1629	1528	-6.60%
Area (μm^2)	287.622	563.134	48.92%
Power (μw)	10.5	18.3967	42.92%
ADP (ns- μm^2)	468.536	860.46	45.54%
PDP (ns-μw)	17.1045	28.110	39.15%

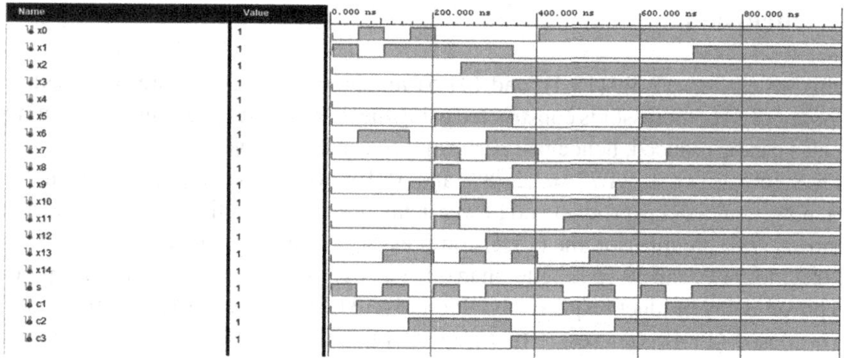

Fig. 9. Simulation results of (15,4) compressor

3.3 (31,5) Compressor

The synthesis results are shown in the Table 4. The proposed (31,5) compressor performs 8.07%, 52.83%, 39.45%, 53.33%, and 40.09% better than other designs in delay, area, power, area delay product and power delay product respectively.

Table 4. Synthesis results of (31,5) compressor

Method	Proposed	[10]	Improve
Delay (ps)	2333	2538	8.07%
Area (μm^2)	653	1384.370	52.83%
Power (μw)	28.016	46.276	39.45%
ADP (ns- μm^2)	1523.44	3264.34	53.33%
PDP (ns-μw)	65.361	109.11	40.09%

The proposed design is tested with some of the test cases and verified using the Xilinx tool and the simulation result of the proposed (31,5) compressor is shown in the Fig. 10.

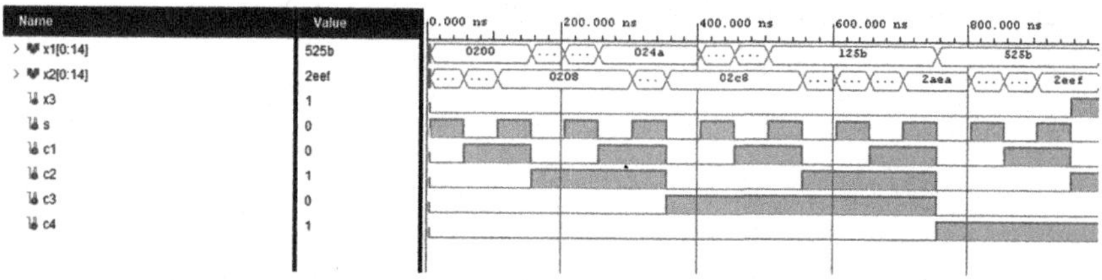

Fig. 10. Simulation results of the proposed (31,5) compressor

4 Conclusion

In this article, the (7,3), (15,4), and (31,5) modified compressors are proposed. The proposed (7,3) compressor is constructed using the revised sorting circuit and the number of gates can be reduced, hence fast performance can be achieved. The (7,3) compressor has is 8.46%, 15.64%, 24.77%, 22.78% and 31.16% better than other designs in delay, area, power, area delay product and power delay product respectively. Further, using the proposed (7,3) compressor, the (15,4) compressor is constructed that performs 48.92%, 42.92%, 45.54%, and 39.15% better than other designs in area, power, area delay product and power delay product respectively. Similarly, (31,5) compressor is constructed using the proposed (15,4) compressor that performs 8.07%, 52.83%, 39.45%, 53.33%, and 40.09% better than other designs in delay, area, power, area delay product and power delay product respectively. The (7,3) and (15,4) compressors are simulated on Xilinx test bench with different input values and verified.

References

1. Kaushik, V., Saini, H.: The proposed full-dadda multipliers. IJIRST Int. J. Innov. Res. Sci. Technol. **7**, 18–26 (2018)
2. Maxwell, J. C.: A Treatise on Electricity and Magnetism, 3rd edn., vol. 2, pp. 68–73. Clarendon, Oxford (1892)
3. Wallace, C.S.: A suggestion for a fast multiplier. IEEE Trans. Electron. Comput. (1), 14–17 (1964)
4. Yorozu, T., Hirano, M., Oka, K., Tagawa, Y.: Electron spectroscopy studies on magneto-optical media and plastic substrate interface. IEEE Transl. J. Magn. Jpn. **2**(8), 740–741 (1987)
5. Kronenburg, M.J.: Toom-cook multiplication: Some theoretical and practical aspects. arXiv preprint arXiv:1602.02740 (2016)
6. Weimerskirch, A., Paar, C.: Generalizations of the Karatsuba algorithm for efficient implementations. Cryptology ePrint Archive (2006)
7. Asif, S., Kong, Y.: Design of an algorithmic Wallace multiplier using high speed counters. In: 2015 Tenth International Conference on Computer Engineering & Systems (ICCES), pp. 133–138. IEEE (2015)
8. Jiang, Q., Li, S.: A design of manually optimized (15, 4) parallel counter. In: 2017 International Conference on Electron Devices and Solid-State Circuits (EDSSC), pp. 1–2. IEEE (2017)
9. Fritz, C., Fam, A.T.: Fast binary counters based on symmetric stacking. IEEE Trans. Very Large Scale Integr. (VLSI) Syst. **25**(10), 2971–2975 (2017)
10. Guo, W., Li, S.: Fast binary counters and compressors generated by sorting network. IEEE Trans. Very Large Scale Integr. (VLSI) Syst. **29**(6), 1220–1230 (2021)

Speed-Invariant Gait Recognition Using Correlation Factor Lists for Classroom Attendance Systems

R. Anusha[1(✉)] and CD Jaidhar[2]

[1] KLE M S Sheshgiri College of Engineering and Technology, Belgaum, India
anur.research@gmail.com

[2] National Institute of Technology Karnataka, Surathkal, India
jaidharcd@nitk.edu.in

Abstract. The way a person walks is an important biometric used in many human detection applications, including classroom attendance systems. In such applications, speed is one of the key factors that can affect the performance of a gait detection system, as the student will enter the classroom at different speeds, depending on various factors. This study proposes an effective approach to reduce the impact of speed variations in a gait detection system. Initially, the proposed approach identifies similar regions between training and test samples. Later, the correlation factor lists are calculated using three proposed features: intensity measure, contour measure, and spatial measure. By capturing minute variations in static data, this method efficiently enhances the performance of a gait detection system. The evaluation of this approach uses CASIA C and OU-ISIR A datasets of gait. The experimental results suggest that this approach shows potential in comparison to other gait recognition methods.

Keywords: Biometrics · Gait Recognition · Human Identification

1 Introduction

Gait is a notable biometric characteristic used in various fields, such as robotics, animation, medical assessments, and more [21]. Gait recognition techniques can distinguish individuals from a distance by analyzing their walking patterns. These approaches are divided into appearance-based and model-based methods. The latter approach entails developing models that represent the subject's body movement through gait sequences. Nevertheless, these methods necessitate high-quality images and possess limited resilience, resulting in high computational costs. The presence of these significant drawbacks causes many researchers to prioritize appearance-based methods. Instead of a human identification model, this method utilizes gait sequence images, simplifying the processing.

Various factors, like speed and viewing angle changes, can modify the way humans walk. Among these factors, one of the challenging issues is changes in

N. Chauhan et al. (Eds.): MIND 2023, CCIS 2128, pp. 281–290, 2024.
https://doi.org/10.1007/978-3-031-62217-5_24

walking speed. Due to differences in hand, hip, knee, and ankle movements, as well as changes in stride length and joint angles, the gait pattern undergoes significant alterations [3,4]. The effectiveness of the gait recognition system is negatively affected by modifications in these variables.

Studies that specifically focus on speed-invariant recognition of gait include the following: Nandy et al. [18] categorized the subject's walking body posture into three parts: leg swing, arm swing, and head areas. These spaces are subsequently utilized as representations of the edges of an n-sided shape for area calculations. The author then generated the convex hull of these features in each space to extract their essential attributes. An approach was proposed by Anusha and Jaidhar [2] where mutual information is extracted from regions of interest between training and testing samples. Their focus was on the less affected regions due to speed variations. Mahikara et al. [14] utilized transformed kinematic and static features to detect speed-invariant gait. Using a training dataset that included individuals of different walking speeds who were not specifically targeted for recognition, they developed a model to transform gait kinematic features.

The learning-based classifier, enhanced locality and a normalized hypergraph algorithm, was introduced by Huang et al. [8]. In their work, Kusakunniran et al. [10] introduced a new descriptor called "higher-order derivative shape configuration". The extraction of gait shape variations involved Procrustes Shape Analysis (PSA). Two key PSA components, the Procrustes Mean Shape and Procrustes distance, were employed for recognition.

Information set features were introduced by Medikonda et al. [17] for capturing temporal and spatial information from gait silhouettes. By extracting a histogram of oriented gradients for the set of gait images and applying the Hanman-Jeevan entropy function, these features are extracted. The main emphasis of Rokanujjaman et al. [19] was on determining body parts that are less susceptible to gait feature extraction. The image's feature vector is generated by combining the derived features from these selected components. A frame-based classification method and wavelet transform signal approximation were suggested by Kovac et al. [9] in their study for analyzing feature signals at various frequency resolutions. The frame-based classification approach tackles the constraints of distance-based methods.

2 Motivation and Contributions

When someone changes their walking speed, dynamic factors like joint angles and stride length change, while static features like the head and torso regions stay the same [3]. As a result, spatial or static data is primarily used to extract distinct gait features in gait recognition methods proposed to acheive speed invariance. Despite containing static and dynamic information, gait silhouette images are favored over Gait Energy Images (GEI) for feature extraction [4]. The reason for this preference is that the information that is dynamic in GEI changes with an individual's speed. However, the drawback arises when all silhouette images are used for feature extraction, leading to higher computational costs. This study overcomes this challenge by extracting spatial regions, known as Data Images, from GEI, and then extracting features from these regions.

Recent literature suggests that deep learning methods are more effective than machine learning for recognition. In the context of developing a gait biometric application for classroom attendance systems, machine learning algorithms prove to be more effective, especially with smaller datasets. The number of students in a classroom can vary across universities, but it typically ranges from 10 to 150.

When the student enters the classroom at a specific time, their gait is recognized and their attendance is recorded. To achieve this, an application can be developed where the time during which the student enters and leaves the class can be noted and the student might enter at different speeds. Thus, proposing an efficient gait recognition approach that is speed-invariant becomes necessary.

This manuscript contributes in the following ways:

1. The data image (DI) is derived from GEI using the marching square algorithm and linear interpolation. The dynamic information that varies with an individual's speed is eliminated by this method.
2. The measure of the correlation between training and testing samples enables the effective extraction of three features that capture gait variations.
3. By incorporating the integration module, the gait detection system's performance is enhanced.

3 Proposed Method

Figure 1 shows the flow of the proposed method. Initially, the GEI images of the training and testing samples are transformed into data images. Here, $a_i = a_1, a_2,...,a_m$ represent the training dataset and $b_i = b_1, b_2,...,b_n$ represent the testing dataset. For each training sample a_i in this method, the three features are extracted by combining training sample a_i and test sample b_i. Thus, the combination of training sample b_i with each test sample yields three discriminative features. This will generate a correlation factor list for the test sample, indicating its similarity to each training sample. The next step involves a module dedicated to classification and integration. By using the integration module approach, the performance of the proposed method is enhanced. By calculating the correct classification rate (CCR) on the testing dataset, we determine the performance of the proposed method.

3.1 Data Image Extraction

Due to the changing dynamic information in GEI, authors in the past utilized silhouette images to extract discriminative features. Here, the inclusion of silhouettes drives up computational expenses. Extracting the static information from GEI can be achieved by implementing the marching squares algorithm [15], thus avoiding this situation. The value is set to 0.6 to generate contour, followed by linear interpolation to obtain the list of coordinates O(x, y). Figure 2 represents the data image DI(x, y) obtained using coordinates O(x, y).

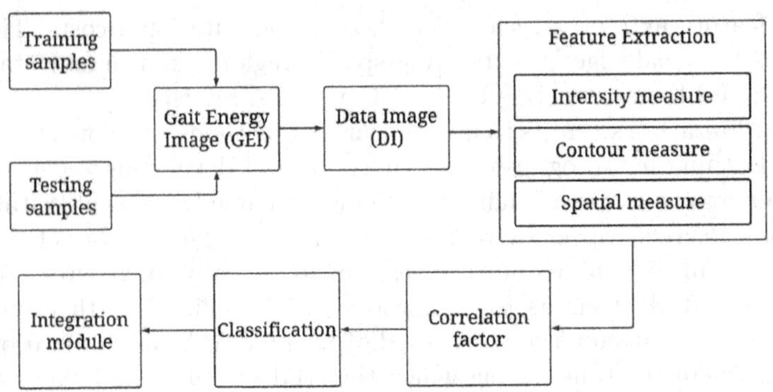

Fig. 1. Framework of the proposed approach.

3.2 Feature Extraction

To determine the resemblance between two pictures of the same individual, one must identify similarities. Extracting three features from a training sample and a testing sample allows for measuring the correlation between two images. The three features extracted include Intensity measure (I_m), contour measure (C_m), and spatial measure (S_m).

Intensity Measure (I_m). The purpose of this measure is to evaluate the intensity variations between the training and test sample. The training sample (TRS) with the lowest (I_m) is designated as the test sample (TES) candidate.

Let a(x_c, y_c) and b(x_c, y_c) represent the pixels of TRS and TES with a_c and b_c as intensities respectively, where c ranges from 1 to d. The intensity measure is determined by adding up the squared differences between intensity values in two images. That is, $M_{is} = \sum_{c=1}^{d}(a_c - b_c)^2$.

Contour Measure (C_m). This metric utilizes the extracted contour to determine the similarity between the TRS and TES. Consider the contours of to images, one belonging to the TRS and other TES. Using the Euclidean distance measure, we can determine the pair of coordinates that overlap between two data images, where one belongs to TRS and the other to TES. Only the pair of coordinates that overlap are considered for deriving this measure. The overlapping consecutive coordinates create the coordinate segment (CS). Contour measures are generated using these coordinates to show the similarity between TRS and TES. Algorithm 1 is used to compute this measure.

When a TRS and TES come from the same subject, the length of overlapping coordinates (v) will be greater. As a result, subtracting the value of v from each element in the overlapping segment produces a vector V_c with negative values. Therefore, the root mean square (rms) of V_c is calculated to transform the vector into a positive single value. The test sample considers the training sample with the highest C_m as a candidate.

Algorithm 1. Computation of contour measure (C_m).

Input: Coordinate Segments $s[i]$, here i ranges from 1 to t
for $i \leftarrow 1{:}t$ **do**
    Let (x_n, y_n) be the coordinates of a CS, where $n = 1, 2, .., m$.
    The arctangent of the x and y coordinates of the segment is used to obtain the vector θ_c. Thai is, $\theta_c = atan2(x_n, y_n)$.
    Let v represent the total number of vertices in the vector.
    Subtracting the number v from each element of the vector θ_c yields vector V_c. That is, $V_c = \theta_c - v$.
    Find the rms value, rms_i of V_c,
end for
Find the sum of rms value obtained for each coordinate segment, $C_m = rms_1 + rms_2 + ... + rms_t$.

Spatial Measure (S_m). This measure is employed to gauge the similarity between TRS and TES. Consider an image that contains the contour of only overlapping coordinates, and let that be converted into a greyscale image. The intensity values of pixels in the greyscale image are represented by I_c. By computing the relative entropy for each row, a vector E is obtained. The value of E can be calculated by

$$E = \sum_{n=1}^{255} p_n^m \log_2 \frac{p_n^m}{q_n^m} \tag{1}$$

In the above equation, p_n^m represents the number of times pixel n appears in m^{th} row and q_n^m represent the probability that pixel n occurs in m^{th} row of the image. The quantification of pixel information in each row of the image is measured by the above equation. A higher level of entropy implies a stronger correlation between TRS and TES. Therefore, the TRS with the highest S_m is chosen as the TES candidate.

3.3 Correlation Factor

The extraction of all features results in three correlation factor lists for each TES. Consider L_{Im}, L_{Cm}, and L_{Sm} as the lists holding TRS measures with each TES. Each TES with measurements related to all TRS contributes to the creation of the lists L_{Im}, L_{Cm}, and L_{Sm}.

3.4 Classification

Sort the lists L_{Im}, L_{Cm}, and L_{Sm} in ascending order and obtain the vector $V = v_1, v_2, v_3, ..., v_n$. Suppose $U = u_1, u_2, u_3, ..., u_n$ consists of the respective subjects. It can be concluded from the above lists that v_1 is the smallest value and u_1 is its corresponding subject. The subject with the smallest value, u_1, is considered the candidate subject for TES. I_m, C_m, and S_m having the least values indicate a higher similarity between the TRS and TES.

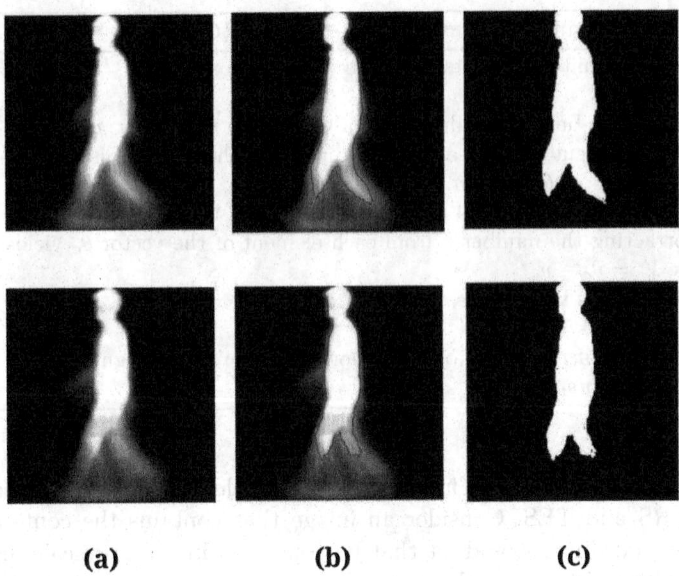

Fig. 2. Sample images repersenting (a) GEI of CASIA B dataset (b) Contour generated from GEI (c) Data image.

3.5 Integration Module

The integration module produces the final result by sorting the correlation factor lists. The computation calculates an integration factor (I_f) for each candidate. The candidate with the highest I_f value is chosen as the final result. The candidate's I_f in each list is determined by combining its measure value with the measure value of the next best subject from the same list.

Each of the three measures has a distinct range of values. Therefore, the normalization of measure values between 0 and 1 is done prior to computing the integration factor. Consider u_a and u_b as candidates from the list u_i, such that u_a is not eual to u_b. Assign u_a as the first-best subject and u_b as the second-best subject from the list. By using the following equation, we can determine the integration factor, I_f.

$$I_f = \frac{u_b - u_a}{u_a} \tag{2}$$

Given that L_{Im}, L_{Cm}, and L_{Sm} are all in ascending order, a smaller u_a and a larger u_b-u_a suggest a higher level of confidence in u_a. In addition, the one with a higher I_f is more expected to be the correct case. The final result depends on the subject with the highest I_f.

Table 1. The proposed method's CCR (%) on CASIA C database and comparison with other methods.

Method	fn/fn	fn/fs	fn/fq	fs/fq
Medikonda et al. [16]	99	97	**96**	90
Tan et al. [23]	98	82	92	–
Shiraga et al. [22]	95	87	83	80
Semwal et al. [20]	94	80	75	71
Chen et al. [6]	88	89	90	–
Kusakunniran et al. [11]	97	92	93	89
Alotaibi and Mahmood [1]	95	89	88	85
Anusha and Jaidhar [2]	99	98	96	94
Liang et al. [12]	99	98	**98**	91
Proposed method	**100**	**100**	**96**	**94**

Table 2. The proposed approach was used to analyze CCR (%) across different walking speeds on the OU-ISIR A database.

TRS/TES	2 km/h	3 km/h	4 km/h	5 km/h	6 km/h	7 km/h
2 km/h	98.00	95.53	86.41	86.00	84.00	83.94
3 km/h	98.00	100.0	96.06	91.00	91.71	87.00
4 km/h	97.84	97.00	98.94	95.00	90.12	87.53
5 km/h	84.06	89.00	96.06	100.0	95.24	91.53
6 km/h	85.53	85.12	86.47	92.24	96.94	96.12
7 km/h	83.00	83.06	86.94	93.53	94.41	97.00

4 Experimental Results

The CASIA C and OU-ISIR A gait databases are utilized to evaluate the performance of the proposed method.

The description of the CASIA C dataset includes 153 subjects walking at different speeds. The speeds 4km/h, 5km/h, and 6km/h are represented by the abbreviations fs, fn, and fq respectively. In the dataset, there are four nm walking sequences, two fs sequences, and two fq sequences. Two out of the four fn sequences are used for training, while the remaining two fn sequences, two fs sequences, and two fq sequences are used for testing. Thus, the TRS's include fn while the TES's include fn, fs, and fq. We compare the performance of the proposed approach on the CASIA C gait database with state-of-the-art methods and present the results in Table 1.

The OU-ISIR A database includes gait sequences from 34 subjects walking in a side view, and this study presents its results. The subjects show speed variations between 2 and 10 km/h, with intervals of 1 km/h [13]. Speeds between

Table 3. CCR (%) for several walking speeds of testing dataset with training dataset speed of 5 km/h on OU-ISIR A database.

Method	4 km/h	5 km/h	6 km/h	7 km/h	Average
Medikonda et al. [16]	88.24	**100.0**	91.18	73.53	88.23
Arora et al. [5]	76.40	88.00	85.20	–	85.90
Huang et al. [7]	70.60	**100.0**	88.20	73.50	82.94
Semwal et al. [20]	85.00	92.00	89.71	81.60	87.07
Anusha and Jaidhar [2]	90.90	97.50	91.24	76.00	88.60
Alotaibi and Mahmood [1]	91.12	94.24	89.70	82.00	89.26
Liang et al. [12]	**96.60**	**100.0**	91.24	83.20	92.76
Proposed method	96.06	**100.0**	**95.24**	**91.53**	**95.70**

2 and 7 km/h fall under the category of walking, while speeds between 8 and 10 km/h are considered running. The exclusive focus of this study is on the walking category.

Additionally, the dataset is divided as follows for experimentation. The TRS's consist of six cycles of gait, while the TES's consist of three cycles of gait. The method is tested on various combinations of walking speeds. The obtained results of all these combinations are presented in Table 2.

The CCR of each training dataset ranges from 88.98% to 94.40%. The average CCR for all entries in Table 2 is 91.67%. The performance of the proposed method is compared with several state-of-the-art approaches in Table 3. By the data comparision Table 3, it is evident that the proposed method performs better than other methods. Table 1 and 3 show a comparison of the proposed method with neural network-based gait recognition methods like GEINet [22] and multilayer perceptron [20]. When compared to other neural network-based approaches, the results show that the proposed method has better performance. Other methods don't specifically reduce the impact of speed variations before recognition. Both spatial and dynamic features are included in the gait template used for recognition. The GEI gait templates contain dynamic information. The misclassification issue arises when the same subject walks at different speeds, caused by speed variations and the use of GEI. This problem is addressed in the proposed method by using data images.

5 Conclusion

An approach is suggested in this work to augment the performance of the speed-invariant gait recognition method. The computation of correlation factor lists that account for spatial changes in GEI of TRS and TES is the key contribution of this paper. The comprehensive experimental results on two gait databases demonstrate that the proposed approach outperforms several existing state-of-the-art approaches in the literature. Additionally, for the recognition system of gait to be useful in real-world settings, the proposed method must be tested on a large-scale database.

Acknowledgements. The authors are extremely thankful to the team behind CASIA [24] and OU-ISIR gait datasets.

References

1. Alotaibi, M., Mahmood, A.: Improved gait recognition based on specialized deep convolutional neural network. Comput. Vis. Image Underst. **164**, 103–110 (2017)
2. Anusha, R., Jaidhar, C.: An approach to speed invariant gait analysis for human recognition using mutual information. In: TENCON 2019-2019 IEEE Region 10 Conference (TENCON), pp. 1616–1621. IEEE (2019)
3. Anusha, R., Jaidhar, C.: Frontal gait recognition based on hierarchical centroid shape descriptor and similarity measurement. In: 2019 International Conference on Data Science and Engineering (ICDSE), pp. 71–76. IEEE (2019)
4. Anusha, R., Jaidhar, C.: Clothing invariant human gait recognition using modified local optimal oriented pattern binary descriptor. Multimedia Tools Appli. **79**, 2873–2896 (2020)
5. Arora, P., Hanmandlu, M., Srivastava, S.: Gait based authentication using gait information image features. Pattern Recogn. Lett. **68**, 336–342 (2015)
6. Chen, C., Liang, J., Zhao, H., Hu, H., Tian, J.: Frame difference energy image for gait recognition with incomplete silhouettes. Pattern Recogn. Lett. **30**(11), 977–984 (2009)
7. Huang, C.P., Hsieh, C.H., Lai, K.T., Huang, W.Y.: Human action recognition using histogram of oriented gradient of motion history image. In: 2011 First International Conference on Instrumentation, Measurement, Computer, Communication and Control, pp. 353–356. IEEE (2011)
8. Huang, S., Elgammal, A., Lu, J., Yang, D.: Cross-speed gait recognition using speed-invariant gait templates and globality-locality preserving projections. IEEE Trans. Inf. Forensics Secur. **10**(10), 2071–2083 (2015)
9. Kovač, J., Štruc, V., Peer, P.: Frame–based classification for cross-speed gait recognition. Multimedia Tools Appli. 1–23 (2017)
10. Kusakunniran, W., Wu, Q., Zhang, J., Li, H.: Speed-invariant gait recognition based on procrustes shape analysis using higher-order shape configuration. In: 2011 18th IEEE International Conference on Image Processing, pp. 545–548. IEEE (2011)
11. Kusakunniran, W., Wu, Q., Zhang, J., Li, H.: Gait recognition across various walking speeds using higher order shape configuration based on a differential composition model. IEEE Trans. Syst. Man Cybernetics, Part B (Cybernet.) **42**(6), 1654–1668 (2012)
12. Liang, J., Fan, C., Hou, S., Shen, C., Huang, Y., Yu, S.: Gaitedge: Beyond plain end-to-end gait recognition for better practicality. In: European Conference on Computer Vision, pp. 375–390. Springer (2022). https://doi.org/10.1007/978-3-031-20065-6_22
13. Makihara, Y., et al.: The ou-isir gait database comprising the treadmill dataset. IPSJ Trans. on Computer Vision and Applications **4**, 53–62 (2012)
14. Makihara, Y., Tsuji, A., Yagi, Y.: Speed-invariant gait recognition. In: Signal and Image Processing for Biometrics, pp. 209–229. Springer (2014)

15. Maple, C.: Geometric design and space planning using the marching squares and marching cube algorithms. In: Proceedings. 2003 International Conference on Geometric Modeling and Graphics pp. 90–95. IEEE (2003)
16. Medikonda, J., Madasu, H., Bijaya Ketan, P.: Information set based features for the speed invariant gait recognition. IET Biometrics **7**(3), 269–277 (2018). https://doi.org/10.1049/iet-bmt.2016.0136
17. Medikonda, J., Madasu, H., Ketan, P.B.: Information set based features for the speed invariant gait recognition. IET Biometrics **7**(3), 269–277 (2017)
18. Nandy, A., Chakraborty, P., Nandi, G.: Speed invariant, human gait based recognition system for video surveillance security. In: International Conference on Intelligent Interactive Technologies and Multimedia. pp. 325–335. Springer (2013). https://doi.org/10.1007/978-3-642-37463-0_30
19. Rokanujjaman, M., Hossain, M.A., Islam, M.R., Hossain, A.A., Ferworn, A.: Part definition and selection for part-based speed invariant gait recognition. In: 2016 9th International Conference on Electrical and Computer Engineering (ICECE), pp. 218–221. IEEE (2016)
20. Semwal, V.B., Raj, M., Nandi, G.C.: Biometric gait identification based on a multilayer perceptron. Robot. Auton. Syst. **65**, 65–75 (2015)
21. Sepas-Moghaddam, A., Etemad, A.: Deep gait recognition: a survey. IEEE Trans. Pattern Anal. Mach. Intell. **45**(1), 264–284 (2022)
22. Shiraga, K., Makihara, Y., Muramatsu, D., Echigo, T., Yagi, Y.: Geinet: view-invariant gait recognition using a convolutional neural network. In: 2016 International Conference on Biometrics (ICB), pp. 1–8. IEEE (2016)
23. Tan, D., Huang, K., Yu, S., Tan, T.: Recognizing night walkers based on one pseudoshape representation of gait. In: 2007 IEEE Conference on Computer Vision and Pattern Recognition, pp. 1–8. IEEE (2007)
24. Zheng, S.: CASIA Gait Database. http://www.sinobiometrics.com (Accessed 27 July 2017)

Network Security

A Novel Unsupervised Learning Approach for False Data Injection Attack Detection in Smart Grid

Aschalew Tirulo[1,2](✉), Siddhartha Chauhan[1,2], Mathewos Lolamo[1,2], and Tamirat Tagesse[1,2]

[1] NIT Hamirpur, Hamirpur, HP 177005, India
{aschalew,sid}@nith.ac.in, matilolamo@gmail.com
[2] Wachemo University, Hosanna 667, Ethiopia

Abstract. Smart grids, enhanced by integrating new technologies like home energy management systems (HEMS) and smart meters, face risks like false data injection attacks (FDIA). These attacks are particularly challenging in decentralized residential demand response (DR) structures, where security breaches are not immediately evident. Traditional security measures are ineffective against FDIAs in these systems due to the diverse data sources, unique household energy use patterns, and dynamic energy forecasts. Using unsupervised learning, we present a new way to find FDIAs in smart grids. It combines K-means clustering with the spectral residual method (KM-SR). This method accurately identifies attack timeframes, as evidenced by a 95% accuracy rate, 88.67% recall, an 88 % precision-recall curve, and a 97% ROC-AUC score. Tested with Austin, Texas, energy data, KM-SR outperforms existing detection methods, showcasing its effectiveness in safeguarding smart grids against FDIA threats.

Keywords: Smart grid · K-means clustering · demand response · spectral residual · False data injection attacks

1 Introduction

The interplay between energy efficiency and conservation has become paramount in the context of increasing concerns over energy deficits and environmental impacts [1]. Smart grids, integrated with demand response (DR) programs, exemplify this shift. These programs incentivize consumers to adjust their energy consumption based on pricing, efficiency, and grid functionality, thereby reducing peak load demands. Home Energy Management Systems (HEMS) is central to these programs, aligning household device usage with cost reduction and convenience goals [2].

The anticipated widespread use of smart meters with embedded agents will mark the evolution of smart grids. These agents facilitate communication between consumers and DR aggregators, enabling flexible loads to participate

N. Chauhan et al. (Eds.): MIND 2023, CCIS 2128, pp. 293–308, 2024.
https://doi.org/10.1007/978-3-031-62217-5_25

in energy markets. Internet of Things (IoT) advancements contribute to this responsive energy environment, aiding utility companies in devising effective DR strategies through improved demand predictions. This has led to the adoption of decentralized systems, empowering users to align their demand predictions with price signals [3].

However, this decentralization and emphasis on privacy in DR programs present significant challenges. The autonomy of HEMS and the reliance on aggregated community demand data create opportunities for adversaries to exploit vulnerabilities for detrimental outcomes or financial gains. A major vulnerability in smart grids is their susceptibility to false data injection attacks (FDIAs), which can cause physical damage, financial losses, and widespread grid disruptions. The ubiquity and interconnectedness of devices like HEMS, IoT devices, and smart meters in modern energy systems make them prime targets for malicious attacks [4].

Addressing these vulnerabilities requires robust detection strategies, especially given the lack of genuine datasets for machine learning in DR systems. Some old ways of finding anomalies, like the Local Outlier Factor (LOF), One-Class Neural Networks (OC-NN), and Isolation Forests, don't work well with changing time series data, like forecasts for household demand [7].

We present a new way to find FDIAs in DR systems that combines K-means clustering with the spectral residual approach (KM-SR). This innovative approach not only improves detection precision but also accurately identifies the timing of attacks. The KM-SR method is more accurate at finding anomalies than other methods when tested with energy data from 168 homes in Austin, Texas. This makes smart grids even more resistant to FDIAs.

2 Related Work

Various methods have been developed to detect FDIAs and irregularities in innovative grid systems. We discussed the critical research on FDIA detection and compared our methodology with existing techniques. FDIAs modify the documented energy consumption figures by implementing partial reductions or specific circumvention methods. Many researchers are harnessing machine learning, utilizing simple and advanced learning detection methods, to counter these issues. For instance, in the primary detection realm, the ARIMA model-based detector boasts an 89 % detection rate [5], while a multi-class SVM detector has marked a commendable 94 % detection rate [6].

In the sphere of advanced learning, neural network models are gaining traction. Feedforward neural network detectors have achieved a 92% detection rate [7], whereas deep recurrent neural networks (RNNs) have reached up to 93% [8]. Pioneering methods using deep vector embeddings also secured a 95% detection rate [9]. Research [10] using a CNN to identify electricity fraud in smart grids reports 92% accuracy. However, it mainly emphasizes accuracy, with limited insights into its dataset. In comparison, our methodology excels in accuracy and also considers other vital metrics, such as precision. Another study [11] examines the Symbolic Aggregation Approximation (SAX) for anomaly detection but fails to produce thorough results. Contrarily, our research provides an exhaustive evaluation of our FDIA detection techniques, backed by extensive findings. The study [12] investigates machine learning methods for detecting non-technical losses but restricts its focus to individual consumers, using only five daily readings. In contrast, our approach emphasizes aggregated community data for a more holistic analysis. The methodology in [16] integrates k-means clustering, the Naive Bayes classification algorithm, and dynamic programming for identifying abnormalities. Nevertheless, we focus on assessing if a particular demand pattern is at risk without strictly relying on statistical attributes.

In [13], supervised and unsupervised learning methods were proposed to distinguish between discrete FDIA and secure operational states. [14] leveraged the conditional deep belief network (CDBN) to reveal the complex temporal characteristics of concealed FDIAs, successfully identifying 90% of these attacks. Recently, [15] used a discrete wavelet transform to show spatial data attributes and a deep neural network to find associations between temporal data for FDIA identification. This approach improved detection accuracy from approximately 70% using Kalman filters [16] to over 90%.

Other research [17] [18,19] presents advanced algorithms and deep learning methods for time-series anomaly identification. However, they often need help with the fluctuating nature of demand forecasts. Deep autoencoder-driven detection systems have reported detection rates ranging between 81% and 95% [18] [19] [20]. Another significant piece of research [21] presents two FDIA detection techniques utilizing a CSR strategy alongside a supervised CNN-based deep learning model. Nevertheless, our KM-SR model surpasses these in efficacy.

In conclusion, our study fills a significant gap in FDIA detection for aggregate consumer demand forecasting. Our method is distinctive, adeptly identifying attacks even with sparse label data, and excels in accuracy, precision, and F1 scores, minimizing false positives. This highlights the effectiveness of our model in detecting FDIAs and enhancing the resilience and security of smart grid infrastructures.

3 Distributed Demand Response System

Utilities use dynamic pricing, like RTP and DAP, to enhance energy consumption [22]. Integrating DDR systems with smart meters automates appliance scheduling. Nevertheless, decentralized systems amplify cyber risks, with FDIAs potentially causing power disruptions and financial issues. System dynamics and attack models are scrutinized.

3.1 System Model

Homes have both manageable (like dishwashers) and unmanageable appliances (like refrigerators). DDR systems control manageable ones to streamline usage and cut costs for households and utilities. As per [23], RTP-focused DR mechanisms effectively create cost-saving schedules. Days are split into 48 half-hour pricing periods, each comprising three ten-minute scheduling sessions. Utilities send 24-hour pricing signals to smart meters daily, prompting households to adjust appliance operations, considering start times, usage rates, and potential delay penalties. HEMS coordinates these operations, including deviation penalties. An optimization exercise begins: households target minimum expenses, including inconvenience penalties, while utilities tweak pricing signals. A shared demand profile relayed via an aggregator aids utilities in refining pricing. The process iterates until collective expenses bottom out. Operation likelihood within that time (Eq. 1) serves as a gauge of aggregate appliance demand during each pricing interval.

$$S_m = \sum_{n=3m-2}^{3m} \sum_{h=1}^{H} \sum_{i=1}^{T_h} \sum_{s=n-l_{h,i}}^{i=1} d_{h,i} \times p(t_{h,i}, s) \tag{1}$$

where $S_m$represents the sum demand for a given pricing interval m. H denotes the total count of households within the community. $T_h$number of tasks per household h. $t_{h,i}$ $i^{t,h}$ task of household h. p_m is the per unit price of electricity. $p(t_{h,i}, s)$ the likelihood of task $t_{h,i}$ commencing during interval 's'. $d_{h,i}$ the amount of task i required by household h in one hour. $l_{h,i}$ represents the duration required to finish task i for household h.

Daily electricity costs are determined by multiplying demand in each pricing period with their unit prices (Eq. 2). Power generation costs align with unit prices despite possible differences. User discomfort, influenced by appliance start time deviations and penalty factors, contributes to the system's total penalty.

$$\text{consumption cost} = \sum_{m=1}^{48} P_m \times S_m \tag{2}$$

$$\text{penalty} = \sum_{h=1}^{H} \sum_{i=1}^{t_h} \sum_{s=1}^{144} |s - b_{h,i}| \times w_{h,i} \times p(t_{h,i}, s) \tag{3}$$

where, $b_{h,i}$ optimal begin time of task i of homestead unit h. $w_{h,i}$ degree of inconvenience if task i did not start at $b_{h,i}$.

Table 1. A relationship between cost and scheduling slots.

Time of the day	00:00 h-=00:29 h			...		23:30 h–23:59 h	
Pricing slot	1			...		48	
Scheduling slot	1	2	3	...	142	143	144

3.2 Attack Model

Smart meters and HEMS, vital for smart grid DR strategies, face FDIA cyber risks due to their wide accessibility [20]. Figure 1 shows potential attacks on

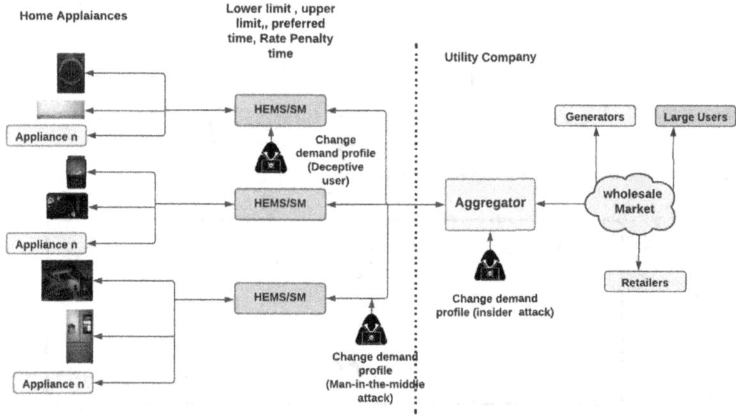

Fig. 1. Numerous possible FDIA situations

devices, communication, and data integrity. Despite encryption and regulations, attackers can modify data, risking DR systems.

Increased HEMS compromises reduce attack detection rates. The attack process involves:

1. Choose an appliance and its operation period(s).
2. Assign both preferred and earliest start times to the start of the selected period(s).
3. Calculate the final permissible end time as:

$$\text{final permissible end time} = \text{earliest start time} + \text{operation duration} - 1.$$

4. Set the device's demand to a new value d^{new} where, $d^{\text{new}} > d_{h,i}$.

After selecting a device and determining its time of operation, the assailant adjusts its demand in the HEMS to a modified version of the original demand d^{new}. This adjustment guarantees that the local optimization will not alter the starting time from the desired time.

4 Methodology

4.1 Problem Statement

With today's intricately interconnected infrastructure, precise demand forecasting is essential. Systems are subject to more cybersecurity risks as they move toward distributed architectures, most notably FDIA in demand response systems. A series of cumulative demand matrices are being examined $(df_1^D, df_2^D, ..., df_N^D$, each with 48 thirty-minute observations (D = 48), to see if there is any manipulated forecast $(df_i^D$ that is a component of an FDIA. We present the KM-SR model for finding problems in energy systems. It uses collected demand data to spot fake data insertions, making interconnected energy infrastructures more resistant to breaches.

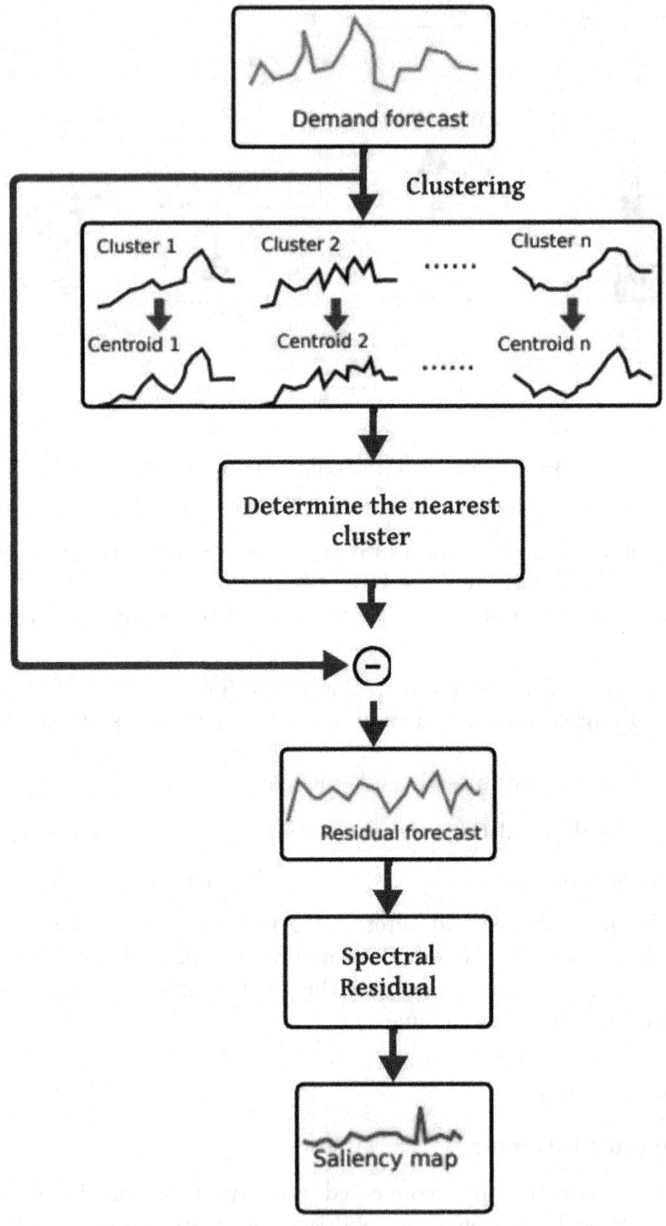

Fig. 2. Proposed KM-SR Model

4.2 Preliminaries

K-Means (KM) clustering is a widely adopted method for grouping data points into clusters, valued for its computational effectiveness and straightforwardness.

Within these clusters, the entities are closer in distance to the centroid of their respective cluster than to any other data points across the entire dataset [24]. This type of data can be present in any space with D dimensions. In the current scenario, while evaluating N demand predictions $df_1^D, df_2^D, ..., df_N^D$, the clustering technique arranges these predictions into k (k<N) groups. This arrangement is facilitated by minimizing the sum of squared deviations within the clusters, as illustrated in Eq. 4. In this equation, T represents a collection of k groupings $T_1, T_2, T_3, ..., T_k$, and μ_i^D represents a cluster's average of the predictions. T_i:

$$\arg\min_{T} \sum_{i=1}^{k} \sum_{df \in T_i} \|df - \mu_i\|^2 \tag{4}$$

To determine the most suitable cluster for a specific demand forecast df_j^D, one should identify the cluster T_i that results in the smallest squared Euclidean dist b/n df_j^D and μ_i^D, where μ_i^D represents the centroid of cluster T_i. This can be computed using Eq. (5):

$$\min \|df - \mu_{i^D}\|^2 \tag{5}$$

Spectral Residual (SR) [25] is an unsupervised method excelling in image recognition, especially visual saliency detection. A study [18] used SR to find outliers in time-series data because it was thought to be useful for finding outliers in data that is easy to see. Given the nature of demand forecasts as time series, we propose using SR to pinpoint FDIAs. This application is expected to improve detection accuracy by highlighting affected periods. The Spectral Residual (SR) method unfolds in three primary stages:

- Applying the Fourier transform to obtain the log amplitude spectrum
- Computing the spectral residual
- Using the Inverse Fourier Transform to Revert the Sequence to its Spatial Domain

For clarity, we describe the steps involved in processing a demand forecast df_j^D.

$$A(f) = \left|F(df_i^D)\right| \tag{6}$$

$$P(f) = \text{Phase}\left(F(df_i^D)\right) \tag{7}$$

Initially, the Fourier transform Γ (Eq. 6 and 7) is applied to the signal to calculate the $A(f)$ and $P(f)$ spectra. The amplitude spectrum is then subjected to a logarithmic transformation (Eq. 8), and the resultant values are averaged to produce $AL(f)$ (Eq. 9).

$$L(f) = \log\left(A(f)\right) \tag{8}$$

Utilizing a matrix h_q (Eq. 10), the Spectral Residual $R(f)$ is obtained by contrasting transformed amplitudes (Eq. 11). Lastly, the inverse Fourier transformation, F^{-1}, is employed to generate the saliency map (Eq. 12).

$$AL(f) = h_q(f) \times L(f) \tag{9}$$

Algorithm 1. KM-SR Model Pseudo Code

Require: A collection of N demand forecast vectors, $df_1^D, df_2^D, ..., df_N^D$, for half-hourly demand predictions (inclusive of both training and testing data sets) Parameters: k, threshold

Ensure: Labels indicate whether the test set's demand forecast is 'attacked' or 'normal.'

Implement the algorithm (referenced in Sec 4.1, b(i)) on the refined train-test data to get k centroids of clusters, denoted as μ_j^D, where $0 \leq j < k + 1$.
for each df_i^D, in the testing set **do**
  Determine the nearest cluster center μ_j^D.
  Determine the remaining by using rs: $rs_i^D = df_i^D - \mu_j^D$.
  Determine the spectrum's amplitude as: as_i = magnitude of the inverse fast Fourier transform of rs_i^D.
  Determine the phase spectrum as: ps_i = phase of the fast Fourier transform of rs_i^D.
  Find the logarithmic spectrum: $ls_i = \log(as_i)$.
  Calculate the average logarithmic spectrum: als_i = convolution of as_i.
  Compute the Spectral Residual: $rs_i = als_i - ls_i$.
  Establish the saliency map as sm_i^D = magnitude of the inverse fast Fourier transform of the exponential of $rs_i + ips_i$).
  if the maximum value of sm_i^D is greater than or equal to the threshold **then**
    Label df_i^D as an "compromised" demand.
  else
    Label df_i^D as a "Not compromised" demand.
  end if
  End the conditional check.
end for
End the loop.

$$h_q(f) = \frac{1}{q^2}\left[\begin{pmatrix} 1 & 1 & \cdots & 1 \\ 1 & 1 & \cdots & 1 \\ \vdots & \vdots & \ddots & \vdots \\ 1 & 1 & \cdots & 1 \end{pmatrix}\right] \tag{10}$$

$$S(df_i^D) = F^{-1}\left(\exp(R(f) + i \times P(f))\right) \tag{11}$$

K-Means-Driven Spectral Residual (KM-SR). We present KM-SR, a distinctive unsupervised technique that combines k-means and SR methodologies. The first tests we did using singular k-means clustering with Euclidean and DTW distances gave us good, sometimes different results. Conversely, the sole SR method struggled to discern authentic peaks from attacks. Hence, we integrated both, resulting in enhanced FDIA detection. While boosting accuracy, this hybrid model only requires tuning two hyper-parameters (besides a threshold), k and q, which can be empirically set. As described in Algorithm 1, we start by forming groups of demand forecasts that are free of attacks using the k-means method. The squared Euclidean distance is then employed to ascertain the nearest cluster centroid for each new prediction. Subtracting this centroid results in residual forecasts. Using SR, we compute saliency maps for these residuals. If the highest value in a saliency map exceeds a set threshold, the related forecast is deemed 'attacked.' In the final step, we normalize the predictions by deducting a mean and adjusting to a unit variance.

$$Z = \frac{df_i}{\sigma} \tag{12}$$

$$\mu = \frac{\sum df_i}{N} \tag{13}$$

$$\sigma = \left(\frac{1}{N}\sum (df_i - \mu)^2\right)^{0.5} \tag{14}$$

5 Experiment

5.1 Dataset and Setup

Numerous energy consumption datasets, like Pecan Street, are available, but there is a dearth of datasets for decentralized device scheduling in DR algorithms. Our research combines synthetic dataset techniques with Pecan Street's empirical data [27], crafting a realistic dataset from 168 Austin homes between June and August 2017. We concentrated on 'manageable' devices like electric cars and washers. To enhance appliance-specific details in the Pecan Street dataset, we use a method [28] to deduce appliance demand, uncovering distinctive consumption patterns. We computed the average appliance demand, producing datasets from 168 households spanning 92 d. Our method consisted of:

- Extract manageable demands and distinct device demands.
- Establishing a probability distribution to ascertain the best device start times and utilizing a Rayleigh distribution for their durations
- Using a uniform distribution for determining initial start times, end times, and penalty factors.
- Creating datasets that encompass 168 homes over 92 d.
- Guaranteeing the data's authenticity for subsequent demand response evaluations.

Our synthetic data, mimicking 48 daily device operations, matches actual demand (Fig. 2) based on national energy market pricing [26]. From 168 households, we produced 92 community demand profiles. We adjusted the daily start times of manageable appliances for genuine demand variability. We also introduced artificial demands, up to 2.5% of total daily demand, simulating

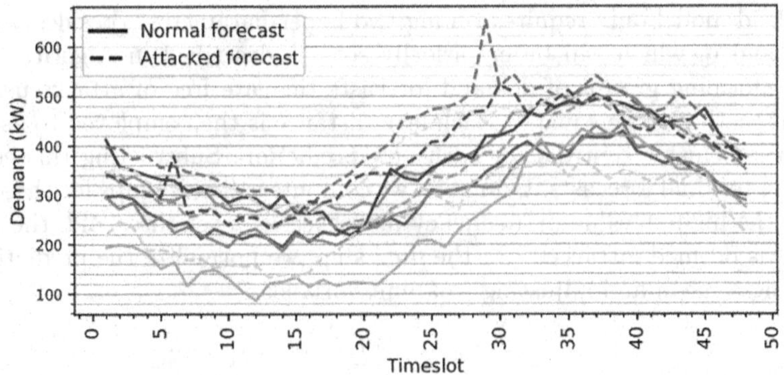

Fig. 3. Contrast between Actual and Simulated Demand across Various Days

false spikes by manipulating appliances in random homes. Our dataset contains 186,096 demand forecasts: 171,096 are normal, and the remainder are attacked. We divided the data 2:1 for training and testing. We also created a clean training set, a pruned version, and a testing set with 5% attacked forecasts.

5.2 Performance Metrics

The performance of the KM-SR model is assessed using the following parameters: accuracy, precision, recall, F1-score, FPR, and AUC values. Furthermore, the duration required for training and testing is also considered.

$$\text{Acc} = \frac{\text{TP} + \text{TN}}{\text{TP} + \text{TN} + \text{FP} + \text{FN}} \tag{15}$$

$$\text{Prec} = \frac{\text{TP}}{\text{TP} + \text{FP}} \tag{16}$$

$$\text{Rec} = \frac{\text{TP}}{\text{TP} + \text{FN}} \tag{17}$$

$$\text{F1 Score} = 2 \times \frac{\text{Prec} \times \text{Rec}}{\text{Prec} + \text{Rec}} \tag{18}$$

$$\text{FPR} = \frac{\text{FP}}{\text{FP} + \text{TN}} \tag{19}$$

5.3 Evaluation

Our KM-SR model was assessed using unsupervised anomaly detection benchmarks, testing various k values from 2 to 1000. Anomalies were identified using peaks on the saliency map and thresholds determined from the Youden Index [27]—a metric that locates the best point on the ROC curve. A comparison was made between the KM-SR model and other unsupervised anomaly detection methods, such as deep learning and traditional methods. Some of these reference points are cutting-edge instruments and a brand-new FDIA detection method [17] that combines Naive-Bayes classifiers with clustering techniques.

In our research on unsupervised anomaly detection, we utilized methods such as DAGMM, LSTM-AD for sequential datasets, and LSTM-ED for detecting multi-sensor anomalies. Additionally, we incorporated AE with replicator neural networks alongside traditional methods like TwitterAD, HBOS, iForest, FB-based detectors, kNN, and LOF. We also benchmarked OC-NN and SR-based techniques designed for time-sequenced data.

We applied the suggested hyper-parameters for the KM-SR model while adhering to the default configurations for the other methods. The assessment of the models was based on criteria such as accuracy, precision, recall, F1 score, and FPR.

6 Results

The performance of the KM-SR model is juxtaposed with other DL-based unsupervised methods in Table 2. The LSTM-ED achieved an accuracy rate of 89.17%, while both the AutoEncoder and KM-SR exceeded 90%. However, due to the data imbalance, using only accuracy gives a partial picture of detection performance. Apart from KM-SR, the precision and F1 scores of other methodologies were under 50%. Three out of the four models under study did not detect half of the attack scenarios. The KM-SR successfully detected over 94% of attacks, marking a 17% advancement compared to the leading auto-encoder that detected only 75% of attacks. An F1 score lower than 50% indicates that many DL-based techniques are not optimal for FDIA detection. Nevertheless, KM-SR registered an F1 score of 68.04%, which is 19.05% higher than the AutoEncoder's. Clearly, KM-SR does better than other DL-based methods, like the AutoEncoder, in terms of accuracy, precision, recall, F1 score, and FPR metrics. Notably, our KM-SR model showed a reduced FPR of 4.0%, which is a 3.89% improvement from the auto-encoder, underscoring its superior accuracy. With a precision rate of 55.53% and an FPR of 4.0%, the KM-SR stands out among all models. However, there is significant potential for further enhancement, and subsequent improvements should prioritize these metrics.

Table 2. Our KM-SR model in comparison to DL-based unsupervised techniques

Model	Acc	Prec	Rec	F1-score	False Positive Rate(FPR)
DAGMM	44.0%	5.0%	55.0%	9.6%	56.7%
LSTM-Auto-Deco	69.0%	9.8%	57.0%	16.8%	30.0%
LSTM-Encoder-Deco	89.0%	26.5%	56.9%	36.0%	9.0%
Auto-Encoder	91.0%	35.6%	76.4%	48.5%	7.9%
Our KM-SR	95.5%	55.5%	87.8%	68.0%	4.0%

Our detailed analysis of nine unsupervised learning methods revealed that only 44% (four out of nine) successfully identified over half the attacks, as highlighted in Table 3. Specifically, the LOF, feature bagging, and KNN exceeded 50% in F1 scores, while most methods, except the LOF, did not surpass 50% precision. Additionally, the KM-SR model showed modest improvements, increasing accuracy, precision, recall, and F1 scores by 0.72%, 4.25%, 4.22%, and 4.93%, respectively, compared to LOF, feature bagging, and TwitterAD. These improvements were substantiated by a remarkable ROC-AUC of 97% and an 88% precision-recall curve. However, the KM-SR model also registered the highest FPR among all evaluated methods. Figures 4 and 5 show that the ROC and precision-recall curves have AUC values of 0.97 and 0.88, respectively. This shows that the KM-SR model can differentiate between classes even when the dataset is unequal. Unsupervised methods, such as KM-SR, work better than others. For example, KM-SR found 550 more cyberattacks out of 4,950 than the LOF and autoencoder models. However, as threat intensity escalates, model performances converge, highlighting the need for comprehensive security assessments during the development of smart grid systems, given the rapidly evolving security landscape of grid technology.

Table 3. A comparative study of our KM-SR model with various unsupervised techniques

Model	Acc	Prec	Rec	F1-score	False Positive Rate
Twitter Auto-Deco	91.9%	7.0%	4.0%	5.0%	3.14%
HBOS	37.0%	5.9%	71.5	10.9%	65.0%
OC-Neural Net	91.0%	12.0%	10.9%	11.3%	4.6%
Isolation Forest (IF)	43.2%	6.2%	67.3%	11.3%	58.2%
Spectral Residual (SR)	90.4%	14.0%	15.2%	14.6%	5.3%
Feature Bagging (FB)	92.0%	39.2%	86.6%	54.0%	7.7%
kNN	94.0%	46.0%	75.0%	5.8%	5.0%
LOF	94.8%	51.3%	82.0%	63.1%	4.5%
Our KM-SR	95.5%	55.5%	87.8%	68.0%	4.0%

7 Discussion

Navigating FDIAs in demand response systems is challenging due to their stealthy nature and ability to disrupt operations. A key strategy in the early stages of development is to create a robust infrastructure and conduct extensive research on preventive measures to strengthen smart grid systems.

Standard detection algorithms operate on the premise that successful, high-impact attacks can be pinpointed by employing aggregate forecasts. However, the potential for attackers to exploit meteorological and demographic data to create FDIAs necessitates a commitment to continuous adaptation and a thorough review of existing methods. The KM-SR model, w/c is the integration of

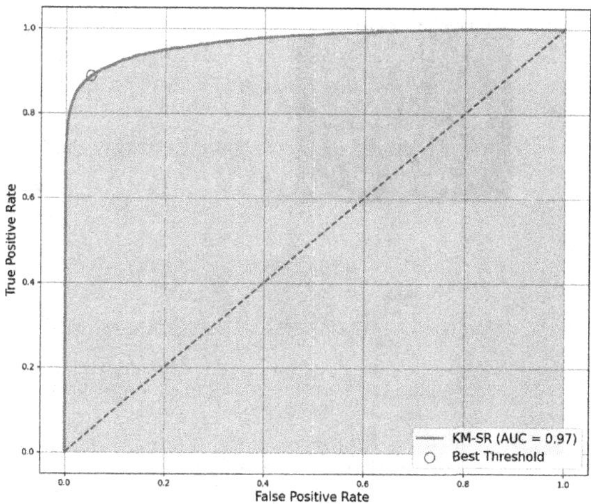

Fig. 4. ROC Curve and AUC Illustration for KM-SR Model: Demonstrating High Efficacy with 97% AUC Score

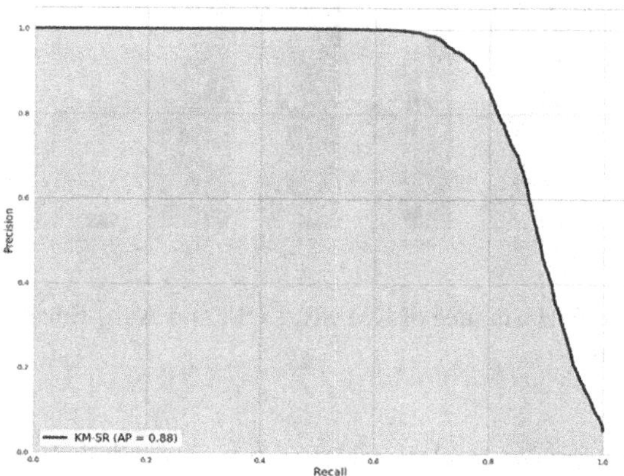

Fig. 5. KM-SR Model's Precision-Recall Curve: Demonstrating High Differentiation Capability with 88% AUC

k-means and spectral residuals and is very good at finding FDIAs in distributed demand response systems. It starts by grouping demand forecasts that are free of attacks using the k-means method. Following that, the Euclidean distance, squared, is employed to determine the nearest cluster center for every new forecast. Subtracting this centroid produces residual forecasts, and spectral residuals are used to calculate saliency maps for these residuals. If the peak value on a saliency map exceeds a predefined threshold, the corresponding forecast is classified as "compromised." While the KM-SR model generally performs well across various metrics, it has yet to improve the FPR. The current landscape of anomaly detection techniques frequently needs help when detecting FDIAs in DR

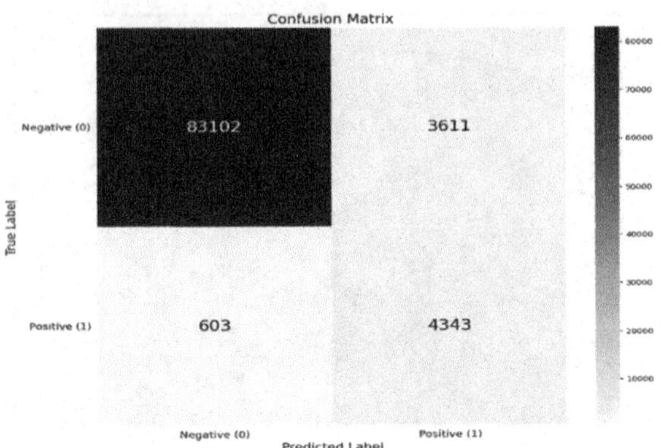

Fig. 6. Confusion Matrix

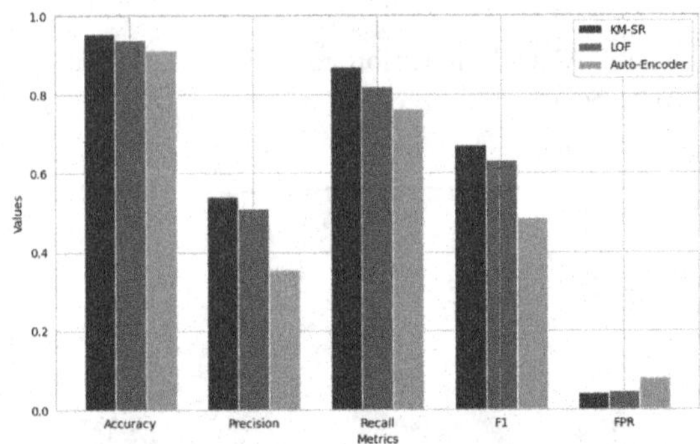

Fig. 7. Comparative Performance of KM-SR, LOF, and Auto-Encoder in FDIA Detection for DDR Systems

frameworks. Unsupervised models, which require less labeled data, offer a practical approach for smart grids. However, these models need to be improved regarding precision and FPR reduction. As a result, it is critical for utility companies to effectively manage tampered forecasts to mitigate the negative consequences of FDIAs.

8 Conclusion

In conclusion, this study underscores the importance of developing innovative unsupervised anomaly detection techniques specifically tailored for identifying FDIAs in smart grids' DR systems. The KM-SR model has showcased exceptional potential. Our results show that our model is better than the other techniques we used to find anomalies. It has better accuracy, precision, recall, F1 score, and FPRs. Nonetheless, there is a pronounced need for continuous enhancements, especially in augmenting the FPR and precision rates. Our research shows that strong FDIA detection systems can make DR systems much more reliable, which will help ensure that transactive energy markets keep running smoothly. We suggest adding more time-sequenced data to the outlier detection scope to understand better how FDIAs affect d/t types of data in energy markets and SG control processes. This research serves as a foundational step and catalyzes further investigations into this vital aspect of smart grid security.

References

1. Honarmand, M.E., Hosseinnezhad, V., Hayes, B., Shafie-Khah, M., Siano, P.: An overview of demand response: from its origins to the smart energy community. IEEE Access, 96851–96876 (2021)
2. Mahmoud, M., Slama, S.B.: Peer-to-peer energy trading case study using an ai-powered community energy management system. Appli. Sci. **4, 13**(13), 7838 (2023)
3. Mhanna, S., Chapman, A.C., Verbič, G.: A fast distributed algorithm for large-scale demand response aggregation. IEEE Trans. Smart Grid. **147**(4), 2094–107 (2016)
4. Dayaratne T, Rudolph C, Liebman A, Salehi M, He S. High impact false data injection attack against real-time pricing in smart grids. In 2019 IEEE PES Innovative Smart Grid Technologies Europe (ISGT-Europe),(pp. 1-5). IEEE, (2019)
5. Dayaratne, T., Rudolph, C., Liebman, A., Salehi, M., He, S.: High impact false data injection attack against real-time pricing in smart grids. In 2019 IEEE PES Innovative Smart Grid Technologies Europe (ISGT-Europe), pp. 1-5. IEEE (2019)
6. Jokar, P., Arianpoo, N., Leung, V.C.: Electricity theft detection in AMI using customers' consumption patterns. IEEE Tran. Smart Grid. **7**(1), 216–26 (2015)
7. Ismail, M., Shahin, M., Shaaban, M.F., Serpedin, E., Qaraqe, K.: Efficient detection of electricity theft cyber attacks in AMI networks. In: 2018 IEEE Wireless Communications and Networking Conference (WCNC), pp. 1-6. IEEE (2018)
8. Ismail, M., Shahin, M., Shaaban, M.F., Serpedin, E., Qaraqe, K.: Efficient detection of electricity theft cyber attacks in AMI networks. In: 2018 IEEE Wireless Communications and Networking Conference (WCNC), pp.1-6. IEEE (2018)
9. Takiddin, A., Ismail, M., Nabil, M., Mahmoud, M.M., Serpedin, E.: Detecting electricity theft cyber-attacks in AMI networks using deep vector embeddings. IEEE Syst. J. **15**(3), 4189–98 (2020)
10. Noor, I., Al-Janabi, S., Al-Khateeb, B.: Electricity-theft detection in smart grid based on deep learning. Bull. Electr. Eng. Inform/ **10**, 2285–92 (2021)
11. Yue, M.: An integrated anomaly detection method for load forecasting data under cyberattacks. In: 2017, the IEEE Power and Energy Society General Meeting, pp.1-5. IEEE (2017)
12. Cai, G., Jiang, C., Yang, D., Liu, X., Zhou, S., Cao, Z., Liu, C., Sun, Z.: Data-driven predictive based load frequency robust control of power system with renewables. Inter. J. Electrical Power Energy Syst. **1, 154**, 109429 (2023)
13. Esmalifalak, M., Liu, L., Nguyen, N., Zheng, R., Han, Z.: Detecting stealthy false data injection using machine learning in smart grid. IEEE Syst. J. **11**(3), 1644–52 (2014)
14. He, Y., Mendis, G.J., Wei, J.: Real-time detection of false data injection attacks in smart grid: a deep learning-based intelligent mechanism. IEEE Trans. Smart Grid. **8**(5), 2505–16 (2017)

15. James, J.Q., Hou, Y., Li, V.O.: Online false data injection attack detection with wavelet transform and deep neural networks. IEEE Trans. Industr. Inf. **14**(7), 3271–80 (2018)
16. Manandhar, K., Cao, X., Hu, F., Liu, Y.: Detection of faults and attacks including false data injection attack in smart grid using Kalman filter. IEEE Trans. Control Netw. Syst. **1**(4), 370–9 (2014)
17. Cui, M., Wang, J., Yue, M.: Machine learning-based anomaly detection for load forecasting under cyberattacks. IEEE Trans. Smart Grid. **10**(5), 5724–34 (2019)
18. Ren, H., et al.: Time-series anomaly detection service at microsoft. In: Proceedings of the 25th ACM SIGKDD International Conference on Knowledge Discovery and Data Mining, pp. 3009-3017 (2019)
19. Zhao, B., Lu, H., Chen, S., Liu, J., Wu, D.: Convolutional neural networks for time series classification. J. Syst. Eng. Electron. **1**, 162–9 (2017)
20. Ismail Fawaz, H., Forestier, G., Weber, J., Idoumghar, L., Muller, P.A.: Deep learning for time series classification: a review. Data Min. Knowl. Disc. **4**, 917–63 (2019)
21. Dayaratne, T., Salehi, M., Rudolph, C., Liebman, A.: False data injection attack detection for secure distributed demand response in smart grids. In: 2022 52nd Annual IEEE/IFIP International Conference on Dependable Systems and Networks (DSN), pp. 367-380. IEEE (2022)
22. Eid, C., Koliou, E., Valles, M., Reneses, J., Hakvoort, R.: Time-based pricing and electricity demand response: existing barriers and next steps. Utilities Policy. **40**, 15–25 (2016)
23. Aneesl, A., Dillon, T., Wallis, S., Chen, Y.P.: Optimization of day-ahead and real-time prices for smart home community. Inter. J. Electr. Power Energy Syst. **124**, 106403 (2021)
24. MacQueen J. Some methods for classification and analysis of multivariate observations. In: Proceedings of the Fifth Berkeley Symposium on Mathematical Statistics and Probability, vol. 1, No. 14, pp. 281-297 (1967)
25. Hou, X., Zhang, L.: Saliency detection: a spectral residual approach. In: 2007 IEEE Conference On Computer Vision and Pattern Recognition, pp. 1-8. IEEE, (2007)
26. Pecan Street Inc.: Dataport. Accessed (2019). https://dataport.cloud/
27. Youden, W.J.: Index for rating diagnostic tests. Cancer **3**(1), 32–5 (1950)
28. He, S., Wallace, M., Gange, G., Liebman, A., Wilson, C.: A fast and scalable algorithm for scheduling large numbers of devices under real-time pricing. In: Hooker, J. (ed.) CP 2018. LNCS, vol. 11008, pp. 649–666. Springer, Cham (2018). https://doi.org/10.1007/978-3-319-98334-9_42

A Review of Authentication Schemes in Internet of Things

Upendra Verma(✉)

Department of Computer Engineering, MPSTME, SVKM'S NMIMS University, Shirpur Campus, Mumbai, M.H, India
upendra4567@gmail.com

Abstract. Internet of Things (IoT) has emerged as one of the most important technological developments in recent years, because of its ability to process a wide range of application domains. IoT is com-posed of several interconnected objects that are able to communicate to one another. A secure communication between these objects is an essential requirement. There are security issues in this situation where several objects share information. User authentication is a key component in an IoT ecosystem as it enables the user to securely interact with one another. This paper presents an extensive examination of IoT authentication schemes. The taxonomy of authentication schemes is presented in terms of various domains including wireless sensor networks (WSN), smart home network, vehicular network, grid network and cloud-based network. Based on the review, limita-tion of existing authentication schemes is highlighted.

Keywords: Internet of Things · User authentication · Taxonomy of authentication · Secure communication

1 Introduction

The evolution of the Internet of Things (IoT) has been aided by wireless connectivity. Wireless communication is the foundation of IoT, which uses radio frequency (RF), Bluetooth, light, and sound to establish connection in both directions for message delivery and data collecting in a regulated manner without physical interaction. [1]. Wireless communication and technology can be used for a variety of IoT applications, including critical industrial missions like power grid automation and oil and gas field control, as well as everyday activities like smart cities, home automation, smart farming, industrial Internet, and many others [2]. The IoT is a well-known and rapidly-growing paradigm that consists of many physical entities that can gather and distribute information through wireless technologies [3].

Kevin Ashton popularized the term "Internet of Things" for the first time at a presentation in 1999 [4]. IoT is a network of physical things that uses RFID, actuators & sensors and connected with each other for achieving some goals [5]. IoT is the emerging technology and attracted a lot of attention to many fields, e.g. smart transportation, smart

N. Chauhan et al. (Eds.): MIND 2023, CCIS 2128, pp. 309–322, 2024.
https://doi.org/10.1007/978-3-031-62217-5_26

healthcare and smart city [6]. According to Cisco's Annual Internet Report, 29.3 billion networked devices will be connected to the internet by 2023 [7].

The most influential research challenges in the IoT domain are privacy and security [8]. Figure 1 shows the core areas in the field of privacy and security of IoT. The core area includes integrity, authentication, cofidentiality, availability, access control, and non-repudiation. These areas depend on the security needs of the IoT application. Particularly, Authentication is considered as a supreme requirement for the IoT. The traditional authentication schemes are infeasible in resource constrained environments. In this paper, the current state of art of authentication schemes in the field of IoT has been presented.

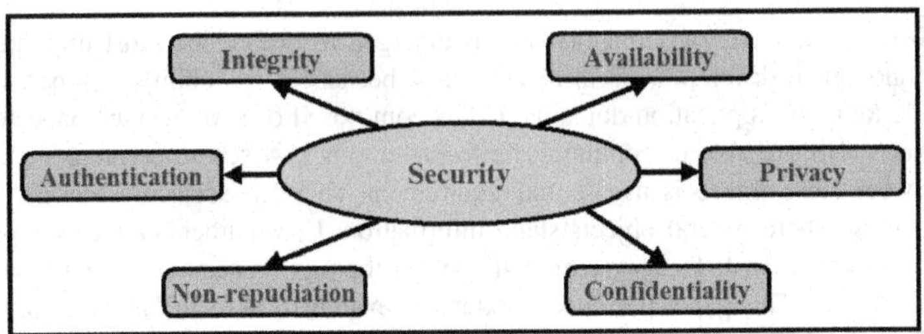

Fig. 1. Security areas in IoT

The rest of the paper is organized as follows: Sect. 2 presents the taxonomy of authentication schemes in the context of IoT and also gives comparative analysis of authentication schemes. The discussion and limitation of existing authentication schemes has presented in Sect. 3. Finally, Sect. 4 presents our conclusions.

2 Taxonomy of Authentication Schemes in IoT

Authentication is a process which ensures proof of identities and It is one of the major pillar for information assurance. In authentication, the entity in a network has to prove its identity. Security is supreme requirement for IoT and in particular authentication is being widely considered amongst most of IoT researchers [9]. Multiple criteria were used to classify IoT authentication, which were chosen based on the commonality and key aspects of existing authentication schemes. The taxonomy of authentication schemes is shown in the Fig. 2. The following abbreviations are used in this article.

- **Architecture: H** for Hierarchical architecture and **F** for Flat architecture
- **L:** IoT Layers- **A** for Application layer, **N** for Network layer, **P** for Perception layer
- **AD:** Application Domain

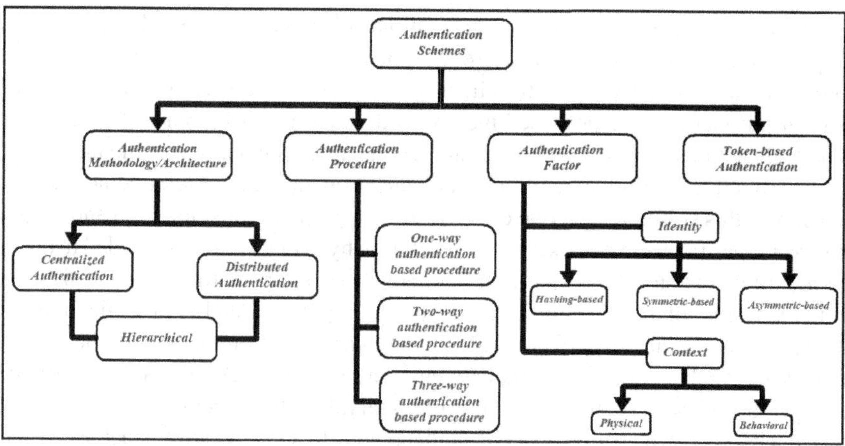

Fig. 2. Taxonomy of IoT authentication schemes

2.1 Authentication Methodology

The authentication methodology has two major classifications namely, centralized and distributed. Centralized authentication provides an authentication method using centralized entity or Trusted Third Party (TTP) or Centralized server e.g. Kerberos authentication protocol, Single sign-on etc. Centralized authentication's major goal is to disseminate and manage credentials. Using centralized server or TTP.

Distributed Authentication allows communication parties to authenticate each other in a distributed & straight-forward manner. So, the entity coordinates autonomously to build the trust e.g. blockchain based distributed authentication. In distributed authentication, there is no centralized entity to build the authentication. In the review article [10], we have already reviewed the centralized and distributed authentication approaches based on the authentication methodology/architecture. In this article, we covered the various authentication strategies based on authentication token, authentication factors, and authentication procedures.

2.2 Authentication Procedures

In one-way authentication procedure, only one of the two parties desiring to communicate authenticates oneself to the other, while the other remains unauthenticated. Mutual authentication is a two-way authentication procedure in which both parties verify each other's identity. The two parties are authenticated by the central authority and central authority assists them in mutually authenticating themselves in the three-way authentication procedure.

2.2.1 Taxonomy of Authentication Schemes Based On One-way Authentication Procedure

Chae et al. [11] developed an authentication method, which is resilience against the replay attack, phishing attack and impersonation attack. However, this authentication method is susceptible to security threats like impersonation and phishing attack. Moghaddam et al. [12] presented scalable and efficient user authentication method for cloud environment. To confirm the user's identity on the client side, a client-based user authentication agent has been introduced. The proposed method is divided into two approaches: First approach deals with the registered devices and second approach deals with the unregistered devices. To reduce the reliance of user authentication and encryption operations on the main server, this solution used two different servers to store authentication and cryptography resources from the main server. A cryptography agent was also included to encrypt data before it was stored on cloud servers. However, the performance analysis of this method was not conducted in order to evaluate computation and communication complexity. Bamasag et al. [13] proposed continuous authentication scheme for the IoT. This authentication scheme provides efficient and secure authentication process for frequent message transmission in short session time intervals. This scheme proposed a secret sharing scheme in which shares act as authenticator tokens and secrets act as authenticators. The performance evaluation of the proposed method shows that the scheme is lightweight with regard to computation and communication complexity. Therefore, the protocol is efficient for resource constrained IoT devices.

Hamidi [14] developed a safe method for device authentication in the Internet of Medical Things (IMT) that relies on people's physical attributes. The authors conducted a review on biometric approaches utilised in smart health and analysed their compatibility with the IMT. Finally, while leveraging biometric attributes for authentication, the authors specified open issues for researchers. However, the computational time of the proposed method was relatively high and therefore the computational cost was also increased. Brian et al. [15] suggested a two-factor authentication technique based on a smartphone as the first issue and the user's fingerprint as the second issue. The smart library system uses both factors to verify a user's identity. If the fingerprint matches the individual data, the user is permitted access to the internal library network, allowing them to request books and receive the rack position (location) where the book is located. However, a remarkable failure was noted in this method that collected data are stored in the plain text form over the mobile phone. Sbeyti et al. [16] presented a new behavioural pattern-based authentication mechanism for mobile phone users. They began by gathering data on the behaviour of mobile phone users in terms of the applications used at a specific time and for a specific length of time, and then converting that data into a unique pattern that could be used to authenticate the person and the phone. The proposed method will be utilised in conjunction with existing mobile phone authentication schemes (pin code, fingerprint, gestures, etc.). However, the computational time of the proposed method was relatively high and therefore the computational cost was also increased. Emerson et al. [17] designed a security technique for IoT network. The threats, such as impersonation and replay attacks, can be mitigated using this method [18]. With the help of a security manager and the OAuth 2.0 protocol, this proposed strategy protects IoT networks from unauthenticated users. However, this authentication scheme is vulnerable to eavesdropping attack. The summarization of aforementioned discussion is illustrated in the Table 1.✔

Table 1. Analysis of IoT authentication scheme based on one-way authentication procedure

Network Model	L	H/F	AD	(✔: Strength)/ (×: Weakness)
Client, Resource owner, Authorization server, Resource server and Mail authentication server [11]	A	H	Smart home network	× Susceptible to impersonation and replay attack, ×No performance evaluation, × Security investigation is not considered
User, Keys server, Authentication server in cloud environment [12]	A	F	Generic IoT application	✔ Resistance to MITM and brute force attack, ✔ Two servers used for storing cryptography and authentication data, ×No performance analysis is considered
Claimer and Verifier in IoT network [13]	A	F	Generic IoT application	✔ Resistance to MITM and replay attack, ✔ Resistance to DoS threat and eavesdropping, × Cost of storage is inefficient
User, Authenticator, FIDO client, User agent, RP web server & app and FIDO server [14]	A + N + P	H	Generic IoT application	✔ Ease of implementation in smart Health, ✔ Resilience to fork and clone attacks, × Higher computation cost
User, Library server, Wi-Fi based LPS and Rank monitors [15]	P	F	NFC based application	✔ Authentication is done with two factors, ✔ Quick finding location of book, × Information gathered is saved as plain text, × Computation cost is not taken into account, × Security analysis is not performed

(continued)

Table 1. (*continued*)

Network Model	L	H/F	AD	(✔: Strength)/ (×: Weakness)
User and Smart devices [16]	P	H	Mobile network and applications	✔ To test the results, a subset of the data is modelled, ✔ Restriction to use android platform only, × Data is saved as clear text in cell phone, × Attacks are not taken into account, × Cost of computation is substantial
User, gateway, security manager and service provider [17]	A	H	Generic IoT application	✔ Resistance to Impersonation, × No evaluation of performance, × Susceptible to eavesdropping

2.2.2 Taxonomy of Authentication Schemes Based on Two-Way Authentication Procedure

Gope et al. [19] developed a user authentication method for WSN. This protocol demonstrated that the existing anonymous authentication solutions are impracticable. The proposed protocol provides following security features: forward and backward secrecy, privacy of user, and untraceability. The protocol is resilience against various cryptographic attacks e.g. node capture attack, stolen smart card and impersonation attack. Moreover, the performance illustrations that the designed method is reliable for WSN in terms of computation and communication cost. In addition, experimentation was done with the help of AVISPA tool and it was proved that this method of authentication was efficient and secure. However, verification delay and message delay are not considered, which was significant factor for WSN. Schmitt et al. [20] propounded a two-way authentication and key agreement method, which gives security for class 1 devices in IoT. This method relies on the Bellare-Canetti-Krawczyk protocol with a secure authentication extension of PSK. Two stages are identified as enrolment and authentication stage. In the enrolment stage, identification of nodes is presented and in the authentication stage, data is exchanged between the device and server. The performance evaluation in terms of memory consumption and energy consumption are considered for WSN. This method is resilience against MITM attack. However, this scheme is susceptible to replay and DoS attack. Lee et al. [21] offered an authentication method based on the use of lightweight encryption algorithm. The authentication protocol is used in RFID application for IoT. This scheme is based on the XOR operation. However, it was found that the security and performance analysis are not considered to validate the security of proposed method. Lai et al. [22] propounded group based lightweight authentication approach (GLARM) for

M2M which comprises of two protocols, 3GPP access case and non-3GPP access case, respectively. This method also minimizes the authentication overhead. The security analysis shows that the proposed method is robust for IoT environment. The performance of this approach is also evaluated to show the method is effective regarding to computation and communication overhead. This method is resilience against the MITM and DoS attack. Device anonymity plays an important role in case of group based authentication. However, this authentication method failed to provide a property of device anonymity. Kumari et al. [23] introduced an approach to perform mutual authentication and key agreement based on chebyshev chaotic maps for WSN. The proposed method provides security features e.g. secure session-key agreement, freely password changing facility and user anonymity. This method of authentication is resilience against user impersonation attack, password & identity guessing attack and replay attack, GWN bypass attack and privileged insider attack. Furthermore, this strategy was proved to be effective in detecting unauthorised logins with incorrect identification and password. The formal security proof is accompanied using BAN. The performance evaluation shows that the scheme is competent for resource constrained networks. In addition, this authentication method is also considered the efficiency comparison based on security features is also considered. However, this authentication scheme failed to provided data integrity, which was played significant role in the case of login and registration phase. Zhu et al. [24] proposed user-friendly authentication method called Duth for android smartphone. The time and location of the user entering patterns on the touch screen are saved in this technique, and the stored data is used to authenticate the user. The experimentation results proved that this method was an efficient in providing the dual factor authentication. However, security analysis is not performed over the cryptographic attacks. Granjal et al. [25] developed ECC based mutual authentication method that supports end-to-end transport layer security communication. This scheme proposed architecture enabled security at the transport layer that supports DTLS security. The proposed method protected low-energy wireless communication environment against internet-originated threats. The TelosB sensing device, Linux host and TinyOS were employed to perform experimental evaluation. However, this scheme is vulnerable to several cryptographic threats such as eavesdropping, cloning & disclosure attack, brute force & forgery attack. Ray et al. [26] demonstrated a flexible approach for the improvement of security in the Internet Key Exchange (IKE) protocol. This approach is based on the ECC-based public key certificate to provide secret key negotiation. The main advantage of this method was to use ECC than RSA, which provides less computation cost, low network traffic and high processing speed. However, this method is vulnerable against brute force attack, forgery attack and disclosure attack. An ECC-based protocol for device-to-device communication in smart cities has been devised by Dang et al. [32]. They claimed that cryptographic attacks cannot defeat their strategy. However, the security features like location privacy and anonymity could not be provided by the protocol. Their protocol is also susceptible to DoS attack. The summarization of aforementioned discussion is illustrated in the Table 2.

Table 2. Analysis of IoT authentication scheme based on two-way authentication procedure

Network Model	L	H/F	AD	(✔: Strength)/ (×: Weakness)
User, Gateway node, Cluster Head and Sensor node in WSN [19]	P + N + A	F	Wireless Sensor Network	✔ Security of smart card stolen is considered, ✔ Resistance to impersonation attack and node capture attack, × Verification delay is not considered, × Message delay is not considered
Devices, RFID tags and Sensor Nodes in IoT environment [20]	P + N + A	F	Wireless Sensor Network	✔ Resistance to MITM attack, ✔ Performance measurement is considered, × No consideration of Replay and DoS attack
User, RFID tag, RFID reader in IoT environment [21]	P + N	F	Generic IoT application	✔ Authentication of RFID tag and RFID reader, × No regard of location privacy, × Security and performance analysis is not considered
User, MTC server, 3GPP, Home AAA server, Proxy AAA server, Local authentication server in IoT network [22]	P + N + A	F	Generic IoT application	✔ Protection from MITM and DoS threat, Identity security is ignored, × Location privacy is not considered
User, Gateway Node, Sensor Node in WSN [23]	P + N	H	Wireless Sensor Network	✔ Identity security is implemented, ✔ Cost of computation and storage is taken into account, × No consideration for data integrity

(*continued*)

Table 2. (*continued*)

Network Model	L	H/F	AD	(✔: Strength)/ (×: Weakness)
User, Android smartphone in mobile environment [24]	P	H	Mobile Network application	✔ Dual factor authentication is introduced, ✔ Improvement in security without addition of any hardware, × Security analysis is not performed over cryptographic attacks
Sensor, Access control server and Certification authority [25]	A + N + P	H	Internet-integrated sensing application	✔ Efficient in resource constrained network due to employment of ECC, × Vulnerable to eavesdropping, cloning attack, disclosure attack, brute force attack and forgery attack
Initiator and Responder in Internet [26]	A + N + P	H	Internet application	✔ ECC-based certificate requires less computation cost and high processing speed compared to RSA, × Vulnerable to brute force attack, forgery and disclosure attack
Device and Server in smart cities [32]	N + P	H	Smart city	✔ Efficient key management, Resilience to replay, MITM and forgery attacks × Location privacy and anonymity not considered, × Susceptible to DoS attack

2.2.3 Taxonomy of Authentication Schemes Based on Three-Way Authentication Procedure

Lai et al. [27] developed a group temporary key to enable a group-based authentication technique for LTE networks. This method offered a secure and efficient AKA protocol called SE-AKA to fit in the LTE networks. This authentication scheme also provides the privacy-preservation based on ECDH algorithm, which achieves forward/backward confidentiality. However, the identity privacy is not examined and this method cannot authentication cluster of machines at the same time. Shao et al. [28] and [29] propounded an authentication mechanism for VANETs. During vehicle communication, the method is specified by the usage of a group signature technique to achieve authentication, traceability and anonymity. However, the performance evaluation in terms of communication overhead is not carried out. Nicanfar et al. [30] presented a protocol for connecting smart meters to the smart grid network, as well as a novel key management method. This method considered two important features while constructing a smart grid: data transmitted to the control unit should come from a genuine smart meter and there should be no means of revealing the customer's style by analysing his electricity use. This method is efficient in respect to computation and communication cost, according to the performance analysis. Du et al. [31] presented a framework for analysing the security of WSN key predistribution schemes, which increases the network's resiliency over earlier systems. This scheme is flexible & scalable, and implemented on MICAz sensor nodes. However, this method is not efficient in terms of energy. A user authentication system for cloud-IoT model based healthcare services was proposed by Sharma and Kalra [33]. The feature of anonymity for sensor nodes is not ensured by their approach. A safe mutual authentication method was created in 2021 by Shamshad et al. [34] for healthcare services. They claimed that their strategy is resistant against offline password guessing, replay, insider, and masquerade cryptography attacks. However, it is discovered that their strategy is unable to use AVISPA to give formal security verification. The summarization of aforementioned discussion is illustrated in the Table 3.

Table 3. Analysis of IoT authentication scheme based on three-way authentication procedure

Network Model	L	H/F	AD	(✔: Strength)/ (×: Weakness)
Sensor Nodes in WSN [31]	N	H	Wireless Sensor Network	✔ Strength to tolerate node capture attack, × Not Energy efficient
Mobile phone, home evolved node, mobile management entity, serving gateway and home subscriber server [27]	A + N + P	F	Mobile network and Application	✔ Protection from redirection attack, DoS, & MITM attacks, The privacy of identity & location is not considered, × Impossible to authenticate a large number of devices at once

(continued)

Table 3. (*continued*)

Network Model	L	H/F	AD	(✔: Strength)/ (×: Weakness)
Central authority, tracing manager, road side unit and on-board unit in vehicular ad hoc network [28, 29]	N + P	H	Vehicular Networks	✔ Cost of computation cost is low, ✔ Defending against replay attack, × Communication overhead is not examined
Authentication agent, smart grid and security associate in smart grid communication [30]	N + P	F	Smart Grid Application	✔ Resistance to various attacks e.g. DoS, replay, brutforce and MITM, ✔ Key management is safe, ✔ Low communication cost, × Integrity & Confidentiality are not taken into account
Cloud server, gateway node and sensors [33]	A + N + P	H	Cloud-IoT based networks	✔ Protection from MITM, brute force, dictionary and offline password guessing attacks, ✔ Provides session key management × Unable to provide user anonymity
Patient and server [34]	A + N + P	H	Healthcare network	✔ Provide device anonymity, ✔ Resilience to MITM, brute force, dictionary & offline password guessing attacks, × Provides session key agreement

3 Discussion

From the above discussions, it is very clear that the existing schemes available for authentication faced a lot of challenges. The existing authentication schemes are not feasible for resource constrained networks due to higher storage, communication and computation overhead. The authentication schemes required lightweight cryptographic primitives to reduce the computation and storage overhead in resource constrained environment. The schemes [19, 23, 32, 33, 34] make use of lightweight cryptographic primitives, which indicates the schemes are well-suited for resource constrained networks. Moreover, some schemes have used certificate based authentication and RSA based authentication but this type of authentications are not feasible in resource constrained network. There are some existing schemes [25, 26, 33, 34] based on ECC and hash function, which is feasible for IoT enabled networks. ECC and hash functions are used by authentication schemes, which enable faster computing operations as compared to RSA and digital certificates. The schemes employed for authentication are not resilience against various cryptographic attacks and security threats. In some authentication schemes, Informal security analysis and formal security verification have not performed for showing the strength of authentication scheme.

4 Conclusions

Supporting trusted and authenticated communication between IoT objects is a key of successful and wide deployment of services provided over IoT. This paper presents a taxonomy and a literature review of authentication schemes in the IoT context. The authentication schemes are categorized as various factors including authentication procedure, authentication factor and token based authentication. Various authentication schemes such as cloud-based IoT, lightweight, decentralized blockchain-based, and biometrics-based remote user authentication were analyzed. Researchers proposed various authentication schemes, which might be different from each other and applicable across different domains. Finally, the survey highlights the main issues and challenges in IoT authentication, which recommends future research directions.

References

1. Kogias, D.G., Michailidis, E.T., Tuna, G., Gungor, V.C.: Realizing the wireless technology in internet of things (IOT). In: Emerging Wireless Communication and Network Technologies: Principle, Paradigm and Performance, pp. 173–192 (2018)
2. Tripathi, A., Singh, A.K., Choudhary, P., Vashist, P.C., Mishra, K.K.: Significance of wireless technology in Internet of Things (IoT) Mach. Learn. Cognitive Comput. Mobile Commun. Wireless Netw., 131–154 (2020)
3. Amarilli, F., Amigoni, F., Fugini, M.G., Zarri, G.P.: A semantic-rich approach to IoT using the generalized world entities paradigm. In: Managing the Web of Things, pp. 105–147. Morgan Kaufmann (2017)
4. Taha, W. et al.: Acumen: An Open-Source Testbed for Cyber-Physical Systems Research. In: Mandler, B., et al. (ed.) Internet of Things. IoT Infrastructures. IoT360 2015. LNICST, vol. 169. Springer, Cham (2016). https://doi.org/10.1007/978-3-319-47063-4_11
5. Lopes, N.V., Pinto, F., Furtado, P., Silva, J.: IoT architecture proposal for disabled people. In: IEEE 10th International Conference on Wireless and Mobile Computing, Networking and Communications (WiMob), pp. 152–158. IEEE (2014)
6. Wang, J., Wang, H., Zhang, H.: A trust and attribute-based access control framework in internet of things. Int. J. Embedded Syst. **12**(1), 116–124 (2020)
7. https://www.cisco.com/en/us/solutions/collateral/executive-perspectives/annual-internet-report/white-paper-c11-741490.html
8. Abomhara, M., Køien, G.M.: Security and privacy in the Internet of Things: Current status and open issues. In: International conference on privacy and security in mobile systems (PRISMS), pp. 1–8. IEEE (2014)
9. El-Hajj, M., Fadlallah, A. Chamoun, M., Serhrouchni, A.: A survey of internet of things (IoT) authentication schemes. Sensors **19**(5), 1141 (2019)

10. Verma, U., Bhardwaj, D.: Centralised and distributed authentication scheme in internet of things: review and outlook. Inter. J. Internet Technol. Sec. Trans. **12**(2), 127–160 (2022)
11. Chae, C.-J., Choi, K.-N., Choi, K., Yae, Y.-H., Shin, Y.: The extended authentication protocol using e-mail authentication in OAuth 2.0 protocol for secure granting of user access. J. Internet Comput. Serv. **16**(1), 21–28 (2015)
12. Moghaddam, F.F.: A scalable and efficient user authentication scheme for cloud computing environments. In: IEEE Region 10 Symposium, pp. 508–513. IEEE (2014)
13. Bamasag, O.O.; Youcef-Toumi, K.: Towards continuous authentication in Internet of things based on secret sharing scheme, In Proceedings of the WESS'15: Workshop on Embedded Systems Security, Amsterdam, The Netherlands, 4–9 October, (2015)
14. Hamidi, H.: An approach to develop the smart health using Internet of Things and authentication based on biometric technology. Future Gen. Comput. Syst. **91**, 434–449 (2019)
15. Brian, A., Aro, L., Arockiam, L., Malarchelvi, P.D.S.K.: An IOT based secured smart library system with NFC based book tracking. Inter. J. Emerging Technol. Comput. Sci. Electr. (IJETCSE) **11**(5), 18–21 (2014)
16. Sbeyti, H., El Hage, B., Fadlallah, A.: Mobile user signature extraction based on user behavioural pattern (MUSEP). Inter. J. Pervas. Comput. Commun. **12**(4), 421–446 (2016)
17. Emerson, S., Choi, Y.-K., Hwang, D.-Y., Kim, K.-S., Kim, K.-H.: An OAuth based authentication mechanism for IoT networks. In: International Conference on Information and Communication Technology Convergence (ICTC), pp. 1072–1074. IEEE (2015)
18. Chae, C.J., Choi, K.N., Choi, K., Yae, Y.H., Shin, Y.: The extended authentication protocol using E-mail authentication in OAuth 2.0 Protocol for Secure Granting of User Access. J. Internet Comput. Serv., **16**, 21–28 (2015)
19. Gope, P., Hwang, T.: A realistic lightweight anonymous authentication protocol for securing real-time application data access in wireless sensor networks. IEEE Trans. Industr. Electron. **63**(11), 7124–7132 (2016)
20. Schmitt, C., Noack, M. Stiller, B.: TinyTO: two-way authentication for constrained devices in the Internet of Things, Internet of Things, pp. 239–258 (2016)
21. Lee, J.Y., Lin, W.C., Huang, Y.H.: A lightweight authentication protocol for internet of things. In: International Symposium on Next-Generation Electronics (ISNE), IEEE, pp. 1–2 (2014)
22. Lai, C., Lu, R., Zheng, D., Li, H., Shen, X.S.: GLARM: Group-based lightweight authentication scheme for resource-constrained machine to machine communications. Comput. Netw. **99**, 66–81 (2016)
23. Kumari, S., Li, X., Wu, F., Das, A.K., Arshad, H., Khan, M.K.: A user friendly mutual authentication and key agreement scheme for wireless sensor networks using chaotic maps. Futur. Gener. Comput. Syst. **63**, 56–75 (2016)
24. Zhu, H., Lin, X., Zhang, Y., Lu, R.: Duth: a user-friendly dual-factor authentication for Android smartphone devices. Security and Communication Networks **8**(7), 1213–1222 (2015)
25. Granjal, J., Monteiro, E., Sa Silva, J.: End-to-end transport-layer security for Internet-integrated sensing applications with mutual and delegated ECC public-key authentication. In: IFIP Networking Conference, pp. 1–9. IEEE (2013)
26. Ray, S., Biswas, G.P.: Establishment of ECC-based initial secrecy usable for IKE implementation. In Proceedings of the World Congress on Engineering, vol. 1 (2012)
27. Lai, C., Li, H., Lu, R., Shen, X.S.: SE-AKA: a secure and efficient group authentication and key agreement protocol for LTE networks. Comput. Netw. **57**(17), 3492–3510 (2013)
28. Shao, J., Lu, R., Lin, X., Zuo, C.: New threshold anonymous authentication for VANETs. In: IEEE/CIC International Conference on Communications in China (ICCC), pp. 1–6. IEEE (2015)
29. Shao, J., Lin, X., Rongxing, L., Zuo, C.: A threshold anonymous authentication protocol for VANETs. IEEE Trans. Veh. Technol. **65**(3), 1711–1720 (2015)

30. Nicanfar, H., Jokar, P., Leung, V.C.M.: Smart grid authentication and key management for unicast and multicast communications. In: IEEE PES Innovative Smart Grid Technologies, pp. 1–8. IEEE (2011)
31. Du, W., Deng, J., Han, Y.S., Varshney, P.K., Katz, J., Khalili, A.: A pairwise key predistribution scheme for wireless sensor networks. ACM Trans. Inform. Syst. Sec. (TISSEC) **8**(2), 228–258 (2005)
32. Dang, T.K., Pham, C.D., Nguyen, T.L.: A pragmatic elliptic curve cryptography-based extension for energy-efficient device-to-device communications in smart cities. Sustain. Cities Soc. **56**, 102097 (2020)
33. Sharma, G., Kalra, S.: A lightweight user authentication scheme for cloud-IoT based healthcare services. Iranian J. Sci. Technol. Trans. Electr. Eng. **43**, 619–636 (2019)
34. Shamshad, S., Ayub, M.F., Mahmood, K., Kumari, S., Chaudhry, S.A., Chen, C.M.: An enhanced scheme for mutual authentication for healthcare services. Digital Commun. Netw. **8**(2), 150–161 (2022)

A Multi-stage Encryption Technique Using Asymmetric and Various Symmetric Ciphers

Habibur Rahman[1], Kazi Md. Rokibul Alam[1(✉)], and Yasuhiko Morimoto[2]

[1] Department of Computer Science and Engineering, Khulna University of Engineering and Technology (KUET), Khulna 9203, Bangladesh
rahman2107552@stud.kuet.ac.bd, rokib@cse.kuet.ac.bd

[2] Graduate School of Advanced Science and Engineering, Hiroshima University, Higashi-Hiroshima 739-8521, Japan

Abstract. Retaining privacy is essential to protect sensitive data from tampering or unauthorized access. The multi-stage encryption (MSE) technique reinforces data privacy against continual cyber-attacks by incorporating multiple encryption techniques consecutively. For this purpose, this paper proposes an MSE technique that embodies asymmetric, chaotic, and substitution ciphers together. Here, the first one uses a public key, but the later ones rely on a dynamic and an apathetic shared key, respectively. Thus, the plain data is (*i*) first reformed into the asymmetric cipher, (*ii*) then converted into the chaotic cipher, and (*iii*) further transformed into the substitution cipher, respectively. As a result, the designed MSE technique is proficient enough to protect text, images, etc., forms of data against different security attacks by enhancing the confusion level. Various experimental results, security analyses, comparisons with existing works, etc., prove the efficacy of the designed technique.

Keywords: Asymmetric cryptosystem · Chaotic neural network · Substitution cipher · DNA bases · Security analyses

1 Introduction

Owing to resource sharing and workload distribution, regularly data migrates among various computing sites. Unknown access paths, undefined perimeters, the anonymity of attackers, etc., threats [1] lead to cause various cyber-attacks. Here, encryption techniques restrain unauthorized entities from grasping the delicate data and thus assure data confidentiality. However, the usage of feebly encrypted data causes data leaks or data hacking. Regarding this issue, the recent data breach incidents of First American Financial Corp., Capital One Bank, Bangladesh Biman email server hack [2, 3], etc., are noteworthy. Hence, a reinforced data encryption technique is important for numerous computer systems developed based on computer networks, parallel, distributed, pervasive, ubiquitous, etc., computing.

Classical cryptosystems, *e.g.*, Caesar cipher, Vernam cipher, etc., exploit a private key where methods are fast and inexpensive. However, due to limited key sizes, they are not

N. Chauhan et al. (Eds.): MIND 2023, CCIS 2128, pp. 323–335, 2024.
https://doi.org/10.1007/978-3-031-62217-5_27

flexible and breach without difficulty [4]. Likewise, symmetric cryptosystems, *e.g.*, DES, AES, etc., also rely on a shared secret key and can quickly process massive amounts of data. Yet, they are inefficient with key exchange, the strength of secrecy, various attacks, etc. In contrast, the public-private key-pair-based asymmetric cryptosystems, *e.g.*, RSA, ElGamal, etc., assure better secrecy. But they are also supposed to be vulnerable to various malicious attacks, tricky cryptanalysis, high-speed computations [5], etc. Here, all these perform only single-stage encryption. Whereas, successively integrating distinct encryption methods, a multi-stage encryption (MSE) technique can offer enhanced data secrecy [6]. Although it may require slightly higher computations than the single-stage ones, by assuring enriched data privacy, it is capable enough to confine attackers from mounting various cyber-attacks. Hence, the MSE technique is admired.

This paper proposes an MSE technique that successively combines asymmetric, chaotic, and substitution ciphers. From the input data, it yields (*i*) the initial cipher through Paillier encryption, then (*ii*) re-encrypts it via the chaotic neural network (ChNN), and finally, (*iii*) masks it into DNA bases by using the substitution cipher. Here, the Paillier encryption can generate a relatively larger key size and yield probabilistic encryption output as well and its cryptanalysis is quite hard [6]. Besides, the ChNN is too sensitive to initial conditions and generates highly unpredictable encryption output [7]. Also, the substitution by DNA bases enriches the level of confusion. Thus, the entangling of the asymmetric and various symmetric ciphers reinforces the final cipher to resist various undefined cyber-attacks. The evaluation results ensure its efficacy.

The remaining part of this paper is organized as follows. Section 2 surveys the related works. Section 3 describes the required cryptographic tools. Section 4 illustrates the proposed MSE technique. Section 5 explains the evaluation along with the NIST security test analyses and Sect. 5.4 finally concludes the paper.

2 Related Works

To enhance data privacy, combining multiple encryption methods is already available. Namely, considering symmetric and asymmetric encryption methods, the works proposed in [8–10] leveraged the strength of both ones. For instance, by employing DES and RSA, the encryption method proposed in [8] assured a better performance for horizontally partitioned data than using the single DES or RSA. Similarly, the work in [9] engaged the Blowfish symmetric cryptosystem along with RSA for encryption, and stored this data over the cloud. Also, by using the HMAC hash technique and employing a combination of AES and RSA, the work in [10] developed a well-secure system. However, symmetric encryption methods usually produce deterministic output if they exploit the same key. At the same time, RSA also produces the deterministic encryption output [19]. Hence, these works were suitable to encrypt secret data only, and not appropriate to hide any sort of public data.

Likewise, uniting chaos with symmetric or asymmetric encryption methods, various MSE techniques were proposed [11, 12]. The work in [11] used the Arnold chaos sequence to produce multiple round keys, first encrypting the plain image via a modified AES method, and then performing further encryptions via the round keys, and is capable to resist attacks, *e.g.*, brute force, various statistical ones, etc. By incorporating chaos with an asymmetric encryption method, the work in [12] first produced a compressed image, then encrypted via a 4D chaos map, and re-encrypted by the elliptic curve ElGamal scheme. However, Arnold's chaotic map is not so robust against external noise and a small perturbation can amplify and affect the system's behavior quickly. Also, some works use a symmetric cryptosystem to encrypt the data that encrypt the key via an asymmetric cryptosystem, usually, known as hybrid cryptosystems [6].

Besides, considering various chaotic models along with DNA bases, several MSE techniques were also proposed to encrypt the image. Namely, the work proposed in [14] produced a pseudo-random sequence by using a logistic-based chaos model to process the image and then applying rule-based DNA bases to mask this processed image. However, herein the usage of the logistic chaos model possessed inferior chaotic behavior and distinguishability [15]. Another work proposed in [16] utilized a 5D hyper-chaos model and DNA bases with a fixed secret key. Then, it executed both pixel-level and DNA-level diffusion and permutation while rearranging the pixel values. But, here the usage of a fixed secret key degraded the level of flexibility.

Moreover, by merging multiple chaos models, DNA bases with chaos, multiple DNA bases, etc., diverse encryption methods are available. Namely, the work in [13] considered medical image as its input and exploited multiple chaos models, *i.e.*, the Logistic map and the Lorenz attractor to accomplish the initial and the final encryption, respectively. By integrating a chaos model with the DNA bases and considering the text data, the work in [7] developed an MSE method. It produced the initial cipher through a random key generated via the chaos and then substituted that one via DNA bases. Considering an asymmetric encryption method with multiple DNA bases, *i.e.*, dynamic sequence table and dynamic DNA encoding, the encryption method in [5] analyzed its applicability for text data only.

Unlike the above ones, the proposed MSE technique (*i*) considers both text and image as the input, and (*ii*) combines asymmetric with various symmetric ciphers to enrich the data privacy. Initially, it transforms the plain data into a numeric value, divides it into smaller blocks and encrypts it via an asymmetric cryptosystem. Now for re-encryption, it converts these ciphers into binary values for executing the XOR operation with a key randomly generated via a chaos model. Finally, it substitutes these outputs with DNA bases. Here, the usage of (*i*) the Paillier encryption to produce the asymmetric cipher assures a promising strength because of its complex security parameters and probabilistic encryption output, (*ii*) the ChNN with time-varying delay to yield a symmetric cipher confers a higher pseudo-randomness and makes harder for intruders to guess the correct sequence of the key, and (*iii*) the DNA bases as the substitution cipher extends the key space. Thus, it can resist various attacks.

3 Cryptographic Building Blocks

For data encryption, the proposed MSE technique relies on Paillier encryption, delayed ChNN and DNA bases to produce the asymmetric and various symmetric ciphers, respectively. Their descriptions are as below.

3.1 Paillier Encryption.

The Paillier encryption [6] usually considers plain data in integer form as its input, produces probabilistic encryption output, and is renowned for its strong security properties. Its strength relies on the Decisional Composite Residuosity Assumption (DCRA), which is computationally hard to resolve. It consists of three stages, *i.e.*, key generation, encryption, and decryption, and their descriptions are as below.

Key Generation. At first two large primes p and q are chosen to calculate the modulus n as $n = p.q$ and a random number g is selected as the generator of the multiplicative group of integers modulo n. Now, the least common multiple (lcm) of (p-1) and (q-1) is calculated as $\lambda = \text{lcm}\ (p\text{-}1)(q\text{-}1)$. To ensure that n divides the order of g, the existence of the multiplicative inverse $\mu = (L(g^{\lambda} \bmod n^2))^{-1} \bmod n$ is calculated where $L(x)$ is defined as $L(x) = (x\text{-}1)/n$. At last, (n, g) is declared as the public encryption key and (λ, μ) is kept as the private decryption key.

Encryption. To encrypt the message m $(0 \leq m < n)$, a random integer r $(0 < r < n)$ is opted where gcd $(r, n) = 1$. Now the ciphertext c is calculated as $c = g^m.r^n \bmod n^2$.

Decryption. The ciphertext c is decrypted, *i.e.*, the message m is retrieved as $m = L\ (c^{\lambda} \bmod n^2).\mu \bmod n$.

3.2 Chaotic Neural Network (ChNN).

The ChNN is capable of generating a very complex random key and usually receives the input data in binary form. Due to being highly sensitive to initial conditions, it is difficult to predict or replicate its key, which turns it into an effective data encryption tool. The proposed MSE technique adopts a hopfiled ChNN with time delay functions [7] to protect against various potential attacks of the asymmetric cipher. It also consists of key generation, encryption, and decryption stages, and is described below.

Key Generation. First, it generates random sequences from trajectories and then transforms them into binary sequences where Eq. (1) denotes the trajectories. Here, n (≥ 2) number of neural networks (NNs) is employed where $y(t) = (y_1(t), y_2(t)\ldots, y_n(t))^{\mathrm{T}} \in R_n$ represents the state vectors. The activation function, the external input vector, and the delay are represented as $f(y(t))$, I, and $\tau(t)$, respectively. The initial conditions to implement the NN are $y_i(t) = \alpha_i\ (t) \in C([-r, 0], R)$ where $r = \max_{((1 \leq i), (j \leq n), (t \in \mathrm{R}))}\{\tau_{ij}(t)\}$ and $C([-r, 0], R)$ is the set of continuous functions from $[-r, 0]$ to R, C is a diagonal matrix, A is the weight matrix for each connection, and B is the delayed connection.

$$y(t) = -Cy(t) + Af(y(t)) + Bf(x(t - \Gamma(t))) + 1 \tag{1}$$

which can be extended as

$$y(t) = -c_i y_i(t) + \sum\nolimits_{j=1}^{n} a_{ij} f_i(y_i(t)) + \sum\nolimits_{j=1}^{n} b_{ij} f_i\big(y_i\big(t - \tau_{ij}(t)\big)\big) + I_i;\ i = 1, 2, \ldots, n \tag{2}$$

To generate the binary random sequence the method available in [7] is adopted that shows both independence and uniformity. In the interval of $[s, t]$, a map $y(.)$ is defined as in Eq. (2) where $(y - s) / (t - s) \in [0, 1]$ results in a binary outcome.

$$\frac{y-s}{t-s} =, 0.a_1(y).a_2(y)\ldots, a_i(y), y \in [s, t]a_i(y) \in \{0, 1\} \tag{3}$$

In *Eq.* (3), the ith bit $a_i(y)$ is explained as

$$a_i(y) = -\sum_{j=1}^{2^i-1} (-1)^{j-1} \varnothing_{(t-2)(j\div 2^i)+s}(y) \tag{4}$$

The random binary sequence generates through a sequence of nth iteration where the threshold function is represented by $\varnothing_t(y)$. If $(y < \text{t})$ then $\varnothing_t(y) = 0$, , and while $(y \geq T)$ then, $\varnothing_t(y) = 1$. The binary sequence is represented as $R_n^i = \{a_i(y_n)\}_{n=0}^{\infty}$.

To solve Eq. (2) the fourth-order Runge-Kutta (RK) method is applied. Also, to obtain the trajectories $y_1(t)$ and $y_2(t)$, the number of NN (n) is set to 2, and the time step h is set to 0.01. The other parameters are chosen as A = [2.0, − 0.1], [−5.0, 3.0], B = [−1.5, − 0.1], [−0.2, − 2.5], C = [1, 0], [0, 1], $f_1(y_i(t)) = \tanh(y_i(t))$, and $\tau = 1 + (0.1 \times \sin(t))$ with initial function $\phi(t) = [0.4, 0.6]^T$ and a time interval of [−1.1, 0]. The binary sequence is generated according to Eq. (3) by iterations where each binary bit is computed by Eq. (4). The output of this sequence will be 42 bit-long (s), from which the initial 32-bit is kept as the shared key (k) to be used for both encryption and decryption purposes. The next 9 bits determine a decimal value (d), and the last bit of the sequence (l) represents the selected trajectory.

Encryption. For encryption, initially, the message is transformed into the corresponding binary value (if it is in different form), and then it is divided into fixed length chunks (each one denoted as p equal to 32 bit). Here, the length of p and k must be the same. Now, each chunk is left circular shifted up to d times and an XOR operation is performed with the 32-bit key k to generate the cipher. Finally, the resulting chunk ciphers are concatenated.

Decryption. For decryption, at first the concatenated cipher is divided into fixed-sized chunks (equal to k, *i.e.*, 32-bit), now the cipher of each chunk is XOR-ed with the 32-bit key k. Then, each resulting data is right circular shifted up to d times which retrieves the binary message of each chunk. Finally, after concatenation, the entire message is regained.

3.3 DNA Bases as Substitution Cipher

For encryption, the substitution cipher replaces the contents of a message with other symbols. When DNA bases are used for substitution cipher, its four bases, *i.e.*, A, C, T, and G, are used to represent a binary message. The three stages, *i.e.*, key generation, encryption, and decryption to process this cipher are as below.

Key Generation. The value of the four DNA bases are assigned as 00 = A, 01 = G, 10 = C, and 11 = T.

Encryption. While encryption, the entire message in binary form is substituted according to the keys. Then, the ciphertext remains in the pattern of four DNA bases.

Decryption. For decrypting, the ciphertext in DNA form is altered in the reverse order of the encryption process. Thus, the plaintext is retrieved in its binary form.

4 The Proposed MSE Technique

To enhance data privacy, *i.e.*, to encrypt the text, the image, etc., data, the proposed MSE technique successively applies multiple distinct encryption methods through deploying their keys accordingly. The overall process is organized through three major stages, *i.e.*, key setup, encryption, and decryption which are described below.

4.1 Key Setup

As previously discussed, for successive encryption (and later on decryption) purposes, the proposed technique relies on the following keys, *i.e.*, (*i*) the public-private key-pair of Paillier encryption, (*ii*) the shared-key of ChNN, and (*iii*) the static swap-keys of DNA bases. Here, how the entities, *e.g.*, the receiver and the sender generate these keys are described below. Algorithm 1 describes the overall procedure.

Algorithm 1: Key Setup of the Proposed MSE Technique	
Input: Various parameters (*e.g.*, p, q, g, s, A, G, C, T, *etc.*) used by the sender for encryption **Output:** Various parameters (*e.g.*, λ, μ, s, A, G, C, T) used by the receiver for decryption	
Step 1: Generation of Paillier Keys	
1.	Receiver creates private key (λ, μ) and announces public key (n, g) of Paillier encryption
Step 2: Generation of 42 bit shared Key of ChNN	
1.	Sender generates a 42-bit shared-key (s) including (k, d, l) of ChNN
Step 3: Initiation of DNA swap Keys	
1.	Establish swap-keys of DNA bases (*i.e.*, 00 = A, 01 = G, 10 = C, and 11 = T)

Step 1: At first, to generate the public-private key pair of Paillier encryption, the receiver picks two sufficiently large primes (p, q), and a generator g. Now it calculates the public key (n, g) to disclose to be used by the allied sender for encryption. At the same time, it calculates the private key (λ, μ) to keep to itself to be used for decryption purposes. These are performed based on the key generation of Sect. 3.1 (*i.e.*, Algorithm 1, Step 1, line 1).

Step 2: To be used by both the sender and the receiver, *i.e.*, to encrypt and decrypt the chaotic cipher, the shared-key of ChNN is generated as follows. For this purpose, at first, the sender (or an entity who is considered trusted for the system) generates two trajectories, randomly picks any one of them, and converts the picked one into its corresponding binary value via iteration which generates the ultimate 42-bit shared-key (denoted as s). From s, the first 32 bits (denoted as k) are dedicated for XOR-ing with the data, the next 9 bits (denoted as d) are used for the left circular shifting of the data, and the last bit (denoted as l) is used to choose the trajectory. Finally, by using the

Paillier encryption key the sender encrypts the value of s, *i.e.*, (k, d, l) and sends them to the receiver from which through decryption the receiver regains these parameters (*i.e.*, Algorithm 1, Step 2, line 1).

Step 3: Analogous to the previous step, *i.e.*, while dealing with the substitution cipher, the sender (or a trusted entity) and the receiver jointly settle the swap-keys of DNA bases as A = 00, G = 01, C = 10, and T = 11, in advance (*i.e.*, Algorithm 1, Step 3, line 1).

Thus, through the utilization of these keys, successively the plain data turns into the ultimate cipher data.

4.2 The Encryption Process

To initiate the proposed encryption process, first, the sender needs to encrypt data via the receiver's Paillier public key (n, g), re-encrypt the cipher data by ChNN's shared.

key s, and finally, swap the re-encrypted cipher with DNA bases A, G, C, and T. The overall process is presented in Algorithm 2 and it is described below.

Algorithm 2: Multi-stage Encryption	
Input: Text or image in plain form **Output:** Text or image in highly confused cipher form	
Step 1: Formation of Asymmetric Cipher	
1.	Create data blocks using four consecutive values
2.	Transform each data block by using the Paillier public key (n, g)
Step 2: Construction of Chaotic cipher	
1.	Convert the asymmetric cipher blocks into binary values
2.	Divide each block into 32-bit chunks and apply zero padding if rightmost chunk is less than 32 bits
3.	Execute d times left circular shift operation over each chunk
4.	Apply XOR operation over it with ChNN's 32-bit key k
Step 3: Production of Substitution cipher	
1.	Swap the output with static DNA keys
2.	Merge chunks of DNA bases to produce the final cipher

Step 1: First, scan data to convert it into numeric (integer) form (*i.e.*, Algorithm 2, Step 1, line 1).

(a) If the input data is text, replace each character/symbol within the plain form with its corresponding 3-digit ASCII value. Now, create each block by considering every four 3-digit ASCII values (*i.e.*, $4 \times 3 = 12$ digits).
(b) If the input is an image, convert each pixel into R, G, and B channels. Then, by joining the channel values create each block by selecting four 3-digit values (*i.e.*, $4 \times 3 = 12$ digits).

Here, in both cases, the rightmost block may contain less than four values.

Step 2: Encrypt each block (according to the encryption of Sect. 3.1) using the public key (n, g) of Paillier encryption to produce the asymmetric cipher (*i.e.*, Algorithm 2, Step 1, line 2).

Step 3: Convert it into the corresponding binary values (*i.e.*, Algorithm 2, Step 2, line 1).

Step 4: Split the binary values within each block cipher into 32-bit chunks. Apply zero padding over the rightmost chunk if its' size is smaller than 32-bit. Keep track of the padded position to let the receiver know it (*i.e.*, Algorithm 2, Step 2, line 2).

Step 5: Perform d times left circular shift operation over every 32-bit chunk (*i.e.*, Algorithm 2, Step 2, line 3).

Step 6: Perform XOR operation between this 32-bit output of each chunk and the generated 32-bit shared key k to produce the chaotic cipher (*i.e.*, Algorithm 2, Step 2, line 4).

Step 7: Split the resultant ciphers into two-digit binary groups and apply DNA swap keys to substitute the binary groups with the static DNA bases (as in Sect. 3.3) (*i.e.*, Algorithm 2, Step 3, line 1).

Step 8: Finally, concatenate them to produce the ultimate (substitution) cipher. (*i.e.*, Algorithm 2, Step 3, line 2).

4.3 Decryption Process

Usually, any decryption process works in the opposite order of the encryption process. Herein, the receiver already has (*i*) the static DNA keys, (*ii*) the shared keys (k, d, l) of the ChNN, and (*iii*) the private decryption key (λ, μ) of Paillier encryption. Now deploying these separate keys, the receiver consecutively retrieves the plain data through the following decryption process.

Step 1: First, scan the ultimate cipher to substitute each DNA base with the corresponding two-digit binary values by static DNA swap-keys (as in Sect. 3.3).

Step 2: Merge all binary values and divide them into 32-bit chunks to regain the chaotic cipher.

Step 3: Perform XOR operation between every 32-bit chunk and the generated 32-bit shared key k.

Step 4: Perform d times right circular shift operation over every resultant chunk.

Step 5: Remove Zero padding from the tracked position (if any).

Step 6: Transform each binary cipher chunk into integer values to retrieve the asymmetric cipher.

Step 7: Decrypt the asymmetric cipher of each chunk (according to the decryption of Sect. 3.1) by using Pailler's secret key (λ, μ).

Step 8: Divide them into 3-digit blocks.

(a) If the data is text, convert each block into its corresponding character based on the ASCII value to regain the plain form.
(b) If the data is an image, arrange the blocks in R, G, and B channels to reconstruct the plain from.

5 Prototype Evaluation

5.1 Experimental Setup

A prototype of the proposed MSE technique was implemented with the settings of Intel(R) Core (TM) i5-1135G7 2.40 GHz 64-bit processor with 8GB RAM operating on Windows 11 operating system using Python 3.0 programming language. For the experiment, 60-digit or less sized text and 256 × 256 size images of various formats, *i.e.*, 'jpg', 'jpeg', and 'png' was used as the input. While executing the MSE technique, the Paillier encryption was implemented through 1024-bit keys. Then, every 32-bit chunk of this cipher was XOR-ed separately through a 32-bit binary key produced by ChNN.

5.2 Output of the Proposed Encryption Process

Considering a plaintext "Khulna University of Engineering and Technology" and plain Lena image, the corresponding output of the MSE is presented in Table 1 and Table 2.

5.3 Output of the Proposed Decryption Process

Table 3 and Table 4 show the outcomes of the decryption process for the same text and the same image considered in Table 1 and Table 2, respectively.

Table 1. Output of the encryption process for plain text.

Steps	Operations
Step 1	Plain Text- "Khulna University of Engineering and Technology" Transform into ASCII and divide into multiple blocks, *i.e.*, 075104117108, 110097032085*
Step 2	Encrypt using Paillier encryption key, *i.e.*, 11520*, 1688*
Step 3	Transform into binary, *i.e.*, 1110111*, 1110111010*
Step 4	Split into 32-bit chunks, *i.e.*, 11011110100110000011011*
Step 5	Execute left circular shift, *i.e.*, 10011001101111101001100*
Step 6	Execute XOR operation, *i.e.*, 11011001000101011110000*
Step 7	Divide into 2-digit binary, *i.e.*, '11', '01', '10', '01', '00'* Substitute with DNA bases, *i.e.*, 'T', 'G', 'C', 'G', 'A',*
Step 8	Merge DNA bases, *i.e.*, TGCGAGGG*

Only a portion of the data is exposed
*

5.4 Runtime Comparisons

For similar five plain text of Table 1 and ten alike images of Table 2, the average time required for the proposed MSE technique and the comparisons with existing works are shown in Fig. 1(a) and (b), respectively. Here, encryption takes a longer time than decryption. For text data, the proposed MSE technique takes comparatively less time than [5] for both encryption and decryption. For image, the proposed technique is slower than [13] because [13] is a multi-stage chaotic approach, doesn't deploy any asymmetric crypto-technique, and hence its underlying operations are not so robust.

5.5 NIST Statistical Security Test Analyses

The robustness of the ciphertext is essential for maintaining the confidentiality of any.

Table 2. Output of the encryption process for plain image.

Steps	Operations
Step 1	Plain Image-
	Transform into RGB channel and divide into multiple blocks, *i.e.*, 154101061*, 100059*
Step 2	Encrypt using Paillier encryption key, *i.e.*, 1783887250*
Step 3	Transform into binary, *i.e.*, 101110001*, 111100 *
Step 4	Split into 32-bit chunks, *i.e.*, 1011100011010101100*
Step 5	Execute left circular shift, *i.e.*, 1001100110111101001100*
Step 6	Execute XOR operation, *i.e.*, 111010110111000110101*
Step 7	Divide into 2-digit binary, *i.e.*, '00', '01', '10', '01', '01'* Substitute with DNA bases, *i.e.*, 'A', 'G', 'C', 'G', 'G'*
Step 8	Merge DNA bases, *i.e.*, AGGCGG*

* Only a portion of the data is exposed

Table 3. Output of the decryption process for cipher text.

Steps	Operations
Step 1	Read cipher data (in DNA form), *i.e.*, TGCGAGGG* Transform DNA into binary, *i.e.*, '11', '01', '10', '01', '00'*
Step 2	Merge values and split it into 32-bit chunks, *i.e.*, 110110*
Step 3	Execute XOR operation, *i.e.*, 11011001000101011111000*
Step 4	Execute right circular shift, *i.e.*, 100110011011110100110*
Step 5	Remove zero padding (if any), *i.e.*, 10011*
Step 6	Transform into integer, *i.e.*, 11520*, 1688*
Step 7	Decrypt asymmetric cipher, *i.e.*, 075104117108*
Step 8	Divide into 3-digit groups, *i.e.*, '075', '104', '117', 108'* and convert into characters Retrieved plain text- "Khulna University of Engineering and Technology"

* Only a portion of the data is exposed

data. To verify the randomness of any ciphertext, the NIST [18] statistical test suite is considered as standard by many researchers. It consists of 15 different tests. The test results depend on the value of P. If the value > 0.01 for an individual test, it is considered as random, if not, it is considered as non-random. For the proposed MSE technique, these 15 tests have been executed. The results are presented in Table 5 for both text and image data considered in Table 1 and Table 2, respectively. To perform the test, first, the final cipher needs to transform into binary as the NIST test suite can consider only the binary data. The results in Table 5 show that, for text data the proposed technique successfully

Table 4. Output of the decryption process for cipher image.

Steps	Operations
Step 1	Read cipher data (in DNA form), i.e., AGGCGG * Transform DNA into binary, i.e., '00', '01', '10', '01'*
Step 2	Merge values and split it into 32-bit chunks, i.e., 00110*
Step 3	Execute XOR operation, i.e., 1110101101110001101 01*
Step 4	Execute right circular shift i.e., 1001100110111101001*
Step 5	Remove zero padding (if any), i.e., 10111*
Step 6	Transform into integer, i.e., 19533405*
Step 7	Decrypt asymmetric cipher, i.e., 1783887250*
Step 8	Arrange into RGB channels, i.e., [154 101 061], [100 * and reconstruct the plain image Retrieved plain image-

* Only a portion of the data is exposed

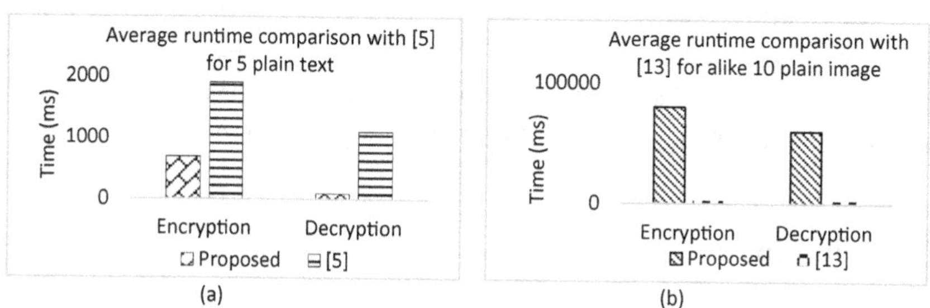

Fig. 1. Runtime comparisons for (a) text, and (b) image data.

shows random behavior for 12 tests out of 15. Alongside, for image it shows random behavior for 11 tests out of 15. Here, (√) and (-) indicate the test result is random and non-random, respectively.

Table 5. NIST Statistical Test Suite.

Statistical Test	*P*-Value(text)	Status	*P*-Value (image)	Status
Frequency (Monobit)	0.69431	√	0.01675	√
Block Frequency	0.68932	√	0.23580	√
Runs	0.42959	√	0.17950	√
Longest Run (Block)	0.89012	√	0.09671	√
Binary Matrix Rank	0.91558	√	0.17016	√
Discrete Fourier Transform (Spectral)	3.30806	–	1.00251	√
Non-Overlapping Template Matching	0.85586	√	0.27665	-
Overlapping Template Matching	0.53437	√	0.02526	√
Maurer's Universal Test	−1.0	-	1.57601	-
Linear Complexity	0.51211	√	0.1977	-
Serial	0.49896	√	0.0	√
Approximate Entropy	1.44951	-	0	-
Cumulative Sums (Forward)	0.09432	√	0.01145	√
Cumulative Sums (Backward)	0.07557	√	0.02512	√
Random Excursions Test (State +1.0)	0.78898	√	0.15499	√
Random Variant Test (State −1.0)	0.88523	√	0.80625	√

6 Conclusion

The proposed multi-stage data encryption technique consecutively incorporates asymmetric, chaotic and substitution ciphers to assure adequate privacy for various forms of data, *e.g.*, text, image, etc. Here, to generate the asymmetric cipher the utilization of the Paillier encryption technique is capable enough to produce sufficiently larger keys along with probabilistic encryption output which is desirable concerning privacy. Further, to reinforce the strength of the encryption the usage of the chaotic neural network effectively produces the random key along with a more complex crypto-system that can resist various unwanted attacks. Finally, the deployment of DNA swap-keys to produce the ultimate cipher yields a highly confused cipher output. Here, experimental results, comparisons with state-of-the-art works, NIST statistical test suite, etc., exhibit the effectiveness of the proposed technique. A future plan is to perform various security analyses, and deploy the proposed technique to encrypt the data in the environment of cloud, fog, etc., computing while considering other types of data, *e.g.*, audio, files, video, etc.

References

1. Kim, Y., Kim, I., Park, N.: Analysis of cyber attacks and security intelligence. In: Park, J., Adeli, H., Park, N., Woungang, I. (eds.) Mobile, Ubiquitous, and Intelligent Computing. LNEE, vol. 274, pp. 489–494. Springer, Berlin, Heidelberg (2014). https://doi.org/10.1007/978-3-642-40675-1_73
2. Kost, E.: 10 Biggest Data Breaches in Finance [Updated August 2022]. https://www.upguard.com/blog/biggest-data-breaches-financial-services, (Accessed 03 Sep 2023)
3. Correspondent, S.: Biman's email server hacked for five days, probe opens. https://bdnews24.com/aviation/h9x9b0dsjn, (Accessed 06 May 2023)
4. Andress, J.: The Basics of Information Security: Understanding the Fundamentals of InfoSec in Theory and Practice, 2nd edn. Syngress, Amsterdam (2014)
5. Biswas, M., Alam, K.M.R., et al.: A technique for DNA cryptography based on dynamic mechanisms. J. Inform. Sec. Appli. **48**, 102363 (2019)
6. Mondal, A., Alam, K.M.R., et al.: A multi-stage encryption technique to enhance the secrecy of image. Trans. Internet and Inf. Syst. KSII 13(5), 2698–2717 (2019)
7. Roy, S.S., Shahriyar, S.A., et al.: A novel encryption model for text messages using delayed chaotic neural network and DNA cryptography. In: 20th International Conference of Computer and Information Technology (ICCIT), Bangladesh, pp. 1–6 (2017)
8. Vashi, D., Bhadka, H., et al.: An efficient hybrid approach of attribute based encryption for privacy preserving through horizontally partitioned data. Proc. Comput. Sci. **167**, 2437–2444 (2020)
9. Ghanmi, H., Hajlaoui, N., et al.: A secure data storage in multi-cloud architecture using blowfish encryption algorithm. In: Barolli, L., (eds.) Advanced Information Networking and Applications. AINA 2022. LNNS, vol 450, pp. 398–408. Springer, Cham (2022). https://doi.org/10.1007/978-3-030-99587-4_34
10. Harba, E.S., et al.: Secure data encryption through a combination of AES, RSA and HMAC. Eng. Technol. Appli. Sci. Res. **7**, 1781–1785 (2017)
11. Arab, A., Rostami, M.J., et al.: An image encryption method based on chaos system and AES algorithm. J. Supercomput. **75**, 6663–6682 (2019)
12. Wu, J., Liao, X., Yang, B.: Color image encryption based on chaotic systems and elliptic curve ElGamal scheme. Signal Process. **141**, 109–124 (2017)
13. Tanveer, M.S.R., Alam, K.M.R., et al.: A multi-stage chaotic encryption technique for medical image. Inf. Secu. J. Global Perspect. **31**(6), 657–675 (2021)
14. Maddodi, G., Awad, A., et al.: A new image encryption algorithm based on heterogeneous chaotic neural network generator and dna encoding. Multimedia Tools Appli. **77**(19), 24701–24725 (2018)
15. Rahman, Z., et al.: Chaos and logistic map based key generation technique for AES-driven IoT security. In: Yuan, X., et al. (eds.) Quality, Reliability, Security and Robustness in Heterogeneous Systems, QShine 2021. LNICST, vol. 402. Springer, Cham (2021). https://doi.org/10.1007/978-3-030-91424-0_11
16. Liu, L., Wang D., et al.: An image encryption scheme based on hyper chaotic system and DNA with fixed secret keys. IEEE Access **8**, 46400–46416 (2020)
17. Rajput, S.K., et al.: Known-plaintext attack on encryption domain independent optical asymmetric cryptosystem. Optics Commun. **309**, 231–235 (2013)
18. Bassham, L., et al.: A Statistical Test Suite for Random and Pseudorandom Number Generators for Cryptographic Applications. NIST SP, Gaithersburg. https://tsapps.nist.gov/publication/get_pdf.cfm?pub_id=906762, (Accessed 15 Oct 2023)
19. Alam, K.M.R., Tamura S., et al.: An electronic voting scheme based on revised SVRM and confirmation numbers, IEEE Trans. Dependable Sec. Comput. (TDSC) **18**(1), 400–410 (2021)

Data Sciences

Bridging the Gap: Condensing Knowledge Graphs for Metaphor Processing by Visualizing Relationships in Figurative and Literal Expressions

Vibhavari Kamble(✉) and Yashodhara Haribhakta

COEP Technological University, Pune, India
{vvk20.comp,ybl.comp}@coeptech.ac.in

Abstract. Metaphorical expressions, being unique phrases with complex traits like disjointedness, non-compositionality, diversity, and flexible structure, are crucial in natural language tasks like translation, opinion analysis, and summarization. To handle these expressions, an inventive approach is needed. This method, using Design Science Research, relies on identifying patterns in how concepts connect through dependency parsing. It stores this knowledge by organizing it into structured scripts, utilizing Cypher statements to integrate it into a graph database. Neo4j helps visualize various nodes and attributes, allowing the study of their patterns and behaviors in both literal and figurative sentences. The accuracy of this process is assessed using machine learning models like Naive Bayes, k-nearest neighbor, random forest, gradient booster, and support vector machine to classify literal versus metaphoric expressions.

Keywords: Knowledge graph · Machine learning · Metaphorical expression · Figurative language processing

1 Introduction

Metaphors compare unrelated concepts and are used for emphasizeing points, expressing emotions and making communication more appealing. The Natural Language Processing (NLP) community is increasingly interested in processing figurative language for effective human-computer interaction. Computational metaphor processing identifies and interprets metaphors. Empirical studies contradict the idea that metaphors are just embellishments in poetry, showing that around 20 percent of everyday language is metaphorical. A metaphor processing application can interpret the intended meaning of a metaphor. However, well-known NLP applications such as opinion mining and machine translation often struggle to process metaphors in the text despite their prevalence in human communication. Let us consider an example phrase, "Life is a highway," Google translates[1] it as "Jivana ha eka rajamarga ahe." in Marathi. It simply performs a

[1] https://translate.google.co.in/.

N. Chauhan et al. (Eds.): MIND 2023, CCIS 2128, pp. 339–351, 2024.
https://doi.org/10.1007/978-3-031-62217-5_28

word-to-word translation without considering the metaphorical meaning of the original phrases. To avoid such inaccuracies, it is essential to use machine translation tools with caution and always consider their limitations. When it comes to translating figurative language, it is recommended to rely on professional human translators who have a deep understanding of the source and the target languages. Further one should be familiar with the cultural and social context in which the language is being used.

1.1 Challenges in Metaphor Processing

The language can have both literal and metaphorical or implied elements as a system of communication. Similes, metaphors, idioms and proverbs are used to convey a specific impact or creative description to attain a phrase's figurative meaning. Hence, a mechanism is required to describe a grammatical structure accurately. However, the problem of metaphor recognition is highly challenging due to the numerous complex characteristics of metaphor, such as:

- **Non-compositionality**: The intended meaning of the metaphoric expression, cannot be derived.
- **Discontinuity**: The phrases are not structured sentences and lack a subject or verb, so it has syntactic flexibility.
- **Heterogeneity**: The phrases of the sentences and the metaphorical phrases are semantically different from each other.

The main limitation is the simile sentence collection. However, the model is designed in such a way that it can efficiently be implemented for processing a more extensive collection. Besides, there is a limitation in directly measuring the impact of the comprehension of the narrative format and results from the database. Another limitation is difficulty in handling creative language use. Metaphors are often used in creative and imaginative ways that may not follow strict grammatical rules. It is challenging to develop a model that can capture these nuances and detect metaphors accurately. An organized and systematic approach is critically essential with respect to the above scenarios to generate a knowledge graph for metaphor processing, which strengthens the potential for future research on two aspects: metaphor identification and metaphor interpretation.

The present paper has been divided into six sections. Section 2 provides insights into related works through the literature review. Section 3 introduces the methodology based on Design Science Research used in the proposed computing model. Section 4 illustrates the computing model application in metaphor processing with use cases. Section 5 presents experimental results and KG evaluation. Finally, Sect. 6 provides conclusions highlighting the present limitations that motivate researchers to work on future scope.

2 Literature Review

The proposed model aims to bridge the gap between unstructured or semi-structured text and structured knowledge in the field of figurative language, thereby bringing the new sun in the research with new possibilities [1].

2.1 Building Metaphor Resources

Simile and metaphor are the figures of speech used to compare two dissimilar things. The main difference is that a simile uses the words-"like" or"as" while a metaphor directly compares one thing with another. For example,"Life is as long as a highway" is an example of a simile, while"Life is a highway" is an example of metaphor. Explicit similes can be useful in comprehending and generating non-explicit metaphors [2]. One of the approaches to understanding metaphors is the extraction of attributes of concepts from similes using heuristic patterns or annotated examples [3]. While pattern-based methods have limitations, approaches with neural multi-task learning have shown promises in simile classification and component extraction [4].

2.2 Conceptual Mapping

Lakoff and Johnson [5] proposed a conceptual model on traditional "similarity based meaning extension". As opposed to prior theories, the Conceptual Metaphor Theory (CMT) articulates metaphor as a "conventional conceptual mapping" between the target domain and the source domain, which can be demonstrated as "TARGET CONCEPT IS SOURCE CONCEPT". For instance, if "great idea" is a concept, it can be re-conceptualized metaphorically as "gold" and then the conceptual metaphor becomes "GREAT IDEA IS GOLD". Thus, a conceptual metaphor is constructed by systematically mapping relatively abstract or vague concepts from the target domain and more concrete, clearer, and more familiar concepts from the source domain. It is worth noting that conceptual metaphors can take different linguistic expressions, but they all relate to the same underlying conceptual metaphor [6]. Another example that demonstrates the various ways in which metaphor manifests as linguistic expressions "An atom (target/ tenor) is a solar system (source/vehicle)." [7] This sentence maps an atom to the solar system, depicting the analogy"electrons: atom:: planets: sun" to provide one possible interpretation.

2.3 Building Knowledge Graph

Several researchers [8,9] have noted the advantages of knowledge mapping, which mainly includes effective storage and more efficient knowledge traversal. Gardner (2018) [10] introduced AllenNLP, an NLP library that offers deep learning methods for NLP research. Although AllenNLP performs reasonably well for general-purpose text, it doesn't suit Metaphor Processing. Kertkeidkachorn and

Ichise (2018) [11] presented a framework called T2KG that takes unstructured text as an input and automatically generates a knowledge map. The key components used by T2KG to construct the knowledge graph for named entities are mapping for entities, coreference, and triplet extraction. Existing work can generate knowledge graphs without creating a repository, and it is not applied to metaphor processing. On the other side, the FRED tool [12] links other knowledge bases to existing knowledge entities. In the past few years, deep learning, including its capability to inevitably learn successful feature representation from information, has also made accomplishments in numerous fields, for example, computer vision and NLP [13]. Some pre-trained language representation models, such as BERT [14] and GPT-3 [15], are considered state-of-the-art methods that can overcome the limitations of other language models. However, existing models like WEC [16] that use word embedding-based clustering to detect topics have limitations such as restricting the search information to text only, requiring a complex setup, and lacking a permanent repository creation.

3 Metaphor Knowledge Graph Framework

The Design Science Research (DSR) [17] methodology is widely adopted by prominent information system development methods. The DSR involves a cyclical process that starts with identifying a problem or an opportunity, followed by a design phase where a solution is proposed and developed and then an evaluation phase where the solution is evaluated and refined. The process continues until a satisfactory resolution is achieved. The proposed framework for knowledge management in figurative language processing, specifically metaphor processing depicted in Fig. 1, is inspired by the DSR methodology to create visually comprehensible knowledge graphs for the metaphoric text.

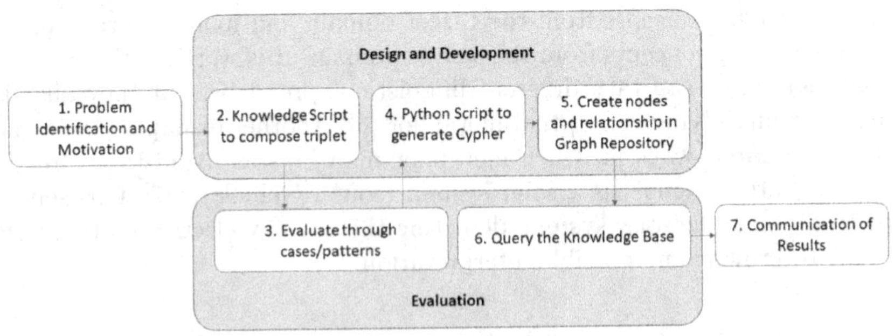

Fig. 1. DSR approach for Metaphor Knowledge Graph framework development.

Metaphor Knowledge Graph framework (MKG framework) begins with a problem identification related to knowledge management in metaphor processing. It translates the problem into a design requirement for a solution based on knowledge script composition and Python scripting for Cypher statement generation. This work establishes a system design based on NLP techniques and applies it as a prototype, demonstrating its applicability to a metaphor dataset as a case study. An evaluation is conducted by performing visual navigation and searching the graph database developed for this study. The findings of the assessment are communicated through the DSR approach, also serves as the study's theoretical contribution. Overall, the study proposes an effective solution design for knowledge management in metaphor processing, using a graph database and NLP techniques. The computing model uses a validated DSR approach to develop a graph database for storing knowledge from a collection of metaphorical sentences involving three phases and the evaluation followed the DSR methodology described previously.

1. Dataset creation
2. Simile Processing to Build Metaphor Resources
3. Generation of Cypher statements, graph database, and visualization

The proposed computing model for developing a graph database implementing the MKG framework is outlined in Fig. 2. The first step involves obtaining a set of unstructured text consisting of simile and non-simile sentences from various sources, including dictionaries and educational websites. It involves cleaning the input by pre-processing it to removing any unwanted text and punctuation marks. The next step is to construct a knowledge script that identifies the target concept, source concept, and attribute for each metaphor triplet. Then, a Python script is used to generate Cypher statements which are used to store this information in the graph database. In the end, the data is visualized in the Neo4j repository. This process enables to successfully develop a graph database for managing knowledge in metaphor processing.

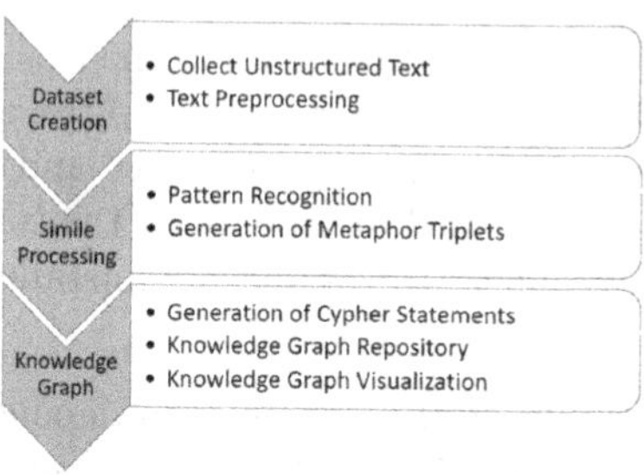

Fig. 2. Workflow of the computing model for developing a knowledge graph database.

3.1 Dataset Creation

This research study has performed a Systematic Literature review (SLR) to understand the relationship between similes and metaphors. A simile is a type of figurative language that employs explicit comparators like 'like' and 'as.' It is believed that studying explicit similes can aid in understanding and producing non-explicit metaphors [18]. A metaphor sentence comprises source and target concepts, whereas similes contain attributes. Let us consider this sentence: "The sky was as blue as the ocean". In this sentence, the "sky" is the target, the "ocean" is the source, and the common attribute shared by both concepts is the colour "blue". The comparators being explicit in similes are easier to locate. Metaphors, on the other hand, lack direct comparators. However, having comparators in a sentence does not give the sentence a figurative meaning. For example, consider these sentences: "The girl looks like her mother". The meanings in this sentence is literal and not figurative. Therefore, each sentence is categorized as a simile or non-simile by manually labeling it. Within simile sentences, further annotation is made based on simile components viz. source, target and attribute. The source and the target concepts are currently limited to single nouns. The attributes are limited to verbs or adjectives. In labeling the simile components, two annotators labeled simile sentences, of which 95% of extracted triples agreed.

3.2 Simile Processing to Build Metaphor Resources

The dataset created in the study consists of unstructured data. The knowledge script consists of a sequence of findings. The Key findings of sentences are written to build the Cypher with simple and systematic rules. The syntax for each sentence is as follows: "Target Node, Relationship Name, Source Node". The "POS tag" is used to define the property of each node, and the "dependency type" is used to define the property of each relation. To extract more metaphor triples automatically from sentences, the proposed model employs a pipeline approach that utilizes comparators. The condition to retain triples is to have all three types of simile components in the same sentence.

POS Tagging. Initially, tokenization is performed on the sentences, followed by the application of POS tagging. POS tagging plays a vital role in NLP as it helps in comprehending the meaning of a sentence and analyzing its structure. Part-of-speech tagging is performed by employing the Natural Language Toolkit (NLTK) wrapper module, which utilizes a locally installed Stanford POS tagger.

Dependency Parsing. The dataset undergoes dependency parsing, a procedure that analyzes the grammatical structure of a sentence and identifies the relationships between the terms. The CoreNLP, a Java-based NLP tool, can be utilized with NLTK to parse dependencies in Python. Each sentence in the dataset is parsed, resulting in a triple of the form ((head word, head POS), relation, (dependent word, dependent POS). An open-source tool called Graphviz[2] is used for visualizing graphs. It can be used with Python 3.7+ and it also provides a wholly Python-based user interface.

[2] https://graphviz.org/.

Concept-Attribute Associations. Concept-attribute association refers to how attributes or characteristics are linked or associated with particular concepts or objects. The proposed model relie on dependency parsing patterns to extract concept-attribute association. For instance, a simile sentence, "The sky was as blue as the ocean" has "blue" as an adjective, which is regarded as an attribute, whereas, "sky" and "ocean" nouns are considered concepts. All extracted Dependent POS tag ← Head POS tag collocations are referred to as concept-attribute associations. The following patterns are recognized to identify these associations.

1. Adjective ← Noun
2. Noun ← Adjective
3. Noun ← Verb
4. Adjective ← Verb(be)

Extracted the concept attribute associations in this form: (concept, attribute), e.g., (lion, brave), (cool, cucumber), (war, fighting), and (arrow, straight). Some attributes, such as " become" and "good," are commonly used by many concepts and do not convey the specific properties of a particular concept.

3.3 Cypher Statements' Generation, Graph Database and Visualization

The present study also attempts to analyse a non-relational graph-based repository, Neo4j[3] as a structured repository to store the extracted knowledge. The graph store is constructed using entities that are represented as nodes and the relationships that connect these nodes. It includes properties of entities and relationships, which are stored as key-value pairs to provide detailed information. In comparison with the other structured data sources, Neo4j offers efficient traversal of nodes and relationships. Generated Concept-Attribute pairs are semi-structured knowledge representations in the form of a knowledge script that both humans and computers can interpret, but it becomes a time-consuming process. Therefore, to generate Cypher Statements, the knowledge script is passed through a Python script, which generates Cypher statements. The Cypher statement creates unique nodes if a concept node already exists. Initially, concept nodes with their properties are created, where properties are set to the POS tag of the word. The source node and target node of a connection are then defined. Finally, relationships are linked, by setting relationship property to attribute. Creating the nodes and the links with Cypher can be challenging for humans; hence, the Python script serves as a bridge to generate human-readable formats by translating all Concept-Attribute pairs to Cypher queries. This approach provides a more efficient way to establish nodes and links in the graph database.

[3] https://neo4j.com/.

4 Metaphor Identification

The quality "fit for purpose" of the knowledge graph is evaluated by building a knowledge-based application namely metaphor identification. Generated dataset $D = \{X, Y\}$, where X is a collection of sentences $S \epsilon X$ and $S = w_1, w_2, w_3 ... w_n$ and Y is 0 for non-metaphoric sentence and 1 for metaphoric sentence. Then, the generated metaphor graph$G = (C, A)$ contains a Metaphorical triplet. Here C denotes a nonempty node set, and A is an ordered pair. This article demonstrates Metaphor identification as a triplet $T = (t, a, s)$ classification task. Here, t is a set of target concepts $t \subseteq C$, s is a set of source concepts $s \subseteq C$ and a is a shared attribute. Five classifiers are used to perform classification tasks: Naive Bayes, K-nearest neighbours (KNN), Random Forest, Gradient Boosting, and Support Vector Machine (SVM).

5 Experiments

This section, determins whether proposed model can judge an unseen triplet (target, attribute, source) and whether it is metaphoric or non-metaphoric.

5.1 Dataset

The metaphor unstructured data is generated to evaluate the performance of the proposed model, English sentences and essays are collecred from educational websites, books and social media sources written in diverse genres. The dataset contains 3415 sentences, whereas each sentence is manually labeled as metaphorical or non-metaphorical. Furthermore, 2892 triplets (target, attributes, source) are extracted from the dataset. Three annotators are labelled 1558 metaphorical triplets and 1334 non-metaphorical triplets. Three engineering college students are selected to validate these triplets manually. Then, the dataset is split into two subsets, i.e., MKG_trn for training and MKG_tst for testing. Table 1 depicts the statistics of the constructed triplets.

Table 1. The statistics of the constructed triplets. # indicates the number of, % indicates percentage of and Avg indicates average.

Data	#triplets	#sent	% Meta triplets	Avg sent len	#Meta triplets	#Non meta triplets
MKG Dataset	2892	3415	53.87	16	1558	1334
MKG_trn	2313	2732	53.86	16	1246	1067
MKG_tst	579	683	53.88	16	312	267

5.2 Knowledge Graph Evaluation

The essential quality requirements of the metaphor knowledge graph for serving the purpose of knowledge discovery are evaluated using the framework proposed by Chen et al. [19]. Accordingly, subjective dimensions like representation conciseness are manually evaluated through sampling, so here the technical description outlines the representation of a graph database of metaphor triplets using the Neo4j database management system. The resulting knowledge graph comprises nodes and relationships that depict source and target concepts, and their attributes are shown through links. For instance, the Metaphor triplet (throat, dry, desert) is presented in Fig. 3 as (Target concept, Attribute, and Source concept) knowledge graph. The Cypher statements have created 1826 nodes and 1531 relationships, which are stored permanently with the POS tag property of each in the Neo4j database.

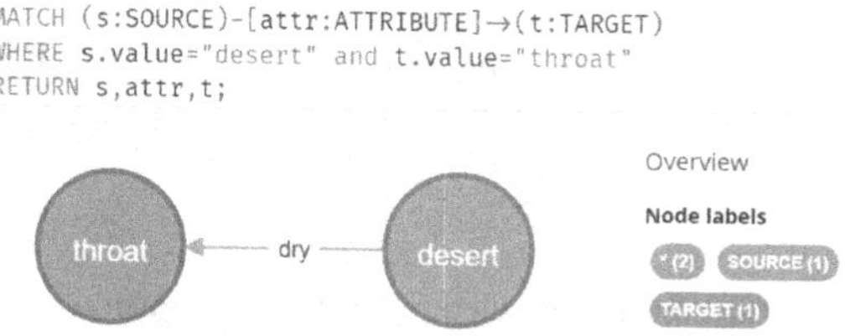
MATCH (s:SOURCE)-[attr:ATTRIBUTE]→(t:TARGET)
WHERE s.value="desert" and t.value="throat"
RETURN s,attr,t;
throat
dry
desert
Overview
Node labels
* (2)
SOURCE (1)
TARGET (1)

Fig. 3. Knowledge Graph for triple (throat, dry, desert).

A Cypher Query "MATCH (n) RETURN n" is used to retrieve all the information in the database in a visual graph form. The resulting graph visualization clearly represents the concepts and the relationships between them. The use of coloured nodes helps to clearly distinguish or identify knowledge about the source concept (Orange node) and target concept (Lavender node). The graph structure is amenable to traversal for the purpose of querying information. The inherent flexibility in creating a graph and the subsequent extraction of information from it afford considerable advantages in facilitating sophisticated search operations. This study manually validate the triplets for syntactic validation and semantic accuracy, relevance, and understandability. As it can be seen in Figs. 3 and 4, the triplet is brief and comprehensive and gives a lot of information. Further, the cipher use merge statements to avoid duplicate nodes and links as shown in Fig. 5, so the metaphorical knowledge graph is concise, contextual, clear and concentrated. Furthermore, KG is also evaluated for robust and diversity dimensions. The proposed KG is robust because it can easily be expanded without affecting the existing graph. Additionally, it is diverse because KG is constructed on metaphorical knowledge which is extracted from unstructured data collected from multiple sources.

5.3 The Results of Metaphor Identification

This section, implements the proposed MKG framework approach for metaphor identification. The Five different classifiers have been trained, namely Naive Bayes, KNN, Random Forest, Gradient Boosting, and SVM classifiers.

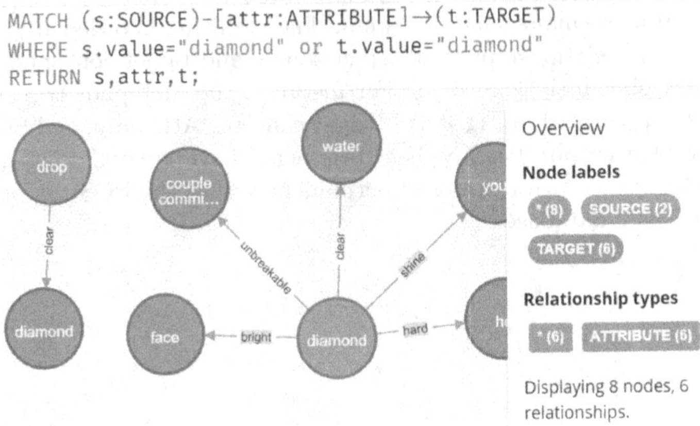

Fig. 4. Metaphorical knowledge for the node value 'diamond'.

A comparative analysis has been carried out for metaphor detection regarding precision, recall, and F1 score. For non-metaphorical triplet classification, the Support Vector Machine classifier with FastText embedding outperforms in terms of precision 0.98 and F1 score of 0.95, whereas the K-nearest neighbour classifier with Word2Vec embedding outperforms in terms of recall of 0.97. For metaphorical triplet classification, the Support Vector Machine classifier with FastText embedding and ELMO embedding outperforms in terms of recall of 0.98, and F1 score 0.96, whereas the K-nearest neighbour classifier with Word2Vec embedding and Glove embedding outperform in the precision of 0.96. Overall, the Support Vector Machine classifier with FastText embedding and ELMO embedding outperforms in terms of the accuracy of 0.95 (Table 2).

Table 2. The metaphor and non-metaphor identification results, the best results are shown in boldface.

Model	Nonmeta Triplets			Meta Triplets			Accuracy
	P	R	F1	P	R	F1	
NB + TF-IDF	0.93	0.91	0.92	0.92	0.95	0.93	0.93
NB + Word2Vec	0.85	0.81	0.83	0.85	0.88	0.86	0.85
NB + Glove	0.83	0.76	0.80	0.81	0.87	0.84	0.82
NB + ELMO	0.86	0.81	0.82	0.84	0.87	0.86	0.84
NB + FastText	0.88	0.73	0.80	0.80	0.91	0.85	0.83
KNN + TF-IDF	0.86	0.86	0.86	0.88	0.88	0.88	0.87
KNN + Word2Vec	0.74	**0.97**	0.84	**0.96**	0.71	0.82	0.83
KNN + Glove	0.82	0.96	0.88	**0.96**	0.81	0.88	0.88
KNN + ELMO	0.87	0.95	0.91	0.95	0.88	0.92	0.91
KNN + FastText	0.85	0.95	0.90	0.95	0.86	0.90	0.90
RF + TF-IDF	0.94	0.76	0.84	0.82	0.96	0.89	0.87
RF + Word2Vec	0.95	0.85	0.90	0.88	0.96	0.92	0.91
RF + Glove	0.92	0.85	0.89	0.88	0.94	0.91	0.90
RF + ELMO	0.93	0.89	0.91	0.91	0.94	0.92	0.92
RF + FastText	0.92	0.89	0.91	0.91	0.94	0.92	0.92
GB + TF-IDF	0.96	0.60	0.73	0.74	0.98	0.84	0.80
GB + Word2Vec	0.95	0.85	0.90	0.88	0.96	0.92	0.91
GB + Glove	0.90	0.86	0.88	0.89	0.92	0.90	0.89
GB + ELMO	0.92	0.88	0.90	0.90	0.94	0.92	0.91
GB + FastText	0.94	0.91	0.93	0.93	0.95	0.94	0.93
SVM + TF-IDF	0.95	0.87	0.91	0.90	0.96	0.93	0.92
SVM + Word2Vec	0.97	0.90	0.93	0.92	0.97	0.95	0.94
SVM + Glove	0.93	0.89	0.91	0.91	0.95	0.93	0.92
SVM + ELMO	0.97	0.91	0.94	0.93	**0.98**	0.95	**0.95**
SVM + FastText	**0.98**	0.92	**0.95**	0.94	**0.98**	**0.96**	**0.95**

6 Conclusion

Automating the process of building the repository is one of the challenging parts, which is attempted in this study with MKG framework as the proposal. This framework leverages the DSR approach. The unstructured knowledge is stored by building semi-structured knowledge scripts, generating the Cypher statements, and then integrating the same with existing knowledge in the graph database. This approach demonstrates that the automation of graph database creation out of knowledge extracted from the simile sentences can form a better perception of the metaphor in the figurative language processing domain. This can indeed be a vast support for researchers in the same domain. Moreover, transforming humanly readable knowledge script into the Cypher query language helps to facilitate the comprehension process and elevates interest in this research domain. Visualizing of the relationship between the source and the target is based on the knowledge graph. At the same time, the related knowledge is integrated as properties or relationships of the entities, which is a more comprehensible form of this related knowledge. The system can be designed for Multi-lingual Metaphor Detection, while also incorporating language-specific features and developing knowledge graphs that can capture the intricacies of metaphorical language use in each language. Another potential avenue for research in metaphor detection is to focus on generating novel metaphors, which can have applications in creative writing and marketing to communicate complex ideas more easily and digestibly.

References

1. Wang, Q., Mao, Z., Wang, B., Guo, L.: Knowledge graph embedding: a survey of approaches and applications. IEEE Trans. Knowl. Data Eng. **29**(12), 2724–2743 (2017)
2. Veale, T., Hao, Y.: Comprehending and generating apt metaphors: a web-driven, case-based approach to figurative language. In: AAAI 2007: Proceedings of the 22nd National Conference on Artificial Intelligence, A. Cohn, ed., pp. 1471–1476. AAAI Press, Canada (2007)
3. Li, H., Zhu, K., Wang, H.: Data-driven metaphor recognition and explanation. Trans. Assoc. Comput. Linguist. **1**, 379–390 (2013)
4. Zeng, J., Song, L., Su, J., Xie, J. Song, W., Luo, J.: Neural simile recognition with cyclic multitask learning and local attention. In: The Thirty-Fourth AAAI Conference on Artificial Intelligence (AAAI-20), Association for the Advancement of Artificial Intelligence, Brussels, Belgium, pp. 9515–9522 (2020)
5. Lakoff, G., Johnson, M.: Metaphors We Live By. University of Chicago Press (2008)
6. Rai, S., Chakraverty, S.: A survey on computational metaphor processing. ACM Comput. Surv. **53**(2), 1–37 (2020)
7. Gentner, D.: Structure-mapping: a theoretical framework for analogy. Cogn. Sci. **7**(2), 155–170 (1983)
8. Balaid, A., Rozan, M., Hikmi, S., Memon, J.: Knowledge maps: a systematic literature review and directions for future research. Int. J. Inf. Manage. **36**(3), 451–475 (2016)
9. Maksutov, A., Zamyatovskiy, V., Vyunnikov, V., Kutuzov, A., Algorithms, K.B.C.U.N.L.P.: 2020 IEEE Conference of Russian Young Researchers in Electrical and Electronic Engineering (EIConRus), pp. 405–407. IEEE (2020)
10. Gardner, M., et al.: AllenNLP: a deep semantic natural language processing platform. In: Proceedings of Workshop for NLP Open Source Software (NLP-OSS), Association for Computational Linguistics, Australia, pp. 1–6 (2018)
11. Kertkeidkachorn, N., Ichise, R.: An automatic knowledge graph creation framework from natural language text. IEICE Trans. Inf. Syst. **E101**(1), 90–98 (2018)
12. Gangemi, A., Presutti, V., Recupero, D., Nuzzolese, A., Draicchio, F., Mongiov, M.: Semantic web machine reading with FRED. Semantic Web **8**(6), 873–893 (2016)
13. Farooq, N., Selwal, A.: Image steganalysis using deep learning: a systematic review and open research challenges. J. Ambient. Intell. Humaniz. Comput. **14**, 7761–7793 (2023)

14. Devlin, J., Chang, M., Lee, K., Toutanova, K.: BERT: pre-training of deep bidirectional transformers for language understanding. In: Proceedings of NAACL-HLT 2019, Association for Computational Linguistics, Minnesota, pp. 4171–4186 (2019)
15. Zhu, Q., Luo, J.: Generative pre-trained transformer for design concept generation: an exploration. arXiv arXiv:2111.08489 (2021). 1825–1834
16. Comito, C., Forestiero, A., Pizzuti, C.: Word embedding based clustering to detect topics in social media. In: WI 2019: IEEE/WIC/ACM International Conference on Web Intelligence, Association for Computing Machinery, pp. 192–199 (2019)
17. Peffers, K., Tuunanen, T., Rothenberger, M., Chatterjee, S.: A design science research methodology for information systems research. J. Manag. Inf. Syst. **24**(3), 45–77 (2007)
18. Niculae, V., Yaneva, V.: Computational considerations of comparisons and similes. In: Proceedings of the ACL Student Research Workshop, Association for Computational Linguistics, Sofia, Bulgaria, pp. 89–95 (2013)
19. Chen, H., Cao, G., Chen, J., Ding, J.: A practical framework for evaluating the quality of knowledge graph. In: Zhu, X., Qin, B., Zhu, X., Liu, M., Qian, L. (eds.) CCKS 2019. CCIS, vol. 1134, pp. 111–122. Springer, Singapore (2019). https://doi.org/10.1007/978-981-15-1956-7_10

Effectiveness of Influencer Marketing on Gen Z Consumers

Paras Jeena, Santoshi Sengupta(✉), and Mohit Joshi

School of Management, Graphic Era Hill University, Bhimtal, India
santoshisengupta@gmail.com

Abstract. With the growing popularity of influencer marketing among Gen Z consumers, there are many challenges posed with it in addition to its high claimed benefits. This study attempts to investigate the effectiveness of influencer marketing among the Gen Z consumers. Precisely, it tries to find out the most popular platforms where influencer marketing is popular, the factors behind choosing an influencer, and the kind of decisions and buying behavior of Gen Z are influenced by influencers. Data collected from Gen Z consumers was analyzed to reach interesting results and insights.

Keywords: Influencer marketing · Gen Z · patterns · decisions

1 Introduction

Influencer marketing is a form of marketing that utilizes influential people on social media platforms to promote a product, service or brand [1]. Influencer marketing has gained immense popularity because of social media platforms such as Instagram, TikTok, YouTube, and others. Influencers are people who have a significant following on social media, and their audience is often highly engaged and attentive to what they say and promote. Indeed, one can see how influencer marketing has immersed as an essential feature of the marketing mix for several organizations, and it has grown rapidly in popularity.

One reason why influencer marketing has become so popular is the decline of traditional advertising methods [2]. Television, print, and radio advertising have become less effective as consumers have become more adept at filtering out traditional advertising messages. In contrast, influencer marketing has proven to be more effective because it is less intrusive and more engaging. Influencers can promote products and services in a way that feels more authentic and natural, and the people who follow them are more likely to believe their recommendations.

Another reason for the increasing popularity of influencer marketing is the rise of social media platforms [3]. Instagram, TikTok, and YouTube are just a few examples of platforms that have become hugely popular in recent years. These platforms have provided a way for influencers to reach a huge client base and for companies to reach potential customers in a more targeted and engaging way. Instagram, for example, has over 1 billion active users, and many of these users follow influencers in their niche.

N. Chauhan et al. (Eds.): MIND 2023, CCIS 2128, pp. 352–361, 2024.
https://doi.org/10.1007/978-3-031-62217-5_29

The growth of influencer marketing has also been driven by the changing demographics of consumers [1, 2]. Younger consumers, particularly millennials and Generation Z, are less likely to respond to old advertising methods and are likely to be influenced by social media [3]. These consumers have grown up with social media, and they are more likely to trust recommendations from people they follow on social media than from traditional advertising channels.

Influencer marketing has also become more accessible to companies of all sizes [2]. In the past, influencer marketing was mainly reserved for large companies with significant marketing budgets. However, the rise of micro-influencers has made influencer marketing more accessible to small and medium-sized businesses. Influencers are often more affordable for companies to work with and can provide a more targeted audience for niche products and services.

In all, the popularity and fame of influencer marketing because of a combination of factors, including the decline of traditional advertising methods, the rise of social media platforms, and the changing demographics of consumers. Influencer marketing has proven to be an effective form of marketing for many companies. The rise of micro-influencers has made influencer marketing more accessible to small and medium-sized businesses, allowing them to compete with larger companies in the digital marketplace. Influencer marketing is likely to continue to grow in popularity as social media platforms continue to evolve, and consumers become more comfortable with using social media as a primary source of information and entertainment.

2 Literature Review

2.1 Importance of Studying the Effectiveness of Influencer Marketing on Gen Z Consumers

In today's digital age, social media has become an integral part of people's lives, especially for the younger generation. Gen Z, born between the mid-1990s and mid-2010s, is the first generation to have grown up with the internet and social media. They spend a significant amount of time on social media platforms, and their buying behaviour is heavily influenced by social media content. This has led to the rise of influencer marketing, a marketing strategy. The effectiveness of influencer marketing on Gen Z consumers is of great importance to marketers, and in this article, we will discuss why.

Firstly, Gen Z is the largest consumer demographic in the world, with an estimated purchasing power of over $140 billion. They are also the most diverse and socially conscious generation, which means that they are more likely to support brands that align with their values. Influencer marketing is an effective way to reach this demographic as they trust and relate to influencers more than traditional advertising. According to a study by Kantar, 63% of Gen Z consumers said that they have made a purchase based on an influencer's intensions [4].

Secondly, Gen Z is a highly digital and mobile-savvy generation. They spend an average of 3 h a day on their smartphones and are more likely to make purchases on mobile devices than any other generation. Influencer marketing is a mobile-first marketing strategy that can be easily integrated with social media platforms [3]. This makes it easier for brands to connect with Gen Z consumers on the platforms where they spend most of their time [4].

Thirdly, influencer marketing is a cost-effective marketing strategy [1] that can provide a high return on investment (ROI). According to a study by Influencer Marketing Hub, for every $1 spent on influencer marketing, businesses can earn an average of $5.78 in earned media value. This is because influencer marketing generates high engagement rates and reach, which can lead to increased brand awareness and sales.

Fourthly, Gen Z consumers are highly sceptical of traditional advertising and tend to rely on peer recommendations and reviews before making a purchase. Influencer marketing can help brands overcome this scepticism by using influencers as a bridge between the brand and the consumer. Influencers are perceived as more authentic and trustworthy than traditional advertising, which can lead to increased brand loyalty and repeat purchases [5].

Finally, the effectiveness of influencer marketing on Gen Z consumers can provide valuable insights for marketers on how to connect with this demographic [5]. By analyzing the engagement rates, reach, and conversion rates of influencer marketing campaigns, marketers can gain a better understanding of what resonates with Gen Z consumers and how to improve their marketing strategies.

2.2 Types of Influencer Marketing

There are several different types of influencer marketing, each with its own benefits and drawbacks. Here are some of the most common types:

1. Sponsored Content: Sponsored content is one of the most common types of influencer marketing. Brands pay influencers to create content, such as a post, video, or story, that promotes their products or services. Sponsored content can be a great way to reach a large audience quickly, but it can also be expensive.
2. Affiliate Marketing: Affiliate marketing involves influencers promoting a brand's products or services and earning a commission for every sale made through their unique affiliate link. This type of influencer marketing is a cost-effective way for brands to reach new customers, but it can also be challenging to track the results.
3. Product Reviews: Product reviews involve influencers testing and reviewing a brand's products or services. They may receive the product for free or at a discounted price in exchange for their review. Product reviews can be an effective way to build trust with consumers and increase sales, but they can also be time-consuming.
4. Giveaways and Contests: Giveaways and contests are a popular way to increase engagement and reach on social media. Brands can partner with influencers to host a giveaway or contest that requires followers to like, share, or comment on a post to enter. This type of influencer marketing can be a great way to generate buzz around a new product or service, but it may not necessarily translate into increased sales.
5. Influencer Takeovers: Influencer takeovers involve an influencer taking over a brand's social media account for a set period. During the takeover, the influencer creates content that promotes the brand's products or services. Influencer takeovers can be an effective way to reach new audiences and build brand awareness, but they can also be risky if the influencer doesn't align with the brand's values.

6. Influencer Reviews and Testimonials: Brands can collaborate with influencers to provide honest reviews and testimonials about their products or services. Influencers can share their personal experiences and opinions, which can carry significant weight and influence their followers' purchasing decisions.
7. Influencer Co-Creation: Brands can involve influencers in the co-creation of new products, services, or campaigns. This collaboration allows influencers to contribute their expertise, creativity, and insights to develop offerings that resonate with their audience. By involving influencers in the creative process, brands can tap into their influence and ensure the final product aligns with the preferences of the target audience.
8. Event Partnerships: Brands often partner with influencers for event-based campaigns. This could involve influencers attending and covering brand-sponsored events, trade shows, or festivals, sharing real-time updates and behind-the-scenes content. Event partnerships provide opportunities for increased exposure, engagement, and amplification of the brand's message.
9. Social Advocacy: In social advocacy campaigns, brands collaborate with influencers who align with a specific cause or social issue. These campaigns aim to raise awareness, drive social change, or support charitable initiatives. Influencers use their platforms to promote and advocate for the cause, encouraging their followers to get involved and support the brand's efforts.
10. Micro-Influencer Collaborations: Micro-influencers are those influencers those have a very highly engaged group but very small in number, and thus they can be valuable partners for brands. Collaborating with micro-influencers allows for more niche targeting and fosters a sense of authenticity and relatability, as their followers perceive them as peers rather than celebrities.
11. Virtual Influencers: Virtual influencers are computer-generated characters with a distinct personality and style. Brands collaborate with these virtual influencers to create content and promote their products or services. Virtual influencers are popular on social media [3] platforms and can provide a unique and futuristic approach to influencer marketing.

2.3 Challenges Related to Influencer Marketing

Finding the right influencer requires brands to search for individuals whose values, audience, and niche align with their own, a process that can be complex and time-consuming [6]. As influencer marketing grows more widespread, maintaining authenticity is crucial; influencers must disclose sponsored content and align it with their personal brand to keep audiences engaged [7]. Transparency is also key for brands to maintain trust with their audience by openly disclosing financial relationships with influencers. However, measuring the return on investment (ROI) from influencer marketing campaigns poses challenges, as quantifying the direct impact on a brand's bottom line is often unclear. Furthermore, managing relationships with influencers, especially when working with multiple influencers simultaneously, demands transparency, communication, and mutual respect [8].

The reputation of a brand is at risk if an influencer engages in negative behavior or becomes involved in scandals. Additionally, the cost of influencer marketing can be high, particularly for influencers with large followings or those highly sought after in their niche, requiring brands to carefully consider their budget and negotiate accordingly [9, 10]. Compliance with regulations, such as the Federal Trade Commission's (FTC) guidelines on sponsored content, is essential to avoid legal issues and damage to brand reputation. The quality of content produced by influencers must align with the brand's image and messaging to ensure it positively impacts the brand and achieves the desired outcomes. With social media platforms constantly evolving, brands and influencers must adapt their strategies to remain effective, considering changes in algorithms or policy updates that could affect content reach. Ensuring brand safety is crucial when partnering with influencers to avoid association with controversial or offensive content. Despite these challenges, influencer marketing continues to offer significant benefits for those who navigate its complexities effectively.

2.4 Research Objectives

1 To determine the pattern of influencer marketing among Gen Z consumers and the platforms used.
2 To identify the factors behind choosing an influencer.
3 To determine what kind of decisions and buying behaviour of Gen Z are influenced by influencers.

3 Research Design

It is important to design a detailed plan for the research and to carry out in a meaningful, planned and a phased manner. The phases of the research undertaken have been monitored on the basis of design that enabled data collection, processing of information and objective analysis of data. The detailed description of the process of data collection and the tools used have been incorporated in the research design. The research study is descriptive in nature. Random sampling is a method of choosing a sample of observations from a population to make assumptions about the population. It is also called probability sampling. The counterpart of this sampling is non-probability sampling or Non-random sampling. The data is collected from 144 students. The selected sample size is supposed to be representative of the target population. The sample size was 200 but the responses gathered were 144.This was a good amount to conduct the research. The responses were from different kinds of individuals which became helpful finding the answers to the question. To find out the pattern of the effectiveness of influencer marketing on Gen z consumer among students, it was important to use a questionnaire to gather the information. The questionnaire finalised for the study was distributed among the student sample to get the data.

4 Findings and Analysis

The analysis of data gave us some interesting findings.

The pie chart in Fig. 1 illustrates that 73% students follow at least one influencer and 27% do not follow, as influencers are leading model in today's world and has gain

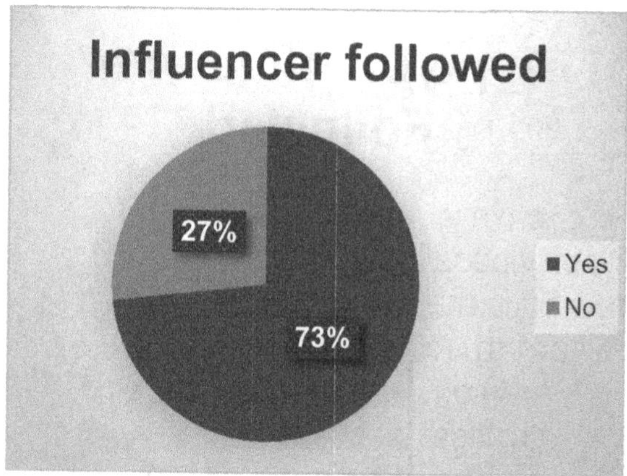

Fig. 1. Influencer followship

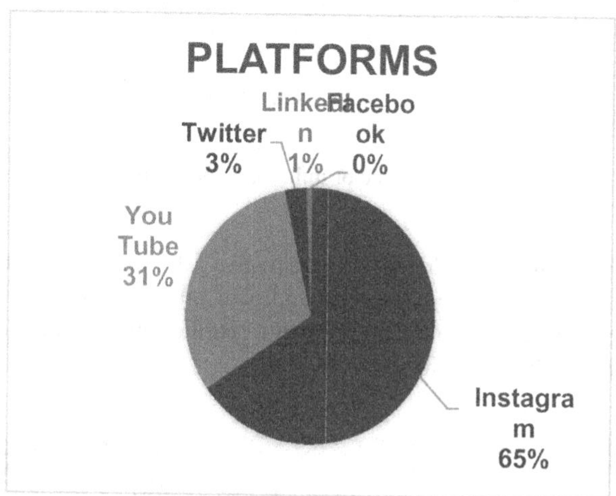

Fig. 2. Popularity of platforms

a very high rise in recent times. That's why the young generation like us love to follow them and watch them.

From the pie chart in Fig. 2 it clear that majority of participants prefers Instagram to follow their favourite influencer i.e.-65%. After Instagram, You Tube is the second most liked platform by the participants i.e.-31% whereas, Twitter is at the third number i.e.-3% and LinkedIn is the least used social media platform i.e.-1% and facebook is used by none of the participants as the platform where they can follow there favourite influencer.

As evident from the pie chart in Fig. 3, our research findings suggest that students have a huge interest on the influencers who make travel videos or show anything related to the travelling on their feeds i.e.-79.90%. On the second number lifestyle influencers i.e.-73.60% and food influencer's i.e.-71.50%, next is Fitness influencers i.e.-63.90% and

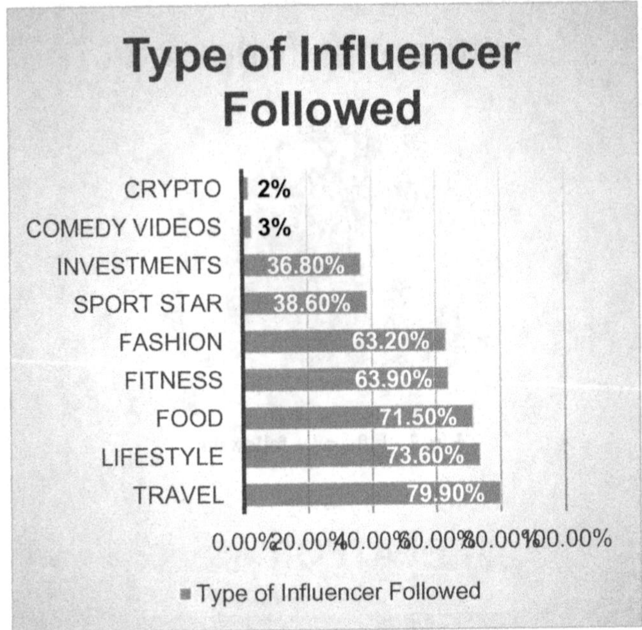

Fig. 3. Type of influencer followed

Fashion influencer followed by 63.20% participants of the survey. Under the last second number sport stars influencers i.e.-38.60% and investment influencers are followed by 36.80% %participant students and least number of public follows and like crypto i.e.-2% and comedy videos influencers followed by 3%.

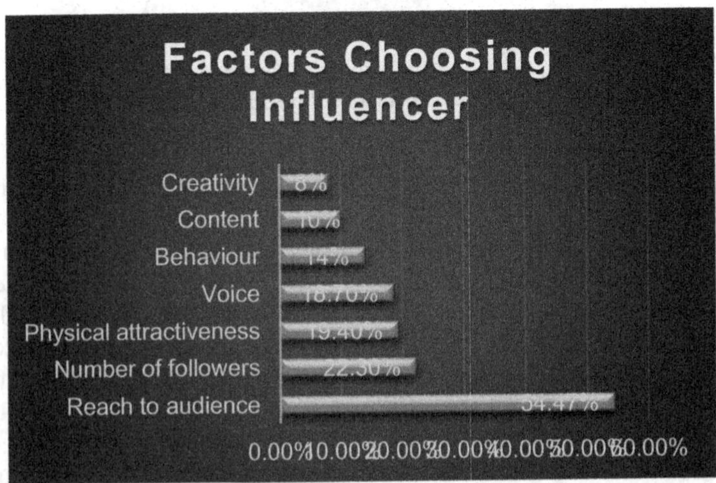

Fig. 4. Factors for choosing influencer

The graph in Fig. 4 help us understand clearly that a person consider while choosing his/her favourite influencer on social media is "Reach to the audience" i.e.-54.47% after that "number of follower" is the another factor that influence the audience i.e.-22.3%, "physical attractiveness" is followed by 19.4% and least is voice i.e.-18.7%. Other than is there are various factors that influence the audience which are very low in percentage.

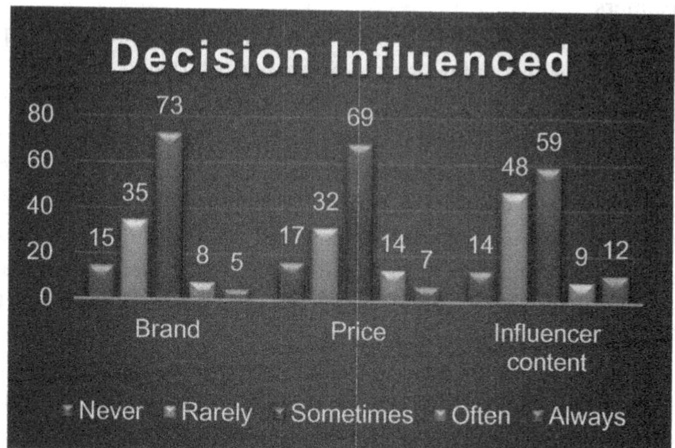

Fig. 5. Decision influenced by influencer marketing

The above chart in Fig. 5 provide information on how far the decision of the participants is influenced by social media on various categories i.e.- Brand, Price and Influencer Content. Discussing the first bar in the graph, it shows the percentage of participants who never got influenced by the product/brand on social media. The second bar represents the percentage of participants who rarely got affected by the product or brand they saw on social media. The third bar represents the percentage of students who sometimes got affected by the brand/product which they get to interact with om social media platforms. The green bar in the chart is for the students who often got influenced by the product/brand on social media. The last bar in the graph shows the percentage of students who always got affected by the brand/product they interacted with on social media platforms.

5 Discussion

Influencer marketing has become a prominent strategy for businesses to reach their target audience, especially Gen Z consumers. Gen Z, typically defined as individuals born between the mid-1990s and early 2010s, is a generation that has grown up in the digital age and is highly influenced by social media and online content creators. There are implications of influencer marketing on Gen Z consumers and how it can impact marketers and businesses. First, Gen Z consumers prioritize authenticity and value genuine connections with brands and influencers. They can easily spot inauthentic endorsements, and it can lead to a loss of trust in both the influencer and the brand.

Marketers and businesses need to carefully choose influencers and have an authentic connection with their audience. Second, Gen Z consumers often look up to influencers as role models and seek inspiration from their lifestyles, fashion choices, and experiences. Marketers and businesses can leverage this by partnering with influencers who embody the aspirational qualities and values that resonate with their target audience. By doing so, they can effectively market their products in a manner that feels relatable and desirable to Gen Z consumers.

Gen Z consumers heavily rely on peer recommendations and social proof before making purchasing decisions. Influencers, who are seen as trusted individuals within their communities, can provide that social proof by showcasing their positive experiences with products or services. Marketers and businesses can leverage influencer marketing to tap into this aspect and drive brand awareness and sales among Gen Z consumers. In addition to this, traditional forms of advertising may not resonate as well with Gen Z consumers, who have grown up in an era of ad-blocking and ad-skipping. Influencer marketing allows for native advertising, where promotional content is seamlessly integrated into the influencer's narrative. This approach can be more effective in capturing the attention of Gen Z consumers and driving engagement.

Gen Z is a diverse generation that values inclusivity and representation. They appreciate seeing influencers who reflect a range of backgrounds, cultures, and body types. Marketers and businesses can demonstrate their commitment to diversity and inclusion by partnering with influencers who represent different identities, thereby expanding their reach and connecting with a wider Gen Z audience. While macro-influencers with massive followings still hold influence, Gen Z consumers are also drawn to micro-influencers who have smaller but highly engaged communities. Micro-influencers often focus on niche topics or interests, allowing marketers and businesses to target specific segments of Gen Z consumers with tailored messages and products.

As with any marketing strategy, it is essential for marketers and businesses to track and measure the effectiveness of influencer marketing campaigns. They need to consider metrics such as engagement rates, reach, conversions, and brand sentiment to evaluate the success of their campaigns and optimize their strategies accordingly. Gen Z consumers are not just passive recipients of content; they actively participate in creating it. Influencer marketing allows businesses to involve Gen Z consumers in their campaigns by encouraging user-generated content. By collaborating with influencers and their followers to create content, businesses can foster a sense of community and engagement, making Gen Z consumers feel like valued contributors rather than just consumers. Moreover, Gen Z consumers are passionate about social causes and expect brands to take a stand on issues they care about. Influencer marketing provides an avenue for businesses to align with influencers who champion social causes. By partnering with influencers who genuinely advocate for these causes, businesses can showcase their commitment to social responsibility, which resonates strongly with Gen Z consumers and can help enhance brand perception.

While influencer marketing can yield short-term gains, cultivating long-term partnerships with influencers can be even more beneficial. Gen Z consumers appreciate consistency and value authenticity over time. By forging ongoing relationships with influencers, businesses can establish a sense of continuity and foster brand loyalty among

Gen Z consumers who see their favorite influencers consistently endorsing and using their products or services. Influencer marketing offers numerous opportunities for marketers and businesses targeting Gen Z consumers. By considering these implications and adapting strategies to align with the values and preferences of this generation, businesses can effectively leverage influencer marketing to connect, engage, and build lasting relationships with Gen Z consumers.

6 Conclusion

In conclusion, continued research on influencer marketing and its effectiveness on Gen Z consumers is essential to keep up with the evolving digital landscape, optimize marketing strategies, and ensure ethical practices. By gaining deeper insights into the psychology, preferences, and behaviours of Gen Z consumers, businesses can harness the power of influencer marketing to forge meaningful connections and drive success in the rapidly changing marketplace.

References

1. Leung, F.F., Gu, F.F., Palmatier, R.W.: Online influencer marketing. J. Acad. Mark. Sci. **50**(2), 226–251 (2022)
2. Vrontis, D., Makrides, A., Christofi, M., Thrassou, A.: Social media influencer marketing: a systematic review, integrative framework, and future research agenda. Int. J. Consum. Stud. **45**(4), 617–644 (2021)
3. Esteban, O.O..: The rise of social media. Our World in Data (Sep 2019)
4. Nguyen, C., Nguyen, T., Luu, V.: Predicting the relationship between influencer marketing and purchase intention: focusing on gen Z consumers. In: International Econometric Conference of Vietnam, pp. 467–481. Springer International Publishing, Cham (2022). https://doi.org/10.1007/978-3-030-98689-6_31
5. Pradhan, D., Kuanr, A., Pahi, S.A., Akram, M.S.: Influencer marketing: when and why gen Z consumers avoid influencers and endorsed brands. Psychol. Mark. **40**(1), 27–47 (2023)
6. Zietek, N.: Influencer Marketing : the characteristics and components of fashion influencer marketing', Dissertation (2016)
7. Jin, S.V., Muqaddam, A., Ryu, E: Instafamous and social media influencer marketing. Marketing Intell. Planning **37**(5), 567–579 (2019)
8. Vrontis, D., Makrides, A., Christofi, M., Thrassou, A.: Social media influencer marketing: A systematic review, integrative framework and future research agenda. Inter. J. Consumer Stud. **45**(4), 617–644 (2021)
9. Campbell, C., Farrell, J.R.: More than meets the eye: the functional components underlying influencer marketing. Bus. Horiz. **63**(4), 469–479 (2020)
10. Bakker, D.: Conceptualising influencer marketing. J. Emerging Trends Marketing Manag. **1**(1), 79–87 (2018)

Author Index

N. Chauhan et al. (Eds.): MIND 2023, CCIS 2128, pp. 363–364, 2024.
https://doi.org/10.1007/978-3-031-62217-5

Printed in the United States
by Baker & Taylor Publisher Services